Peter R. Moore
The Lame Storyteller, Poor and Despised

D1666964

Peter R. Moore

The Lame Storyteller, Poor and Despised

Studies in Shakespeare

Verlag Uwe Laugwitz

To the Memory of Peter R. Moore
1949 – 2007

Editor:
Gary Goldstein

special issue no. 1 of NEUES SHAKE-SPEARE JOURNAL
All rights for this edition reserved by Verlag Uwe Laugwitz,
Matthias-Claudius-Weg 11B, 21244 Buchholz, Germany
www.laugwitz.com

ISBN 9783-933077-25-7

Contents

Part Two: An Oxfordian Foundation

Editor's Introduction

Peter Moore established himself as a scholar of the Renaissance in England by contributing articles to six peer reviewed journals in Europe and the United States for a fourteen year period, from 1993 to 2006. The journals are *The English Historical Review* and *Notes and Queries* (Britain), *Neophilologus* and *English Studies* (Holland), *Cahiers Élisabéthains* (France) and *The Elizabethan Review* (United States). I edited and published four of the pieces which appear in this collection in *The Elizabethan Review*, and found Peter's incisive thinking, tenacious research and lucid prose a revelation. In fact, he was that most rare of Shakespeare scholars—a literary historian, and each article printed here reflects the benefits of that inter-disciplinary background.

Born February 28, 1949 in Bern, Switzerland, where his father was serving as the US military attaché, Peter's career as an independent scholar was dissimilar from the typical Shakespeare scholar in profound ways: he was a professional military officer, graduating University of Maryland with a degree in engineering and achieving the rank of lieutenant colonel in the US Army's 82nd Airborne Division. He also graduated from the University of Maryland with a masters degree in economics, served as a legislative aide to US Senator John East of North Carolina, then became an official at the Georgia Department of Education. He ended his career by serving as a director at a national non-profit organization in Washington, DC dedicated to working with troubled teenagers. On November 29, 2007, he died in Virginia at the age of 57 from cancer.

Given such a rigorous public service background applied to non-literary concerns, one might have expected Peter to neglect the traditional authorites in his chosen field of scholarly research. On the contrary, he absorbed the full measure of their achievments before advancing his own ideas, and the references that fill these papers will impress with the scope and depth of his reading.

What spurred Peter to become a Shakespeare scholar was reading Charlton Ogburn Jr's *The Mysterious William Shakespeare* in the late 1980s, which persuaded him of the case for Edward de Vere, 17th Earl of Oxford as William Shakespeare. More to the point, Peter considered the authorship question the pre-eminent issue in the Humanities.

As a result, Peter embarked on an eight-year investigation into the Oxfordian case that generated 18 papers which appeared in *The Shakespeare Oxford Society Newsletter* and *The Elizabethan Review*. After finishing his book on the *Sonnets*, Peter was faced with rejections from publishers who insisted his lack of academic credentials prevented them from printing his discoveries. (The core of that book is presented here in four articles.) At that point, Peter decided to earn his research *bona fides* by gaining acceptance in European academic journals. In a dozen years, he published 11 notes, articles and monographs on William Shakespeare, Andrew Marvell, and historical figures of the Tudor period, such as the Earl of Surrey and Sir Walter Ralegh, in five journals.

The first section of this book focuses on Shakespeare's plays and sonnets without regard to authorship. The second section focuses on the case for Oxford as Shakespeare. The intellectual work Peter was inspired to perform because of the authorship question informs all of his writing in the field.

To peer at Peter's extra-literary knowledge is to understand how original insights into Shakespeare can emerge by integrating humanistic and scientific concepts, as in his concluding thoughts in «Hamlet and Surrey's ‹Psalm 8.›»

> If Surrey's influence on Shakespeare is granted, then one question remains. Did Shakespeare simply regard Surrey's pieces as useful quarries for his own work, or did he take an interest in their author? I believe that the answer lies in the character of Hamlet that Shakespeare fashioned—poet, courtier, scholar, soldier—and in the consistently negative twist or reversal Shakespeare gives to Surrey's thoughts as expressed by Hamlet, matching the contrast between

rash Surrey and indecisive Hamlet. That is, I believe that Hamlet is an intentional anti-Surrey, but not one who is opposite in every respect like a photographic negative. Rather Hamlet is opposite to Surrey in one important characteristic, but otherwise identical, as in the concept in physics known as anti-matter.

Peter contributed much more to the in-depth study of Shakespeare and his works—he employed objective historical methods to place the man and the canon within the context of Elizabethan England, and thereby generated significant new discoveries: the detection of concealed identities in poetry and drama; the identification and explication of literary and philosophical sources that together reveal the author's original intent; knowing how and when literature can serve as historical evidence; and integrating Shakespeare's plays and sonnets into their personal and political roles as defined by the era in which they were composed. This meant an examination not only of Shakespeare, his dramatic rivals and their literary output, but the social, religious and political environment prevailing in England and the Continent. Unifying these often disparate strands of intellectual study is rarely attempted, but highly rewarding, as the papers in this book show.

This, then, is why we publish the papers of a man who was neither formally trained in Shakespeare studies nor an experienced instructor of Shakespeare—the marvelous results of his research.

1 Identifying Shakespeare's Rival Poet in the *Sonnets* as Robert Devereux, Earl of Essex; confirming the case for Henry Wriothesley, Earl of Southampton, as the friend to whom the first 126 sonnets were addressed; showing that Sonnet subseries 1 to 126 as well as 127 to 152 (the Dark Lady sonnets), are both in their proper order, though the latter was penned before the midpoint of the first subseries; and demonstrating that Sonnets 78 to 100 can be dated to events in the life of the Earl of Southampton between his return from the Azores voyage in late 1597 and his departure for Ireland in early 1599.

2 Presenting a revised chronology of the complete plays of William Shakespeare by moving their initial date of composition back five

years and the terminus date back eight years from Sir E. K. Chambers' chronology of 1590 to 1613 — to a new framework spanning the years 1585 to 1604.

3   Identifying many of the literary and biblical sources of Hamlet's soliloquies — the Earl of Surrey's «Psalm 8,» *Piers Plowman*, etc. — while revealing how Shakespeare sets religious logic against human emotion throughout the play to establish the inner dynamic of *Hamlet*.

4   Identifying the sources and explicating the debate between Christian and pagan philosophies that undergirds *King Lear*, showing how pagan values may be rendered into Christian terms and vice versa through the mediation of nature.

5   Demonstrating how Shakespeare employed the concepts of time and Epicureanism in devising the dramatic action of *Macbeth*.

6   Offering a theory of Shakespeare's motivation for the composition of *Two Noble Kinsmen* — and why he failed to finish it.

7   Identifying Elizabethan playwright Thomas Dekker — rather than William Shakespeare — as the object of Ben Jonson's ire in the poem, «On Poet Ape.»

The discoveries embodied in the *Sonnets* articles were the results of research from the late 1980s and early 1990s; his chronology of the plays from the mid-1990s; the four articles on *Hamlet* involved a full decade of labor, from the mid-1990s to the mid-2000s; while the insights on *King Lear* and *Macbeth* came at the end of his life, during 2005-07 (his paper on *Macbeth* was finished the year of his death, and lacks Peter's concluding thoughts).

Peter was unique in another sense — he was the first Oxfordian scholar in 80 years to publish in such a wide variety of traditional academic journals on Shakespeare and the Tudor period, albeit by not acknowledging his authorship position. That Oxfordian sensibility informs all of his writing and his historical approach to literary scholarship, and compels us to present a synopsis of the Oxfordian case and Peter's thoughts on the matter.

Edward de Vere, 17th Earl of Oxford (12 April 1550 – 24 June 1604) was an Elizabethan courtier, playwright, poet, sportsman, patron of numerous writers, and sponsor of at least two acting companies, Oxford's Men and Oxford's Boys, as well as a company of musicians.

Oxford was one of the leading patrons of the Elizabethean age and, during his lifetime, 33 works were dedicated to the Earl, including publications on religion, philosophy, medicine and music. The focus of his patronage, however, was literary, with 13 of the books presented to him either original or translated works of world literature. Authors dedicating their works to De Vere include Edmund Spenser, Arthur Golding, John Lyly, Anthony Munday, and Thomas Churchyard, the latter three writers all having been employed by De Vere for various periods of time. His extensive patronage, as well as possible mismanagement of his estates, forced the sale of his ancestral lands. In 1586, the Queen granted the Earl an annuity of £1,000 for the remainder of his life.

In 1920, J.T. Looney's book, *Shakespeare Identified in Edward de Vere, 17th Earl of Oxford*, introduced the Oxfordian case for authorship of the Shakespeare canon, which has since gained adherents as varied as John Galsworthy, Sigmund Freud, Orson Welles, Sir Derek Jacobi, Sir Michael York, and US Supreme Court Justices John Paul Stevens and Antonin Scalia.

The case for Oxford's authorship is based on numerous similarities between Oxford's biography and events in Shakespeare's plays, sonnets and longer poems; parallels of language, idiom, and thought between Oxford's letters and the Shakespearean canon; and underlined passages in Oxford's Geneva Bible that may correspond to quotations in Shakespeare's plays. Oxfordians point to the acclaim of Oxford's contemporaries regarding his talent as a poet and a playwright, his reputation as a concealed poet, and his connections to London theatre and the contemporary playwrights of Shakespeare's day. They also note his long term relationships with Queen Elizabeth I and the Earl of Southampton, his knowledge of Court life, his extensive education, his academic and cultural achievements and his wide-ranging travels through France and

Italy, both of which form the background for ten of the plays, from *Merchant of Venice* and *Othello* to *Taming of the Shrew* and *Much Ado About Nothing*.

Lewis Lapham, former editor of *Harpers Magazine*, published a cover story on the authorship question in the April 1999 issue, and later summed up the intellectual consensus regarding the controversy in 2003, when he hosted a public debate on the issue: «On one side we have a voice but not a man; on the other, we have a face but not a man. Why is your candidate the most likely author? You have some servings of documents on behalf of William Shaksper. The Oxfordians have internal evidence and the personal life. Both sides present a circumstantial case. Neither is conclusive.»

Peter proceeded from the position that sufficient circumstantial evidence had accumulated since 1920 to demontrate that Edward de Vere, 17th Earl of Oxford was the author William Shakespeare. On the other hand—as indicated by Lapham's comments—Peter thought the case required more conclusive proof to be persuasive to academicians, who had invested much prestige over time in another candidate.

Peter's contributions to the Oxfordian case were significant, and based on scouring primary documents in Elizabethan archives as well as extensive reading of modern scholars writing about the era's social and political environment, its ideas and sensibility. In the second section of this book, papers 1-6 sum up Peter's negative case against Shakspeare; papers 7-13 embody Peter's positive argument for Oxford; papers 14-16 comprise Peter's response to orthodox authorities such as Professor Alan Nelson of UC, Berkeley and Claremont College's Shakespeare Authorship Project; and, finally, papers 17-18 represent Peter's recommendations regarding engagement with the Shakespeare establishment and future research efforts that seek to prove the Oxfordian hypothesis.

In general, I think Peter's numerous discoveries and insights demonstrate that the Shakespeare authorship issue demands an interdisciplinary perspective to be properly researched and resolved.

On the reason for the Oxfordian «cover-up» Peter was definite—the 17th Earl of Oxford's goal was to secure his son's inheritance and title to the earldom while preserving the reputation of his three daughters so that they could marry well. On both scores Oxford was successful. This was both a social and political issue for Oxford, for publicly acknowledging his poetry and dramas would clearly violate the rules of behavior of the English aristocratic class, which held it *infra dig* for any member of the nobility to be associated with the world of the theater as anything but patron—defined in Elizabethan law as the lowest of society's professions.

In this regard, Peter understood that for an Elizabethan nobleman to appear in public—in print as author or on stage as performer—would invite general ridicule of the class that governed England. German author Robert Detobel cites John Selden's *Table Talk*, written in the 17th century, in support of this argument: «Tis ridiculous for a Lord to print verses, 'tis well enough to make them to please himself but to make them publick is foolish. If a man in a private Chamber twirles his Band string, or plays with a Rush to please himselfe 'tis well enough, but if hee should goe into Fleet streete & sett upon a stall & twirle his bandstring or play with a Rush, then all the boyes in the streete would laugh at him.» In other words, to expose one's verses in print to the public view or to act upon a stage would be as ridiculous for a nobleman as playing children's games in public.

Forfeiting one's status was something not to be taken lightly, as Victor Kiernan writes in his book, *The Duel in European History* (1988): «Every superior class, even the most secure, holds over its members the menace of forfeiture of status if they deviate from its prescriptions. Even a Brahmin can lose caste.» (14) Equally important is his observation that, «niceties of social behavior were given an importance now scarcely comprehensible.»

Peter highlighted the reason for Shakespeare's fall from grace at the end of his article on the Garter Elections:

The 17th Earl of Oxford had been a man of popularity and prestige, but he fell from favor and honor twice, first in 1581, then again after 1588. Shakespeare's personal sense of disgrace is found throughout his *Sonnets*: the poet is barred from «public honour and proud titles» (25), he wants his name buried with his body (72), he knows himself to be «vile esteemed» (121). Finally, Shakespeare alludes to the cause of his dishonor several times, most clearly in Sonnet 110: «I ... made myself a motley to the view.»

By writing for the stage, Oxford had thereby gained a public notoriety that was incompatible with his status as a courtier—and which required intervention to prevent loss of all privileges for his family.

To find his way back to favor meant Oxford would be compelled to transfer that shameful reputation for poetry and playwrighting to a low-born rustic, where it could rest without social violation—and thereby free himself of the consequences of loss of caste. Moreover, to maintain the earldom in the family meant the dissimulation had to endure beyond Oxford's own lifetime. Of course, being forced to surrender that identity by his class created an authorship issue that still confronts us four hundred years after Oxford's death in 1604.

This book is Peter Moore's intellectual legacy.

Gary Goldstein

Part One:
New Shakespearean Vistas

The Rival Poet of Shakespeare's *Sonnets*

My research on the *Sonnets* resulted in a series of four articles: the first demonstrates why Robert Devereaux, 2nd Earl of Essex, was the Rival Poet of Sonnets 78 to 86. The second shows that Sonnets 78 to 100 can be dated quite firmly to events in the life of the Earl of Southampton between his return from the Azores voyage in late 1597 and his departure for Ireland in early 1599. The latter article will be largely independent of the theory that Essex was the Rival, and both articles will be independent of the Shakespeare authorship controversy. The third article discusses the implications of the first two articles with regard to the authorship controversy and will bring the 17th Earl of Oxford into the picture (particularly with regard to some of the later Sonnets). The concluding article argues that the *Sonnets* as published in 1609 are in the right order. This fourth article is partly motivated by original material, but also by the fact that most learned commentators believe the question of the order of the *Sonnets* is one of subjective literary judgment. In fact, there exist a number of completely objective, non-judgmental reasons for believing that the *Sonnets* are properly ordered.

Shake-speares Sonnets appeared in 1609, apparently published without the author's consent, and probably suppressed by the authorities as they were not republished until 1640. There are 154 sonnets; the first 126 address a young aristocrat, commonly called the Fair Youth, with whom Shakespeare was infatuated (though whether the motivation was sexual is quite unclear—I join the majority who believe it was not). The next 26 describe Shakespeare's relations with his unfaithful mistress, the Dark Lady. These sonnets were apparently written during rather than after the Fair Youth series, and so Sonnet 126 may be taken as the closing poem. Sonnets 78 to 86 concern a Rival Poet who competed with Shakespeare for the affections of the Fair Youth. Sonnets 153 and 154 are an unrelated finial.

The principal questions about the *Sonnets* are the identities of the Fair Youth, Dark Lady, and Rival Poet, the dates of their composition, the problem of whether their 1609 order is correct, and what, if any, topical allusions are found in them. This article supports the consensus that the Fair Youth was Henry Wriothesley, 3rd Earl of Southampton, a vain and reckless young man who, following a treason conviction and two years of imprisonment, matured into a model husband, a courageous champion of Parliamentary rights, and a hard working patron and director of the Virginia colony. He was born in 1573 and died on campaign in the Netherlands in 1624. Shakespeare's only dedications (of *Venus and Adonis* in 1593 and *The Rape of Lucrece* in 1594) were written to Southampton. No substantial candidate has emerged for the role of the Dark Lady. The most often proposed Rival Poets are George Chapman and Christopher Marlowe, but the arguments for them are thin; even weaker cases have been offered for virtually every other contemporary professional poet. The conventional wisdom is that the *Sonnets* were begun in the early or mid-1590s and continue past the death of Queen Elizabeth and the advent of King James in 1603 (which events are referred to in Sonnet 107). This series of articles will argue that the conventional wisdom is correct. As has been indicated, I also feel that within the two subseries (Sonnets 1 to 126 and 127 to 154) the *Sonnets* are in the right order.

And now to the Rival Poet.

Robert Devereux, 2nd Earl of Essex, was the brilliant but flawed star of the late Elizabethan firmament. He was the Queen's most illustrious (though not her best) military and naval commander during the 1590s; he was her last great favorite; and he attempted to take over her government from the astute and cautious dynasty of Sir William Cecil, Lord Burghley and his son Sir Robert. Desperation and mental instability led him into a botched coup that cost him his head in February 1601. He was intelligent, handsome, athletic, improvident, charming, a generous patron of writers, a commander of real talent, a confirmed womanizer, a devout Protestant who leaned toward Puritanism, a ditherer on several critical occasions, and a dangerously unstable egotist who finally lost touch with reality. He was also the best friend and hero of the youthful 3rd Earl of Southampton. He was also a poet whose talent was admired by his contemporaries.

Essex exerted a major gravitational force on his age, and he influenced William Shakespeare, who praised Essex in *Henry V*. Contemporaries also saw a resemblance, intended or not, between Essex and Bolingbroke in *Richard II*. It has plausibly been suggested that *Love's Labour's Lost* had something to do with Essex's circle, that the description of Cawdor's execution in *Macbeth* evokes the death of Essex, and that «The Phoenix and the Turtle» glorifies Essex's love for Elizabeth. Above all, Essex appears in books about Shakespeare as the hero of Southampton, Shakespeare's sole dedicatee. There are more than ten good reasons for proposing Essex as the Rival of the Sonnets, and, in Ben Jonson's words, «I therefore will begin.»

First, Sonnets 78 to 86 describe a man who was Shakespeare's rival for the affections of Southampton during the 1590s. The man who is known to have had Southampton's affection during that period was the heroic and charismatic Earl of Essex. Southampton attempted to serve under Essex in the Cadiz expedition of 1596, but was forbidden by the Queen; he did serve under and was knighted by Essex on the Azores expedition of 1597. Southampton sought Essex's counsel when in financial difficulties, agreed to marry Essex's penniless cousin (whom he had gotten with child) in 1598, and named his daughter after Essex's sister. During the failed Irish campaign of 1599, Essex made Southampton his General of the Horse and was furious when Queen Elizabeth vetoed his decision.

In December 1599 Essex was near death with fever and wrote Southampton a moving letter of counsel. This letter, published in Thomas Birch's *Memoirs of the Reign of Queen Elizabeth*, holds several points of interest. Like Shakespeare's Sonnets 2 and 4, it addresses Southampton in terms of the Parable of the Talents. It also contains the following passage, which confirms that on some previous occasion Essex eulogized Southampton: «What I think of your natural gifts... to give glory to God, and to win honour to yourself... I will not now tell you. It sufficeth, that when I was farthest of all times from dissembling, I spoke freely, and had witnesses enough.»[1]

Southampton was Essex's right-hand man during the 1601 uprising, and they were tried and sentenced together; they kissed hands and embraced at the start of the trial, and Essex did what he could to protect Southampton. Both were adjudged to die, but Southampton was spared, though deprived of titles, estates, and liberty.

Second, Essex was rated a gifted poet by his contemporaries and was admired as a writer by Ben Jonson (who called him «noble and high») and as a critic by Gabriel Harvey. Essex's friend and sometime secretary Sir Henry Wotton wrote that it was «his common way... to evaporate his thoughts in a Sonnet.» Essex wrote poems for specific occasions. Rather than out of any dedication to poetry, he penned his verses only for his own circle and the Queen, so little of his poetry survives. Thus the puzzling disappearance of the poems of Shakespeare's Rival is quite understandable if Essex wrote them. Rival Poems by a professional like Chapman should have survived.

Essex's verse is hardly in a class with Shakespeare's, nor is it close, but it is technically accomplished, sincere, and moving. It may be protested that Essex's talent was so slender that Shakespeare could not possibly have regarded him as a rival, but this objection ignores the fact that the rivalry lay in the eyes of Southampton and not in the views of literary critics. Any poetic praise from Essex was bound to make Southampton ecstatic, given his idolization of Essex. This is a sufficient answer to the objection, but two lesser points may be added. First, *Shakespeare's Sonnets* contain criticism that may not have been welcome to Southampton, e.g., «thou dost common grow» (Sonnet 69, line 14). Next, Southampton was quite an active young man in the 1590s: jouster, athlete, gambler, patron, womanizer, brawler, arid above all, a would-be warrior who finally got his chance and distinguished himself on the Azores voyage. But Shakespeare's praise is all of passive qualities such as being fair and beauteous. His poetics may endlessly fascinate, but his subject matter can be tedious. Praise of Southampton's martial prowess by the great Essex might have been more agreeable.[2]

Third, the Rival is said to be «learned» (78, 7); it is implied that he knew the art of rhetoric, a major academic subject in those days (82, 10), and he had a «polished form of well-refined pen» (85, 8). Essex received his MA from Cambridge in his midteens, maintained a lifelong interest in intellectual matters, and surrounded himself with educated men.

Fourth and fifth, the Rival was «of tall building and of goodly pride» (80, 12), and his pride is further alluded to in Sonnet 86. Several contemporaries recorded that Essex was notably tall. His pride was inordinate even by the standards of Elizabethan nobility—it consumed and finally destroyed him.

Sixth, Shakespeare contrasts himself to his mighty Rival with much nautical metaphor in Sonnets 80 and 86. Shakespeare is a «saucy bark» (80, 7), while the Rival is «the proudest sail» (80, 6) whose «great verse» is called «the proud full sail» (86, 1). So we may suppose that the Rival was something of a sailor. Essex distinguished himself on the Lisbon voyage of 1589, won further glory as co-commander of the 1596 Cadiz expedition, and was sole commander of the ill-managed Azores venture of 1597. (Essex unjustly placed the blame on his Rear Admiral, Sir Walter Ralegh[3]).

Seventh, Sonnet 86 says that the Rival has an «affable familiar ghost/ Which nightly gulls him with intelligence» (lines 9-10). Seekers of the Rival Poet always take this passage as indicating occult practices and try to show that their candidates were up to such activities. The task is not difficult, as almost everyone back then was more or less superstitious by modern standards, but a far more mundane explanation is available. Essex maintained his own international intelligence service as part of his rivalry with the Cecils, who commanded the official intelligence agency. It was Essex's aim to be better informed than the government and to be the first to tell the Queen of foreign events. Essex's chief of intelligence was the erudite Anthony Bacon, who had friends all over Europe, and who lived in Essex's mansion in the Strand from 1595 to 1600.

Thus, without conjuring up necromancers and astrologers, we find the «affable familiar ghost»: an intelligence director whose greatest asset was his legion of overseas friends (hence, «affable»), and who lived as part of Essex's household (a «familiar» in the old-fashioned sense). «Ghost» is appropriate for a man who was active behind the scenes, but who suffered from so many ailments (dying in 1601) that he became a virtual recluse after moving to Essex House and was forced to decline invitations from the Queen to present himself at Court.

Eighth, the Rival was a «spirit, by spirits taught to write» (86, 5), and had friends «Giving him aid» (86, 8). Various people are believed to have assisted Essex with his writing, including his personal secretary Henry Cuffe, an occasional poet and former professor of Greek, Anthony Bacon, who is known to have written some sonnets, and Lord Henry Howard (later Earl of Northampton), a part-time consultant of Essex's. It is perfectly possible that Essex received aid from the professional poets he patronized, including George Chapman, in which case some of the other Rival Poet theories would be part right. But there is one poet who is known to have ghost written serious essays and also a masque for Essex: Anthony Bacon's brother Francis.

Ninth, we can find support for the new theory of the Bacons as The Rival Poet's Ghost Writers by considering some word play in the passage, «affable familiar ghost/Which nightly gulls him with intelligence.» «Ghost» and «gulls» are linked by alliteration, but also by the superstition (prevalent then and now) that gulls are inhabited by the ghosts of drowned sailors. «Gulls» is thus a bridge between the two sets of imagery, nautical and ghostly, used in Sonnet 86. These words also harbor an appropriate Latin pun (all of the principals mentioned in this article were fluent in Latin), since the Latin for «familiar ghost» is «Lar» or «Lans,» usually encountered in it plural form «Lares»: the Latin for «ghost» or «specter» is «larva.» The Latin for «gull» is «larus»; the modern scientific name for the gull family is «Laridae.» The Latin for «bacon» is variously «laridum,» «lardum,» or «larida.» It may be added that making puns, anagrams, and acrostics on names was a popular sport in that age.

Tenth comes the following passage on the Rival: «He lends thee virtue, and he stole that word/From thy behavior» (79, 9-10). Essex's mottoes were *Virtutis Com Invidia* (literally «virtue with envy» or, more loosely «manliness draws envy») and *Basis Virtutum Constantia* («loyalty [is] the basis of virtue or manliness»).

The remaining items of evidence concern not only the identity of the Rival, but also the question of the dates of the Rival Poet Sonnets. My hypothesis is that Sonnets 78 to 86 were written soon after Essex and Southampton returned from the Azores in late October 1597.

Eleventh, despite objections by William Shakespeare, cosmetics were used by men as well as women in the Elizabethan Age. Judging by contemporary poetry, the fashionable complexion consisted of a face as white as lilies, a touch of roses in the cheeks, and lips like rubies (teeth were usually compared to pearls). Those not blessed by nature with such an appearance could paint their faces with white lead and redden their lips and cheeks with rouge. Sonnets 82 («And their gross painting might be better used/Where cheeks need blood; in thee it is abus'd,» lines 13-14) and 83 («I never saw that you did painting need,» line 1) disparagingly associate the Rival with the use of cosmetics.

There are two portraits of Essex in the National Portrait Gallery in London, both believed to have been painted around 1597. In any event, they are later than August 1596, as Essex is wearing the beard grown on the Cadiz voyage. One is a full-length portrait of Essex standing in the robes of a Knight of the Garter; it is reproduced in color in *National Portrait Gallery in Colour*, edited by Richard Ormond, who dates the portrait circa 1597. The other is a head and shoulders portrait of Essex in a white satin doublet (he wears the same garment in the standing portrait), with a ruff over a transparent collar over a wide blue ribbon that suspends his St. George medal; it is reproduced in color in *The Horizon Book of the Elizabethan World*, by Lacey Baldwin Smith and bears the date 1597. During the early part of that year, Essex should have had something of a tan left over from his several months at sea during the summer of 1596. During the latter part of 1597, Essex should have been bronzed by his voyage to the Azores. However, the standing portrait shows Essex with a ghastly pallor; his face has obviously been painted white, and his lips have probably been carmined as well. The head and shoulders portrait shows him with lips of a bright, artificial red, unquestionably carmined, and a face that is not quite as pallid as in the other portrait, but that is far too pale for a man who had been making summer voyages to the latitude of southern Spain.

Yet Essex had another link to cosmetics at that time. At the beginning of 1598, the Queen gave him all of the available stock of cochineal, partly as an outright gift and partly by selling it to him at a reduced price. She then banned any further imports for two years; the total profit to Essex was reportedly the immense sum of 40,000 pounds. Cochineal is a bright red dye used then for textiles but also for painting the lips and cheeks. The two portraits of Essex are of around 1597, and the Elizabethan year 1597 was, by modern reckoning, April 4, 1597 to April 3, 1598, so the two portraits may show Essex wearing his own product. In short, Shakespeare simultaneously complains about the Rival Poet and face paint, while Essex used cosmetics and had a monopoly on rouge.

Twelfth is Shakespeare's assertion in the nautical Sonnet 80 (lines 3-4) that his Rival «spends all his might/...speaking of your [Southampton's] fame.» Hyperbolic praise was common in Elizabethan poetry, but the first incident in Southampton's career that would reasonably justify lauding his fame was his return from the Azores in late October 1597 with a knighthood and the spoils of one of the few prizes taken on that voyage.

We also know that Southampton's success was exaggerated. The prize that he looted and abandoned was quite small, but one courtier sent a friend the following information. «This morning my Lord Essex's letters came to court of his safe landing in Plymouth. He had unfortunately missed the (Spanish) King's own ships with the Indian Treasure but fell on the merchant fleet. Four of them he hath taken, and sunk many more, my Lord of Southampton fought with one of the King's great Men of War, and sunk her.» So it appears that Essex was indeed puffing the fame of the Fair Youth.

Thirteenth, the theme of Sonnet 79 may be stated as follows: «You [the Fair Youth] owe the Rival Poet no thanks for his praise, because he is simply repaying his debt to you.» A partisan of Southampton's who was resentful of Essex could very well make such an argument in the wake of the Azores expedition, in which the value of the loot was far less than the cost of the voyage. The five prizes taken kept the expedition from being a total failure, and one of them was seized by Southampton while his ship was detached from the fleet. So Shakespeare would feel justified in telling Southampton that Essex was simply giving him his due by knighting and praising him.

Fourteenth, and rather tenuously, we may note Shakespeare's remark in the same sonnet that «my sick Muse doth give another place» (79, 4). This line may be paraphrased in two ways, either «my sick Muse yields to another Muse,» or «my sick Muse yields to another sick Muse.» It is impossible to be certain as to whether the pronoun «another» includes the adjective «sick» as well as the noun «Muse,» but such a reference would be highly appropriate. When Essex returned from the Azores he found that the Queen blamed him for the expedition's failure and that two of his rivals at court had stolen marches on him during his absence. He responded by shutting himself up in his house for several weeks, claiming to be ill. So Shakespeare would be quite justified in implying that his Rival's Muse is sick.

Shakespeare's Sonnets describe a rival who was Southampton's friend, a poet, learned, tall, proud, probably a sailor, who had an affable familiar ghost who dealt in intelligence, who received assistance in his writing from friends whose name makes a plausible Latin pun on Bacon, who was associated with the word «virtue» and with cosmetics, who boosted Southampton's fame while being in his debt, and who could be said to have a sick muse. This is quite a detailed portrait, and Essex matches it perfectly.

Endnotes

1   Thomas Birch, *Memoirs of the Reign of Queen Elizabeth* (London: A. Millar, 1754) 484.

2   The most recent and thorough analysis of Essex's surviving poems is in «The Poems of Edward DeVere, Seventeenth Earl of Oxford and of Robert Devereux, Second Earl of Essex,» by Steven W. May, *Studies in Philology*, LXXVII, Early Winter 1980, No.5.

3   If the arguments offered in this article in favor of Essex as the Rival are applied one by one to Sir Walter Ralegh, it will be seen that a surprisingly strong case can be made for him as the Rival Poet. At any rate, the case for Ralegh is far superior to the arguments that have been offered in favor of Chapman, Marlowe, or any other professional poet. I mention this not to suggest Ralegh as a backup candidate behind Essex, but to underscore the dereliction of orthodox Shakespeare scholars. The courtier poets of the Elizabethan Age held high prestige, while the leading candidates for the role of Shakespeare's Fair Youth (Southampton and the Earl of Pembroke) were both courtiers. Yet it never occurred to the Shakespeare establishment that the Rival Poet might be a courtier.

Dating Shakespeare's Sonnets 78 to 100

This article is sequel to «The Rival Poet of Shakespeare's Sonnets,» which showed that the Rival of Sonnets 78 to 86 was Robert Devereux, 2nd Earl of Essex. Four of the fourteen points made in that article assist in the problem of dating, as well as in identifying the Rival Poet: Essex's cosmetic connections, his exaggeration of Southampton's exploits on the Azores voyage, his figurative debt to Southampton resulting from that voyage, and his subsequent illness allow the Rival Sonnets to be dated between November 1597 and January 1598. The next significant event in the life of Southampton (to whom the Sonnets were addressed) was his departure for the Continent with a two-year travel warrant in February 1598. Indeed, we observe that the first sonnet after the Rival Sonnets, number 87, begins with the word «Farewell.»

Southampton left for France accompanying Sir Robert Cecil on a diplomatic mission to King Henri IV, after which he intended to tour Italy. Elizabeth Vernon, his mistress and Essex's first cousin, was reduced to tears by his departure. Cecil and Southampton located Henri IV at Angers, were unsuccessful in their mission, and so Cecil returned to England in April, while Southampton headed for the fleshpots of Paris. In August, the visibly pregnant Elizabeth Vernon, one of the Queen's Maids of Honour, left the Court for refuge at Essex House, and old Lord Burghley died that same month. On September 3, Cecil wrote to Southampton in Paris, saying that the Queen was aware that Southampton had secretly returned to England, married his mistress, and returned to France—and that he was to come back to England forthwith. Meanwhile, the new Countess of Southampton was jailed in the Fleet prison. Southampton was desperately trying to recoup huge gambling losses, and so he delayed his return from Paris. He came back to England prior to November 8, suffered a short spell of imprisonment, and his wife bore a daughter. From April through September 1599, Southampton sought glory by campaigning under Essex in Ireland.

If Sonnet 87 refers to February 1598, then we can continue in the following vein. Sonnets 88 to 91 tend to confirm the separation of Shakespeare and the Fair Youth, i.e., «thou didst forsake me for some fault» (Sonnet 89, line 1), «Be absent from thy walks» (89,9), and «If thou wilt leave me» (90, 9). Sonnets 88 («place my merit in the eye of scorn,» line 2), 89, and 90 («Then hate me when thou wilt,» line 1) indicate a quarrel between Shakespeare and the Fair Youth, which is consistent with the fact that Southampton remained a devoted follower of Essex despite Shakespeare's attacks on him in the Rival Poet Sonnets. Sonnet 92 begins, «But do thy worst to steal thyself away,» which is plausible as a reference to Southampton's furtive visit to England in August and his secret return to France. Sonnets 93 and 94, and especially 95 and 96, discuss the Fair Youth's sinfulness, but before pondering that fact we should pause at the much discussed Sonnet 94:

> They that have power to hurt and will do none,
> That do not do the thing they most do show,
> Who, moving others, are themselves as stone,
> Unmoved, cold, and to temptation slow;
> They rightly do inherit heaven's graces,
> And husband nature's riches from expense;
> They are the lords and owners to their faces,
> Others but stewards of their excellence.
> The summer's flower is to the summer sweet,
> Though to itself it only live and die,
> But if that flower with base infection meet,
> The basest weed outbraves his dignity:
>> For sweetest things turn sourest by their deeds;
>> Lilies that fester smell far worse than weeds.

The first eight lines (the octave) describe politic persons who achieve power, and it is impossible to avoid tying them to the most politic Englishmen of the age, Lord Burghley (whose magnificent funeral coincided with Southampton's marriage) and his son and political heir Sir Robert Cecil. These two remarkable men were crafty, cautious, farsighted, moderate in the use of power, no more unscrupulous than the age they lived in, and were dedicated to the state and to the fortunes of their family. Under Queen Elizabeth I and King James, they governed England wisely from 1558 to 1612. Soon after Burghley's death, a member of his household wrote a panegyric memoir of his late master, which includes the following passages: «His natural disposition was ... slow to anger, ever shunning revenge, and never doing anything in fury or choler, neither yielding to passion, but always tempering his affections ... He was ... never moved with joyful or ill news. He could better cover his griefs than help it, and whatsoever was in his mind would never appear in his countenance or speech.» It would be difficult to find a closer match to Sonnet 94's octave, and Sir Robert Cecil shared his father's poker-faced nature.

Burghley, the Lord Treasurer of England, was also Master of the Court of Wards from 1561 until his death. Discussions of the harshness and corruption of many Tudor institutions commonly make allowance for the times, but the Court of Wards was a scandal in its own day. It was a moribund feudal institution, revived by Henry VII, strengthened by his descendants, and destroyed by the Civil War.[1] It seized upon underage heirs, sold them to officials and courtiers, and caused their estates to be legally plundered. Burghley kept the best of the lot, six young earls, under his own guardianship. All six, two of whom were Southampton and Essex, were intellectually gifted, each received a superb education under Burghley's guidance, and five eventually turned against Burghley or his son. Burghley spied on and attempted to dominate his former wards after they became adults, he tried to make Southampton marry his granddaughter, and he reportedly assessed a huge fine to punish Southampton's rejection of the lady (which was a lawful penalty for a ward who turned down a suitable spouse). The passing of the great Lord Burghley was a landmark in the reign of Elizabeth I and it must have been a monumental event to his former wards; let the octave of Sonnet 94 (especially line 5) be Shakespeare's epitaph on William Cecil, Lord Burghley.

Otherwise, we may note that the octave of Sonnet 94 has nothing to do with its sestet, unless one strives to force a link. It is a reasonable conjecture that revelatory material (presumably identifying Burghley and Southampton) was chopped out of two sonnets, with the remnants being joined to form the present Sonnet 94.

Some unspecified sins of the Fair Youth are harped upon in Sonnets 93 to 96: «thy sweet virtue answer[s] not thy show» (93, 14); «Lilies that fester smell far worse than weeds» (94, 14); «shame ... canker ... spot ...sins ... lascivious comments ... dispraise ... ill report ...vices ... blot» (95); «fault ... wantoness ... faults ... faults ... errors» (96). This paternalistic chiding meshes perfectly with the scandal caused by Southampton's secret marriage to a pregnant Maid of Honour, and perhaps also with his excesses in Paris. Additionally, Shakespeare's remark about «the beauty of thy budding name» (95, 3) is most appropriate to the condition of the new Countess; the name of Wriothesley was indeed budding.

The first lines of Sonnets 97 and 98 mention Shakespeare's absence from the Fair Youth, and so one might suppose that Shakespeare departed while his friend remained. However, line 12 of Sonnet 97 says «thou away» and line 13 of Sonnet 98 says «you away,» which indicate the contrary. Sonnet 97 relates that the friend was gone during a summer and a «teeming autumn,» i.e., harvest time or early autumn, while Sonnet 98 informs us that the friend was also away during the spring. Spring, summer, and early fall were precisely the seasons of Southampton's absence from England in 1598. Shakespeare's comment about the «teeming autumn» implies a good harvest, but the years 1594 through 1597 were years of disastrous weather and ruined crops, known as «the great dearth.» On the other hand, the year 1598 witnessed a good harvest that must have been all the more welcome after four bad years.[2]

We will close the evidence with Sonnet 100's couplet:

> Give my love fame faster than Time wastes life;
> So thou prevent'st his scythe and crooked knife.

Southampton sought fame at the risk of his life in Ireland in 1599.

It should be pointed out that finding the dates of Sonnets 78 to 100 was remarkably easy and could have been done in complete ignorance of the identity of the Rival Poet. A standard method of trying to date the *Sonnets* starts by noting that Sonnets 1 to 17 urge the Fair Youth to wed, which can be linked to unsuccessful efforts between 1590 and 1594 to get the underage Southampton to marry, while Sonnet 107 was almost certainly penned in 1603. One then examines Sonnets 18 to 106 for apparent references to external events and tries to tie them to Southampton's recorded life from 1590/94 to 1603. Sonnets 93 to 96 show the Fair Youth in trouble for wanton and lascivious behavior, and the only known sex scandal in Southampton's life was his secret marriage to a pregnant Maid of Honour in August 1598. Had anyone linked these two facts, no matter how tentatively, then everything else would have fallen into place. One could then note the coincidence of that wedding and Lord Burghley's funeral, and the fact that Sonnet 94's octave is a perfect description of Burghley. One could realize that «thy budding name» is a plausible reference to an expecting wife. One could see the references to absence, to stealing away, and to the seasons, and tie them to Southampton's trip to France. Finally, one could note the opening reference to warships in Sonnet 86 and the closing reference to fame and danger in Sonnet 100, and connect these to Southampton's sea and land campaigns in 1597 and 1599.

The twentieth century's dean on the subject of William Shakespeare was the late Sir Edmund Chambers. In his magisterial *William Shakespeare: A Study of Facts and Problems*, Chambers granted that «the case for him (Southampton) as the friend of the sonnets is now very generally accepted ... I do not think it a convincing one. If it were sound, one would expect to find some hints in the sonnets of the major interests of Southampton's early life; his military ambitions, his comradeship with Essex, the romance of his marriage.»[3] Sir Edmund's excellent criteria are now met.

The two hypotheses offered in these articles — Essex as the Rival and the dates of Sonnets 78 to 100 — are based on research in a university library rather than in the archives. However, the papers of Anthony Bacon,

Lord Henry Howard, and others connected to Essex still exist, and it would be extraordinary if these theories could not be confirmed, expanded, or, for that matter, refuted by the archives.

Endnotes

1   Further details are found in Joel Hurstfield's *The Queens Wards*. (London: Longmans, Green 1958).

2. The sufficiency of the 1598 harvest is indicated by Y.S. Brenner, «The Inflation of Prices in England, 1551-1650,» *The Economic History Review*, December 1962, 281-2; and by Peter Ramsey, *Tudor Economic Problems* (London: Gollancz, 1936), 116.

3   E. K. Chambers, *William Shakespeare: A Study of the Facts and Problems* (Oxford: Clarendon Press, 1930), Vol. I, 565.

Every Word Doth Almost Tell My Name

This article follows two earlier pieces, «The Rival Poet of Shakespeare's Sonnets» and «Dating Shakespeare's Sonnets 78 to 100.» They showed that Shakespeare's Rival was Robert Devereux, Earl of Essex, they confirmed the case for Henry Wriothesley, Earl of Southampton, as the friend to whom the first 126 sonnets were addressed, and they showed that Sonnets 78 to 100 date from 1597 to 1599. These points are made without regard to the Shakespeare authorship controversy, which we now will enter.

The *Sonnets* are Shakespeare's only direct autobiography; indeed, aside from two short formal dedications, they are his only surviving utterances in the first person. They are passionate, tormented, sometimes sordid, occasionally reticent (see Sonnets 33 and 88), and are manifestly heartfelt. They are the ultimate fusion of intense emotion and poetical skill, and they ought to form the centerpiece of any biography of their author. Others have written eloquently on why the *Sonnets* make no sense as the testament of William Shakspere of Straftord, but do fit what we know of Edward de Vere, 17th Earl of Oxford. That this is so is testified to by the silence, variously glib, stony, or embarrassed, of orthodox biographers when they come to the *Sonnets*. This article will not present a full discussion of the *Sonnets* and the Oxford authorship theory, but will be limited to specific points that have come out of my research. The first two items were omitted from my first two articles, as the latter were purposely kept independent of the authorship controversy.

My article on the Rival Poet listed fourteen reasons for Essex, but there is a fifteenth that relates to Oxford and also to the matter of dating. Sonnet 85 says that Shakespeare «holds his rank before» the Rival (line 12). This passage has a clear surface meaning about love, but can also be taken as an allusion to certain events at the end of 1597. In October of that year, Queen Elizabeth elevated her Lord Admiral, Howard of Effingham (victor over the Armada and co-commander at Cadiz) to Earl of Nottingham, which made him the junior earl, close behind Essex. However, his office of Lord Admiral (as well as a new office, Lord Steward) gave him precedence of all earls save Oxford, the Lord Great Chamberlain. Essex was infuriated by this relative demotion (as the Queen undoubtedly intended), and so he claimed sickness and refused to attend court, council, or Parliament until he was made Earl Marshal in December. The journal of the House of Lords therefore recorded that on January 11, 1598, Essex «having been creted Earl Marshal ... took his place according to his said office, viz. next after the Earl of Oxon, Chamberlain of England, and before the Earl of Nottingham, Lord Steward and Lord Admiral.» Thus, Oxford «held his rank before» Essex.

My article on dating discussed Lord Burghley's character and Mastership of the Court of Wards, and noted that the octave of Sonnet 94 describes him with a remarkable balance of animosity and respect. I also pointed out that Essex and Southampton had been his wards, but, of course, Oxford too had been his ward, then became his son-in-law, and, from his point of view, had cause to resent Burghley. It is difficult to see why Will of Stratford would care, know, and dare enough to write those eight lines (besides satirizing Burghley as Polonius in *Hamlet*), but it is clear why Oxford would do so.

In Sonnet 122, Shakespeare apologizes for giving away some «tables» presented to him by Southampton, which are also called «tallies thy dear love to score» (line 10); Southampton is assured that Shakespeare has retained their contents. The standard Stratfordian explication of this sonnet is truly bizarre. We read that the «tables» are a commonplace book, a blank notebook in which people in those days jotted down virtuous, wise, or clever thoughts, sayings, or fragments of literature for future mental and moral profit. As for the «tallies,» the experts call this a reference to notched sticks used to count the score in an alehouse or to record debts among the unlettered. In other words, Shakespeare, apologizing as gracefully as he can for parting with a notebook filled with the Earl of Southampton's profoundest thoughts, likens the book to the IOU of an illiterate or a drunkard. One hardly knows whether to laugh, cry, or declare that we are beginning to get at the cause of the occasional quarrels between the Bard and the Fair Youth. As was pointed out some years ago, the only way to reconcile Shakespeare's equation of Southampton's «tables» with scoring tallies is by considering it as a reference to the ornamental sheets used to tally scores in a tournament. As it happens, Southampton and another earl were the top performers in King James' 1604 Accession Day Tournament. For Southampton to present his scoring sheet to Oxford, an undefeated tournament champion in his youth, seems quite appropriate. Moreover, Oxford, by then three months from death and perhaps no longer enamored of chivalric prowess, might have given the gift away.

Next, we should consider four sonnets, numbers 117, 119, 120, and 126, that seem to allude to events of February 8 and 19, 1601. On the former date, Essex and Southampton attempted a coup that failed, and they surrendered that night. On the latter date, they were unanimously convicted of treason by a jury of twenty-five peers, the senior one of which was Oxford. A bit of background information is needed to understand how the verdict may have affected later relations between Oxford and Southampton.

First, Essex and Southampton were manifestly guilty of treason, and the judges and prosecutors easily destroyed their legalistic attempts to justify their actions. Also, impartiality of judges and jurors, the right to counsel, the rules of evidence, and other legal niceties were either non-existent or were scrapped during treason trials in that period. A suspected traitor might clear himself during the pre-trial investigation, but if the case went to court, then guilt had already been determined; the trial was a public display of the wickedness of the accused and the power of the government. No Elizabethan treason trial produced any verdict but guilty (though there was one acquittal under Eiizabeth's not too competent sister Mary, while another occurred right at the start of James' reign). Also, a unanimous verdict was necessary to convict a commoner, but only a majority was needed to convict a peer.

More important, the situation facing Southampton was quite different from that of Essex. The latter was the leader of the uprising, his third serious offense in as many years, and had let himself become politically isolated, so that no important people were likely to ask the Queen to show him mercy. On the contrary, the most powerful man in England, Sir Robert Cecil, wanted him dead, while other major figures like the Earl of Nottingham were his enemies. On the other hand, the rebellion was Southampton's first major offense, he was a follower rather than the leader, he was liked by many influential people, beginning with Cecil, and despite his twenty-seven years and three campaigns, he was considered young and not fully responsible for his actions. In addition, he and Essex both claimed that their lives were threatened by their enemies, and that they rose up in self-defense. This plea was nonsense in Essex's case, but was partly true for Southampton. His enemy Lord Grey (a member of the jury) had attempted to slaughter him in the Strand in January and was punished with three weeks in jail. In short, Southampton had no chance of acquittal but did have a good chance of escaping execution.

Now we must consider the situation of a juror who wished to save Southampton. If the juror argued and voted for acquittal, then Southampton would have been convicted by a vote of twenty-four to one, the juror would have failed in his duty to Queen and country, he would probably have been imprisoned for a while (as happened to the jurors who acquitted Sir Nicholas Throckmorton in Queen Mary's reign), and, above all, he would have forfeited every ounce of credit with the Queen and Cecil. The only rational course was to vote for conviction and then join those pleading with the Queen to spare Southampton.

If Southampton was the Fair Youth, if Oxford was Shakespeare, and if the latter behaved as has been suggested during and after the trial, then what should we expect of later relations between the two? Southampton must have realized that Oxford took the only sensible course and helped to save his life. But emotionally, Southampton could not have completely forgiven those who voted, not so much for his death, as for the death of his hero, Essex. After the trial, Essex's bravado was broken by his chaplain who insisted that Essex could not die in a state of grace unless he confessed and repented his crimes. Essex did so, and accused his sister and his closest followers of pushing him into rebellion; this was also true of Southampton, but with him alone Essex kept faith. We should therefore expect that later relations between Oxford and Southampton would be uneasy and scarred by unhealed wounds, and this is precisely what we find in some of the final sonnets.

Sonnet 126, Shakespeare's *envoi*, presumably alludes to the Essex uprising and Southampton's imprisonment by saying that the Fair Youth «hast by waning grown» (13). More significantly, Sonnet 117 pleads, «But shoot not at me in your wakened hate» (110), which plausibly describes how Southampton may have felt about a friend who voted to condemn Essex. In Sonnet 119, Shakespeare is still dealing with the wakened hate in general terms: «What potions have I drunk of siren tears/Distilled from limbecks foul as hell within … Still losing when I saw myself to win/What wretched errors hath my heart committed» (lines 1-5). But Sonnet 120 gets much more specific on the same theme:

> That you were once unkind befriends me now,
> And for that sorrow which I then did feel
> Needs must I under my transgression bow,
> Unless my nerves were brass or hammered steel.
> For if you were by my unkindness shaken,
> As I by yours, y'have passed a hell of time,
> And I, a tyrant, have no leisure taken
> To weigh how much I suffered in your crime.
> O that our night of woe might have remembered
> My deepest sense how hard true sorrow hits,
> And soon to you, as you to me, then tendered
> The humble salve which wounded bosoms fits!
>> But that your trespass now becomes a fee;
>> Mine ransoms yours, and yours must ransom me.

What earthly reason could Shakspere of Stratford have had for writing such a poem to the Earl of Southampton, particularly line 5? However, it is obvious why the Earl of Oxford would have written it, especially line 5.

Let us now consider some implications. The author of *Shakespeare's Sonnets* was intimate for a period of years (I would guess about ten) with the Earl of Southampton, whom he freely criticized, as he criticized Lord Burghley, and actually challenged the Earl of Essex. He wrote sonnets like 85, 117, 119, and 120 that defy elucidation under the Stratford theory, but which are easily explainable if Oxford wrote them. Of course, the foregoing sentence also applies to sonnets such as 125, which have been discussed by others. We also have some plausible dates for the later sonnets: March or April 1603 for Sonnet 107, late 1603 for Sonnet 111, and April 1604 for Sonnet 122. It rather looks as if Sonnet 126 was written on a deathbed around June 1604.

As it came to me that Sonnets 78 to 100 were written around 1598, I naturally tried to find out what Oxford was doing that year. However, save sitting in Parliament in January, his recorded life is an irritating blank. Yet it is otherwise for our friend from Stratford; we do know something of his activities (even including threats from the Rival Poet), and perhaps Shakspere's advocates can still save the day. In February 1598, as Shakespeare was penning his touching farewell to Southampton in Sonnet 87, Shakspere was being cited in Stratford for hoarding grain in time of famine. Feelings against the hoarders were so strong that one Warwickshireman prayed that «my Lord of Essex» would hang them at their own doors. Doubtless (to use a favorite Stratfordian word), the Rival Poet was contemplating revenge.

The Order of *Shakespeare's Sonnets*

This is the fourth and concluding article in a series about the *Sonnets*. Its contention is that Sonnets 1 to 126, written to the Earl of Southampton, were published in the correct chronological order of composition in 1609 by Thomas Thorpe. A lesser contention is that Sonnets 127 to 152, written about the Dark Lady, are also in order, though they appear to have been penned before the midpoint of the first series. This article will also consider the apparent problem caused by Sonnet 104, with regard to the theory that Southampton was the friend of the first 126 sonnets. Some of the arguments are not new; in such cases, the material will be summarized and references will be provided for those who wish to pursue things further. My most important source is John Kerrigan's New Penguin edition of the *Sonnets*, which I have found to be the best single edition, and which first made me aware that the question of the order of the *Sonnets* could be investigated with objective arguments.

The first reason for believing that the *Sonnets* are correctly ordered is that a sonnet cycle was supposed to be ordered, with the individual sonnets being numbered. Thorpe was a quality publisher[1] and he produced his volume of the *Sonnets* and «A Lovers Complaint» in a familiar format.[2] The simplest explanation for Thorpe's 1609 order is that he followed the author's order. One scholar, J. B. Leishman, wrote that only Shakespeare himself could have kept the *Sonnets* in order, as if they were written on 154 otherwise blank sheets of paper. However, Shakespeare was writing within an established convention of numbered sonnets, and he may well have numbered 1 to 126 as he went along, and/or he may have written them sequentially in a notebook.

That Shakespeare numbered his sonnets as he wrote them is supported by Rene Graziani, who argues that some of the sonnets take themes from their numbers.[3] For instance, the week is divided into seven days, and Sonnet 7 is the first to describe the sun's daily journey across the sky. The clock divided the day into two periods of twelve hours, and Sonnet 12 begins, «When I do count the clock that tells the time.» The year is divided into fifty-two weeks, and Sonnet 52 mentions «the long year.» The hour is divided into sixty minutes, and Sonnet 60 says «So do our minutes hasten to their end.» The inexorable passage of time is, of course, an obsessive theme of the first 126 sonnets, which adds to the likelihood that these links are intentional. These and other possibilities suggested by Graziani are not conclusive but constitute a highly plausible argument that Shakespeare numbered the *Sonnets*.

The next reason in favor of Thorpe's order is the existence of distinguishable groups within the *Sonnets*. Sonnets 1 to 17 urge the friend to get married; 27 and 28 deal with insomnia; 33 and 34 mention clouds masking the sun; 40, 41, and 42 describe the friend's seduction by the Dark Lady; 44 and 45 consider the four elements; 46 and 47 use the eye and heart as their theme; 50 and 51 concern riding a horse; 63 and 64 begin with the hand of Time; 67, 69, and 70 discuss some sins of the friend; 71 to 74 all anticipate the poet's death; 78 to 86 attack the Rival Poet; 87, 89, and 90 allude to separation of the poet from his friend; 88 to 90 all speak of a quarrel between the two; 93 picks up 92's theme of the possible falseness of the friend; 93 to 96 harp on the friend's sins; 97 and 98 specify the seasons of the Separation; 100 to 102 apologize because the poet had written no sonnets for a time; 104 and 105 both play on the symbolic number three; 109 to 112 confess the poet's faults; 113 and 114 refer to the eye; 115 and 116 return to Time; 116 and 117 feature nautical imagery; 117, 119, and 120 defend against the friend's hate; and 123 and 124 again return to Time. These groups are obvious, but far more subtle links can be found between neighboring sonnets. Here it is necessary to put the *Sonnets* under a microscope, so to speak, and one can then discover a world invisible to the casual reader.

Consider, for example, the rhymes of Sonnets 36 to 39: twain/remain and one/alone are used as rhymes in 36 and 39; spite/delight is a rhyme in 36 and 37, while 38 rhymes sight/delight; thee/me is used in all four sonnets; and give/live crops up in both 37 and 39. These sonnets are not linked by theme, but are most certainly linked by rhymes. Kerrigan gives a detailed discussion[4] of the minute but unmistakable links among 106 to 109, which are superficially unrelated, but we can actually begin earlier and continue further. Sonnet 100 ties to 101 as both address Shakespeare's muse and both apologize for a lapse of time; 102 and 103 also excuse the time lapse; 102 and 104 both refer back to the beginning of the friendship; 104 and 105 discuss three; 104 and 108 close with the same rhyme and both imply that the friend is aging; 106 and 107 both rhyme time/rhyme and both mention prophecies; 107 and 108 both make a rhyme on age; 109 returns to a lapse of time, like 100 to 103; 109 and 110 both speak of the poet wandering; 110 and 111 both apologize for the poet's dramatic career; and 110 to 112 all discuss the poet's disrepute. These sort of links can be found all through the first 126 sonnets; readers may try the game themselves or look at Stephen Booth's Yale edition of the *Sonnets*[5] or his essay on *Shakespeare's Sonnets*.[6] It is, to put it mildly, difficult to see how such groupings and echoes could survive re-ordering.

We now turn from internal to external evidence by examining the sequential ties between the *Sonnets* and the life of Shakespeare's friend, the Earl of Southampton. When these two first met is unknown, but clearly not later than 1593, the year Shakespeare dedicated *Venus and Adonis* to Southampton. Sonnets 1 to 17 strongly urge the friend to wed and produce sons, which can be linked to a very active campaign waged between 1590 and 1594 to get Southampton married. The second article in this series showed that Sonnets 78 to 100 can be neatly mated to Southampton's life between late 1597 and early 1599. The only proposed date and set of events that truly explains Sonnet 107 is 1603: the death of Queen Elizabeth, the coming of King James, the freeing of Southampton from the Tower, and the references to prophecies, fears of the uncertainty, joy, and the coming of peace (this last item alone disposes of earlier suggested dates). The second quatrain of Sonnet 111 can be plausibly linked to the trial of Sir Walter Ralegh in November 1603. The second article in this series established a perfectly plausible tie between Sonnet 122 and James' Accession Day tournament of 1604. Sonnet 126 closes the series, and the Earl of Oxford died in 1604, with about a week's notice to get his affairs in order. Everything fits in place.

Let us focus on Sonnets 127 and 152 about the Dark Lady. In a sense, I am less concerned about the sequence of these sonnets, but still we find evidence of order. Internal evidence is again found in groups. Sonnets 130, 131, and 132 all deal with blackness; Sonnets 133 and 134 both concern the Fair Youth; 135 and 136 pun obsessively on the word «will»; 140, 141, and 142 all discuss the eye and heart; lines of 14 in 147 and 148 both denounce the Dark Lady; 149, 150, and 151 all speak of the Lady's hate or criticism of the poet. Rhyme links are found across as well as within these groups. For example, name/shame is a rhyme in 127, while shame/blame is used in 129; sounds/confounds is a rhyme in 128, while sound/ground is in 130; groan/alone makes a rhyme in both 131 and 133; face/place is found in 131, and face/grace is in 132. The foregoing list can be extended right across the Dark Lady Sonnets up to friend/friend (144), end/friend (145), spend/end (146), and friend/spend (149). (Incidentally, various scholars have from time to time sought to evict some of the sonnets from the cycle. The fifteen line Sonnet 99, the octosyllabic 145, and the religious 146 have all been questioned, but all possess rhyme links to their neighbors. Also, G.P.V. Akrigg in his valuable biography of Southampton[7], argues that the couplet to Sonnet 96, which is identical to that of 36, does not belong and may have resulted from censorship. Yet that couplet's sort/report rhyme ties to the sport/resort rhyme of lines 2 and 4 and to the sport/report rhyme of Sonnet 95.)

External evidence that both the Dark Lady and Fair Youth Sonnets are correctly ordered can be found by comparing the themes of some of the sonnets of these two groups. Sonnet 8 ties to 128 by their mutual references to music. Sonnet 21 links to 130 as both decry the exaggerated praise of beauty by other sonneteers. Sonnets 40 to 42 speak of the Youth's seduction by the Lady, as do 133 and 134. Sonnets 46 and 47 share the eye and heart theme of 140 to 142, and lines 7-8 of 142 concern the law of property, the principal metaphor of 46. Meanwhile, 141's mention of the five wits and live senses of man may be connected to 44 and 45's listing of the four humors of which man is composed. Sonnet 62 reminds of 146 in its concern with the sin of physical vanity. These links preserve order; an early Fair Youth sonnet matches an early Dark

Lady sonnet, later Fair Youth sonnets tie to later Dark Lady sonnets—no cross-cutting is found.

I have isolated and examined the rhyme cluster in all 154 sonnets, a cluster being an identical or similar rhyme used in neighboring sonnets. The results are too lengthy to be detailed here, but it can be shown that the clusters in the Dark Lady Sonnets can be tied in approximately correct order to rhyme clusters in Sonnets 9 to 52.

A final piece of evidence for the correctness of the order of the first 126 sonnets, as well as of the place of the Dark Lady Sonnets with regard to the first 126 is provided by MacD. P. Jackson[8]. Jackson counted the number of commas within the lines of each sonnet (as opposed to punctuation marks at the end of lines), and found that the number of internal commas (which yield evidence of syntactical complexity) was independent of the shifts of the two compositors who set up the 1609 edition of the *Sonnets*. The results are that Sonnets 1 to 25 have an average 2.8 internal punctuation marks per sonnet, Sonnets 26 to 50 average 4.7 per sonnet, Sonnets 51 to 75 average 4.9, Sonnets 76 to 100 average 5.5, Sonnets 101 to 126 average 5.4, and Sonnets 127 to 154 have 3.6 on average.

We have now seen considerable evidence that the original edition placed the *Sonnets* (within the two main groups) in the correct order, but let us contemplate the alternative. Suppose that Thomas Thorpe obtained the Sonnets in a bundle of 154 numbered sheets, decided (rightly or wrongly) that he has inherited a hodgepodge, and carefully created the present sequence by grouping the *Sonnets* by themes, placing all of the marriage sonnets at the beginning, all of those on the Dark Lady at the end, etc. In doing so, he would also have created the numerical themes noted by Graziani, the rhyme and other subtle word links noted by Kerrigan, Booth, and others, the ordered ties between the *Sonnets* and Southampton's life story, the ordered ties of themes and rhymes between the Fair Youth and Dark Lady groups, and the progression in internal punctuation noted by Jackson. I would regard such results as virtually impossible to obtain intentionally and astronomically unlikely to occur by accident. The type of evidence presented here is not capable of proving that every last sonnet is in its proper place, but I feel that it does place a large burden of proof on those who favor minor, much less major reordering. Also, we have seen tests that may establish that a given sonnet does belong where it is.

We will now turn to Sonnet 104, which proclaims that three years have passed since Shakespeare and his friend first met: «Three winters cold ... three summers' pride ... three beauteous springs ... Three April perfumes in three hot Junes burned,/Since first I saw you fresh, which yet are green.» This sonnet follows the 1597-99 group of Sonnets 78 to 100 and precedes the 1603 Sonnet 107. But Shakespeare met Southampton no later than 1593, so some explanation is called for. Some say that Sonnet 104 is an argument against Southampton as the Fair Youth, but the evidence in favor of Southampton (which I have never seen collected in one place) has always been strong, and the additional arguments in this series of articles should make the case decisive. Some, including Charlton Ogburn, Jr., argue that Sonnet 104 belongs earlier in the series, but, as has been shown, there is a strong presumption that the *Sonnets* are correctly ordered and there exist rhyme and thematic links between 104 and its neighbors. A third possibility was suggested but not developed as long ago as 1910 by Sir Sidney Lee: that there was a sonnet convention that the full duration of an affair of the heart was three years.[9] I find this theory highly persuasive and would like to develop it.

French sonneteers exerted a strong influence on Shakespeare and his compatriots, and Pierre de Ronsard and Philippe Desportes observed the three-year convention, which went back to Horace and was also used by Samuel Daniel. Ronsard and Desportes were the premier French poets of the day and were widely imitated in England; Daniel (along with Sir Philip Sidney) was the model English sonneteer; and Horace was a towering presence in Renaissance literature. If these poets used a three-year metaphor, then it can be taken as an established convention. Yet, would Shakespeare have found the convention useful?

The *Sonnets* repeatedly and vividly tell of Shakespeare's dread of the destructive passage of time. Defeating time by procreation and by the immortality of poetry (also an ancient poetic convention) are among the major themes of the *Sonnets*. Another method of defying time is joked about in Sonnet 138, especially in the original version of that poem (published in The *Passionate Pilgrim* of 1599):

> Thus vainly thinking that she thinks me young
> Although I know my years be past the best,
> Outfacing faults in love with love's ill rest.
> But wherefore says my love that she is young?
> And wherefore say not I that I am old?
> O, love's best habit's in a soothing tongue,
> And age in love loves not to have years told.
> > Therefore I'll lie with love, and love with me
> > Since that our faults in love thus smothered be.
> > > (lines 5-14, 1599 version)

> Therefore I lie with her, and she with me,
> And in our faults by lies we flattered be.
> > (lines 13-14, 1609 version)

Shakespeare's willingness to try to ignore the passage of time is also found in the sonnets to Southampton. The earlier ones speak much of his friend's youth, but later sonnets (including 104) appear to acknowledge that he was aging: «Thou hast passed by the ambush of young days» (70, 9); «To me, fair friend, you never can be old ... Such seems your beauty still» (104, 1, 3); «y'have passed a hell of time» (120, 6). It is significant that Southampton was thought to be youthful longer than most people. He was lightly bearded through his twenties, and many saw him as a misguided youth at the time of his treason trial in 1601, despite his being a twenty-seven year old husband, father, and veteran of three campaigns. In fact, the tacit acknowledgement of aging found in the opening of 104 (see above) and in its closing (see below) make far more sense if written to the twenty-nine year old Southampton in late 1602 or early 1603, after his experience of marriage, fatherhood, war, rebellion, trial, and imprisonment than if written to the callow twenty-two year old of 1596.

> Ah, yet doth beauty, like a dial hand,
> Steal from his figure, and no pace perceived;
> So your sweet hue, which methinks still doth stand,
> Hath motion, and mine eye may be deceived;
> For fear of which, hear this, thou age unbred:
> Ere you were born was beauty's summer dead. (104, 9-14)

A completely different line of argument comes from Shakespeare's use of number symbols and wordplay (which were common to his age). Sonnet 105 deals with the concept of «three ... in one»; Sonnet 136 is concerned with unity and multiplicity (lines 7-9); «The Phoenix and the Turtle» discourses on unity and duality in a complex and fascinating way (lines 25-48). There is much play on «three» in I, ii of *Love's Labour's Lost*, in which the clever Moth collapses «three years» into two words or one hour. That play also transforms the nine Worthies into three (V,ii, 485-97). Several sonnets as well as «The Phoenix and the Turtle» express the common belief that two lovers become one. So Shakespeare clearly believed that a larger number could be changed to a smaller. It should also be noted that three was a multiple symbol of importance as defining God's nature (three in one), as the male number (two was female), and as the trefoil was the symbol of hope and the herald of spring (which, by the way, Shakespeare called Southampton in Sonnet 1; see the *OED* for the meanings of the trefoil.) Elizabethans also used «thrice» to mean «very» or «completely,» as in phrases like «thrice noble,» «thrice happy,» or «thrice famed» (*2 Henry VI*, III,. ii, 157).

The Earl of Oxford shared the belief in number symbols, as testified to by the flourishes of his signature. For most of his life he used a sub-flourish consisting of a long horizontal slashed by seven short verticals (which I take as a tally mark for seventeen), and a supra-flourish of four lower case i's (roman number four, iiii). He dropped these after the death of Queen Elizabeth and switched to trefoil, a symbolic threesome, shortly after the likely date of composition of Sonnets 104 and 105.

When we combine Shakespeare's hatred of the passage of time, his determination to defeat time, his jokes about simply lying time away, the evidence that Southampton was aging, the prolific numerology of the age, the special status of the number three, and Shakespeare's tendency to alter larger numbers to smaller, and then ask whether Shakespeare would have taken advantage of an established sonnet convention that three years could be used to cover a longer time, then I think that the answer is obviously in the affirmative. As earlier in this article, it is useful to consider the alternative. If Sonnet 104 was indeed composed in 1603 or thereabouts, I believe that Shakespeare would have absolutely recoiled at the thought of writing: «Ten winters cold ... ten summers' pride ... ten beauteous springs ... Ten April perfumes in ten hot Junes burned,/Since first I saw you fresh, which yet are green.»

Endnotes

1   William Shakespeare, *Shakespeare's Sonnets*. Ed. John Kerrigan (NY: New Penguin, 1986), 427.
2   *Op. cit.*, 14.
3   Rene Graziani, «The Numbering of Shakespeare's *Sonnets* 12, 60 and 126,» *Shakespeare Quarterly* 35 (1984), 79-82.
4   Kerrigan, 8-9.
5   William Shakespeare, *Shakespeare's Sonnets*. Ed. Stephen Booth (New Haven: Yale UP, 1977).
6   Stephen Booth, *An Essay on Shakespeare's Sonnets* (New Haven: Yale UP, 1969).
7   G.P.V. Akrigg, *Shakespeare and the Earl of Southampton* (London: H. Hamilton, 1968).
8   Kerrigan, 430. See also MacD. P. Jackson, "Punctuation and the Composition of Shakespeare's Sonnets," *Library* 30 (1975), 1-24.
9   Sir Sidney Lee, *The French Renaissance in England: An Account of the Literary Relations of England and France in the Sixteenth Century* (NY: Octagon, 1968) 267.

Hamlet and the Two Witness Rule

In an analysis of the *Spanish Tragedy*, S. E Johnson implies in a brief parenthetic remark that Hamlet's acts of vengeance against Claudius are justified by Numbers 35, one of several chapters of the Old Testament dealing with *avengers of blood*.[1] Eleanor Prosser in a footnote in her *Hamlet and Revenge* disagrees with Johnson, maintaining that Numbers requires the avenger to act immediately and without hatred or malice.[2] However, Johnson is quite right, as several aspects of the Mosaic law on avengers of blood were in Shakespeare's mind when he penned *Hamlet*, particularly the biblical requirement for two witnesses against a killer, as well as the apparent requirement that the avenger act immediately. We will begin with the law of Moses.

Numbers 35 and Deuteronomy 19 permit or command a man whose next of kin has been slain to kill the slayer. However, if the slayer escapes to one of six cities of refuge he will be given trial. If found guilty of murder, he will be excecuted by the avenger. But if he is found to have killed his victim without premeditation or by accident, then he is safe from the avenger as long as he remains within the bounds of the city of refuge for a statutory period, after which he may return in safety to his home. This divine establishment of sanctuary originates in a promise made in Exodus 21:12-14, a chapter best known as the source of the *lex talonis*, which is repeated at the end of Deuteronomy 19. The cities of refuge are also mentioned in Deuteronomy 4:41-2, and the doctrine concerning them is summarized in Joshua 20.

We will pass over the requirement for immediate action on the part of the avenger for the moment, and will consider Prosser's curious stipulation that the avenger of blood kill the slayer without enmity. Prosser has misunderstood Numbers 35:19-20. Verse 19 allows or requires the avenger to kill the slayer «when he meteth him,» and verse 20 begins, «But if he thrust him of hate...»,[3] which Prosser takes as continuing what verse 19 says regarding the avenger. In fact, verses 20 to 23 deal with the slayer, not the avenger, and establish the distinction between murder and manslaughter, leading up to verses 24 and 25, which describe the trial the slayer is to receive in the city of refuge. The misreading is an easy one to make, at least in the English Bible, especially if one stops at verse 20. However, Deuteronomy 19 clarifies the matter unambiguously, and a marginal note next to the Geneva Bible's Numbers 35: 20 directs the reader to «Deu. 19, 11.»

Numbers 35, Deuteronomy 19, and Joshua 20 begin to replace the old tribal code of familial vengeance with a national legal system, and I would hardly argue that Elizabethans regarded them as having equal standing with later parts of the Bible in terms of governing Christian behaviour. The authorized version of Shakespeare's age, the Bishops' Bible, explains in a marginal note to Exodus 21:21 that the vengeance doctrine was a necessary evil:

> In these ciuill lawes, we muste not seeke for absolute perfection, whiche God tempered accordyng to the rudenesse of ye people, amongest whom many thinges were to be winked at for the tyme.

Yet, as Johnson puts it, «Protestants believed [the Mosaic code] to be quite as much the word of God as anything else in the two testaments,» (29) to which it may be added that Catholics were of the same opinion. Moreover, these texts provide biblical warrant for Hamlet's actions, especially given that the source of national law in his Denmark is King Claudius, the slayer.

Prosser's attention to Numbers 35 leads us to the realization that Hamlet follows an important religious rule that appears to have gone unremarked. Numbers and Deuteronomy both state that serious crimes require two witnesses for conviction:

> Whosoeuer killeth anie persone, the *iudge* shal slay the murtherer, through witnesses: but one witnes shal not testifie against a person to cause him to die. (Numbers 35:30)

> One witnes shal not rise against a man for any trespas, or for any sinne, or for any faute that he offendeth in, *but* at the mouth of two

witnesses or at the mouth of thre witnesses shal the matter be stablished. (Deuteronomy 19:15)

This two witness rule or variants is also found in Deuteronomy 17:6, Matthew 18:16 (where Jesus says, «by ye mouth of two or thre witnesses euerie worde may be confirmed»), 2 Corinthians 13:1, Hebrews 10:28, and Revelation 11:3. Abuse of the two witness rule is chronicled in 1 Kings 21, the judicial murder of Naboth, while the antidote to perversion of the rule by a pair of perjurers is described in the Book of Susannah. That two witnesses were necessary under God's law for certain capital convictions was an ingrained English belief in Shakespeare's age, the importance of which cannot be appreciated without considering some examples.[4]

In 1529 the House of Commons presented a petition to Henry VIII complaining of sundry clerical abuses, among them false charges of heresy:

> And if it fortune the said party so accused to deny the said accusation, ... then for the most part such witnesses as are brought forth for the same, be they but two in number, never so sore diffamed, of little truth or credence, they shall be allowed ... and therefore sufficient cause be found to proceed to judgment,

The bishops defended the practice:

> To this we reply, the Gospel of Christ [Matthew 18:16] teacheth us to believe two witnesses; and as the cause is, so the judge must esteem the quality of the witnesses; and in heresy no exception is necessary to be considered if their tale be likely;[5]

In 1541 two doctors of the Church accused Sir Thomas Wyatt the Elder and John Mason of committing treason during an embassy in which the four participated in 1538. The accusation was pressed by Wyatt's enemies, who were eager to strike at any ally of the recently executed Thomas Cromwell, and though the charges are absurd to the modern eye, they represented deadly peril to Wyatt and Mason. The two doctors, learned scholars that they were, concocted their depositions together so as not to fall into the trap laid by Daniel for Susannah's two accusers. Wyatt wrote a speech in his defence, apparently to be used in court, in which he referred to the number of his accusers:

> But theye are ii, we ar also ii [himself and Mason]. As in spirituall courtes mene ar wonte to purge there fames, let vs trie our fames for our honesties — and we will give them oddes.

Wyatt refers to the comparative reputations for honesty of the accusers and the accused, as the Commons did in 1529. The doctors had ensured that they could pass Daniel's test, that the two accusers, questioned apart, must agree in matters of substance. So Wyatt devised a new test:

> Confer [compare] their depositions, yf theie agre worde for worde. That is harde yf theie were examyned aparte, on lese [unless] theie had conspired more than became faythefull [honest] accusares.[6]

That is, Wyatt argues that if the agreement between the two accusers goes beyond matters of substance to their very words, then collusion is evident. Wyatt eventually confessed on promise of pardon in order to escape a trial and its inevitable outcome.

A few weeks after the arrest of the Earl of Surrey in 1546, the Imperial Ambassador to England was privately informed by Lord Chancellor Wriothesley (the grandfather of Shakespeare's patron, the Earl of Southampton) that «two ... gentlemen of faith and honour» had revealed that Surrey and his father, the Duke of Norfolk, had attempted to enlist them in a conspiracy to overthrow the King and murder the Privy Council.[7] These two gentlemen with their direct testimony of high treason are never heard from again in the surviving documents and accounts of the investigation and trial of Surrey, who was convicted and executed for alleged words of disaffection and the use of an old royal coat of arms. In short, the pair of faithful and honourable witnesses seems to have been a fiction designed to persuade foreign rulers that biblical standards of justice had been met in the destruction of Surrey and Norfolk.

In November 1603, as the second Quarto of *Hamlet* was going to press, Sir Walter Ralegh stood trial for treason, believing that he had a chance of acquittal as there was only one witness against him. Ralegh was counting on a couple of treason statutes passed in the reign of Edward VI requiring two witnesses, as called for by the Bible:

> no parsone ... shalbe ... convicted for anny offence of Treasone ... oneles the same offendor ... be accused by twoo sufficyent and lawfull witnesses, or shall willinglye withowt vyolence confesse the same.[8]

However, the law had been changed in the time of Mary I, and the prosecution brought forward only the deposition of its unreliable single witness of Ralegh's guilt. Ralegh cited the Bible's two witness rule as overriding human law, and he demanded to be confronted by the sole witness, reminding the court of the story of Susannah, but to no avail.

At the start of a 1604 play that filches scraps from *Hamlet*, the villain explains how he rid himself of his virtuous wife:

> You know the cause on't, two sufficient men
> Swore her a harlot, and the partiall Bench
> Inspirde by my good Angels (Angels wings
> Sweepe a cleare passage to the seat of Kings)
> Seald our diuorce.[9]

In 1628, Ralegh's prosecutor, Sir Edward Coke, completed his *Third Institute,* stating of treason:

> Also it is most necessary (as many doe hold) that there should be two lawfull accusers, that is, two lawfull witnesses ...

> And it seemeth that by the ancient common law one accuser, or witnesse was not sufficient to convict any person of high treason: ...

> And that two witnesses be required, appeareth by our books, and I remember no authority in our books to the contrary: and the com-

mon law herein is grounded upon the law of God expressed both in the old and new Testament: *in ore duorum aut trium testium peribit qui interficietur: nemo occidat ur uno contra se dicente testimonium,*[10]

Shakespeare uses this rule in *Cymbeline*, where Belarius relates that he was banished for treason based on the testimony of «two villains, whose false oaths prevail'd,»[11] but we cannot take Shakespeare's knowledge of the rule as evidence of familiarity with any particular part of the Bible. It may be added that in the biblical passages cited, the rule applies to murder and other crimes, while the English examples concentrate on treason. Regicide, the crime of which Claudius is guilty, is the ultimate form of high treason; note the response of the spectators when Hamlet wounds Claudius, «*All.* Treason! treason!» (V.ii.328).

Now to the play. After hearing the testimony of the Ghost in Act I, Hamlet does not determine to kill Claudius. Instead, he decides to verify the Ghost's story, and, as events fall out, he devises the play-within-the-play or mousetrap. Just before the play begins, Hamlet summons Horatio, who knows Hamlet's suspicions, and instructs him to watch Claudius for signs of guilt:

> Give him heedful note;
> For I mine eyes will rivet to his face,
> And after we will both our judgments join
> In censure of his seeming (III.ii.84-7)[12]

After Claudius's guilt is revealed, Hamlet is in a state of elation bordering on euphoria, but he still takes the time to request and receive confirmation from Horatio:

> *Ham.* O good Horatio, I'll take the ghost's word for a thousand
> pound. Didst perceive?
> *Hor.* Very well, my lord.
> *Ham.* Upon the talk of poisoning?
> *Hor.* I did very well note him. (III.ii.280-4)

The requirement for two witnesses has now been met.

Among Shakespeare's other plays, *Much Ado About Nothing* seems most relevant to the question of Shakespeare's attention to the rule of two or three witnesses. Hero's supposed crime is witnessed by Don John, Don Pedro, and Claudio; Borachio's admission of guilt is overheard by two members of the Watch; Borachio confesses to Don Pedro and Claudio that Hero «is dead upon mine and my master's false accusation»;[13] and Beatrice and Benedick are each tricked into love on the testimony of a trio. Some of these examples can be explained by the needs of the stage or by common sense, without invoking the Bible. Nevertheless, Borachio's statement that Hero died upon the accusation of himself and Don John is an odd way to explain the event unless Borachio has the biblical rule in mind. Moreover, Claudio's plan to shame Hero «before the whole congregation»[14] has Mosaic resonances, for Numbers 35:12 and Joshua 20:6 and 9 call for the slayer to receive judgement in the city of refuge «before the Congregacion.» Shakespeare's first two uses of the word «congregation» are in *Much Ado*, while his next use is in *Hamlet* (II.ii.302-3); Shakespeare's only other use of the word is in *Coriolanus* (III.ii.11).

Hamlet's use of Horatio as a witness is not motivated by the dramatic needs of Act III, scene ii. The audience has known of Claudius's guilt since his confession in an aside in the previous scene (49-54), and would need no help in understanding the implications of the mousetrap. Hamlet certainly has no doubt of his uncle's guilt after the trap is sprung. The simplest explanation for Horatio's role as a witness is to demonstrate Hamlet's biblical rectitude in determining the truth of the Ghost's accusations. It could be argued that Horatio needs to know the truth in order to fulfill Hamlet's dying command to «Report me and my cause aright» (V.ii.344), but that argument acknowledges the larger purpose of Horatio's role in *Hamlet*— as a witness who can testify.

Are we justified in believing that Shakespeare and Hamlet are following the Bible, and not merely English custom, in enlisting Horatio as a second witness? The answer is found by returning to Numbers 35.

Prosser reads Numbers 35:19 and 21 as requiring immediate response: «the reuenger of the blood shal slay the murtherer when he meteth him»; the language of the Geneva and Bishops' Bibles is identical. In other words, if the avenger fails to kill the slayer at their first meeting, then he has disobeyed God's imperative—or missed his only chance. Some would not interpret these words in that manner, but Prosser's reading is literally correct, and Matthew's Bible of 1530, Coverdale's Bible of 1535, and the Great Bible of 1539 all put the matter even more strongly than the Geneva: the avenger «shall slay» the killer «as soon as he findeth him.»[15] That, *pace* Prosser, is exactly what Hamlet intends to do. After Claudius rushes out of the play, Hamlet elicits Horatio's testimony, and next encounters Claudius at prayer, whereupon he draws his sword, saying, «And now I'll do't.» (III.iii.74)

Yet Hamlet recoils from killing Claudius, saying that he will not have his revenge result in Claudius going straight from prayer to heaven. Hamlet decides that he will delay his vengeance until he catches Claudius in a state of mortal sin, so that he can send him to hell. Hamlet's next opportunity to kill Claudius, so be believes, is when he hears him behind the arras in his mother's chamber, and this time he thrusts without hesitation. The result, of course, is the death of the wrong man, but the point is clear. Shakespeare causes Hamlet to follow the two witness rule, whether in obedience to the Bible or to English custom, and then Shakespeare twice gives Hamlet the intention of slaying Claudius as soon as he finds him, exactly as called for by Numbers 35.

Two more items in *Hamlet* may also indicate the presence of Exodus 21 and Deuteronomy 19 in the mind of the author. Hamlet's refusal to slay his uncle at prayer is often contrasted to Claudius's approval of the readiness of Laertes «To cut [Hamlet's] throat i'th church»; as Claudius says, «revenge should have no bounds.» (IV.vii. 125-6) Exodus 21:12-14 calls for murderers to be taken from the altar to execution, but not to be slaughtered at the altar itself, and so Claudius clearly exceeds the bounds of Mosaic revenge. Hamlet's destruction of his old schoolfellows, Rosencrantz and Guildenstern, is clearly planned on the principle of the *lex talonis*. He intends to see them «Hoist with [their] own petard,» and continues his sapper metaphor by saying that he «will delve one yard below their mines/And blow them at the moon.» (III.iv.209-11) Of course, Hamlet is as good as his word. Discovering that the commission carried by his erstwhile friends commands his immediate execution, he substitutes an order for them to be «put to sudden death,/Not shriving-time allow'd.» (V.ii.46-7) However, another passage is relevant here besides the «eie for eie» of Exodus 21 and Deuteronomy 19, namely the penalty meted out to false accusers: «Then shal ye do vnto him as he had thoght to do vnto his brother.» (Deuteronomy 19:19) The fate of Rosencrantz and Guildenstern may seem unjust, unless they were aware of the contents of their commission. That matter aside, Hamlet follows the law of Moses, just as he did on the procurement of a second witness to the guilt of Claudius and as he intended to do on the matter of immediate vengeance.

Given the widespread public awareness of the two witness rule in Shakespeare's age, many, perhaps most, of *Hamlet's* original audiences would have understood why Horatio is enlisted as a witness. Numbers 35 and Deuteronomy 19 were not considered esoteric by the sixteenth century, as they were the source of the two witness rule and provided a precedent to judge the contemporary custom of sanctuary, while the *lex talonis* ensured the continuing relevance of Exodus 21. Given the popularity of Bible reading in that era, some of the audience must also have realized why Hamlet draws his sword immediately after the mousetrap. But what should these things mean to us?

If the arguments of this note are accepted, then we gain insight into one of the more notorious questions concerning Hamlet, namely, why he is rebuked for delay by both himself and his father's ghost, as well as how his name has become a byword for indecision. The Arden editor, Harold Jenkins, discusses this issue at some length, observing that:

> It is often remarked that through all the excitements of Shakespeare's unfolding drama it would never occur to us that Hamlet was neglecting his revenge if he refrained from saying so himself. (137)

Shakespeare creates the tension in the first three acts of *Hamlet* by setting the apparent Mosaic requirement for immediate vengeance against the Mosaic requirement for two witnesses. Hamlet is not in the position of the Old Testament avenger contemplated by Numbers and Deuteronomy, one without doubt of the fact of homicide or of the identity of the slayer. Rather, as Elizabethan audiences knew, the testimony of the Ghost may derive from a demon bent on Hamlet's damnation. Hamlet overcomes this obstacle by springing the mousetrap with two witnesses, which carries us up to his drawing his sword on his praying uncle, and on through the killing of Polonius. Yet now things become more complicated, for Shakespeare has already created another dilemma in Act I that continues through Act V. Is it more heinous to kill a person unprepared for death or one in church? More broadly, given the act of killing or of causing death indirectly, is the killer responsible for the soul as well as the body? Shakespeare sets religious logic against human emotion on these questions throughout the play.

Endnotes

1   S. F. Johnson, ‹*The Spanish Tragedy*› in *Essays on Shakespeare and Elizabethan Drama*, ed. Richard Hosley (Columbia, Missouri, 1962), 29-30.

2   Eleanor Prosser, *Hamlet and Revenge* (Stanford, 1971), 18 n. 52.

3   All scriptural quotations are from the Geneva Bible unless otherwise specified. *The Geneva Bible, a facsimile of the 1560 edition* (Madison, Milwaukee, and London, 1969).

4   Johnson discusses the two witness rule as applied to *The Spanish Tragedy*, op. cit., 30 n. 10.

5   J. A. Froude, *History of England* (New York, 1899), 1, 206-7, 219.

6   Kenneth Muir, *Life and Letters of Sir Thomas Wyatt* (Liverpool, 1963), 192, 196-7.

7   CSP Spanish, VIII, 533.

8   1 Edward VI, c. 12, §22; see also 5 & 6 Edward VI, c. 11, §9. The definition of treason placed in article III, section 3 of the United States Constitution in 1787 is substantially the same: «No Person shall be convicted of Treason unless on the Testimony of two Witnesses to the same overt Act, or of Confession in open Court.»

9   John Day, *Law Tricks* (1608; Malone Society Reprints, Oxford, 1950), lines

46-50. Day's borrowings from *Hamlet* are mostly trivial and incidental, for example, he mentions a poison that acts like «speeding Physicke in thine eare.» (1127) Another example: «when we *counterfeited ourselues lunaticke* to escape their furie I proued not false when wee were *cast naked a shore.*» (292-4, my emphases) Compare «cast naked a shore» to *Hamlet* IV.vii.42-3, «set naked on your kingdom.» Taken separately, neither of the two emphasized items is definitely from *Hamlet*, after all, King David also feigned madness. However, when found together they presumably are from *Hamlet*.

10 Sir Edward Coke, *The Third Part of the Institutes of the Laws of England* (London, 1797), ch. 2, 25. The Latin is Deuteronomy 17:6, «At ye mouth of two or thre witnesses shal he that is worthy death, dye: *but* at the mouth of one witnes, he shal not dye.»

11 The Arden *Cymbeline*, ed. J. M. Nosworthy (1955), III.iii.66.

12 All citations from *Hamlet* are from the Arden edition, ed. Harold Jenkins (1982).

13 The Arden *Much Ado Abut Nothing*, e d. A. R. Humphreys (1981), V.i.236-7.

14 *Much Ado*, III.iii.156-7; see also III.ii.113-14 and IV.ii.51-2.

15 Actually, Prosser feels that God tolerates, but does not command, immediate revenge by a next of kin acting in hot blood. In this matter she is in approximate agreement with the Bishops' Bible; with John Calvin in *Commentaries on the Four Last Books of Moses*, tr. C. W. Bingham (Edinburgh, 1852), III, 65, and *Commentaries on the Book of Joshua* (1854), 239-40; and with Martin Luther in *Luther's Works*, ed. Jaroslav Pelikan (Saint Louis, 1955), IX, «Lectures on Deuteronomy,» 195-7. One sympathizes with this preference for law over private vengeance, but every English Bible available to Shakespeare, including Wycliffe's, uses the imperative «shall slay» rather than the permissive «may slay,» while the Vulgate's «*interficiet*» is future, active, indicative. Luther, Calvin, and the Elizabethan bishops were clearly afraid of the implications of a literal reading of Numbers 35.

Ophelia's False Steward

In Act IV, scene v of *Hamlet,* the maddened Ophelia speaks and sings distractedly of this and that, including the remark: «It is the false Steward that stole his masters daughter» (lines 172-3). Scholars have been unable to discover the ballad or story referred to by Ophelia. For example, Philip Edwards's 1985 Cambridge edition of *Hamlet* notes that, «it is embarrassing that no one has been able to throw light on the false steward.» It is impossible to prove the matter fully, but Ophelia's source could very well be Ben Jonson's *The Case Is Altered.*

One of the subplots of this early play of Jonson's concerns a supposed beggar, Jaques de Prie, and his daughter Rachel. However, in a soliloquy at the beginning of Act II, Jaques explains to the audience:

> But now this maid, is but suppos'd my daughter:
> For I being Steward to a Lord of France,
> Of great estate, and wealth, call'd Lord *Chammount,*
> He gone into the warres, I stole his treasure;   35
> (But heare not, any thing) I stole his treasure,
> And this his daughter, being but two yeares old,[1]

At the play's conclusion, Rachel's true identity is revealed and she is therefore worthy to marry her lover, Lord Paulo Ferneze.

The Rachel de Prie subplot of *The Case Is Altered* exactly fits Ophelia's words. We find a steward who stole his master's daughter, and the theft took place before, rather than during, the action of the play, which agrees with Ophelia's use of the past tense, *stole.*

The Case Is Altered conflates the plots of two of Plautus' plays, *Aulularia (The Pot of Gold)* and *Captivi (The Captives).* Rachel de Prie is modelled on Phaedria of *Aulularia,* but the latter is not a stolen child and lives with her real father. The stolen child gambit comes from *Captivi,* in which a boy, Tyndarus, was stolen by his father's runaway slave, Stalagmus, and sold into slavery at age four. So, despite her late father's familiarity with Plautus («*Senaca* cannot be too heavy, nor *Plautus* too light» — II.ii.366-7), Ophelia is not referring to the work of the Roman dramatist. In other words, Shakespeare did not simply borrow from the same source as Jonson.

The earliest surviving notice of *The Case Is Altered* is in Thomas Nashe's 1598 *Lenten Stuff*. It was perhaps written a year or so earlier, which is consistent with estimates on the date of composition of *Hamlet*.

Endnote

1   *Ben Jonson*, eds. C. H. Herford and Percy Simpson (Oxford, 1927), Vol. III, 126.

Hamlet and Surrey's Psalm 8

As indecisiveness is Hamlet's best known trait, so rashness is regarded as the hallmark of Henry Howard, Earl of Surrey. Both men were poets, and Ophelia's well known words on Hamlet could just as well have been carved on Surrey's grave:

> O, what a noble mind is here o'erthrown!
> The courtier's, soldier's, scholar's, eye, tongue, sword,
> Th' expectancy and rose of the fair state,
> The glass of fashion and the mould of form,   155
> Th' observ'd of all observers, quite, quite down! (III.i.152-156)[1]

Overthrown nobleman, poet, courtier, soldier, scholar—Hamlet or Surrey—take your pick. Moreover, «glass of fashion and mould of form» also apply to Surrey, the most often portrayed courtier of Henry VIII.[2] In his edition of a selection of Surrey's poems, Emrys Jones comments on the vision of hills, men and beasts figured in the clouds in lines 9 to 12 of Surrey's paraphrase of Psalm 8: «The thought is developed into something which anticipates the cloud fantasies of *Hamlet* (III.ii.380-4) and *Antony and Cleopatra* (IV.xiv.2-11).»[3]

Jones does not argue that Hamlet or Mark Antony had Surrey's words in mind, as other works of literature available to Shakespeare discuss what is, after all, a common human experience. Moreover, if Shakespeare needed a model for Hamlet, Sir Philip Sidney would have served nicely, and suggestions have ranged from the second Earl of Essex to Castiglione's Courtier.

Nevertheless, a very real link exists between Hamlet and Surrey, specifically Hamlet's use of Surrey's paraphrase of Psalm 8 in two related speeches, first, «What piece of work is a man... this quintessence of dust» (II.ii.298-308), and then in the soliloquy, «How all occasions do inform against me... What is a man.» (IV.iv.32-39) The bond between the two men strengthens as we turn our attention to a poem that Surrey's son called his father's last verse.

I

We will begin by looking at the first five verses of Psalm 8 in Miles Coverdale's translation from the Great Bible of 1540, followed by the same verses from the Vulgate. These verses of Psalm 8 prefigure Hamlet's speech, «What piece of work is a man ... this quintessence of dust,» but we shall see that Surrey's paraphrase of Psalm 8 provides a much closer match. The Vulgate was the basis of Surrey's paraphrase, though he seems also to have known Coverdale's translation.[4] The latter was incorporated in a work familiar to Shakespeare, the Book of Common Prayer, where it remains to this day. In all of the quotations that follow the emphases have been added to highlight suggested parallels.

Coverdale

O Lorde our gouernoure, howe excellent is thy name in all the *world,* thou that hast sett thy glory aboue the *heavens,* * Out of the mouth of very babes and sucklynges hast thou ordeyned strength because of thyne enemyes, that thou myghtest styll the enemye and the auenger. For I consydre thy heavens, euen the worcke of thy fyngers: the moone & ye starres whych thou hast ordeyned. * *What is man,* that thou art myndfull of hym; and the sonne of man, that thou visytest him; Thou madest hym *lower than the aungels,* to crowne hym with glory & worshyppe.

Vulgate

2 Domine, Dominus noster,
Quam admirabile est nomen tuum in universa *terra!*
Quoniam elevata est magnificentia tua super *caelos.*
3 Ex ore infantium et lactentium perfecisti laudem propter inimicos tuos,
Ut destruas inimicum et ultorem.
4 Quoniam videbo caelos tuos, opera digitorum tuorum,
Lunam et stellas quae tu fundasti:
5 *Quid est homo,* quod memor es eius?
Aut filius hominis, quoniam visitas eum?
6 *Minuisti eum paulo minus ab angelis;*
Gloria et honore coronasti eum;

Hamlet's speech on the universe and the nature of man reads (II.ii.298-308):

> ... this goodly frame the *earth* seems to
> me a sterile promontory, *this most excellent canopy*
> *the air,* look you, this brave *o'erhanging firmament*   300
> this majestical roof fretted with golden fire, why, it
> appeareth nothing to me but a foul and pestilent con-
> gregation of vapours. *What piece of work is a man,*
> how noble in reason, how infinite in faculties, in form
> and moving how express and admirable, in action   305
> *how like an angel,* in apprehension how like a god:
> the beauty of the world, the paragon of animals —
> and yet, to me, what is this *quintessence of dust?*[5]

Hamlet begins by mentioning the «earth» and the «canopy of the air,» then asks «What piece of work is a man,» answering, «how like an angel.» Coverdale mentions the «world» and the «heavens,» then asks «What is man,» answering, «lower than the aungels.» The parallelism of ideas is clear, but the word choice differs, while, in the comparison to angels, Hamlet rates man somewhat more favorably than does Coverdale.[6]

We now turn to the first twenty-five lines of Surrey's paraphrase of Psalm 8.

> Thie name o Lord how great is fownd before our sight
> yt fills the *earth* and *spreades the ayre* the great workes of thie might
> ffor even vnto thie powre the *hevens* have geven a place
> and closyd it above their heades a mightie lardge compace
> Thye prayse what clowde can hyde but it will sheen agayne   5
> Synce yonge and tender sucking babes have powre to shew it playne
> whiche in dispight of those that wold thie glorie hyde
> hast put into suche Infantes mowthes for to confound their pryde
> wherefore I shall beholde thy figur'de heaven so hye
> whiche shewes suche printes of dyvers formes within the Clowdye
>   skye   10
> As hills and shapes of men eke beastes of sondrie kynde

Monstruous to o[r] outward sight and fancyes of our mynde
And eke the wanishe moone whiche sheenes by night also
and eache one of the wandring sterres whiche after her doth goe
And how to kepe their cource and whiche are those that stands   15
because they be thie wond'rous workes and labours of thie hands
but yet among all theise I aske *what thing is man*
whose tourne to serve in his poore neede this worke thow first
    began
Or whate is Adames sonne that beares bis fathers marke   20
for whose delyte and compfort eke thow hast wrought all this warke
I see thow mynd'st hym moche that doste rewarde hym so
beinge but *earth* to rule the *earth* wheare on hym self doth go
ffrom Aungells substance eke thow mad'ste hym differ small
Save one dothe chaunge his lif a whyle the other not at all[7]   25

The strong parallels between Surrey and Shakespeare are obvious.
Surrey begins by naming the «earth,» as does Hamlet, followed by the
«spread [of] the air,» similar to Hamlet's «most excellent canopy the air
... o'erhanging firmament.» Surrey asks, «what thing is man,» close to
Hamlet's «What piece of work is a man.» Surrey says that we are made
of earth, but are almost of the same substance as angels, while Hamlet
likens us to angels in our actions, adding that man is a «quintessence of
dust,» that is: «the ‹fifth essence› of ancient and mediaeval philosophy,
supposed to be the substance of which the heavenly bodies were composed».(*OED*).

Many other sources have been suggested for Hamlet's «quintessence of
dust» speech, of which a good summary is given by Harold Jenkins in
the Arden *Hamlet.* I will not quote the best of them for purposes of
comparison, but will offer these points instead. First, both Jenkins and
Alice Harmon, whom Jenkins cites,[8] regard the suggested sources as
analogues rather than sources. Next, no suggested source covers both
halves of Hamlet's speech, rather, different sources are suggested for
the description of the heavens and earth and for the nature of man.
Finally, no suggested source carries over from the «quintessence of
dust» speech to Hamlet's return to the question, «What is a man.»

Hamlet continues his discussion on the nature of man in a later soliloquy (IV.iv.32-39), and again we will find the presence of Surrey's
Psalm 8:

> How all occasions do inform against me,
> And spur my dull revenge. *What is a man*
> If his chief good and market of his time
> Be but to *sleep* and *feed*? A *beast,* no more.   35
> Sure *he that made us* with such large discourse,
> *Looking before and after,* gave us not
> That capability and godlike reason
> To fust in us unus'd.

The sequence of interest, indicated by emphases, is sleep/feed/beast/
God (i.e., «he that made us»)/looking. King David's Psalm 8 mentions
beasts and God, but not sleep, feed, and looking.

Surrey's Psalm 8 carries on from where we left off at line 25 by praising
God's creations made on behalf of mankind: the sun, moon, stars, air,
water, earth, metals, sheep, oxen, horses, all other beasts, fishes and
birds. Here is Surrey's equivalent to Hamlet's continuation on the
nature of man:

> and as hym list eache other *beast* to serve bis turne also
> The fysshes of the sea lykewyse to *feede* hym ofte   35
> and eke the birdes *whose ffeathers serve to make his sydes lye softe*
> On whose head *thow* hast sett a Crowne of glorye to
> to whome also *thow* did'st appoint that honour shuld be do
> and thus *thow* mad'ste hym lord of all this worke of thyne
> of man that goes, of beast that creapes whose *lookes doth downe declyne*

So Surrey's sequence is: beast/feed/sleep (i.e., on feather beds)/God/
looking.[9] Thus we find that elements of Surrey's Psalm 8, in their proper
order, carry us across both halves of Hamlet's «What piece of work is a
man ... quintessence of dust» speech, as well as his reprise in the
soliloquy, «How all occasions do inform against me.»

In short, unless better sources for Hamlet's speeches can be found, it seems clear that Shakespeare was relying on Surrey's Psalm 8. Moreover, we may note for future reference that Hamlet takes a melancholy or pessimistic view of Surrey's expansion of David's joyous Psalm.

II

We will now examine the date of composition of Surrey's Psalm 8, which will be shown to have been written in the Tower of London in December 1546 or, more likely, January 1547. Surrey was arrested on a dubious charge of high treason that December, and was tried, convicted, and beheaded in January. We will then turn to Surrey's last poem, which begins: «The stormes are past these cloudes are overblowne.» It will be seen that this poem was written after Surrey's conviction and is quite plausibly a companion or prologue to Psalm 8. Finally, we will return to Hamlet's meeting with Rosencrantz and Guildenstern which contains the «quintessence of dust» speech, and we shall find that «The stormes are past» is also present.

Surrey is credited with paraphrases of three other Psalms, numbers 55, 73 and 88, all of which were clearly written while he was in the Tower. Their contents, especially Surrey's additions to the words of the Psalmists, reflect his thoughts on his own plight. Surrey's Psalm 8 survives in only one contemporary copy, the Arundel Harington MS., where it is grouped with the other three, which also survive in another manuscript formerly belonging to the Harington family.[10] However, Surrey's 1928 editor, F. M. Padelford, feels that Psalm 8 «has none of the intense emotions of the other three Psalms, and may have been written at an earlier period.»[11]

Ruth Hughey, who rediscovered the Arundel Harington MS., argues that Psalm 8 «is of so impersonal a nature that it might have been composed at any time, ... The other Psalms and the two prologues [to 73 and 88] undoubtedly were composed shortly before Surrey's execution. (2: 101)»

Emrys Jones concurs on the time of composition of Psalm 8: «It would seem not to have been written, as the other three almost certainly were, during Surrey's final imprisonment.» (158)

These scholars are right as far as they go, but there is more to be said on the subject. Surrey's Psalm 55 ends with a reference to some other Psalm which Surrey identifies by two characteristics, both of which rule out Psalms 73 and 88, but both of which apply to Psalm 8. Furthermore, Hughey's observation on the «impersonal ... nature» of Surrey's Psalm 8 neglects its closing couplet, which was written by a man facing death.

Surrey's Psalm 55 concludes with an attack on one of his foes, followed by the line, «but in the other psalme of david fynd I ease.» (Hughey, 1.130-132, line 47) Now Psalm 55 is entitled, «A Psalm of David,» while 73 is «A Psalm of Asaph» and 88 is «A Psalm of the Sons of Korah,» so a Psalm of David's is missing, and 8 is entitled «A Psalm of David.» Moreover, we should consider the themes of these four Psalms, both as they were originally written, and as Surrey added to them. Psalm 55 is about anger and betrayal, and a good deal of anger is also found in 73, while 88 is about sorrow and penitence. Yet the missing Psalm of David is one in which Surrey found «ease» regarding his impending death. Moreover, Psalm 8 is a hymn of rejoicing at the glory of the world that God has created for us; it is indeed a Psalm in which a condemned man might find ease.[12]

Surrey's Psalm 8 closes with six lines that owe nothing to King David, being accurately described by Hughey as «a free rendition of the *Gloria*» (2: 101-102), a prayer recited or sung after the singing of Psalms in church. The ending of the *Gloria Patri* in Latin and in Cranmer's 1544 English translation is:

Sicut erat in principio, et nunc, et semper, et in saecula saeculorum. Amen.

As it was in the beginning, is now, and ever shall be, world without end. Amen.

Surrey renders these words in his closing couplet as:

> And as the same is now even heare within our tyme   51
> and ever shall heare after be when we be filth and slyme

The *Gloria* refers to the everlasting future but makes no mention of the death of the worshipper reciting the prayer. Surrey, in contrast, closes with the decomposition of the body after death, and he abases himself by his choice of the words «filth and slime,» rather than the Bible's more neutral earth, ashes and dust. Surrey's words are exceedingly personal and are very apt coming from a man adjusting his mind and soul to imminent death.

In sum, I think there can be little doubt that Surrey wrote his paraphrase of Psalm 8 in the Tower; moreover, it should logically or theologically have been his last Psalm. Christians facing death in those days, whether on the scaffold, the battlefield or the sickbed, were expected to put aside all earthly considerations such as anger and revenge in order to concentrate wholly on religion.[13] Surrey's Psalms 55, 73 and 88, like their originals, are full of worldly concerns, especially bitterness at betrayal and hope of rescue, but Surrey's Psalm 8 passes beyond the cares of the world; it is the composition of a man ready to die.

We will now take up Surrey's final poem, a companion to Psalm 8, which was used by Shakespeare in the sub-scene of *Hamlet* that includes the «quintessence of dust» speech.

Bomum est mihi quod humiliasti me.

> The stormes are past these cloudes are overblowne,
> And humble chere great rygour hath represt:
> For the defaute if set a paine foreknowne,
> And pacience graft in a determed brest.
> And in the hart where heapes of griefes were growne,   5
> The swete reuenge hath planted mirth and rest,
> No company so pleasant as myne owne.
> [...]

Thraldom at large hath made this prison fre,
Danger well past remembred workes delight:
Of lingring doutes such hope is sprong pardie,   10
That nought I finde displeasaunt in my sight:
But when my glasse presented unto me.
The curelesse wound that bledeth day and nyght,
To think (alas) such hap should graunted be
Unto a wretch that bath no hart to fight,   15
To spill that blood that hath so oft bene shed,
For Britannes sake (alas) and now is ded.[14]

The time of composition of this poem, the end of Surrey's life, is a matter that can be settled by several firm pieces of evidence. Around 1589, Surrey's second son, Lord Henry Howard, future Earl of Northampton, stated that «*Domin est michi quod humiliasti me*» was the «last thing [my father] wrote before his end.»[15] Its opening line marks it as a likely sequel to Surrey's Psalm 73 prologue, which begins, «The soudden stormes that heave me to and froo.» That Psalm attacks Surrey's enemies, and its prologue is addressed to George Blage, one of several friends who turned on Surrey. Next comes the Latin title found, along with the text, in Tottel's 1557 *Songes and Sonnettes*. Tottel supplied English titles for the other 270 poems in his edition of 1557, and those titles refer to the authors of the poems in the third person. *Bonum est mihi* is the only Latin title, it refers to the poet in the first person, and it is the first half of verse 71 of the Vulgate's Psalm 118 (Psalm 119 in Protestant Bibles). Moreover, verses 69 and 70 of that Psalm attack proud persons who have perjured themselves against the Psalmist, all of which indicate that the title is Surrey's. Therefore, without delving into the text of «The stormes are past,» we find strong evidence for dating it to Surrey's final imprisonment.

Yet further evidence for the date of «The stormes are past» lies within the lines of the poem. Line 8 indicates that it was written in prison, though Surrey's hot temper and rowdy ways had cost him several earlier spells of confinement. On the other hand, lines 12-17 lament the fact that his blood is dead, a clear reference to the attainder or corruption of blood that accompanied a treason conviction. A condemned traitor lost not only his titles, property, and life, but also his posterity, and the latter, in turn, lost their ancestry. As Lord Chief Justice Coke explained concerning convicted traitors:

> Thirdly, he shall lose his children (for they become base and ignoble.) Fourthly, he shall lose his posterity, for his blood is stained and corrupted, and they cannot inherit to him, or any other Auncestor.[16]

Moreover, the day before Surrey's trial and conviction, his father, the Duke of Norfolk, confessed to high treason. Consequently, not only were Surrey's four children legally fatherless (his wife was pregnant at the time with a fifth child), but Surrey's sister and brother would be in the same condition as soon as a bill of attainder against the Duke could be rushed through Parliament. The Duke of Norfolk was a veteran of many campaigns, having fought the French, Scots and Irish, not to mention English rebels, and Surrey was his father's worthy heir, well known for his reckless courage in battle. The blood that had often been shed for Britain's sake, as Surrey puts it, was dead.

The last six lines of «The stormes are past» have caused unnecessary problems to some of Surrey's editors. Padelford (223-224) felt that the «wretch» of line 15 was Surrey's initial accuser, Sir Richard Southwell, «whom Surrey had offered to fight when accused by him of treason.» Jones notes of lines 14-17, «[t]he personal allusion has not been satisfactorily traced» (131). However, Surrey says clearly enough in line 12 that he writes of what he sees in his mirror while alone in the Tower. Manifestly what he saw was himself, and his remaining lines continue as one long sentence. The wretch is himself, who no longer desires to fight Southwell, and whose hap or fate is to have his blood spilled by the headsman.

To conclude, it seems clear that «The stormes are past» was written by Surrey in the Tower after his conviction, and that poem harmonizes well with Psalm 8. In both cases we find a cheerful beginning leading up to acceptance of impending death.

It is now time to go back to Act II, scene ii of *Hamlet,* more specifically to lines 239-315. This sub-scene begins with the entry of Rosencrantz and Guildenstern and the exit of Polonius. Hamlet then converses with his two sometime friends, now turned traitor, he utters his «What piece of work is a man ... this quintessence of dust» speech, and then the talk turns to the arrival of the troupe of players. In this space of just under eighty lines, we will find three ideas borrowed from lines 6-8 of Surrey's «The stormes are past,» moreover two of these ideas enclose the «quintessence of dust» speech like a pair of parentheses.

Surrey, «The stormes are past:»

> The swete reuenge hath planted *mirth and rest,*   6
> *No company so pleasant as myne owne.*
> [...]
> *Thraldom at large* hath made *this prison* fre,

Shakespeare, *Hamlet,* II.ii:

> *Ham.*   ... What have you,
>   my good friends, deserved at the hands of Fortune   240
>   that she sends you to *prison* hither?
> *Guild. Prison,* my lord?
> *Ham.* Denmark's a *prison.*
> *Ros.* Then is the world one.
> *Ham.* A goodly one, in which there are many confines,   245
>   wards, and dungeons, Denmark being one o'th'
>   worst.
> *Ros.* We think not so, my lord.
> *Ham.* Why, then 'tis none to you; for there is nothing
>   either good or bad but thinking makes it so. To me   250
>   it is a *prison.*
>   ....
> *Ham.*   ... I have of late, but where-   295
>   fore I know not, lost all my *mirth, forgone all custom*
>   *of exercise.*

[Here follows the «quintessence of dust» speech, 298-308.]

> *Man delights not me — nor women neither,* though
> by your smiling you seem to say so.　　　　　310
> Ros. My lord, there was no such stuff in my thoughts.
> Ham. Why did ye laugh then, when I said *man delights*
> *not me?*
> Ros. To think, my lord, if *you delight not in man,* what
> Lenten entertainment the players shall receive from　　　　315
> you.

The first passage from *Hamlet* (239-251) directly endorses Surrey's observation that «Thraldom at large hath made this prison fre,» except that Surrey was on the inside looking out, while Hamlet is on the outside expressing the same thought. The meaning of Surrey's words is that with tyranny abroad throughout the land, he is just as free in prison as anyone is outside. Hamlet, at liberty, proclaims that Denmark and the rest of the world are prisons, because «thinking makes is so,» which, of course, was exactly what Surrey was doing to console himself.

The two items from the second passage from *Hamlet* (295-297 and 309-314) refashion what Surrey says in lines 6 and 7, with Hamlet's usual melancholy twist. Surrey, in the forced idleness of prison, says that his mind has given him «mirth and rest.» Hamlet, on the other hand, complains that he has lost his mirth and has given up his exercises, that is, he is compelled to rest. Surrey continues to make the best of things in his isolation, finding «No company so pleasant as myne owne.» Hamlet, with all the company of the Court available to him, finds no pleasure in men or women; presumably he would prefer to be alone.

If it is asked how Shakespeare came to know Surrey's «The stormes are past,» the obvious answer is that he read it in Tottel. As to Psalm 8, Shakespeare presumably saw that in manuscript. However, I suggest that Shakespeare read the two compositions together in manuscript, or, at any rate, was aware that they were companion pieces.

III

We will close with a review of the arguments offered concerning Surrey's influence on *Hamlet,* which are based primarily on economy and sequence. Surrey's Psalm 8 contains the elements of Hamlet's «quintessence of dust» speech, first the heavens and earth, then the nature of man, and, when Hamlet returns to the latter subject in the soliloquy, «How all occasions do inform against me,» we find again that the elements are in Psalm 8. Moreover, we see that Hamlet follows the sequence in which Surrey brings up these various elements. We then examined good evidence showing that «The stormes are past» is a companion to Psalm 8, and, returning to the sub-scene containing the «quintessence of dust» speech, we discover Hamlet uttering almost the thoughts and words that Surrey placed in three adjacent lines of this poem.[17]

If Surrey's influence on Shakespeare is granted, then one question remains. Did Shakespeare simply regard Surrey's pieces as useful quarries for his own work, or did he take an interest in their author? I believe that the answer lies in the character of Hamlet that Shakespeare fashioned—poet, courtier, scholar, soldier—and in the consistently negative twist or reversal Shakespeare gives to Surrey's thoughts as expressed by Hamlet, matching the contrast between rash Surrey and indecisive Hamlet. That is, I believe that Hamlet is an intentional anti-Surrey, but not one who is opposite in every respect like a photographic negative. Rather Hamlet is opposite to Surrey in one important characteristic, but otherwise identical, as in the concept in physics known as antimatter.

Endnotes

1 The Arden *Hamlet,* ed. Harold Jenkins (London: Methuen & Co. Ltd, 1982).

2 On Surrey's portraits, see Sir Roy Strong, *Tudor and Jacobean Portraits* (London: H. M. Stationery Office, 1969) 2: 307.

3 Emrys Jones, *Henry Howard, Earl of Surrey, Poems* (Oxford: Clarendon Press, 1964) 158.

4 *The Byble in Englyshe* (London: Richard Grafton, 1540). *Biblia Sacra, Juxta*

Vulgatam Clementinam (Paris: Desclée & Co., 1927). Surrey's various editors have noted his preference for the Vulgate. In the case of Psalm 8, we may cite the Vulgate's plural «*opera*» in verse 4, Coverdale's singular «worcke,» and Surrey's «workes» in line 16. More telling is the Vulgate's «*paulo minus*» («little less») in verse 6, compared to Coverdale's blunt «lower than»; Surrey's line 24 clearly follows the Vulgate. On Surrey's knowledge of Coverdale, see Jones, 159-160. For a more detailed discussion of Surrey's sources, see H. A. Mason, «Wyatt and the Psalms — II,» *Times Literary Supplement* (6 March 1953): 160, and his *Humanism and Poetry in the Early Tudor Period* (London: Routledge and Kegan Paul, 1959) 241-249. The rest of this article will refer to the English Bible, the established source of Shakespeare's scriptural knowledge.

5   For line 303 the Folio reads, «What *a* piece of work is a man,» while the Second Quarto is, as above, «What piece of work is a man.» Jenkins, the Arden editor, resolves the crux in favor of the Quarto, calling the Folio version a modernization. Most editions, such as the recent Cambridge and Oxford, follow the Folio.

6   Shakespeare also knew the Geneva Bible, but the latter differs from both Coverdale and Hamlet's speech in one critical passage. Where Coverdale writes, «Thou madest hym lower than the aungels,» the Geneva has, «For thou hast made him a litle lower then God.» As Hamlet follows his comparison of man to angels with «how like a god,» it seems likely that Shakespeare also consulted his Geneva Bible. *The Geneva Bible, A facsimile of the 1560 edition* (Madison, Milwaukee, & London: U of Wisconsin P, 1969).

7   Ruth Hughey, *The Arundel Harington Manuscript of Tudor Poetry* (Columbus: Ohio State UP, 1960) 2: 125-126.

8   Alice Harmon, «How Great Was Shakespeare's Debt to Montaigne?,» *PMLA*, 57 (1942): 994-996.

9   Surrey describes the downward look of four-footed beasts, which Hamlet reverses to the *Iliad's* superior vision of upright humanity, able to look forward and backward in both space and time. Hamlet's echo of the *Iliad*, 3.109 and 18.250, cited by Jenkins, was first noticed by Theobald.

10   On the Park MS. or British Library Additional MS. 36529, see Hughey, 1: 8.

11   F. M. Padelford, *The Poems of Henry Howard, Earl of Surrey* (Seattle: U of Washington P, 1928) 231.

12   Charles A. Huttar noticed that a modified version of Surrey's Psalm 88 was published in an anthology of around 1550, followed by paraphrases of Psalms 31 and 51, which Huttar argues are also by Surrey. In my opinion, these other two paraphrases are not Surrey's work, though it is always

possible that they contain fragments of his. This issue is beyond the scope of the present article, but, more to the point, while 31 and 51 are both Psalms of David, neither is very easeful. 31 is a Psalm of grief and anger, while 51, which was commonly recited on the scaffold in those times, is a Psalm of sorrow and contrition. See Huttar, «Poems by Surrey and Others in a Printed Miscellany Circa 1550,» *English Miscellany* 16 (1965): 9-15. See also Michael Rudick, «Two Notes on Surrey's Psalms,» *Notes and Queries* 220 (July 1975): 291-294.

13 Beach Langston provides an excellent discussion of the sixteenth century's views on the proper preparation for death in «Essex and the Art of Dying,» *Huntington Library Quarterly* 2 (February 1950): 109-129. Hamlet's father did not go to heaven because he died unprepared, while Hamlet declines to kill his uncle at prayer lest he send him straight to heaven. On the necessity of setting aside worldly cares when facing death we may note Michael Williams's speech on the eve of Agincourt. He fears that few soldiers die well in battle: «some swearing, some crying for a surgeon, some upon their wives left poor behind them, some upon the debts they owe, some upon their children rawly left» (the Arden *Henry V*, ed. J. H. Walter (London: Methuen & Co. Ltd, 1954), IV.i.140-143)

14 Richard Tottel, *Songs and Sonnets (Tottel's Miscellany) 1557* (Menston, Yorkshire: A Scolar Press facsimile, 1970) D.iii.v. As indicated, one line, and possibly more, is missing between lines 7 and 8.

15 Bodleian Library MS 903 (arch A 170) (2953) Delta 264, fol. 6r and v. I am indebted to William A. Sessions for the exact wording and reference.

16 Sir Edward Coke, The *Third Part of the Institutes of the Laws of England* (London: W. Lee and D. Pakeman, 1644) 211. The *OED*'s earliest example of the phrase «restore in blood» is from 1591, see *Blood, sb. 13*. Under *Restore, v., 4.b.*, the first example is from 1594, while the definition of *Restitution, 4.b.* gives 1633 as the first use of the phrase, «Restitution in blood.» But these usages are much older. For examples from Surrey's period, see *The Statutes of the Realm* (London, 1817) 34 & 35 Henry VIII (1542-1543), Chapter XXV, section 32. «An Acte for restituicion in name and bloode to Walter Hungreforde and Edwarde Nevyle» (3:894), or 1 Mary 1 (1553), St. 2, sections 21, 23, 25-28 and 30, all for «Restitutionl Restitucion in Bloudd» of various persons, the first being Surrey's older son (4: 200).

17 Actually the lines are not fully adjacent, as a line is missing amidst them. If the full text of «The stormes are past» ever surfaces, I suspect that the contents of the missing line will also be found in Hamlet's mouth.

Hamlet and *Piers Plowman*:
A Matter of Conscience

William Langland's *Piers Plowman* and William Shakespeare's drama, especially *Hamlet,* seem poles apart in the worlds they portray and the ways they portray them—in their pictures and in their poetry. Langland presents us with the grimy underside of medieval England, in virtually the last masterpiece of an alliterative verse tradition extending back to *Beowulf.* Shakespeare, on the other hand, addresses us in elegant blank verse—a Renaissance medium to describe a Renaissance court. Yet a recent *Piers Plowman* editor, A. V. C. Schmidt, finds three distinct similarities between the two poets: «expressive verse rhythms,» «frequent wordplay,» and «use of expanded metaphor and thematic and structural imagery.»[1]

Some years earlier, E. M. W. Tillyard observed that «one of the best analogies with the total landscape of *Hamlet* is Langland's description of the fair field full of folk at the opening of *Piers Plowman.*»[2] Tillyard's comparison may seem rather odd, until we consider that Langland's wandering dreamer describes society as seen from below, while Prince Hamlet, of course, views from above. Nevertheless, *Hamlet's* gravediggers are certainly close cousins to the «dikers and delvers that done their deeds ill» at the end of Langland's Prologue. If, however, Hamlet's own words are compared to Langland's text, we discover that Schmidt's third item of comparison—expanded metaphor and imagery—is no coincidence, for Shakespeare is significantly indebted to Langland in this regard. The metaphors and imagery revolve, moreover, around a particular topic—broadly speaking, the nature of moral dilemmas—but, more precisely, the theme is conscience, a major presence in *Piers Plowman.*

Langland's alliterative poem was written in the late fourteenth century and survives in three consecutive states, called A, B, and C. The A and C versions of *Piers Plowman* remained in manuscript until the nineteenth century, but the B version was published in 1550 in a black letter edition of three impressions by Robert Crowley and again in 1561 by Owen Rogers. It is divided into a Prologue and twenty sections called *passus,* Latin for «step.» The B version's 7,439 lines (in Crowley's edition) describe a series of eight dreams experienced by the wandering narrator. Not surprisingly, Shakespeare seems to have known the B version, though I cannot demonstrate that he read the printed edition rather than a manuscript. However, Shakespeare probably would have preferred a printed book with modernized orthography, and certainly the printed texts were readier to hand; hence, we will deal with Crowley's edition. Incidentally, Shakespeare's knowledge of the popular *Piers Plowman* is hardly odd in light of his familiarity with the works of Langland's contemporaries, Geoffrey Chaucer and John Gower. However, while the latter pair provided Shakespeare with tales set in classical times, Langland contributed ethical quandaries to the Prince of Denmark.

Among the dilemmas that Shakespeare created in *Hamlet* are whether Hamlet should kill his murderous uncle at prayer (III.iii) and whether humans should suffer a host of troubles, oppose them, or commit suicide (III.i). In considering the first problem, Shakespeare borrowed words or ideas from a question raised in *Piers Plowman,* namely, whether the rich may go to heaven (Passus xiv). Regarding the second dilemma—that is, the «To be, or not to be» soliloquy—Shakespeare assembled imagery and concepts from three parts of *Plowman*: first, the assault of Anti-Christ on humanity (Passus xx); next, a confrontation between conscience and corruption (Passus iii); and finally, a discourse on the eight functions of the human soul (Passus xv). Hamlet's most famous soliloquy is, in fact, an attempt to integrate William Langland's scattered observations on the human conscience, with William Shakespeare picking up where *Piers Plowman* left off. After examining each dilemma separately, Langland's ideas on conscience may be connected to Hamlet's decision regarding his uncle's fate. That decision, however, is much more obviously and directly indebted to Langland's words and metaphors, making it the preferred starting point in demonstrating the existence of that debt.

I. Hire and Salary

Having tricked Claudius into revealing his guilt, Hamlet discovers his uncle at prayer and draws his sword, but Hamlet decides not to send Claudius to heaven by killing him in a state of grace, explaining:

> Why, this is *hire and salary,* not revenge.
> A took my father grossly, *full of bread,*
> With all his crimes broad blown, *as flush as May;*
> [...]
> Up, sword, and know thou a more *horrid hent.* (III.iii.79-81, 88)[3]

The words «hire and salary» signify some sort of antithesis to revenge. They have caused editorial problems ever since the 1604 Second Quarto of *Hamlet,* which changed them to «base and silly.»[4] Harold Jenkins, the 1982 Arden editor, felt that Dover Wilson's 1934 suggestion, «bait and salary,» offered a plausible alternative, while in the 1985 New Cambridge *Hamlet,* Philip Edwards conjectured that the 1604 editors were doing the best they could with an illegible manuscript passage. G. R. Hibbard in the 1987 Oxford edition followed G. L. Kittredge's 1939 explanation, «as if I had hired him to murder my father and am now paying him his wages.» T. J. B. Spencer in the 1980 New Penguin *Hamlet* glosses «hire and salary» as, «like a payment for services, instead of punishment for crimes,» which happens to be correct as far as it goes.[5] However, the full explanation for this puzzling expression appears in its source, which is also the origin of the other three phrases emphasized above: Passus xiv of the B version of Langland's *Piers Plowman.*

Passus xiv contains a passage on how contrition may reduce deadly sin to venial, including, «And though a man might not speak [yet] contrition might save/And bring his soul to bliss»[6]—words of obvious relevance to the state of Claudius's soul. Langland continues with a discussion of the difficulty of the rich getting into heaven, as they have already received their reward here on earth, where they often failed to help the poor and otherwise lead good lives:

So I say by you ryche, it semeth not that ye should
Haue heauen in your here beryng, and heuen hereafter
Right as seruant taketh his *salary* before, & sith wold claim more
As he that none had, & hath *hire* at ye last
                              (Ixxiii^v, 140-43, my emphases)

But Langland decides of the deserving rich and others:

And al ye done her deuour wel, have *double hire* for her travel
Here forgiuenes for her sins, & heuen blis after
                              (Ixxiiii^r, 153-54, my emphasis)

Here is the source and also the explanation for Hamlet's words about «hire and salary, not revenge.» Langland's simile depicts an appointed servant with a regular salary, paid at the start of the month or quarter (who «taketh his salary before»), lining up with his master's day labourers to receive wages in the evening («hire at the last»). «Hire and salary» thus means double payment—before and after. If Hamlet kills Claudius in a state of grace, then Claudius would have had heaven on earth by gaining the crown and his brother's wife, to be followed by «heaven hereafter.» This section of Passus xiv also yields the sources of the other three items noted above: «full of bread,» «as flush as May,» and «horrid hent.»

Edmond Malone was the first to notice that «full of bread,» meaning «in a state of sin,» comes from Ezekiel 16:49, but Passus xiv of *Piers Plowman* includes the same metaphor. Eight lines before the passage on how contrition can reduce deadly sin to venial, Langland refers to the verse in Ezekiel that Malone cited:

And ouer plenty maketh pryde amonges pore & rych
Therfor mesure is so mich worth it mai not be to dere
For the mischife & the mischaunce amongs men of Sodom
Wext throughe *plenty of payne* [bread] and of pure Slouth
*Osiositas et **habundantia panis**, peccatum turpissi[mum nutriuit.*
For they measured not hemselfe of y^t they eat & drancke

(Ixxii^v, 74-78, my emphases; «Sloth and *abundance of bread*
                                    nourished the worst sins.»)

The reader then turns one page to see what Langland has to say about
hire and salary, leading up to:

> And al y^t done her deuour wel, have double hire for hir trauel
> Here forgiuenes for her sins, & heuen blis after
> And it is but seld sene, as by sayntes bokes
> That god rewarded double rest to any rych man
> For much myrth is among rych, as in meat & clothes
> *And much myrth in May* is amongest wylde beastes
>
> (Ixxv^r, 153-58, my emphasis)

So Shakespeare found the inspirations for «full of bread» and «as flush
as May» along with «hire and salary,» and the next page explains «Up,
sword, and know thou a more horrid hent.»

The word «hent» meant «to lay hold of, seize, grasp» and suchlike
(*OED*), and was still current, though probably old-fashioned, in Elizabethan times. Shakespeare uses it in two other places in his works: in
Measure for Measure, «Have hent the gates» (IV.vi.14); and in *Twelfth
Night,* «And merrily hent the stile-a» (IV.iii.120). Yet Hamlet's use of the
word seems idiosyncratic, as if he is telling his sword that at some more
opportune moment it will grip or clutch Claudius, which has led some
modern editors to amend the word to «hint.»[7] Langland uses «hent» in
a routine way several times in his work, such as near the beginning of
Passus xiv, «and out of his poke hent/Vytailes» (Ixxii^r, 36-37). In one
place, however, he associates the word with mortal danger. Turning one
page from the passages on hire and salary and mirth in May brings the
reader to a discussion of the seven deadly sins and the poor. Here
Langland pictures Covetise as a giant with «handes and armes of a
longe length» engaged in a wrestling match with puny Poverty, who
does not come up to his Opponent's navel:

> And if couetise catch the pore, they mai not come togithers
> And by ye nek nameli, ther none mai hent other (Ixxv^r, 239-40)

The image of a huge man with his hands around the throat of a tiny weakling conveys the concept of deadly peril. The image leads to Hamlet's words, «a more horrid hent,» presumably meaning that he will seize his sword on a more horrid occasion, when he can send Claudius straight to hell.

To conclude, Shakespeare noticed fifteen lines of Passus xiv of *Plowman,* 140-54, from which he picked an idea and two key words, «hire» and «salary,» concerning reward in both this life and the next. The phrase is certainly compact in relation to the idea, but so much so as to defy explication unless the words are coupled with their source.[8] Shakespeare went on to select three nearby images of Langland's from which Hamlet constructs three lines. This example reveals Shakespeare to be reading deep inside *Piers Plowman,* not just browsing through the Prologue. Regarding Shakespeare's use of the B version, we may begin by noting that the A version of *Plowman* ends with Passus xi and lacks all the material found in the B version's Passus xiv. Meanwhile, the C version omits the two critical lines explaining «hire and salary.» (Passus xiv, 142-43) The equivalent passage is at the start of its Passus xvi:

> So y sey by yow ryche, hit semeth nat that ye sholle
> Have two heuenes tor youre here-beynge.
> Muche murthe is in May amonge wilde bestes[9]

At two places to come, Shakespeare's words will be seen to agree with the B version but not with the C version. Moreover, Hamlet will borrow images and ideas from two *Passus* not included in the A version.

II. Slings and Arrows, Whips and Scorns

Hamlet's best known soliloquy—«To be, or not to be» (III.i.56-90)—is constructed from pieces of *Plowman.* Most conspicuously, Hamlet's «slings and arrows of outrageous fortune» come from a battle described in Passus xx that features personified Conscience. Less conspicuously, Hamlet's opinion that «conscience does make cowards of us all» turns out to be logically derivable from a confrontation in Passus iii involving the same personified Conscience, which confrontation also includes a description of the «whips and scorns of time.» Finally, the last fifteen lines of Hamlet's soliloquy illustrate the functions of the human soul, including conscience—though not personified—as described in Passus xv. Thus the beginning, middle, and end of Hamlet's soliloquy draw inspiration from three parts of *Plowman* that feature conscience. The Conscience of Passus xx is a hero who prevents people from choosing death over life. The same Conscience in Passus iii is revealed as having a cowardly side. When Hamlet decides in line 83 that conscience makes cowards of us all, he combines these two depictions of Langland's Conscience. The conscience described in Passus xv is also found in Hamlet's soliloquy, but in line 88 as «the name of action.» Shakespeare uses Passus xx in lines 57-69 of the soliloquy, shifting to Passus iii in lines 70-88. The material borrowed from Passus xv, however, comes from lines 57 and 76-90, where it is interwoven with threads from Passus iii. In the interest of clarity, I will describe Shakespeare's use of Passus iii and xx in this section, reserving Passus xv for section iii of my paper. I will then offer an integrated view of the soliloquy, showing how the parts create a unified whole, in my final section.

The «To be, or not to be» soliloquy may be summarized thus: Attacked by Fortune's slings and arrows, humanity must decide whether to fight against a sea of troubles or to escape by choosing death, but conscience prevents the latter (see Appendix 1 for the full text). Many editors of *Hamlet* have been uneasy about the word «slings.» Some editors change it to «stings»; others go out of their way to justify «slings» by citing other writings available to Shakespeare that mention slings and arrows together.[10] However, no editor offers a passage combining slings, arrows, *and* fortune. Editors have also questioned the mixed metaphor of taking arms against the sea. Langland's text sheds light on both editorial issues. For our purposes, Langland's central figure is Conscience the Knight, an allegorical representation of the human conscience, and the chief defender of Holy Church against two principal enemies: Mede the Maid in Passus iii and Anti-Christ in Passus xx. Mede threatens the community with subversion from within, while Anti-Christ brings invasion from without. We will now tie Hamlet's soliloquy to Passus xx.

In Passus xx—the final dream of *Plowman*—the community is attacked by Anti-Christ, who commands the seven deadly sins and other personified evils. Faithful Christians prefer death to life under such conditions (cxi^v, 62-63), but Conscience the Knight urges them to rally at the fortress of Holy Church from which they can fight back (cxi^v, 74-79). Then follows a vivid description of medieval combat, shifting back and forth between literal and allegorical. Battle is joined in the open field, where many Christians are slain. Most of Anti-Christ's warriors, such as Pride and Covetise, strike with their inherent vices, rather than with lance or sword. Two material weapons are described: Fortune sends Lechery (cxiii^r, 110-11), armed with «a bowe [...] & many bloudy arrowes» (cxiii^r, 117), against the faithful, while Fortune's son Sloth (cxiiii^r, 158) wields a sling that shoots a dozen miles (cxiiii^r, 163-64). The people are driven within the walls of the fortress, of which Conscience is the constable or governor. The enemy besiege with two sorts of missiles: Sloth makes a «hard assawte» with his sling, followed by sixty archers shooting «many a shefe of [...]/[...] brode hoked arowes.» (cxiiii^v-cxv^r, 214-26) Death is a ferocious combatant in the battle, and «Age the hoore [Age the Hoary, also called Elde] [...]/[...] bare ye banner before death.» (cxiii^r, 95-96) Whoever temporarily escapes the first must contend with the second, and the dreamer—piteously and hilariously—describes his own sufferings at the hands of Elde.

Consider the parallels between Passus xx and the soliloquy. Like Hamlet, Langland's people are attacked by Fortune's sling and arrows. Both Shakespeare's conscience and Langland's Conscience prevent humanity from choosing death, though Langland's Conscience does so by summoning the people to take arms against their sea of evils. Actually, as we have seen, Langland's people take arms, not against a *sea* of troubles, but rather a *siege* of troubles, which is perhaps what Shakespeare actually wrote.[11] Thus the final appearance of Conscience the Knight in *Plowman* helps clarify two editorial problems in *Hamlet*. Moreover, Hamlet continues his soliloquy by mentioning «that sleep of death,» followed by the «calamity of so long life»—normally considered a blessing—matching Langland's powerful dream vision of Death and his calamitous standard-bearer Elde.

On the other hand, we find contradiction between Shakespeare and Langland concerning the courage of Conscience. In each case, Conscience prevents humanity from choosing death, but Hamlet calls conscience a coward, while Langland's Conscience is a hero. At the end of Passus xx, Conscience is overwhelmed after being let down by comrades like Clergy and Contrition. Their dereliction resulted from Conscience permitting subversive friars into Holy Church; his weakness is a too-trusting nature, not cowardice. Conscience is, however, named a coward in *Plowman's* Passus iii, to which we must travel in search of a solution to our paradox (other suggested sources for Shakespeare's connection of conscience and cowardice are discussed in Appendix 2).

We come to Passus iii by continuing down the soliloquy. Hamlet begins by citing Passus xx's slings and arrows of Fortune (1. 58), continues on to «the whips and scorns of time» (1. 70), listing six specific items, and then asks why we put up with such misery when suicide offers an easy escape:[12]

> But that the dread of something after death,
> The undiscover'd country, from whose bourn
> No traveller returns, puzzles the will,   80
> And makes us rather bear those ills we have
> Than fly to others that we know not of?
> Thus conscience does make cowards of us all,
> And thus the native hue of resolution
> Is sicklied o'er with the pale cast of thought,   85
> And enterprises of great pitch and moment
> With this regard their currents turn awry
> And lose the name of action.

So Hamlet's sequence is a list of six «whips and scorns,» followed by cowardice caused by conscience, resulting in the abandonment of great enterprises. The relevant portion of Passus iii reveals an equivalent succession of themes which should be considered before detailed similarities are sought.

Passus iii describes an encounter before the King between Mede the Maid and Conscience the Knight, each of whose names turns out to have a double meaning. Mede represents material reward, including gifts and the wages paid to honest workers, but also every form of dishonestly earned wages, bribes, theft, plunder, and graft. Conscience stands for the modern meaning of that word, one's inner or religious sense of right and wrong, but in both Langland's fourteenth century and in Shakespeare's time, «conscience» had another meaning which Mede brings out, namely, consciousness, awareness, understanding, or knowledge (this meaning is still current in French). These may be termed the moral and neutral meanings of conscience.

The King has had Mede arrested for her crimes, but then he forgives her and proposes to marry her to Conscience; the maid agrees, but the knight flatly refuses (xiii^{r-v}, 101-21). In lines 122-69, Conscience describes the evils wrought by Mede—that she inspires all sorts of crime and corruption, lechery and treachery, and the oppression suffered by honest folk at the hands of the greedy and powerful. Yet Mede the Maid is always resourceful, and, in lines 170-227, she ripostes by proclaiming that during the French campaign of 1359-60, Conscience, in the neutral sense of «awareness,» caused English soldiers to desert due to cold, rain, and hunger, while she kept up the spirits of the troops who stayed with the King, as they «hope to haue me at wyll» (xiiii^{v}, 200). She adds that if she had been marshal of the army, that is, the King's second-in-command, they would have conquered all of France, but that:

> Cowardlie thou conscience counceledst hym thens
> To leuen his lordshipe for a little syluer
> That is the richest realme that raygneth ouer heigh.[13]

The C version of *Plowman* reads «Caytifliche thow, Conscience» and does not use the word «coward.»[14] Mede continues by explaining that rulers and lords of all sorts rely on her rewards to gain the loyalty of their followers, while all manner of workers and merchants expect their honest meed, concluding, «No wyght as I wene [think] w^{t}outen mede may lyue.» Then, «Quod the king to conscience by Christ as me thinketh/Mede is wel worthy the maistry to haue» (xv^r, 227-29); that is, Mede is winning the debate—though Conscience finally prevails.

The basic argument that Shakespeare had the meeting of Mede and Conscience in mind when he wrote the second half of Hamlet's best known soliloquy is the sequence of Conscience's speech on the evils caused by Mede, which is similar to Hamlet's «whips and scorns of time»; followed by Mede's condemnation of «Cowardly, thou Conscience,» similar to Hamlet's «conscience does make cowards of us all»; both leading to the collapse of important enterprises. Hamlet asks,

> For who would bear the whips and scorns of time,
> Th'oppressor's wrong, the proud man's contumely,
> The pangs of dispriz'd love, the law's delay,
> The insolence of office, and the spurns
> That patient merit of th' unworthy takes […] (III.i.70-74)

Each one of these six «whips and scorns,» save perhaps «the proud man's contumely,» can be matched to Conscience's charges against Mede. I do not claim that these links prove that Shakespeare borrowed from Passus iii, as other descriptions of social corruption were available to Shakespeare—not to mention his own observations—and as Shakespeare cannot be shown to be using Langland's actual words. Nevertheless, the similarity justifies a search for further correspondences.

Against «th'oppressor's wrong» may be cited the accusation that Mede causes the guilty to be freed by bribery,

> And taketh the true by the top and tieth him fast
> And hangeth hem for hatred that harme dyd neuer
>   (xii^v, 140-41; «taketh... by the top» means «seizes by the hair»)

Conscience generally charges Mede with doing material wrong to the innocent, rather than slandering them or covering them with contumely. Yet Conscience does call her «talewyse of her tonge,» (131) that is, a spreader of gossip and slander. As for the «pangs of dispriz'd love,» Conscience says of Mede that:

> Wyues and wdydowes [sic] wantones she teacheth
> And lerneth hem lecherie that loue hyr gyftes [...]
> For she is Tikel of her tayle, ...
> As *commen* as a cartwaye to eche a knaue that walketh
>   (xii^v, 125-32)

Conscience is quite specific on «the law's delay»:

> She leadeth the law as her list & louedaies maketh
> And doth men lese through hyr loue y^t law might win
> The maze for a meane man though he mote her euer
> Lawe is so lordleche, and lothe to make end
>   (xiiii^r, 158-61. *Lovedays were held at manor courts to settle disputes,*
>   *but bribery frequently carried the day. The word «mote» means «moot,»*
>   *that is, pleading in court.*)

On the «insolence of office,» Conscience charges,

> Sisours [*assizers*] and somnours [*summoners*] such men her praiseth
> Shyreues [*sheriffs*] of shires ware shent [*ruined*] if she were not
> For she doth men lese her [*their*] lond and her life bothe.
>   (xiii^v, 134-36)

Lastly, as regards «the spurns that patient merit of th' unworthy takes,» we may note,

> For pore men mai have no powr to plain *hem* when they smarte
> Suche a master is mede among *men* of God[15]

These are Langland's equivalents to Shakespeare's «whips and scorns»; we will now evaluate their respective views on cowardice and conscience.

The connection between cowardice and conscience as explained by Mede and Hamlet helps to demonstrate how their opinions dovetail. Mede, as already noted, says that Conscience, in the neutral sense of knowing or awareness of misery, caused soldiers to run away to escape cold, rain, and hunger. Hamlet, on the other hand, bases his view of conscience on not knowing or unawareness, more specifically, on not knowing what lies in store for us after death, an issue which his father's ghost was forbidden to discuss. In essence, Hamlet's opinion of conscience complements Mede's, or carries it to its logical conclusion. Mede holds that awareness of misery makes us flee it, while Hamlet acknowledges the misery but adds that we do not flee as far as we might, that is, we do not flee misery to the point of choosing death because of our unawareness of where that might land us.

Recent editors of *Hamlet,* including Jenkins, Hibbard, and Edwards, maintain that Hamlet uses the word «conscience» in the moral sense, rather than the neutral. However, as Jenkins notes, a number of distinguished critics, starting with A. C. Bradley, argue that Hamlet has the neutral meaning in mind; Jenkins adds that the «choice between the two has been much debated.» (Jenkins, 492, n. to III.i.83) Shakespeare uses the word «conscience» over one hundred times in his works, almost always in the moral sense. His only clear use of the neutral sense is in *Timon of Athens,* «Canst thou the conscience lack,/To think I shall lack friends?» (II.ii.179-80) Thus one might conclude that Jenkins and the others who support Hamlet's use of the moral meaning of conscience have the better of the argument. Yet the neutral sense of the word cannot be logically refuted, given Hamlet's emphasis on our not knowing what lies on the other side of death, not to mention his slur on «the pale cast of thought.» (III.i.85) The simplest escape from this impasse lies in the theory that Shakespeare had read something that set the two meanings of conscience against each other, namely Passus iii of *Plowman,* in which Mede confronts the moral meaning with the neutral, and to conclude that Shakespeare had both meanings in mind. Hamlet's views on conscience and cowardice make more sense if seen as an extension of those of Mede the Maid.[16]

In fact, Mede stands on firm ground when, in her speech before the King, she defends the meaning of her own name, as material reward is a necessity of life—neither inherently good nor evil. Yet Mede seems to rely on a slippery debating tactic in her attack on Conscience, as she simply brings out a peculiarity of language, that «conscience» has both a moral and a neutral meaning, for she never shows a connection between the two senses. The link is easily deduced, for correct moral decisions are impossible without prior neutral knowledge. Thus Hamlet concludes that humans need an accurate knowledge or «conscience» of the hereafter to make moral decisions in the present life, while his own particular problem is to verify Claudius's guilt before determining how to execute justice. So Mede's speech in Passus iii points to Hamlet's meaning about how conscience prevents us from choosing death, as Conscience the Knight did in Passus xx.

That Shakespeare thought in terms of a two-sided conscience, or, more specifically, that neutral knowledge precedes moral decisions, is spelled out in Hamlet's final soliloquy, «How all occasions do inform against me.» (IV.iv.32-66) Here Hamlet considers whether his irresolution arises from «bestial oblivion,» that is, not thinking at all, or from «some craven scruple/Of thinking too precisely on th' event.» (40-41) In other words, craven scruples, that is, cowardly moral conscience, result from the prior action of the neutral or thinking side of conscience. Moreover, the latter, thinking too precisely or pondering the outcome of an action, «hath but one part wisdom/And ever three parts coward.» (42-43) So the blame seems to fall on the thinking side—«the pale cast of thought.»

Hamlet's soliloquy has further connections to the encounter between Mede and Conscience. The six «whips and scorns» that Hamlet names are generally not problems that he faces himself—as has often been pointed out[17]—nor are they miseries that would be expected to afflict a prince. Hamlet continues from the «whips and scorns» to the unknown land of death:

> When he himself might his quietus make
> With a bare bodkin? who would fardels bear,
> To grunt and sweat under a weary life,
> But that the dread of something after death,
> The undiscover'd country, from whose bourn
> No traveller returns   (III.i.75-80)

Hamlet is clearly speaking about the lowly, those who grunt and sweat with burdens on their backs—precisely the victims of Mede whose misfortunes are detailed by Conscience. Then, rather oddly, Hamlet says that conscience makes us into cowards who abandon «enterprises of great pitch and moment,» (86) which are not the sort of activities that one associates with those who grunt and sweat under fardels. An explanation of this seeming inconsistency lies in Mede's counterattack on Conscience. As Mede relates, the desertion of poor common soldiers—bearing cheap plunder on their backs (xiiii^v; 196)—led to the abandonment of Edward III's conquest of France, which to Langland, just as much as to the author of *Henry V,* was an enterprise of the greatest pitch and moment. Therefore, as with «hire and salary» and «slings and arrows,» a passage in *Plowman* clarifies a puzzle in *Hamlet.*

In sum, the central arguments connecting the second part of Hamlet's «To be, or not to be» soliloquy to Passus iii are similar structural sequences, similar details on life's miseries, complementary views on conscience and cowardice, and, as a bonus, an explanation of aristocratic concern for plebeian problems.

The arguments of this entire section on Hamlet's soliloquy may be summarized as follows. Passus xx depicts humanity attacked by Fortune with slings and arrows in what becomes a siege of troubles. Humanity must take arms or succumb without resistance, and Conscience makes the decision. But Langland's Conscience is, at this point, an uncomplicated hero who rallies humanity against Anti-Christ. Shakespeare's conscience, on the other hand, though choosing life over death, does so out of fear and uncertainty, and we find that Langland's Conscience was called a coward in Passus iii. Shakespeare had, however, other paradigms combining conscience and cowardice. Yet, as discussed in Appendix 2, neither Shakespeare in *Richard III* nor either of the two suggested sources of *Hamlet* examines the link between cowardice and conscience in a manner equivalent to Hamlet's. Hamlet considers six «whips and scorns» inflicted on us in life, followed by his connection of cowardice to conscience, just as Conscience the Knight in Passus iii describes virtually the same miseries, followed by Mede the

Maid's contemptuous equation of Conscience and cowardice. Scholars have argued for a century about whether Hamlet intends the moral or neutral meaning of conscience, but they have not found any work available to Shakespeare that confronts that issue, which is exactly what Langland's Mede does in Passus iii of *Piers Plowman*. Moreover, the parallels continue, as we learn why Prince Hamlet is so concerned with the misfortunes of the lowly, and why he associates them with failed enterprises of great moment. Shakespeare is following Sir Conscience on the downtrodden and Lady Mede on the abandonment of the glorious campaign of 1359-60.

III. The Soul in Action

We will now establish the debt of Hamlet's soliloquy to Langland's Passus xv. I noted at the start of section II that «the name of action» in line 88 of «To be, or not to be» is, according to Passus xv, another definition of Conscience. This item comes from a thirteen-line passage in which the dreamer encounters *Anima* or Soul, who names his eight functions or actions, followed by a five-line Latin quotation from Langland's source, the encyclopedia of Isidore of Seville (1xx^v, 24-39á). All eight functions are found in the soliloquy, which offers an alternate reading of the speech.

Langland first defines and names each function in one or two lines of English, though using the Latin name, while the Latin extract from Isidore's encyclopedia defines each with one or two words.

- First comes *Animus* or Will: defined by Langland as, «whan I wyll and wold, Animus iche hate [I'm called],» and by Isidore as «*vult.*»
- Second is *Mens* or Mind: «for that I can and knowe, called am I Mens,» or «*scit.*»
- Third is *Memoria* or Memory: «whan I make mone to god, Memoria is my name,» or «*recolit.*»
- Fourth is *Ratio* or Reason: «whan I deme domes, and do as trouth teacheth/Than is Ratio my right name, reason on Englische,» or «*iudicat.*»

- Fifth is *Sensus* or Sense: «when I fele y^t folke tellith, my first name is sensus,» or «*sentit.*»
- Sixth is *Consciencia* or Conscience: «when I chalenge or chalenge not, chepe [buy] or refuse / Than am I conscience called, gods clerke & his notary,» or «*negat, vel consentit.*»
- Seventh is *Amor* or Love: «when I love lelly [loyally] our lord and all other/Than is Lelilove my name, and in latin Amor,» or «*amat.*»
- Eighth is *Spiritus* or Breath: «when I flee from the flesh and forsake the caroin/Than am I spirite specheles, spiritus than ich hate» or «*spirat.*»

A correct and full explanation of any of the Latin names requires an understanding of scholastic philosophy that Shakespeare probably lacked. Presumably he simply relied on Langland's English text, supplemented by his own, possibly rusty, schoolboy Latin. Here are the soul's eight functions in the soliloquy (my italics):

To be, or not to be, that is the question:	
Whether 'tis nobler in the *mind to* suffer	*Mens*
[...]	
[...] *Who would fardels bear,*	*Sensus*
To grunt and sweat under a weary life,	
But that the dread of *something after death,*	*Spiritus*
The undiscover'd country, from whose bourn	
No traveller returns, puzzles the *will,*	*Animus*
And makes us rather bear those ills we have	
Than fly to others that we know not of?	
Thus conscience does make cowards of us all,	*Consciencia*
And thus the native hue of *resolution*	*Consciencia*
Is sicklied o'er with the pale cast of *thought,*	*Ratio*
And enterprises of great pitch and moment	
With this regard their currents turn awry	
And lose *the name of action.* Soft you now,	*Consciencia*
The fair Ophelia! *Nymph,* in thy orisons	*Amor, Memoria*
Be all my sins *remember'd.*	*Memoria*
(III.i.56-57, 76-90)	

The soliloquy could be paraphrased thus:

> Why should we go on living? Should *Mens* suffer Fortune's slings
> and arrows or end them by resistance? Death is like a sleep that ends
> our mental and physical miseries. Who would bear Time's many
> whips and scorns, when he could settle things with a dagger? Why
> should *Sensus* endure heavy loads, but that fear of our uncertain
> destination when *Spiritus* is gone puzzles *Animus,* causing us to
> prefer the devil we know. Thus *Consciencia,* deterred by *Ratio,* makes
> us cowards, and great enterprises are diverted by *Consciencia's* inde-
> cision. Here comes Ophelia. *Amor,* aid me with your *Memoria.*

Could this, however, be merely a coincidence resulting from Hamlet's
chosen topic and Langland's occasionally loose definitions? Several
considerations argue that Shakespeare is, as before, borrowing from
Langland. First, after the placement of *Mens* at the beginning of the
soliloquy, the other seven functions are concentrated in the last fifteen
lines. In the intervening eighteen lines (58-75), dealing with Fortune's
slings and arrows and Time's whips and scorns, *Animus* might be
identified in line 64 (i.e., «Devoutly to be wish'd»), and *Spiritus* in line
67 (i.e., «shuffled off this mortal coil»). Such random examples are all
that we should expect if Shakespeare and Langland agree only by
coincidence. Concentrated examples imply intent.

Next, Langland's final list of the soul's functions consists of nine items,
for, in the C version, he added *Liberum Arbitrium* or Free Will, the power
to choose between good and evil. When we consider that what Hamlet
contemplates—even if only philosophically—is a deadly sin, then we
see that Free Will not only could, but should have a place in the
soliloquy. Yet Hamlet includes all eight functions found in the B version—and not the C version's ninth. The two foregoing arguments for
Shakespeare borrowing from Langland are probabilistic or indirect.
Happily, however, Shakespeare's description of two of the functions
follows Langland closely enough to provide direct evidence. As
scholars have remarked, Langland's rendering of *Memoria* as «when I
make moan to God»—that is, «when I pray»—is idiosyncratic, for

Isidore's *memoria* and the verb *recolit* (English «recall» or «recollect») do not imply prayer.[18]

Now note how the soliloquy's final sentence, spoken to the approaching Ophelia, connects prayer to memory: «Nymph, in thy *orisons*/Be all my sins *remember'd*.» After they exchange greetings, Ophelia ironically answers Hamlet's request: «I have *remembrances* of yours/That I [...] long to redeliver./I *pray* you now receive them.» After further discussion, Hamlet says, «I did *love* you once,» and then «You should not have believed me [...] I *loved* you not.» (III.i.115-19) Thus the three items in the soliloquy's *Amor/Memoria* sequence, «Nymph [...] orisons [...] remember'd,» are annihilated in reverse order: «remembrances of [you] [...] pray [take them back] [...] I [never loved you].» So it appears that Shakespeare reacted to Langland's odd definition of *Memoria,* and likewise with Langland and Isidore's definition of *Consciencia.*

Keeping in mind the two definitions of conscience already encountered in Passus iii, we should examine Passus xv's definition of conscience: «when I challenge or challenge not, cheap [buy] or refuse/Then am I Conscience called, God's clerk and his notary,» or «*negat, vel consentit,*» that is, «deny or consent.» We should also remember that Langland and Isidore were concerned with the act of naming functions that already existed. So Conscience is the name given to the mind's capacity to make decisions, or, as Hamlet puts it: «the *name* of action.»

We now have a Conscience of three parts, whose workings are displayed in two later soliloquies. When, just before the «hire and salary» speech, Claudius tries to repent his crimes, he knows the facts and he knows what religion demands of him, but he cannot bring himself to act. (III.iii.36-72) Subsequently, in «How all occasions do inform against me,» Hamlet denounces himself for failing to do what he knows he must do—that is, «the name of action» falters.

However, Shakespeare changes the setting in which his version of Conscience is placed. Langland describes *Anima* or Soul as consisting of eight parts, including Mind or *Mens,* whereas Shakespeare depicts Mind as consisting of seven parts. That is, Shakespeare displaces Soul with Mind as the name of the whole. I can think of several reasons why he might have done this, although none is compelling. But it seems to have been a considered decision, for Ophelia shares Hamlet's view that the mind is the essence of the inner person when she states that «the noble mind» deprecates gifts from unkind givers (III.i.100-101), and again when she observes of Hamlet: «O, what a noble mind is here o'erthrown.» (III.i.152)

IV. Reading *Hamlet* by Langland's Light

We will now consider how our recognition of Langland's contribution to Shakespeare's art affects our understanding of *Hamlet*. I do not, incidentally, maintain that the following interpretation of the light *Plowman* sheds on Hamlet's speeches is the correct reading, much less the only reading. On the contrary, a poet who relies on a source that readers—not to mention audiences—cannot be assumed to know is creating up to three readings. First come readings without knowledge of the source. Next come readings based on knowledge of the source, but which can be defended without recourse to the source. Last come readings that can only be defended by reference to the source.

With regard to readings without knowledge of the source, we may find it interesting to know that Hamlet's six «whips and scorns» may derive from the sins of Mede the Maid enumerated in Passus iii, but our understanding of Hamlet's meaning is probably unchanged. In this example, the source makes little difference, but the case is otherwise with «horrid hent» and «hire and salary.» I follow several editors by interpreting Hamlet's «more horrid hent» as meaning that he will grasp his sword on a more horrifying occasion when he can send Claudius to hell; thus the grasp which will thrust the sword is horrid. This reading can be defended without reference to Passus xiv, though the reference strengthens the argument that «hent» is not a misprint of «hint.» On the other hand, «hire and salary» is unintelligible without knowledge of the source—as three centuries of editors could testify.

In the case of «hire and salary,» Shakespeare picked out a concept from Langland, applied it to a recognizably similar situation in *Hamlet,* and then looked in the immediate vicinity for some suitable images to accompany the principal concept. Yet Shakespeare's construction of «To be, or not to be» from scattered pieces of *Piers Plowman* constitutes adaptation on a truly heroic scale, unfortunately—yet again—out-running his readers' knowledge. As Ben Jonson explained, Shakespeare's powerful wit was not always under control.[19] Sections II and III discussed the soliloquy's debt to Langland in its component parts; now we will look at the poetic form of the whole.

The first thing to recognize about «To be, or not to be» is that, after the opening line, the speech is shaped like a sonnet, partaking, as is often the case with Shakespeare, of both the English and Italian forms.[20] An English sonnet features three quatrains discussing three related ideas, clinched by a couplet. In the soliloquy, the three equivalents to the quatrains are the three sections that begin with questions, while Hamlet's conclusion on conscience is equivalent to the couplet:

> Whether 'tis nobler in the mind to suffer
> The slings and arrows of outrageous fortune, [...]
> For who would bear the whips and scorns of time,
> Th' oppressor's wrong, the proud man's contumely, [...]
> Who would fardels bear,
> To grunt and sweat under a weary life, [...]
> Thus conscience does make cowards of us all [...]

The three quatrains are linked by the downward progression of their contents, as well as by their interrogatory openings. We start with humanity's struggle against non-human enemies: outrageous Fortune and the sea of troubles, adapted from the legions of Anti-Christ. We then descend to our battle against human foes: the whips and scorns of time, otherwise known as Mede the Maid.[21] Then we drop to the conflict within the human mind, which, of course, is where we began: «Whether 'tis nobler in the mind.» The outcome of these three combats is decided in the couplet by our triple conscience: neutral knowledge combined with moral awareness, leading to the power to act—or to fail to act. Thus the English sonnet.

An Italian sonnet is composed of an octave followed by a sestet: a situation is described in the first eight lines, then a restatement is made or a solution is reached in the next six. In this view of «To be, or not to be,» our struggle against external and internal foes, Fortune's slings and arrows and Time's whips and scorns, comprises the octave, while our response is given in the sestet, where coward conscience compels us to go on grunting and sweating under fardels. Ben Jonson compared sonnets to the bed of Procrustes, meaning that a poet's thoughts should not be cut or racked to fit a fourteen line format, but Jonson failed to consider the possibility that the format itself could be treated as malleable.[22]

The format's stylistic skeleton of «Whether [...] For who [...] Who [...] Thus» supports an intricate structure of balance and symmetry. The three quatrains begin with questions concerning three levels of struggle, distinguishing between human and non-human foes. The three types of conscience are set in relationship to one another. The whole soliloquy is shaped in a sonnet form that can be read as English or Italian, as is also the case with some of Shakespeare's Sonnets.[23] A further example of balance is found in the first and second quatrains' distinction between the physical and moral blows suffered by humanity. Thus, the physical whips and moral scorns are exemplified by the oppressor's wrong (physical), contumely (moral), pangs of love (moral), and the law's delay (physical). If we now look at the first quatrain, we can identify heart-ache as a moral blow and shocks to human flesh as physical. These balanced sets generally operate across the soliloquy's different sections, thereby aiding the reader's transition from one part to another.

English sonnets often break crisply between quatrains, while the Italian form positively requires a visible change of direction—called a *volta* or turn—between octave and sestet. But the soliloquy provides careful transitions between sections, sometimes touching content as well as style. The simplest of these transitions consists of beginning the third quatrain in the middle of a line, that is, «[...] Who would fardels bear» in line 76, which Shakespeare also does in his Sonnets 63 and 154. A rather more complicated case lies in the interweaving of images and ideas from Passus iii (70-88) and Passus xv (76-90), adding unity to most of the soliloquy, although the concentration of mental functions, starting at «Who would fardels bear,» joins what I have called the third quatrain and the couplet, resulting in an Italian-style sestet. The weaving or repetition or development of themes continues, tying the soliloquy to the subsequent conversation between Hamlet and Ophelia. The soliloquy proper is often thought to end with the words, «lose the name of action,» while «Soft [...] the fair Ophelia [...]» is considered the beginning of the next sub-scene. However, as we have seen, Hamlet's lines to Ophelia contain *Amor* and *Memoria,* the last two of the mind's functions; then Ophelia throws back at Hamlet the two parts of Langland's *Memoria;* followed by Hamlet's retraction of *Amor.* Finally, we hear Ophelia twice echoing the initial theme of the «noble mind»—once in Hamlet's presence, then after his exit. Thus, the material from Passus xv provides connections beyond the soliloquy.

The most complex transition in the soliloquy occurs, however, between the first two quatrains, and can only be fully appreciated by reference to Passus xx, specifically lines 93-94 and 183-202.

> There's the respect
> That makes calamity of so long life.
> For who would bear the whips and scorns of time,

At first glance, the chronological link between «*long life*» and «whips and scorns of *time*» seems simple enough. But does line 69 mean that calamity has a long life or that long life is a calamity? I chose the latter explanation in section II, which puts me at odds with most of *Hamlet's* editors who prefer the former, although Harold Jenkins allows the possibility of the latter. My choice was, of course, influenced by Langland's vivid description of the onslaught of Death and Old Age, but I believe that both answers are correct. The opening of the soliloquy through line 69 may be paraphrased: Should we suffer Fortune's slings and arrows or end them by resistance; death would be preferable, except for our fear of the uncertainties of the afterlife, and it is *that* consideration that makes long life a calamity. In other words, we are haunted throughout our miserable lives by the fear of what comes next. But if we start with «there's the respect/That makes calamity of so long life» and read through the «whips and scorns of time,» then it seems that Hamlet is saying that calamities are unending—that is, calamity is long-lived. The apparent conflict, however, resolves itself when we recognize that if calamity never ends, then long life must be a calamity. In this view, the «whips and scorns of time» restate and then elaborate the «calamity of so long life.» In short, the «calamity of so long life» is a transitional phrase that can be read as the end to the first quatrain and as the prelude to the second.

Having limited this discussion of transitions to the «To be, or not to be» scene, I now wish to show how the material taken from *Plowman* links that scene to the «hire and salary» scene. Shakespeare carefully read, reordered, and integrated four parts of *Piers Plowman* that feature conscience. The «To be, or not to be» soliloquy is constructed from Passus iii, xv, and xx, while the later «hire and salary» speech uses material from Passus xiv, in which Haukin (Hankin in Crowley's edition), a repentant sinner, is counselled on salvation by two allegorical characters: Conscience and Patience. Given all this, how does the «hire and salary» scene fit in? Passus xiv shows Patience explaining to Haukin that Conscience knows well that contrition and confession can bring a soul to heaven, be its sins «never so deadly.»[24] In other words, Passus xiv is highly relevant to the conscience of Claudius struggling to repent.[25] A further link exists between the two scenes in *Hamlet* that make use of Langland's portrayal of conscience. What Hamlet proclaims in «To be, or not to be»—that conscience makes us cowards and paralyses our ability to make decisions—comes true in the «hire and salary» scene. Hamlet has the opportunity to act, but he thinks first, and then decides not to act. In the words of Hamlet's next soliloquy, he is guilty of «thinking too precisely on th' event.» (IV.iv.41)

I will end this section on the profit of refracting *Hamlet* through the prism of *Piers Plowman* by examining several comments made by that most thorough and perceptive of editors, Harold Jenkins. In each case, Jenkins impinges on a source that he does not suspect—but, remarkably, he seems to guess once or twice that something is missing. I discussed the first example two paragraphs back: that the «calamity of so long life» means both that calamities never end and that long life is a calamity. While favouring the former, Jenkins adds that «it is not easy to exclude the feeling that ‹long life› is itself being regarded as a ‹calamity›» (Jenkins, footnote to III.i.69). Although my interpretation can be defended without reference to *Plowman,* it was Langland's depiction of Elde that put it into my head. Jenkins, on the other hand, sensed it without benefit of source.

My second example concerns another item already discussed, namely that the origin of «sea of troubles» was the siege of evils faced by Langland's community, and I joined Alexander Pope in venturing that perhaps Shakespeare actually wrote «siege of troubles.»[26] In this case, knowing the source offers us a basis for comparison—we are no longer reduced to asking whether Shakespeare was guilty of mixing a metaphor. Jenkins and most recent editors argue, correctly in my opinion, that taking arms against Fortune's might is a hopeless proposition, a guarantee of defeat and death. If resistance offered any chance at all of victory, no matter how long the odds, it would be pointless to ask which course of action was nobler—as opposed to which was more pragmatic. So, bearing in mind that a siege may be defeated by taking arms, did Shakespeare write «sea of troubles» or «siege of troubles?» I will let Jenkins answer: «The absurd futility of the contest is what Shakespeare's much-abused metaphor of taking arms against a sea very vividly suggests.»[27] Until Shakespeare's manuscript becomes available, I think that answer stands.

The third example concerns Jenkins's response to a strand of criticism running from Samuel Johnson to L. C. Knights, holding that Hamlet's soliloquy lacks coherence. Jenkins shows that an intuitive path can traced from the beginning to the end, concluding: «I do not know why it should be made an objection to this speech that it lacks *logical* connection when the progress of its ideas is so supremely natural and lucid.»

(Jenkins, 488n to III.i.56-88) The logical links appear when the relevant portions of *Plowman* are consulted. For example, while working his way through the soliloquy, Jenkins states that, «Who would fardels bear» repeats the rhetorical question, «who would bear the whips and scorns of time» (Jenkins, 487n to III.i.56-88). As we have seen, «Who would fardels bear» is not a repetition, but rather the last step in the downward progression from non-human enemies to human enemies to the individual mind—our starting point and destination.

A striking, final example of Jenkins pointing to something that he senses but cannot see is found in his analysis of the repetition of the word «thus» in: «*Thus* conscience does make cowards of us all,/And *thus* the native hue of resolution.» Jenkins observes that «difficulty has arisen from the transition to a new topic which the repeated 'thus' may disguise.» (Jenkins, 488, n. to III.i.56-88) He decides that the second «thus» leads «to a further reflection on a kindred matter in which the same trait of human nature may be seen.» So it does, but, more precisely, the second «thus» makes the transition from the conscience described in Passus iii, the conscience of neutral and moral knowledge, to the conscience of Passus xv, the ability to make decisions or the name of action.

V. Conclusion

In the four examples given above, Langland's words are needed to complete Hamlet's thoughts, the themes of which turn out to be: the equation of long life and calamity, the futility of opposing malign fate, the inescapability of the human mind, and the failure of knowledge to generate action. These themes may be regarded as the legacy that Shakespeare chose for his Renaissance prince from his medieval predecessor, choices that invite further exploration. As noted at the beginning of this essay, affinities between Plowman and Hamlet were observed by E. M. W. Tillyard, who judged Hamlet to be among the most medieval of Shakespeare's plays. Tillyard's point was not that Hamlet lies on the far side of the great divide between the Middle Ages and the Renaissance, but that the divide has been exaggerated and the continuities between the two ages underestimated.[28]

A. V. C. Schmidt makes a similar argument, noting that Robert Crowley informed readers of his 1550 edition of Plowman that, although the English was old-fashioned and dark, the religious and social criticism was fully relevant to their own times.[29] Crowley followed his address to the reader with summaries of the Prologue and each passus, written in a didactic manner in the present tense. For example, the Prologue «declareth some what of the powre and office of Kinges and Princes,» and «it rebuketh the foly of the commune people that cluster togythers in conspiracies against such as god hath called to office under their Prince.»[30] Crowley clearly felt that the political philosophy of 1370 still applied in 1550, and so continuities tie Langland's world to Shakespeare's—but other factors divide them. Hamlet remarks that humans are beasts who look «before and after» (IV.iv.37), and so we may compare the ways that Langland and Shakespeare looked.

Joseph Wittig points out that, unlike Chaucer, Langland's literary art is «unmistakably medieval very much of his age.»[31] However, Langland's message of criticism and his calls for reform carried forward; as we have seen, the Protestant Robert Crowley found him quite contemporary. A century later, Thomas Fuller hailed Langland as «the morning-star» of the Reformation and a Protestant «by prolepsis.»[32] Fuller and other Protestants were somewhat misled, presumably by their lack of familiarity with the freedom of criticism allowed before the Reformation, as well as by Protestant additions and deletions to the text Crowley set in print, for Langland's religious views were basically orthodox.[33] Nevertheless, whatever his intentions, Langland helped stoke the fires of the Reformation. As to those intentions, Langland was a social conservative who lamented the seeds of destruction of the feudal system that he saw sprouting around him. He denounced lords and ladies who dined in private instead of in the great hall with all their household, he resented middle class buyers of the estates of knights impoverished by fighting for the kingdom, he thought prison an appropriate abode for runaway serfs, and he decried the communism being taught in the schools.[34] In short, Langland—even if willy-nilly—looked both before and after.

What of Shakespeare, particularly in «To be, or not to be?» Although Tillyard has become somewhat unfashionable, his instinct or judgment was on target concerning *Hamlet* and *Plowman*, for Shakespeare assuredly drew inspiration from the fourteenth century. Yet we can identify some changes of outlook between Conscience the Knight and the Prince of Denmark that mark a transition from medieval to Renaissance. To contrast *Hamlet* to all that we know of the Middle Ages would be difficult, to put it mildly, but comparison to *Plowman* is feasible. I will argue that two prominent Renaissance features of Hamlet's soliloquy — *in contrast to Langland* — lie in the shifts from collective to individual, and from religious to secular.

In the Prologue to *Piers Plowman*, the dreamer falls asleep in the hills, only to receive a vision of the bustling community. In Passus ii the dreamer asks Lady Holy Church how he may recognize falsehood, and finds himself viewing the crowded adventures of Mede the Maid. So *Plowman* proceeds until the dreamer is thrust into the fray in Passus xx, with life and salvation invariably portrayed as collective activities. As Wittig remarks, «throughout the poem, Langland emphasizes the horrible consequences of sin for the collective human community.»[35] *Hamlet*, on the other hand, is a play about individuals travelling their own paths, with the hero going it alone by spurning the woman he loves and relegating his trusted friend to the role of witness. The «To be, or not to be» soliloquy expresses intensely personal thoughts, and yet Hamlet's pronouns — «we» and «us» — are collective; here Hamlet speaks of the human condition. Without insisting that Shakespeare was writing under Langland's influence in this regard, we may at least note that this is Hamlet's only collective soliloquy.

Piers Plowman is a thoroughly religious poem. *Hamlet* has a great deal of religious content, and the «To be, or not to be» soliloquy seems religious if viewed against a secular background. On the other hand, the soliloquy is markedly secular if compared to the passages in Langland from which it derives. Hamlet's stated foes are Fortune and Time, not Anti-Christ. Hamlet worries about «whether 'tis nobler to suffer or to take arms,» a concern appropriate to his rank, but Langland viewed taking arms against the siege of troubles as a matter of piety, not nobility. Hamlet expresses a degree of doubt about the afterlife that would have been unthinkable to Langland, and then Hamlet regrets that uncertainty over the afterlife can wreck great enterprises—presumably secular— which amounts to echoing Mede the Maid. Finally, Hamlet replaces Soul with Mind as the essence of humanity.

Thus Shakespeare reflects his own age as well as looking back to Langland's. Though the momentum of *Piers Plowman* projected as far forward as the seventeenth century, we now see the reach of *Hamlet* extending into the twenty-first—still influencing our language and art. As far as Prince Hamlet goes, he carries the troubled conscience of Langland's wandering dreamer.

Appendix I

Passages in «To Be, Or Not To Be» (III.i.56-90)
Apparently Deriving From *Piers Plowman*

[*Bolded words derive from the Passus and lines shown at right; italicized words come from the discussion of the parts of the human soul in Passus xv.*]

To be, or not to be, that is the question:	
Whether 'tis nobler in the *mind* to suffer	*(Mens)*
The slings and arrows of outrageous fortune,	(xx.53-229)
Or to take arms against a sea of troubles	
And by opposing end them. To die—to sleep,	
No more; and by a sleep to say we end	
The heart-ache and the thousand natural shocks	
That flesh is heir to: 'tis a consummation	
Devoutly to be wish'd. To die, to sleep;	
To sleep, perchance to dream—ay, there's the rub:	
For in that sleep of death what dreams may come,	(xx.51-53, 89, 96)
When we have shuffled off this mortal coil,	
Must give us pause—**there's the respect**	(xx.93-94, 183-202)
That makes calamity of so long life.	

For who would bear **the whips the and scorns of time,**
Th' oppressor's wrong, the proud man's contumely,
The pangs of dispriz'd love, the law's delay,   (iii.120-69)
The insolence of office, and the spurns
That patient merit of th' unworthy takes,
When he himself might his quietus make
With a bare bodkin? *Who would fardels bear,*   (iii.189-96, *Sensus*)
To grunt and sweat under a weary life,
But that the dread of *something after death,*   (*Spiritus*)
The undiscover'd country, from whose bourn
No traveller returns, puzzles the *will,*   (*Animus*)
And makes us rather bear those ills we have
Than fly to others that we know not of?
Thus *conscience* **does make cowards of us all,**   (iii.206, xx.61-62, 72-75)
And thus the native hue of *resolution*   (*Consciencia*)
Is sicklied o'er with the pale cast of *thought,*   (*Ratio*)
And enterprises of great pitch and moment   (iii.189-208)
With this regard their currents turn awry
And lose *the name of action.* Soft you now,   (*Consciencia*)
The fair Ophelia! *Nymph,* in thy *orisons*   (*Amor, Memoria*)
Be all my sins *remember'd.*   (*Memoria*)

Appendix II

Other Views on the Connection Between Conscience and Cowardice

Evaluating the likelihood that Shakespeare was influenced by Langland on how conscience causes cowardice requires examination of the views Shakespeare expresses on that subject in *Richard III* as well as consideration of the possibility that Hamlet was reflecting two possible sources for the play: Thomas Bedingfield's translation of Girolamo Cardano's *Cardanus Comforte* and François de Belleforest's story of Amleth in his *Histoires Tragiques* (Jenkins, 95 and 492n to III.i.83). The latter may be addressed first.

The case for Belleforest seems plausible, because Shakespeare did use him as a source for *Hamlet*. The relevant passage reads, «*Et dequoy sert vivre, ou la honte, et l'infamie, sont les bourreaux qui tourmentent nostre conscience et la* poltronnerie *est celle qui retarde le coeur des gaillardes entreprises.*»[36] We do find here the word «enterprises,» which Hamlet uses in line 86 of his soliloquy. However, as Jenkins points out, Belleforest, unlike Hamlet, does not feel that all men are made cowards by their consciences; on the contrary, only those whose actions are held back by cowardice will be tormented in their consciences. Belleforest's concept of conscience is based on honor—not religion—and deals with shame in the here and now, whereas Hamlet's concern is the hereafter. In short, Belleforest's views on cowardice and conscience do not agree with nor even lead to the issues raised by Hamlet. In contrast, *Richard III* and Cardano link conscience to religion and the afterlife.

That conscience or, more broadly, religion was invented by society to keep the strong in awe was held by Elizabethans to be the standard opinion of atheists and Machiavellians.[37] So the murderers of the Duke of Clarence in *Richard III* discuss the issue (I.iv.99-145), while King Richard himself denounces cowardly conscience at Bosworth Field (V.iii.180 and 310-12). The connection between cowardice and conscience in *Richard III* is the uncomplicated argument that fear of divine judgment may deter bold villains from profitable crimes.

Cardano, whose book is no longer generally regarded as a source for *Hamlet,* takes the same position. He discusses the fact that all people must die—rich and poor, good and bad—continuing:

> Onely honesty and vertue of minde doth make a man happy, and onely a cowerdly and corrupt conscience, do cause thine vnhappines. Because the worst that the good man can feare, is the best that the euill can wishe for: whiche is the destruction of the Soule in death.[38]

This outlook differs markedly from Hamlet's concern that conscience can make a coward out of anyone. Rather Cardano shares the opinion of

Richard III and the two murderers. The latter feel that fear of divine punishment may deter crimes, while Cardano says that those who have already committed crimes may be made unhappy by the same fear. In other words, conscience only makes cowards out of criminals.

The view of Cardano and *Richard III* derives from the twofold concept of conscience that the sixteenth century inherited from medieval times. At the basic level, the human soul was believed to possess an instinctive understanding of good and evil, a quality called *synderesis*. Human reason then applied that instinct to determine the good or evil of particular circumstances in a process termed *conscientia*.[39] *Synderesis* performs its normal bedrock function in Cardano and *Richard III*, but Shakespeare mines a stratum of uncertainty lying below it in *Hamlet*.

Endnotes

1   A. V. C. Schmidt, Introduction to William Langland, *The Vision of Piers Plowman* (London: Everyman, 1995), xlvii.

2   E. M. W. Tillyard, *Shakespeare's Problem Plays* (London: Chatto and Windus, 1950), 30.

3   Act III scene iii, my emphases. This and other *Hamlet* quotations are from the second Arden edition, ed. Harold Jenkins (London: Methuen, 1982). Citations from other Shakespeare plays are also from the second Arden series.

4   The First or Bad Quarto of 1603 greatly compresses Hamlet's speech, replacing «hire and salary» with «a benefit,» which is at least an accurate paraphrase, as well as antithetical to «revenge.»

5   Harold Jenkins, 513, n. to III.iii.79. William Shakespeare, *Hamlet, Prince of Denmark*, ed. Philip Edwards (Cambridge: Cambridge Univ. Press, 1985), 173, n. to III.iii.79. *Hamlet*, ed. G. R. Hibbard (Oxford: Oxford Univ. Press, 1987), 275, n. to III.iii.79. *Hamlet,* ed. T. J. B. Spencer (Harmondsworth: Penguin, 1980), 293, n. to III.iii.79.

6   Page lxxii[v], lines 85-86, modernized; all subsequent quotations unmodernized. All B version quotations are from William Langland, *The Vision of Pierce Plowman* (London, 1550; Amsterdam: De Capo Press, 1976), ed. Robert Crowley. Crowley's edition does not have numbered lines, and so, for the convenience of readers using other editions, each quotation includes the numbers for the equivalent lines in William Langland, *Piers Plowman: The B*

Version (London: Univ. of California Press, 1988), eds. George Kane and E. Talbot Donaldson, which are nearly identical to the line numbers in A. V. C. Schmidt's edition. Thus «lxxii^v, 85» means that a quotation comes from the back side of Crowley's leaf 72, Kane and Donaldson's line number 85. Crowley used a manuscript that no longer survives, and his text varies from Kane and Donaldson's, sometimes omitting lines, combining two lines into one, or adding lines. Also, when a line is in Latin, Kane and Donaldson give it the number of the previous line, followed by a. So placing Kane and Donaldson's numbers next to Crowley's lines may appear to miscount.

7 Jenkins glosses «hent» as «a variant spelling of *hint,* occasion, opportunity»; Hibbard changes the word to «hint»; while Edwards sticks with «hent,» meaning «grasp.» For older views, see the notes in H. H. Furness's New Variorum *Hamlet* (London: J. B. Lippincott, 1877).

8 Most modern editors regard the Second Quarto's substitution of «base and silly» for «hire and salary» as resulting from a misread manuscript. The change, however, could have been made intentionally, though without Shakespeare's knowledge. I can find no evidence that «hire and salary» was used proverbially for «double reward»; hence the phrase would have been just as incomprehensible in the Globe as it is today—unless one knows its source. But «base and silly» scans, as well as making sense, for killing a praying man seems ignoble, not to mention foolish if the villain goes to heaven instead of hell. That Shakespeare was not responsible for the change is indicated by the fact that he never used the word «silly,» in the sense of «foolish» rather than «defenseless,» in a serious context. Moreover, throughout the play, Hamlet never questions his duty to kill Claudius—if his guilt can be confirmed.

9 William Langland, *Piers Plowman by William Langland: An Edition of the C-text,* ed. Derek Pearsall (London: Univ. of California Press, 1979), 261, 11. 8-10.

10 Jenkins allows that «slings» may be a misprint, but offers a passage from Golding's translation of Caesar's *Gallic War* that couples slings and arrows as Shakespeare's possible source. Hibbard suggests a Biblical passage that includes bow and sling.

11 R. W. Dent in *Shakespeare's Proverbial Language* (Berkeley: Univ. of California Press, 1981), S177.1, points out that «sea of troubles» was proverbial, and perhaps Shakespeare preferred the proverb. Yet «siege of troubles» is consistent with «War, death, or sickness did lay siege to it,» *Midsummer Night's Dream* (1.1.142), and «the wrackful siege of batt'ring days,» *Sonnets* (65.6), while Shakespeare's other troubled-sea metaphor, «deep-drenched in a sea

of care» *(Lucrece,* 1100), is unmixed. The existence of the proverb opens the possibility that an actor slipped into that usage, which then became established by custom.

12 I do not imply that Hamlet actively considers suicide. Rather he asks philosophically why we tolerate miserable lives, leading to the rhetorical question: Why not kill yourself?

13 Langland, xiiii^v-xv^v; 206-8; «that raineth over high» means «that the rain falls on.» Whether Shakespeare and his contemporaries would have known the specific campaign referred to by Mede is not really important. Robert Crowley identifies the King as Edward III in his preface to the reader, who could easily identify the campaign as that of 1359-60 with a bit of browsing in Holinshed's *Chronicles.* Mede's remark about «a little silver» refers to the treaty of Bretigny of Oct. 1360. The French ransomed their captive King John II and ceded Aquitaine to England, in return for Edward's renunciation of his claim to the French crown.

14 Langland, *Piers Plowman by William Langland: An Edition of the C-text,* iii.241.

15 Langland, xiiii^r, 168-69. The last line should end, «among men of good,» that is, «men of property.» The manuscript Crowley used contained a number of Lollard or Protestant alterations and additions that would have shocked Langland. Crowley corrected this particular mistake in his second impression.

16 My argument on the intended meaning of «conscience» was anticipated by D. G. James in *The Dream of Learning* (Oxford: Clarendon, 1951), 42-48, though without reference to *Plowman.*

17 By, for example, Samuel Johnson and Kenneth Muir; see Jenkins, 488, n. to III.i.56-88.

18 J. E Goodridge's translation, *Piers the Ploughman* (Harmondsworth: Penguin, 1959), suggests that Langland's Latin failed him; 298, n. to Book XV, 3. Derek Pearsall's edition of the C version offers meditation or remembering God during prayer as the link to memory; 268, n. to Passus xvi, 185. A. V. C. Schmidt's translation, *Piers Plowman: a New Translation* (Oxford: Oxford Univ. Press, 1992), argues that the context implies thinking of the divine during prayer; 322, n. to 166-67.

19 Ben Jonson, *Complete Poems,* ed. George Parfitt (London: Penguin, 1975), «Timber, or Discoveries,» 11. 814-20.

20 Shakespeare's Sonnet 99 likewise begins with a superfluous introductory line. Shakespeare also inserted a full-fledged sonnet into the dialogue of one play; see *Romeo and Juliet,* ed. Brian Gibbons (London: Arden, 1980), 1.5.92-105.

21 Or, alternatively, Fortune's slings and arrows may represent all the misfortunes that befall humanity, of which Time's whips and scorns are a subset.

22 Ben Jonson, *Complete Poems*, «Conversations with William Drummond,» 11. 51-53.

23 Although Shakespeare's *Sonnets* use the English rhyme scheme exclusively, he sometimes organizes their content more in the Italian manner. See Michael Spiller, *The Development of the Sonnet* (London: Routledge, 1992), 159; G. Blakemore Evans, ed., Introduction to William Shakespeare, *Sonnets* (Cambridge: Cambridge Univ. Press, 1996), 6-7; and Katherine Duncan-Jones, ed., Introduction to *Shakespeare's Sonnets* (Walton-on-Thames: Arden, 1997), 96.

24 Langland, lxxii^v-lxxii^r, 83-97; I discussed part of this passage in Section 1.

25 The theology of Claudius's crime and Hamlet's revenge is further illuminated by a discussion at the end of Passus xvii of murder as the worst of all sins, especially murder for covetousness; of the ghosts of murder victims calling for vengeance; and of the great difficulty of obtaining forgiveness for murder (lxxxv^v-lxxxvi^r, 283-320). I cannot, however, demonstrate that Shakespeare borrowed from this section.

26 William Shakespeare, *The Works of Shakespear in Six Volumes*, ed. Alexander Pope (London: Jacob Tonson, 1725), vol. 6, 400n to III.i.59.

27 Jenkins, 490, n. to III.i.57-69. His footnote to III.i.59: «the 'mixed' metaphor has been much objected to. But the incongruity of taking arms against a sea is expressive of the idea—the futility of fighting against an uncontainable and overwhelming force.»

28 Tillyard's views on this subject are developed in *The Elizabethan World Picture* (London: Chatto and Windus, 1943), supported by G. M. Trevelyan, *English Social History* (London: Longman's, Green and Co., 1944), 92-98, and by Ernst Robert Curtius, *European Literature and the Latin Middle Ages*, trans. Willard R. Trask (Princeton: Princeton Univ. Press, 1953), especially 23-24.

29 Schmidt, ed., *The Vision of Piers Plowman*, xxiv.

30 Robert Crowley, Prologue to William Langland, *The Vision of Pierce Plowman*, iii^r.

31 Joseph Wittig, *William Langland Revisited* (New York: Twayne, 1997), vii.

32 Thomas Fuller, *Worthies of England*, 3 vols. (1662; London: Thomas Tegg, 1840), vol. 3, 64.

33 See note 25 on alterations to Langland's text. On Langland's orthodoxy, see Robert Adams, «Langland's Theology,» especially 105, in J. A. Alford, ed., *A Companion to* Piers Plowman (Berkeley: Univ. of California Press, 1988).

34 Dining in private, xlvi^v, x.97-103; knights losing their lands, C version,

v.72-74; runaway serfs, lv^r (misnumbered as lvii), xi.27-36; academic communism, cxv^v, xx.273-79á.

35 Wittig, *William Langland Revisited,* 23.

36 Sir Israel Gollancz, *The Sources of Hamlet: With an Essay on the Legend* (1926; New York: Octagon, 1967), 226. «And for what [do we] live, when shame and infamy are hangmen who torture our *consciences,* while *cowardice* holds back the heart of gallant enterprises» (my translation and emphases). Or, given that the French used both meanings of «conscience,» the quotation could also be rendered as, «[...] hangmen who torture our consciousness or memories.»

37 On the status of public opinion, see the Arden Shakespeare, *Richard III* (London: Methuen, 1981), ed. Antony Hammond, 325, n. to V.iii.310-11. See also John S. Wilks, *The Idea of Conscience in Renaissance Tragedy* (London: Routhedge, 1990), 115.

38 Girolamo Cardano, *Cardanvs Comforte* (1576; Amsterdam: De Capo Press, 1969), 102^r.

39 Wilks, *The Idea of Conscience,* 9-14. See also Robert Audi, ed., *The Cambridge Dictionary of Philosophy* (Cambridge: Cambridge Univ. Press, 1995), «synderesis.» *OED's* entries for «synderesis» and «synteresis» testify to the currency of the concept for such contemporary dramatists as Marston, Jonson, and Dekker and Chettle.

The Nature of *King Lear*

Like several of Shakespeare's romances, *King Lear* is set in a pre-Christian pagan land that worships the gods of Rome. These plays include, however, a deity rarely encountered in classical mythology, the goddess Nature. Although foreshadowed in late Latin literature, the goddess Nature was largely created in the poems of two twelfth century French clerical philosophers: Bernard Silvestris and Alan of Lille. Actually, the goddess traced her origin and descent from classical philosophy and literature, but she joined the pantheon as a deputy of the Christian God.[1] In parallel to this exotic addition to Christendom, medieval scholars, most notably Thomas Aquinas, extended the work of their classical predecessors on the non-personified concept of nature. The schoolmen used the philosophy of nature to integrate classical and Christian teachings in an attempt to unite faith and reason[2]—which is akin to Shakespeare's intent in *Lear*. Fortunately, the fruit of this medieval labour crops up in many authoritative sixteenth-century texts, rendering a study of scholasticism unnecessary to an appreciation of the role of nature in *King Lear*.

Dame Nature was a well-known figure in English poetry, appearing, for example, in Chaucer's *Parliament of Fowls* and Spenser's *Faerie Queene*, with both authors referring back to Alan of Lille.[3] In medieval and Renaissance literature, Nature serves as God's vicar, controlling the movement of various heavenly bodies, the weather on earth, and the life processes of birth, growth, ageing, sickness, and death. She also instils in humanity the classical concept of natural law or law of nature, that aspect of human behaviour which, among other things, causes us to love our kin and revere our parents. Shakespeare and his contemporaries often omit the personification, and so «nature» may be thought of as combining physics, meteorology, botany, zoology, sociology, and ethics. Above all, whether personified or not, nature, the creation of almighty God, was good. This arrangement allowed medieval and Renaissance writers to refract the theology and ethics of pagan societies through the prism of a Christianized law of nature.

Using nature and related biblical concepts, this essay examines the following topics in *King Lear:* the meaning of Edmund's first soliloquy; the status of Cordelia with respect to Christ; three sins or errors of Lear's; and the significance of the deaths of Cordelia and Edmund, as well as of the Earl of Kent's question, «Is this the promised end?» The principal biblical references come from St Paul's epistles to the Romans and Corinthians, the two wisdom books in the Old Testament Apocrypha, and the synoptic gospels. The marginal notes in the Geneva Bible provide sufficient explanation of the Renaissance concept of nature, which links the play's pagan setting to the biblical references, creating a form of equivalence between the two religions. The analysis will be assisted by the parallels that Shakespeare created between King Lear and the Earl of Gloucester, as well as by the fact that Shakespeare raised similar issues in several other plays. The topics under consideration may be illuminated by either Christianity or nature, though a full understanding requires both. Moreover, this dichotomy between Christianity and nature aligns with the subplots of the two families, as Lear and his daughters illustrate the Christian side, while pagan nature emerges through Gloucester and his sons. All of these factors unite to shed light on the behaviour and fates of *King Lear's* main characters.

Edmund

In his first soliloquy (I.ii.1-22), the bastard Edmund announces his intention of stealing the birthright of his older, legitimate brother Edgar, specifically the lands and title of their father, the Earl of Gloucester. *King Lear's* modern editors have been unable to make sense of Edmund's selection of the goddess Nature as patron of his planned theft.[4] The character of the evil deity implied by Edmund's words and subsequent deeds has been explored by various scholars, two of whom have been particularly influential. John Danby argues that Edmund's Nature prefigures the nasty and brutish view of humanity's natural state in Thomas Hobbes's *Leviathan* of 1651 or in Darwin's theories. Unfortunately, these references to philosophies yet-to-come would have been of no use at all to Shakespeare's Jacobean audiences. They could observe for themselves the motives that Edmund imputes to his deity, but, absent a contemporary explanation, we must suppose them to have been thoroughly confused by the familiar goddess Nature becoming the sponsor of robbing one's brother, not to mention blinding one's father. It is just as if Edmund appealed to Mars to make him a coward in battle. Following Danby, William Elton opens his discussion of Edmund's Nature with Hobbes, but then turns back to Shakespeare's age, citing a multitude of authorities on the emergence of Epicurean libertinism and the growth of religious scepticism. Although improving on Danby's essentially Whig interpretation of *Lear,* Elton organizes selected Renaissance writings into a pattern, and then tries to fit *King Lear* to it.[5] A better approach would be to start with Shakespeare.

In his scores of uses of the word «nature» or «Nature,» Shakespeare conforms to the beneficent view of this force or deity, although the deformed Richard III understandably slurs her as «frail» (*3 Henry VI,* III.ii.155) and «dissembling» (*Richard III,* I.i.19).[6] Aside from Edmund in *Lear,* however, only one character in Shakespeare's works implies an evil Nature. Queen Margaret denounces Richard III, the murderer of her husband and son, as «The slave of Nature, and the son of hell,» (I.iii.230) which malevolent epithet provides the key to Edmund's Nature. Margaret's meaning was first recognized by Virgil Whitaker,[7] who explained it as referring to Article IX, «Of originall or birth sinne,» of the Thirty-nine Articles of the Church of England:

> Originall sinne standeth not in the folowing of Adam (as the Pelagians do vaynely talke) but it is the fault and corruption of the *nature* of euery man, that *naturally* is engendred of the ofspring of Adam, whereby man is very farre gone from originall ryghteousnes, and is of his owne *nature* enclined to euyll, so that the fleshe lusteth al-wayes contrary to the spirite, and therefore in euery person borne into this worlde, it deserueth Gods wrath and damnation. And this infection of *nature* doth remayne, yea in them that are regenerated, whereby the luste of the fleshe, called in Greke φρόνημα σαρκός, which some do expounde the wisdome, some sensualitie, some the affection, some the desyre of the fleshe, is not subiect to the lawe of God. And although there is no condemnation for them that beleue

and are baptized: yet the Apostle [St Paul] doth confesse that concu-
piscence and luste hath of it selfe the *nature* of synne. [emphasis
added][8]

Thus, the evil definition of human nature, which extends back at least to
Chaucer's time,[9] stands in contrast to the benevolent deity. Article IX
explains both Margaret's words and Edmund's, along with those of
Thomas Hobbes, who drew his bleak inspiration from the same well as
Shakespeare—original sin.[10] The two natures are clearly distinguished
in the marginal notes of the original, 1560 edition of the Geneva Bible.[11]
Genesis 4:1, telling of Adam and Eve after the Fall, is flanked by this
clarification: «Mans nature, the state of mariage, & Gods blessing were
not vtterly abolished through sinne, but the qualitie or conditio[n]
thereof was changed.» Genesis 8:22, describing agriculture and the
seasons after the Flood, is amplified by a note explaining that: «The
ordre of nature destroyed by the flood is restored by Gods promes.»

So the order of nature, also known as the dear goddess Nature, to whom
Lear addresses a prayer (I.iv.275), must contend with the wicked state of
human nature arising from Adam and Eve's expulsion from Eden. We
cannot, however, be certain that the thoughts of Shakespeare or his
audiences on such long established usage on such a widely discussed
topic came from the Thirty-nine Articles or the Geneva Bible's notes on
Genesis. Other sources would be desirable—sources that describe both
forms of nature, and that were popular in Shakespeare's age. These
sources include Thomas à Kempis's *Imitation of Christ* and Theodore
Beza's commentary on the New Testament.

Imitation of Christ, written around 1420, was a centuries-long international best seller in the original Latin, as well as in many translations. It
remained in public favour, in suitably edited form, in Protestant nations
throughout the Reformation, with its Book III appearing in 34 printed
English editions between 1504 and 1609. Thomas à Kempis describes the
conflict between grace and man's state of nature after the Fall in Book
III, Chapters 54, «Of the Diverse Movings between Nature and Grace,»
and 55, «Of the Corruption of Nature and the Worthiness of Grace.» The
relationship between the two forms of nature arose as follows:

For after *nature* was vitiated and defiled by the sin of the first man Adam, the pain thereof descended into all his posterity, so that *nature,* which in the first-created was good and righteous, is now taken for sin and corruption; so far forth, that the motions that are now left unto *nature* always draw man into evil ... [yet] the *natural* reason of man, which is belapped with darkness of ignorance, hath nevertheless power yet to judge betwixt good and evil, and to shew the diversity betwixt true and false. [emphasis added][12]

A summary of this concept appears in an undated sermon by the late sixteenth-century Anglican divine, Richard Hooker: «in a Christian man there is first nature, secondly corruption, perverting nature; thirdly grace correcting, and amending corruption.»[13]

A more thorough discussion of these topics, including what Thomas à Kempis calls «the natural reason of man,» occurs in Theodore Beza's commentary on Chapters 2 and 5 of St Paul's Epistle to the Romans and on Chapter 15 of his First Epistle to the Corinthians, the sources of the doctrine of original sin.[14] Beza's commentary on the New Testament appeared in English in the margins of a 1576 edition of the Geneva New Testament, which soon outsold editions containing the original 1560 notes.[15] In the following passages, the critical words are Beza's,[16] which cannot, however, be understood without St Paul's text.

Romans 2

Text	Marginal Notes
14 [6]For when the Gentiles which haue not the Law, doe by <u>nature</u>, the things *conteined* in the Lawe, they hauing not a Law, are a Law vnto themselues,	6 He preuenteth an obiectione which might be made by the Gentiles, who although they haue not the Law of Moses, yet they haue no reason why they may excuse their wickednes, in that they haue somewhat written in their hearts in stead of a Law, as men, that forbid and punish some things as wicked, and command & commend other some as good.

15 Which shewe the effect of the Lawe [1]written in their hearts, their conscience also bearing witnesse, and their thoughts accusing one another, or excusing)

l This knowledge is a <u>naturall</u> knowledge.

Romans 5

Text

Marginal Notes

12 Wherefore, as by[1] one man[m] sinne entred into the world, and death by sinne, and so death went ouer all men: in whom all men haue sinned,

l By Adam, who is compared with Christ, like to him in this, that both of them make those which are theirs, partakers of that they haue: but they are vnlike in this, that Adam deriueth sinne into them that are his, euen of <u>nature</u>, and that to death: but Christ maketh them that are his, partakers of his righteousnesse by <u>grace</u>, and that vnto life.

m By sinne, is meant that disease which is ours by inheritance, & men commonly call it <u>originall sinne</u> ...

14 [12]But death reigned from Adam to Moses, euen ouer also them that sinned not after the like maner of the transgression of Adam, which was the figure of him that was to come

12 But that this Law was not the vniuersall Law, and that that death did not proceede from any actuall sinne of euery one particularly, it appeareth hereby, that the very infants which neither could euer know nor transgresse that <u>naturall Law</u>: are notwithstanding dead as well as Adam.

15 [14]But yet the gift is not so, as is the offence: for if through the offence of that one, many bee dead, much more the grace of God, and the gift by grace, which is by one man Jesus Christ, hath abounded vnto many.

14 Adam and Christ are compared together in this respect, that both of them doe giue and yeeld to theirs, that which is their own: but herein first they differ, that Adam by <u>nature</u> hath spread his fault to the destruction of many, but Christs obedience hath by <u>grace</u> ouerflowed many.

19 [18]For as by one mans disobedience many were made sinners, so by that obedience of that one shall many also bee made righteous.

18 The ground of this whole comparison is this, that these two men are set as two stockes or rootes, so that out of the one, sinne by <u>nature,</u> out of the other, righteousnesse by <u>grace</u> doth spring forth vpon others.

I Corinthians 15

Text

Marginal Note

21 [12]For since by man *came* death, by man *came* also the resurrection of the dead.

12 An other confirmation of the same consequent: for Christ is to bee considered as opposite to Adam, that as from one man Adam, sinne came ouer all, so from one man Christ, life commeth vnto all: that is to say, that all the faithfull, as they die, because by <u>nature</u> they were borne of Adam, so because in Christ they are made children of God by <u>grace</u> ...

From these scriptural and marginal passages in Shakespeare's preferred translation of the Bible,[17] the following principles may be gleaned. All descendants of Adam are sinful by nature (notes «l,» «m,» «14» and «18» to Romans 5:12, 15, and 19; note «12» to I Corinthians 15:26). While the Jews received the Law of Moses to govern their conduct, gentiles, such as the ancient Britons, were expected to know right from wrong by God's instinctive natural law (notes «6» and «l» to Romans 2:14-15; note «12» to Romans 5:14), which is called «the Law of nature» in note «h» to Romans 5:14 in the 1560 Geneva Bible[18] and «the natural reason of man» by Thomas à Kempis. Thus, the ambiguity of the word «nature,» which signifies both humanity's sinful state of nature after the Fall, and also God's law of nature, embodied in *King Lear's* goddess Nature, which imparts moral law—or, in modern idiom, human nature versus Mother Nature. Contemporary recognition of the ambiguity is demonstrated by Hooker's complaint on its abuse:

> There are certaine woordes [such] as Nature ... which wheresoever
> you find named... you suspect them presently as bugs wordes,
> because what they mean you doe not in deed as you ought appre-
> hend. You have heard that mans Nature is corrupt ... Whereupon
> under coulor of condemning corrupt nature you condemn nature[19]

As shown above, we find substantial unanimity on the subjects of
nature and original sin in the Anglican Article IX and Richard Hooker,
the Catholic *Imitation of Christ,* and the Calvinist commentary of Beza, as
well as assurance of contemporary familiarity with these matters.

Edmund's true position with regard to the two natures stands out
clearly if set against the Ten Commandments, five of which he tramples
in his soliloquy and its immediate aftermath: he dishonours his father
by deceiving him, he exalts adultery, he steals, he bears false witness
against his brother, and he covets their father's estate. According to
medieval and Renaissance theologians, including Thomas Aquinas,
Martin Luther, and John Calvin, the six non-religious commandments—
the second table—epitomized natural law.[20] The 1560 Geneva's marginal note to Romans 1:31 expresses substantially the same opinion:
«Which Law God writ in [men's] consciences, and ye Philosophers
called it the Law of nature ... whereof Moses Law is a plaine exposition.»
When Edmund swears allegiance to the goddess Nature in his opening
soliloquy, seeking her aid in his intended crimes, he really refers to the
depraved state of nature which consists in rejecting the divine law of
nature, including the fifth through tenth commandments. Like Richard
III and «the formal Vice, Iniquity,» Edmund thus «moralize[s] two
meanings in one word» (*Richard III*, III.i.82-3).

Cordelia

Just as Edmund identifies himself as a son of hell, so Cordelia connects
to Christ through several biblical echoes or references. At the beginning
of the play, the King of France dismisses concern over Cordelia's lack of
dowry: «Fairest Cordelia, that art most rich being poor,/Most choice
forsaken and most loved despised.» (I.i.252-3) France's paradoxes con-

cerning Cordelia derive from those uttered by St Paul about Jesus in II Corinthians, specifically: «as poore, and *yet* make many rich: as hauing nothing, and *yet* possessing all things» (6:10) and «that hee being rich, for your sakes became poore, that yee through his pouertie might be made rich.» (8:9)[21] Returning to rescue her father in Act IV, Cordelia responds to news of the approaching British army with: «O dear father,/ It is thy business I go about,» (IV.iv.23-4) echoing Jesus' words in Luke 2:49: «I must goe about my Fathers businesse.»[22] Two scenes later, one of Cordelia's gentlemen, attempting to apprehend the mad king, remarks that he has «one daughter/Who redeems nature from the general curse/ Which twain have brought her to.» (IV.vi.20 1-3)[23] In the narrow sense, the identity of the «twain» must be Lear's other two daughters, Goneril and Regan. On the other hand, the mention of a general curse on nature, that is, all forms of life, elevates the reference to God's judgement on Adam and Eve, «cursed *is* the earth for thy sake,» elaborated by this marginal note: «The transgression of Gods commandement was the cause y^t bothe mankinde and all other creatures were subiect to the curse.» (Genesis 3:17 and note «s», 1560 Geneva) The redeemer of humanity from the general curse is Jesus. Thus, Shakespeare thrice links Cordelia to Christ.

Shakespeare also associates Cordelia three times with a mundane human condition—that of a fool. In consequence of Cordelia's departure for France, Lear is told that his Fool «hath much pined away.» (I.iv.71-2) Although this may simply be a deft way of ascribing a sense of humour to a character whose role precludes that quality, Shakespeare also indicates an affinity between Cordelia and the Fool. The implied similarity or connection receives reinforcement at the end of the play, from which the Fool disappeared in Act III, when Lear reacts to Cordelia's death with, «And my poor fool is hanged.» (V.iii.304) Actually, Cordelia reveals her own foolish nature in the opening scene, when, unwilling to emulate her sisters' hypocritical professions of unbounded love, she exclaims: «I cannot heave/My heart into my mouth.» (I.i.91-2) Here Cordelia echoes the apocryphal Book of Ecclesiasticus, a favourite of Shakespeare's: «The heart of fooles is in their mouth: but the mouth of the wise is in their heart.» (21: 26, 1560 Geneva)[24] Cordelia's words are richly, albeit unconsciously, ironic. Ostensibly she proclaims that she is not a fool, while showing herself to be a complete fool in the worldly sense, throwing away her patrimony and a noble or royal husband by refusing to give her father the dutiful speech of flattery he craves.

In this way Cordelia resembles Christ but is also—in the worldly sense—a fool. Combining these two qualities yields St Paul's self-description in 1 Corinthians of «fools for Christ's sake.» Paul wrote this epistle to recall the Christians of Corinth from the disunity, worldliness, pride, and other sins into which they had fallen. His Chapter 1 stresses that worldly wisdom is foolishness to God, while «God hath chosen the foolish things of the world.» (1:27) Chapter 2 adds that to «the naturall man» spiritual things are «foolishnesse,» (2:14) while a marginal note to the 1560 Geneva edition's verse 2:12, which contrasts the spirit of the world to the spirit of God, explains that: «We are not moued with that Spirit, which teacheth things wherewith the worlde is delited, and which men vnderstand by nature.» Chapter 3 extends the logic to, «If any man amongst you seeme to bee wise in this world, let him be a foole, that hee may be wise,» (3:18) before reaffirming that «the wisdome of this world is foolishnesse with God.» (3:19) Chapter 4 builds the argument to its conclusion:

> 8   Now yee are full: now yee are made rich: ye reigne as kings without vs, and would to God yee did reigne, that wee also might reigne with you.
> 9   For I thinke that God hath set foorth vs the last Apostles, as men appointed to death: for wee are made a gasing stock vnto the world, and to the Angels, and to men.
> 10 Wee *are* <u>fooles for Christes sake</u>, and ye *are* wise in Christ: we *are* weake, and yee *are* strong: yee *are* honourable, and wee *are* despised.
> 11 Vnto this houre we both hunger, and thirst, and are naked, and are buffeted, and haue no certaine dwelling place [emphasis added]

While Cordelia is a fool for Christ's sake on a Christian level of understanding, she may also be seen as a pagan who embraces the law of nature. However, as indicated by the marginal note to 1 Corinthians

2:12, this conclusion may be reformulated by saying that fools for Christ's sake are people who reject humanity's naturally depraved state in favour of the law of nature. Cordelia opposes Edmund not only in their choice of natures, but also in their frames of reference, with Edmund calling on the goddess, while biblical references identify Cordelia.

Lear

With the natures of Edmund, Cordelia, and Nature herself thus clarified, we may consider King Lear's three faults—resigning power to his daughters, despair, and blasphemy—each of which turns out to be illuminated by an analogue in the Earl of Gloucester subplot. Following his first soliloquy, Edmund tricks Gloucester into believing that Edgar seeks to rule him in his old age, which proposal Gloucester sensibly denounces as monstrous and unnatural. (I.ii.75-114) Lear, on the other hand, renounces governance of his realm and his daughters of his own accord, an act of folly and an affront to nature, as his Fool keeps reminding him: Lear deserves a fool's coxcomb for giving his daughters his living (I.iv.106-7); Lear has made his daughters into his mothers (I.iv.163-5); Lear will be an obedient father (I.iv.226); snails do not give away their shells (I.v.29-30). Each example describes a reversal of nature, the agency that brings down the storm on Lear's head in Act III.

In the next case, both Gloucester and Lear succumb to the same sin: despair. Betrayed by Edmund, then blinded and turned out by the Duke of Cornwall, Gloucester despairs and seeks to commit suicide. Edgar rescues his father, who subsequently succumbs to a natural death, but the critical point is, as Edgar explains, that he «saved him from despair.» (V.iii.190) Classical Greeks and Romans held mixed views on suicide, but Edgar's position, «Men must endure/Their going hence even as their coming hither,» (V.ii.9-10)[25] agrees with Brutus's belief in *Julius Caesar* that suicide is a cowardly evasion of the miseries visited on humans by the gods. (V.i.101-8) Shakespeare took Brutus's opinion from Plutarch, who apparently derived it from the knowledge that Brutus was a Platonist in his youth, and Plato opposed suicide.[26] And yet, although

Edgar's resistance to suicide coincides with some classical views,[27] his stress on despair raises a strictly Christian concept, which the 1560 Geneva Bible's marginal notes apply retroactively: Saul (1 Samuel 31:4, note «a») and Judas (Matthew 27:4, note «c») killed themselves in despair, whereas Samson (Judges 16:30, note «o») and Job («Argument») did not despair, nor did Samson commit suicide. While despair may be the cause of self-slaughter, the effect is an offence against natural law, the first rule of which is self-preservation. Such was the judgement derived from Aristotle by Thomas Aquinas, whose opinions became the orthodoxy of the late Middle Ages.[28]

Unlike the Earl of Gloucester, King Lear never becomes actively suicidal, but self-slaughter is simply a likely outcome of the sin of despair, which consists in believing oneself to be beyond God's forgiveness.[29] During his spell as an outcast, Lear rejects appealing for help to Cordelia (II.ii.401-4), he avoids her at Dover and then flees when her servants attempt to apprehend him, at which point Cordelia's gentleman exclaims that she «redeems nature from the general curse.» When the two come face-to-face in the next scene, Lear offers to drink poison, adding: «I know you do not love me.» (IV.vii.72-3) So, clearly Lear had despaired of the forgiveness of his Christ-like daughter, which he nevertheless receives, thus clearing that sin. Although Lear's actions are comprehensible without regard to Christian doctrine, that doctrine aligns them with both Gloucester's despair and Cordelia's Christian status.

However, Gloucester has one more sin to be considered—and so does Lear. After mortally wounding his bastard brother, Edgar reveals his identity and explains to the dying Edmund about their father: «The gods are just and of our pleasant vices/Make instruments to plague us:/The dark and vicious place where thee he got/Cost him his eyes.» (V.iii.168-71) Despite Edgar's pagan reference to the «gods,» Edmund's betrayal of Gloucester is predicted in the apocryphal Wisdom of Solomon's discussion of illegitimacy (on which see below): «For all the children that are borne of the wicked bed [bastards], shalbe witnes of the wickednes against their parents when they be <u>asked</u>.» (4:6, 1560

Geneva; emphasis added) When Gloucester told Edmund of plots on behalf of the outcast Lear, of a dangerous letter, and of his plan to visit and aid the old King, he added: «Go you and maintain talk with the Duke [of Cornwall], that my charity be not of him perceived. If he <u>ask</u> for me, I am ill and gone to bed.» (III.iii.14-16, emphasis added) Indeed, Edmund behaves exactly as predicted by the Wisdom author, promptly revealing the truth to Cornwall.

Shakespeare knew the first seven chapters of the Wisdom of Solomon quite well, using them in about eight other plays, as well as in Act IV, scene iv of *Lear*.[30] The Wisdom of Solomon, as well as the apocryphal Ecclesiasticus, which Cordelia echoed, and the canonical Book of Proverbs, personify Wisdom as a woman with qualities remarkably similar to the goddess Nature. Richard Hooker explains the traditional interpretation of Wisdom: «Some things she openeth by the sacred bookes of Scripture; some things by the glorious works of nature.»[31] So Edgar's discussion of Gloucester's pagan sin of adultery finds an explanation in the Old Testament's equivalent to medieval and Renaissance doctrine on nature.

Just as Gloucester sins by begetting a bastard, so Lear sins by blasphemy, which, like Gloucester's crime, seems initially to fall into the pagan category. Lear opens his first of the storm scenes with his famous lines: «Blow winds and crack your cheeks! Rage, blow!/You cataracts and hurricanoes, spout/Till you have drenched our steeples, drowned the cocks!, (III.ii.1-3) concluding with this imprecation:

> And thou, ail-shaking thunder,
> Strike flat the thick rotundity o' the world,
> Crack nature's moulds, all germens spill at once
> That make ungrateful man (III.ii.6-9)

Comparison offers the best means of assessing Lear's tirade, as Shakespeare gives similar lines to characters in *Winter's Tale* and *Macbeth*.[32] When Perdita fears the collapse of her dignity, Florizel replies:

> It cannot fail, but by
> The violation of my faith; and then
> Let nature crush the sides o' th' earth together,
> And mar the seeds within! (IV.iv.478-81)

Florizel rhetorically emphasizes the firmness of his faith by calling for cataclysmic consequences if it fails, which, obviously, he does not expect to happen. Note, moreover, that Florizel, although speaking under great stress, refrains from calling for violence against nature, instead proposing that nature commit the violent act. Macbeth, unlike Florizel, deals with reality rather than rhetoric when demanding information from the three witches:

> Though you untie the winds, and let them fight
> Against the Churches; though the yesty waves
> Confound and swallow navigation up;
> ....
> though the treasure
> Of Nature's germens tumble all together,
> Even till destruction sicken, answer me
> To what I ask you. (IV.i.52-61)

By this point in his career, Macbeth merits multiple damnation, as he seeks further help from servants of the devil. Now he orders them to topple religion, sink all shipping, and destroy Nature if that is what it takes to answer his question. Macbeth's blasphemy obviously horrifies piety—but, alas, so does Lear's.

With regard to the annihilation of life on earth, Florizel speaks rhetorically, Macbeth speaks conditionally, but Lear speaks imperatively. Earlier, Lear implored the goddess Nature to make Goneril sterile or to give her a vicious, thankless child. Yet, as the storm begins, Lear, enraged against two of his three daughters, commands thunder to strike nature in order to destroy all human seed, that is, to end the human race. However, Lear addresses «all-shaking thunder» with the personal «thou,» implying that he gives his order to Jupiter, hurler of thunderbolts, whose name Lear invoked on three earlier occasions.[33] If thunder is personified in Jupiter, then presumably his directed target is the goddess Nature. While it may seem self-evident that an assault on Nature violates natural law, that law includes human awareness of God or divinity. As Calvin explains, «there is, as the eminent pagan [Cicero] says, no nation so barbarous, no people so savage, that they have not a deep-seated conviction that there is a God.»[34] Thus, Lear's blasphemy clearly breaks nature's law. This sin remains on Lear's account.

The Mystery of Things

We can now link the characters to each other and to the play's themes, starting with the great vexing question of *King Lear*: Why must Cordelia die? Perhaps Shakespeare simply believed that tragedies must end tragically. On the other hand, Cordelia's survival would produce the sort of tragicomedy or romance that Shakespeare wrote in his later years, in which brutal endings give way to bittersweet. That most anti-imaginative of all Shakespeare scholars, E. K. Chambers, proposed a different answer by connecting Lear's miseries, as well as those of Timon of Athens, to a conjectured state of mental depression besetting the author.[35] Although that explanation may well be true, a better solution would lie within the logic of the play itself, which calls for a recapitulation of *Lear's* setting and the commonly understood theology of Shakespeare's England.

King Lear occurs in pagan, pre-Christian Britain, but its inhabitants know right from wrong by the law of nature which God inscribed in their hearts. Edmund rejects natural law in favour of the depraved state of nature into which humanity fell by the sins of Adam and Eve. So Edmund chooses to become a servant of the devil—or an heir of Cain. Cordelia, on the other hand, is a paragon of virtue, which, in the pagan context, means that she perfectly adheres to the law of nature, which makes her, wittingly or not, the servant of almighty God.

More precisely, however, Cordelia is modelled on St. Paul's fools for Christ's sake, implying folly in worldly matters, coupled with wisdom in the ways of God. Furthermore, as discussed earlier, these fools are «appointed to death.» Medieval and Renaissance iconography normally depicts St. Paul bearing a sword, the instrument of his martyrdom, just as St Peter holds two keys. The title page of Coverdale's Bible of 1535 shows St. Paul with his sword in the lower right corner, while he and St. Peter, with sword and keys, sit directly above the title of the King James Version of 1611.[36] Given her Pauline status, alert members of *King Lear's* early audiences would have understood that Cordelia's outlook is ominous—that she is unlikely to end up as Queen of France and Britain. Meanwhile, Cordelia's father retains one unexpiated sin: he prayed for violence against nature, God's creation, in order to end all human posterity. Furthermore, the second commandment says that the Lord «visit[s] the iniquitie of the fathers vpon the children, vpon the third *generation* and vpon the fourth of them that hate me.» (Exodus 20:5, 1560 Geneva) As the full Decalogue was read aloud by the minister at the opening of the Church of England's communion service, these words on fathers and children should have been known to everyone in *Lear's* early audiences.[37]

When Lear and Cordelia enter as prisoners in the final scene, Lear exults at the prospect of confinement with his daughter, seeing their future as observing «the mystery of things.» (V.iii.16) She, however, realizes the gravity of their predicament. In the presence of Edmund, Cordelia asks of Goneril and Regan, «Shall we not see these daughters and these sisters?» (V.iii.7) Had that encounter taken place, Cordelia could very well have addressed St Paul's words from 1 Corinthians, quoted earlier, to her sisters on behalf of their father. Significantly, St Paul calls the Corinthians his «brethren» in verse 6, but his «children» in verse 14.

Now ... you reign as kings without us, ... For I think that God hath set forth us .... as men appointed to death: for we are made a gazing stock unto the world, ... we are weak, and you are strong: you are honourable, and we are despised. Unto this hour we both hunger, and thirst, and are naked, ... and have no certain dwelling place ... (4:8-11)

Then Edmund, who bested the unworldly Cordelia on the battlefield, murders her by the shameful death of hanging. Thus depraved human nature defeats the law of nature, as predicted in the Wisdom of Solomon (1:1, 2:16-20, 1560 Geneva), where «vngodlie» persons, considered as «bastardes» by the righteous, plot to «condemne [the latter] vnto a shameful death.» Yet Edmund's crime also punishes Lear's blasphemy, as the last of his three children perishes, thereby annihilating his own posterity.

While Cordelia is being led to the slaughter, however, the disguised Edgar, another faithful follower of natural law, fatally wounds Edmund, who seeks reconciliation if his victorious foe is of noble blood. Edgar reveals his identity, as well as how he rescued their father from despair before he died. (V.iii.180-98) Edgar then recounts the faithful service of the Earl of Kent to the outcast Lear, whereupon Goneril's murder of Regan and her own suicide are announced, and their bodies brought on stage. Though he never expresses penitence, these events persuade Edmund to do «Some good .../Despite of mine own nature.» (V.iii.24 1-2) Edmund reveals that he and Goneril planned that Cordelia's murder should appear as suicide induced by despair. Hence Cordelia's reputation is saved, as the future—and Shakespeare's audiences—will know that she did not die a damnable death, unlike Goneril, Lady Macbeth, and Cymbeline's Queen.[38]

The religious significance of Edmund's demise is found in the Wisdom of Solomon's discussion of illegitimacy: «the bastard plantes shal take no depe roote, nor laye any fast fundacion. For thogh they budde forthe in the branches for a time, yet they shal be shaken with the winde: for they stand not fast, and thorowe the vehemencie of the winde they shalbe rooted out.» (4:3-4, 1560 Geneva) Just so Edmund: when confronted and arrested by the Duke of Albany and his army, Earl Edmund has only his stolen title. Moreover, «the children of adulterers... the seed of the wicked bed shalbe rooted out... If they dye hastely [young], they haue no hope, nether comfort in the day of tryal [judgement].» (3:16-18) The dying Edmund does, in fact, grasp for a final consolation; upon seeing the bodies of Goneril and Regan, he exclaims: «Yet Edmund was beloved.» (V.iii.238) Hence, the love of two murderers will be his comfort at the Judgement Day.

Concerning the fates of Cordelia and Edmund, we should note the differing dichotomies of wisdom and folly in the biblical books discussed so far. St. Paul in 1 Corinthians opposes the fools for Christ's sake to the worldly-wise; the latter will enjoy prosperity on earth, while the former will go to heaven. The Old Testament wisdom books of Proverbs, Wisdom of Solomon, and Ecclesiasticus offer a very different contrast. The wise are those who know and heed God's word, that is, the righteous, in contrast to the fools who neither know nor heed the word, that is, the wicked. The righteous wise are encouraged to develop good habits such as honesty, industry, and sobriety that the wicked fools lack. Although exceptions will occur, the wise may expect prosperity, followed by salvation, while the fools will suffer both here and in the hereafter. Edmund may qualify as worldly-wise from St. Paul's perspective, but Wisdom would call him a fool.

The Promised End

Then the dying Edmund is carried away, as Lear, who narrowly escaped being murdered by Edmund and Goneril, enters with Cordelia's body in his arms. Kent asks, «Is this the promised end?» Edgar responds, «Or image of that horror?» Albany concludes, «Fall, and cease.» (V.iii.26 1-2) Editors of *Lear* note that Kent and Edgar refer to Christ's predictions of the Judgement Day in the synoptic gospels, and they also direct readers to *Macbeth,* specifically to Macduff's comparison of Duncan's body to the «great doom's image.»[39] In order to understand these references properly—to measure their full meaning—we must start with *Macbeth*; then examine Edmund's words, «the image and horror of it,» shortly after his first soliloquy; then proceed to Kent, Edgar, and Albany; and finally return to Edmund.

Just before exclaiming upon the «great doom's image,» (II.iii.77) Macduff compared Duncan's slaughtered corpse to «The Lord's anointed Temple,» (II.iii.67-9) the destruction of which is first on Jesus' list of the signs of impending doom.[40] Moreover, Macduff continues by calling on the sleeping Malcolm and Banquo to rise as from their graves and walk like spirits, (II.iii.78) another incident of the Judgement Day.[41] In other words, Macduff supports his metaphor of Duncan's body as «doom's image» by accurately citing two associated events.

King Lear displays similar accuracy. After his opening soliloquy, Edmund is joined by Gloucester, whom he treacherously turns against the faithful Edgar. Gloucester, shocked at Edgar's disloyalty, notes that recent eclipses of the sun and moon portend an upheaval of nature, leading to brother against brother, son against father, and the severing of all natural bonds uniting humanity. (I.ii.103-17) Gloucester exits, Edmund scoffs at the omens, (I.ii.118-33) Edgar enters, and Edmund warns him that he has offended their father. But Edmund also adapts Gloucester's omens, claiming to have just read «of unnaturalness between the child and the parent, death, dearth, dissolutions of ancient amities» and more. (I.ii.143-9) Edgar doubts his brother's new-found interest in astrology, but Edmund warns him to «go armed,» adding that «I have told you what I have seen and heard—but faintly; nothing like the image and horror of it.» (I.ii.170-4) The biblical significance of these exchanges between Gloucester and his sons will emerge when linked to the final scene.

Does the biblical imagery of Kent, Edgar, and Albany equal Macduff's precision? Mark 13:12 provides the appropriate omen of the Judgement Day: «Yea, and the brother shall deliuer the brother to death, and the father the sonne, and the children shall rise against their parents, and shall cause them to die.»[42] So Kent's. «Is this the promised end?» quite correctly identifies the familial slaughter around him, including the Christ-like Cordelia, with the signs forecasting doomsday. Edgar's response, «Or image of that horror,» might be paraphrased as: «No, this is not the promised end, but this is what it will look like.» Edgar apparently intends to correct Kent's implication that the end may be nigh, which can hardly be the case, given that *Lear* precedes the birth of the Messiah. Nevertheless, the basic portents of doomsday are predicted in Daniel 9, and so were known before the time of Christ.[43] Albany's «Fall, and cease» seemingly refers to another omen in Mark 13:25: «And the starres of heauen shall fall.»[44] Hence, Albany's words could be para-phrased as: «Let this be the end.»

The host of calamities predicting the last days is, however, summarized in the margins of the Geneva Bible in the 1560 edition, as well as in the later editions with Beza's notes. The 1560 Geneva places a note against Matthew 24:29, which tells of the darkening of the sun and moon and of the stars falling from heaven, explaining: «as it were, an alteration of ye ordre of nature.» Against the falling stars of Mark 13:25, the 1560 edition notes: «This teacheth y^t there shalbe a change of ye whole ordre of nature.» These notes agree with the overturning of natural human relations that Gloucester predicted in Act I, scene ii, from the recent eclipses of the sun and moon. Theodore Beza reversed the concept of the 1560 Geneva. Where Matthew 24:32 describes the sprouting fig tree as the harbinger of summer, Beza notes: «If God hath prescribed a certain order to nature, much more hath he done so to his eternall iudgements, but the wicked vnderstand it not, or rather make a mocke at it: but the godly doe marke it, and wait for it.» Edmund's mockery of nature and the omens of judgement in Act I, scene ii, identify him as one of the wicked, while Kent, Edgar, and Albany mark and wait.

Conclusion

Although the Geneva Bible's notes were only one of many sources on natural law available to Shakespeare and his audiences, those notes sufficiently connect nature to the relevant biblical texts—Paul's first three epistles and the synoptic gospels—to explicate the theology or philosophy of *King Lear*. Four additional conclusions arise from the arguments in this essay: two narrow and two broad. First, Edmund's nature springs from the Wisdom of Solomon. Next, Shakespeare's understanding of three of the apocryphal passages discussed above depended on the English translations available to him. Next—the main theme of this essay—pagan values may be rendered into Christian terms and vice versa through the mediation of nature. Finally, nature's regime encompasses the social order, and a disturbance in either destabilizes the other.

The Wisdom of Solomon devotes a total of fifteen verses to bastards, ascribing five characteristics to them; Edmund matches four of those five characteristics. Specifically, he testifies against his father when asked, he condemns Cordelia to a shameful death, he springs up only to be toppled for lack of roots, and he dies young with no likelihood of comfort at doomsday.[45] Hence, the passages on bastards in Chapters 2-4 of Wisdom merit recognition as a source for Shakespeare's portrayal of Edmund, whose illegitimacy is inessential to the plot. Nothing would be lost were Edmund a legitimate younger son, unless his base birth held some significance for the audience, which the Wisdom of Solomon provides as the Bible's principal statement on illegitimacy.[46]

As regards the Geneva text, the interpretations of three of the apocryphal passages cited in this essay would fail if more recent translations were used. First, the Geneva, like the King James Version (KJV), translates Ecclesiasticus 21:26, the verse paraphrased by Cordelia, with literal precision, twice rendering the Greek καρδία into English «heart.» However, as John Calvin explains, the Greek and Hebrew «heart» is the seat of intellect and understanding, as well as of emotions.[47] Consequently, the 1989 New Revised Standard Version (NRSV) translates this verse as: «The mind of fools is in their mouth, but the mouth of the wise is in their mind» — in other words: Think before you speak. This evergreen piece of good advice is, however, entirely consistent with such worldly-wise practices as hypocrisy, dissembling, and deceit. The Geneva's «the mouth of the wise is in their heart» denotes the naive, including fools for Christ's sake. This overly literal translation shifts the meaning of this verse from the Old Testament's distinction between wisdom and folly to St Paul's dichotomy.

Next, Wisdom 4:6 explicates Edmund's betrayal of Gloucester by saying that bastards will testify against their parents «when they be asked.» Behind the quoted phrase lies the Greek εν εξετσμω, normally translated into English as «when examined,» which appears as «in their trial» in the KJV and «when God examines them» in the NRSV. The Geneva's casual «when ... asked» demotes the occasion from Judgement Day to any day, and the questioner from God to anyone.

Finally, Wisdom 2:16-20 says that the righteous will be brought to a shameful death by «bastardes.» But these evildoers are named in the Greek text as κίβδηλον, literally, counterfeits or frauds, which the KJV renders as «counterfeits,» while the NRSV reads «something base.» The Geneva translators conceivably had in mind the contemporary adjectival meaning of bastard: «counterfeit, spurious.»[48] Nevertheless, whether intentionally or not, the Geneva translation falsely accuses the illegitimate.

The Great Bible of 1539 and the Bishops Bible of 1568 agree with the Geneva on Ecclesiasticus 2 1:26 and Wisdom 4:6, but both translate κίβδηλον as «vain persons.»[49]

More generally, this essay has attempted to show that much that seems to be Christian in *King Lear* can be explained by natural law or the goddess Nature acting in a pagan context, although that law was Christian doctrine, while the goddess was a Christian literary conceit. The play's catastrophe offers an apparent choice between the gospel-based interpretation of omens by Kent, Edgar, and Albany, and the astrology espoused by Gloucester in Act I, scene ii. On the other hand, we find the relevant portions of the gospels in both editions of the Geneva Bible flanked by marginal notes linking the portents of the Judgement Day to the overturning of the order of nature, which is precisely what Gloucester had in mind. In *Winter's Tale,* Polixenes explains that the art of grafting can improve the flowers of nature, and yet the art of grafting is itself a part of nature. (IV.iv.88-97) The morality as well as the course of events in *King Lear* may be explained by nature rather than by religion, and yet nature and religion share one creator. Thus, Edmund's rise and fall turn out to be exactly as predicted by Dame Nature's biblical overseer, Wisdom.[50] Gloucester errs regarding the fidelity of his two sons, but at least he understands the natural law principle at stake: that parents rule their children. Lear totally overlooks this point concerning his daughters, but that principle is also the fifth commandment. Later Gloucester and Lear both fall prey to the sin of despair, leading the former to offend against natural law by attempting suicide. Moreover, Shakespeare puts the Christian term «despair» into the mouth of the pagan Edgar, while describing the condition without the label in the case of Lear and his Christ-like daughter. Thus, paganism shades into Christianity. Gloucester pays the price for adultery, a violation of natural law and the seventh commandment, as Lear suffers for blasphemy, also offending natural law, and, so long as Lear's offence may be regarded as consisting only of evil words—and not attempted deicide—he further breaks the second and third commandments.

However, the theological unity of *Lear* also depends upon the Manichean duality of nature: uncorrupted nature or law of nature versus the nature of man after the Fall. This duality builds another bridge within the play between paganism and Christianity. Thus, Edmund calls on a seemingly pagan goddess, when he really refers to original sin, as he violates most of the second table of the Ten Commandments, which is part of natural law. Coming from the opposite direction, Cordelia quotes Ecclesiasticus, thereby showing herself a fool for Christ's sake, while a note in the 1560 Geneva Bible places such fools in Opposition to «nature,» meaning depraved human nature.

Otherwise, two broad religious themes stand out in *King Lear,* aside from the obvious fact that sin will be punished. First, the social order is part and parcel of the divinely ordained fabric of nature. Next, disturbances in the order of nature foretell disaster for humanity. The tragic old King and the malcontent Edmund are the two principal offenders against the order of society. Yet these parallel sinners arouse opposite emotions in audiences. Although some modern critics feel otherwise,[51] a Jacobean audience would spare no sympathy for Edmund's resentment of his lack of inheritance. The status of a nobleman's acknowledged illegitimate son was well understood in Shakespeare's age. Such boys were normally raised as gentlemen in some other household, with the prospect of a career among the privileged elite; a number of contemporary examples could be cited. A society in which even small farmers followed primogeniture would not view Edmund as a rising star but as Lucifer in miniature. Actually, biblically minded auditors of *Lear* would receive a more precise understanding. Although he represents radical freedom in his own eyes, Edmund simply plays the bastard's role inscribed in the Wisdom of Solomon—and suffers the successful bastard's prescribed fate.

Lear attempts to escape his responsibilities as a ruler and father, while maintaining his privileges, with horrifying results. No matter how much the outcome disturbs us, Shakespeare implies that a king's sins and errors may damage or destroy all around him. Yet theatregoers from 1681 to 1826 refused Shakespeare's tragic catastrophe in favour of Nahum Tate's happy-ending version of *King Lear*. Samuel Johnson shared this preference, remarking that he was so shocked by Cordelia's death as to be unable to read the conclusion of *Lear* for many years.[52] Yet we accept the deaths of Ophelia and Desdemona, heroines fully equal to Cordelia, whose longer roles give us more time to become attached to them. I suggest that our greater distress at Cordelia's death lies in its effect on Lear, so close to happiness after such torment—and then cruelly blasted. Whatever our reaction, we need to seek an explanation within the play. Lear's death, when it finally comes, is merciful. His continued existence could only be in misery or madness; as the faithful Kent says, «Vex not his ghost; O, let him pass. He hates him/That would upon the rack of this tough world/Stretch him out longer.» (V.iii.312-14) Our sorrow is not for Lear's death, but for the havoc wreaked upon him—which grew in a chain reaction from his vain assault on the natural order of society.

Just as rents in the social order lead to calamity, so disturbances in the heavens portend disaster for humanity. Shakespeare critics often remark that scepticism regarding the significance of heavenly omens and the unity of nature is the mark of a villain. To describe belief in such portents as mere superstition misses or trivializes its underlying philosophy of universal interdependence; as a prominent contemporary explained, nothing «in the universe could be like an island, separated from connexion with the rest» ... «so that at last nature seems to end as it were in unity.»[53] Moreover, none of Shakespeare's virtuous believers in omens consults the Renaissance equivalents of today's daily horoscopes; rather, they draw conclusions from events around them.[54] We need not share Shakespeare's belief in the celestial omens cited by

Gloucester, and yet we must grasp his philosophy, aspects of which are relevant today, if we are to understand *King Lear.*

Endnotes

1 Curtius, 106-27. Lewis, 34-40. Economou, 1-6, 26, 40-93. Alan of Lille [Alanus de Insulis], 31-64.

2 Wippel, 31.

3 Chaucer, *Parliament,* lines 316-18, and «Physician's Tale,» lines 9-29. Spenser, Book 7, canto 7, stanza 9; Book 7 appeared in 1609, a year after *King Lear.*

4 Foakes, ed., 45 and note to I.ii.1-2; all *Lear* quotations are from this edition. Muir, ed., note to I.ii.1. Duthie and Wilson, eds., xliii-xlviii. Hunter, ed., 17-20. Halio, ed., 17-18 and note to I.ii.1. Wells, ed., note to scene ii, line 1, which cites a 1667 definition of «nature» from the *Oxford English Dictionary (OED).*

5 Danby, 20, 31-2, 38-52. Elton, 116-30, esp. 126-7.

6 For all play citations, see Shakespeare, *Arden Complete Works,* which includes the Foakes text cited in note 4.

7 Whitaker, 79-80.

8 Hardwick, 301-2.

9 On the evil meaning of the word, see *Middle English Dictionary* (henceforth *MED*) «natur(e) n.» 4.(b). *MED's* first example is from Chaucer, «Parson's Tale,» line 461: «We ben alle of o fader and of o moder, and alle we ben of o nature, roten and corrupt.»

10 A few pages after his famous remark about «nasty, brutish, and short,» Hobbes discusses original sin, without naming it, including these words: «For God Almighty, having promised Paradise to those men (hoodwinkt with carnall desires,) that can walk through this world according to the Precepts, and Limits prescribed by him.» Hobbes's «carnall desires» are the «φρόνημα σαρκός» of Article IX. Hobbes's next paragraph describes «meer Nature» as «a condition of Warre of every man against every man.» Hobbes, pt. 1, chaps. 13-14, pp. 186, 195-6.

11 *Geneva Bible, 1560.*

12 Kempis, Book 3, chap. 55, p. 1 60. This translation appeared, in whole or in part, twelve times between 1531 and 1585.

13 Hooker, «Remedie,» 376.

14 *Geneva Bible, 1602;* all biblical quotes are from this source unless otherwise specified. For information on Beza's notes, see Anderson, 11-13. See also

Daniell, 351-7. The Geneva New Testament with Beza's notes is usually referred to by the name of its publisher, Laurence Tomson. Italics in the biblical text indicate words added to the Greek text for clarity; see note 16 below on the italicized marginal notes; other emphases are mine.

15 Noble, 8-9. Shaheen, 31-2. Daniell, 369.

16 Attribution of the marginal notes is complicated because, as explained on the title page, most were written by Beza, while others were derived by Pierre de Villers L'Oiseleur from longer annotations by Beza and Joachim Camerarius, then they were translated from Latin to English by Tomson. The next page, «The Printer to the Diligent Reader,» explains that all marginal notes keyed to a number (in roman type) are by Beza, while all notes keyed to a letter (in italic) derive from Beza or Camerarius. See Backus, 13-28, and Daniell, 352-6.

17 On Shakespeare's biblical preference, see Shaheen, 39, 44, 49.

18 Natural law may also be defined empirically as those rules common to all human societies; Luther, Vol. 47, 89-90; Calvin, *Institutes*, Book 4, chap. 20, sec. 16.

19 Hooker, «Autograph Notes,» sec. 5, p. 17; the note was written in 1599 or 1600. *OED*, «bug-word»: «a word meant to frighten or terrify.»

20 Finnis, 51, 101, 128. See also Aquinas, *Treatise*, 718; Luther, Vol. 35, 164-8; Vol. 47, 88-95, 110-11; Vol. 54, 293; Calvin, *Institutes*, 4.20.16, and *Commentary*, 48-51.

21 Noble, 229. Shaheen, 608.

22 Shaheen, 616.

23 Danby, 125. Shaheen, 618.

24 Noble, 229. Shaheen, 607. On Shakespeare's liking for Ecclesiasticus, see Noble, 43; Shaheen, 20, 799-800; and Milward, 87.

25 See also Gloucester's words at IV.vi.75-7: «I'll bear/Affliction till it do cry out itself/‹Enough, enough› and die.»

26 Maxwell, 128. Miles, 125-7.

27 Although generally opposing suicide as a cowardly pre-emption of the gods, many classical authors allowed it to escape extreme dishonour or misery. However, even those like Socrates and Aristotle, who permitted no exceptions, did not oppose suicide with the vehemence of St Augustine and subsequent Christian doctrine. Nevertheless, the unqualified aversion of Socrates and Aristotle justifies the opposition to suicide in the society Shakespeare creates in *King Lear*. See Plato, *Phaedo*, 61B-63A, and Aristotle, 3.7.13. On the qualified view of suicide, see Plato, *Laws*, 9.873C, and Cicero, 1.30.74.

28 Murray, 125-7, 213, 229-31, 240-1.

29 On despair, see Snyder, especially 18 and 50-7. See also Murray, 321, and Foakes, note to V.iii.190.

30 Shaheen, 617-18, 798-9.

31 Hooker, *Ecclesiastical Polity*, 2.1.4.

32 Shakespeare, *Arden Complete Works*.

33 In his note to III.ii.5-6, Foakes, makes the point about «thou» personalizing Lear's command. Lear's earlier invocations of Jupiter are at I.i.179, II.ii.211, and II.ii.417.

34 Calvin, *Institutes*, 1.3.1. See also Aquinas, *Summa*, 2.5-11 (Ia, Question 2); Luther, Vol. 35, 164, 168; Vol. 47, 89, 90, 94; Hooker, *Ecclesiastical Polity*, 1.5.5, 1.16.5, 3.8.6.

35 Chambers, 85-6.

36 On the meaning of St Paul's sword, see Ferguson, 248, and Appleton, 14. The two title pages are in Daniell, plates 10 and 27.

37 *Book of Common Prayer, 1559*, 248-9.

38 Shakespeare and his age were not fully consistent on topics like suicide, regarding those of Lucrece, Romeo, and Juliet as noble or romantic, rather than damnable, while Shakespeare's good bastard in *King John* does not fully agree with the bastard in *Lear*.

39 For example, Foakes, note to V.iii.261, cites Matthew 24, Mark 13, Luke 21.

40 Matthew 24:1-2, Mark 13:1-2, Luke 21:5-6. See also Daniel 9:26.

41 John 11:24.

42 See also Matthew 10:21 and Luke 21:16.

43 As alluded to in Matthew 24:15 and Mark 13:14, the coming of the Messiah, his death, and the destruction of the Temple are described in Daniel 9. References to doomsday in pre-Christian Britain may still seem anachronistic, and yet the Fool's mention of Merlin (III.ii.95-6) licenses anachronism in *Lear*.

44 See also Matthew 24:29 and Luke 21:25.

45 Wisdom 2:16-22, 3:16-19, 4:3-6. Besides the characteristics applicable to Edmund, Wisdom 2:19 says that bastards rebuke and torment the righteous.

46 Wisdom 4:3-6 «has exerted a not always salutary influence as the main biblical comment on illegitimacy,» Barton and Muddiman, eds., 656. The Bible's canonical books say little on bastards: Deuteronomy 23:2 excludes them from the congregation, but Judges 11-12 tell of Jephthah, the bastard who became Judge of Israel, while Hebrews 12:8 uses the word figuratively.

47 Calvin, *Commentary*, 2:15, p. 49.

48 *OED*, «bastard,» B.4. The modern, pejorative definition of bastard dates

from the nineteenth century.

49 *Great Bible* and *Bishops Bible.*

50 Although the passages in question from chaps. 2-4 of Wisdom of Solomon are in the voice of the author, who assumes the identity of Solomon, yet the author's knowledge derives from the female Spirit of Wisdom.

51 See Foakes, 44, 180, and Duthie and Wilson, xlvi.

52 Johnson, 702-4.

53 Bacon, 321.

54 The one character who cites an astrological pamphlet is Edmund (I.ii.140-1), thereby arousing Edgar's suspicion of his brother's new interest. Otherwise, both Gloucester (I.ii.103-4) and Edmund (I.ii.141) simply refer to «these eclipses» as observed events.

References

Alan of Lille [Alanus de Insulis]. *The Plaint of Nature.* Translated by James J. Sheridan. (Toronto: Pontifical Institute of Mediaeval Studies, 1980)

Anderson, Marvin. «The Geneva (Tomson/Junius) New Testament Among Other English Bibles of the Period.» In *Geneva Bible: The Annotated New Testament, 1602 Edition,* edited by Gerald T. Sheppard, 5-17. (Cleveland, OH: Pilgrim Press, 1989).

Appleton, LeRoy. *Symbolism in Liturgical Art.* (New York: Charles Scribner's Sons, 1959).

Aquinas, Thomas. *Summa Theologiae.* Edited by Thomas Gilby. Vol. 2, translated by Timothy McDermott. (New York: McGraw-Hill, 1964).

—. *Treatise on Law.* Translated by Richard J. Regan. (Indianapolis, IN: Hackett Publishing Co., 2000).

Aristotle. *Nicomachean Ethics.* Translated by H. Rackham. (Cambridge, MA: Harvard UP, 1947).

Backus, Irena D. *The Reformed Roots of the English New Testament: The Influence of Theodore Beza on the English New Testament.* (Pittsburgh, PA: Pickwick Press, 1980).

Bacon, Francis. *Of the Dignity and Advancement of Learning.* 1605, 2.13. In *Works of Francis Bacon.* Vol. 4, edited by James Spedding, Robert Ellis, and Douglas Heath. (London: Longman, 1858).

Barton, John, and John Muddiman, eds. *Oxford Bible Commentary.* (Oxford: Oxford UP, 2001).

Bishops Bible. The Holy Bible: Conteyning the Olde Testament and the Newe. (London: Christopher Barker, 1595).

Book of Common Prayer, 1559: The Elizabethan Prayer Book. Edited by John E. Booty. (Charlottesville, VA: University of Virginia Press, 1976)

Calvin, John. *Commentary upon the Epistle of Saint Paul to the Romans.* Edited by Henry Beveridge, translated by Christopher Rosdell. (Edinburgh: Calvin Translation Society, 1844).

—. *Institutes of the Christian Religion.* Edited by John T. McNeill, translated by Ford Battles. (Philadelphia, PA: Westminster Press, 1960).

Chambers, E. K. *William Shakespeare: A Study of Facts and Problems.* Vol. 1. (Oxford: Clarendon, 1930).

Chaucer, Geoffrey. *Parliament of Fowls;* «Physician's Tale»; «Parson's Tale.» In *Canterbury Tales in Riverside Chaucer,* edited by Larry D. Benson. (Boston, MA: Houghton Mifflin, 1987).

Cicero, Marcus Tullius. *Tusculan Disputations.* Translated by J. E. King. (Cambridge, MA: Harvard UP, 1950).

Curtius, Ernst Robert. *European Literature and the Latin Middle Ages.* Translated by Willard R. Trask. (Princeton, NJ: Princeton UP, 1953).

Danby, John. *Shakespeare's Doctrine of Nature: A Study of «King Lear».* London: Faber and Faber, 1949.

Daniell, David. *The Bible in English.* (New Haven, CT: Yale UP, 2003).

Duthie, George, and John Dover Wilson, eds. *New Shakespeare King Lear.* (Cambridge: Cambridge UP, 1969).

Economou, George D. *The Goddess Natura in Medieval Literature.* (Cambridge, MA: Harvard UP, 1972).

Elton, William R. *King Lear and the Gods.* (Lexington, KY: University of Kentucky Press, 1966).

Ferguson, George. *Signs and Symbols in Christian Art.* (New York: Oxford UP, 1955).

Finnis, John. *Natural Law and Natural Rights.* (Oxford: Clarendon, 1980).

Foakes, R. A., ed. *Third Arden King Lear.* (Walton-on-Thames, Surrey: Thomas Nelson and Sons, 1997).

Geneva Bible, A Facsimile of the 1560 Edition. Introduction by Lloyd E. Berry. (Madison, WI: University of Wisconsin Press, 1969).

Geneva Bible: The Annotated New Testament, 1602 Edition. Edited by Gerald T. Sheppard. (Cleveland, OH: Pilgrim Press, 1989).

Great Bible: A Facsimile of the 1539 Edition. Edited by Yoshio Terasawa. (Tokyo: Elpis, 1991).

Halio, Jay L., ed. *New Cambridge King Lear.* (Cambridge: Cambridge UP, 1992).

Hardwick, Charles. *A History of the Articles of Religion.* (London: George Bell & Sons, 1884).

Hobbes, Thomas. *Leviathan*. Edited by C. B. Macpherson. (Harmondsworth: Penguin, 1981).

Hooker, Richard. *Ecclesiastical Polity*. In *Folger Library Edition of the Works of Richard Hooker*, Vol. 1, edited by W. Speed Hill and Georges Edelen. (Cambridge, MA: Harvard UP, 1977).

—. «Hooker's Autograph Notes on *A Christian Letter*.» In *Folger Library Edition of the Works of Richard Hooker*. Vol. 4, edited by John Booty. (Cambridge, MA: Harvard UP, 1982).

—. «A Remedie Against Sorrow and Feare» In *Folger Library Edition of the Works of Richard Hooker*. Vol. 5, edited by Laetitia Yeandle and Egil Grislis. (Cambridge, MA: Harvard UP, 1990).

Hunter, G. K., ed. *New Penguin King Lear*. (Harmondsworth, Middlesex: Penguin Books, 1972).

Johnson, Samuel. *The Yale Edition of the Works of Samuel Johnson*. Vol. 8, edited by Arthur Sherbo. (New Haven, CT: Yale UP, 1968).

Kempis, Thomas à. *Imitation of Christ*. Translated by Richard Whitford. (Mt. Vernon, New York: Peter Pauper Press, 1947).

Lewis, C. S. *The Discarded Image: An Introduction to Medieval and Renaissance Literature*. (Cambridge: Cambridge UP, 1964).

Luther, Martin. *Luther's Works*. Edited by Jaroslav Pelikan and Helmut T. Lehmann. (Philadelphia, PA: Fortress Press, 1960).

Maxwell, J. C. «Brutus's Philosophy.» *Notes and Queries* 215, 110. 2 (April 1970): 128.

Middle English Dictionary, edited by Hans Kurath and Sherman M. Kuhn. (Ann Arbor, MI: University of Michigan Press, 1952).

Miles, Geoffrey. *Shakespeare and the Constant Romans*. (Oxford: Clarendon, 1996).

Milward, Peter. *Shakespeare's Religious Background*. (Bloomington, IN: Indiana University Press, 1973).

Muir, Kenneth, ed. *Arden Shakespeare King Lear*. (Cambridge, MA: Harvard UP, 1959).

Murray, Alexander. *Suicide in the Middle Ages*. Vol. 2. (Oxford: Oxford UP, 2000).

Noble, Richmond. *Shakespeare's Biblical Knowledge*. (London: Society for Promoting Christian Knowledge, 1935).

Oxford English Dictionary, 2nd ed., edited by J. A. Simpson and E. S. C. Weiner. (Oxford: Clarendon Press, 1989).

Plato. *Phaedo*. In *Plato I*. Translated by Harold Fowler. (Cambridge, MA: Harvard UP, 1914).

—. Laws. In *Plato IX*. Translated by R. G. Bury. (Cambridge, MA: Harvard UP, 1952).

Shaheen, Naseeb. *Biblical References in Shakespeare's Plays.* (Newark, NJ: University of Delaware Press. 1999)

Shakespeare, William. *The Arden Shakespeare Complete Works.* Edited by Richard Proudfoot, Ann Thompson, and David Kastan. (Walton-on-Thames, Surrey: Thomas Nelson, 1998).

Snyder, Susan. «The Left Hand of God: Despair in Medieval and Renaissance Tradition.» *Studies in the Renaissance* 12 (1965): 18-59.

Spenser, Edmund. *Faerie Queene, Two Cantos of Mutabilitie.* In *Complete Poetical Works of Edmund Spenser,* edited by R. E. Neil Dodge. (Boston, MA: Houghton Mifflin, 1908).

Wells, Stanley, ed. *Oxford Shakespeare King Lear.* (Oxford: Oxford UP, 2000).

Whitaker, Virgil K. *Shakespeare's Use of Learning.* (San Marino, CA: Huntington Library, 1953).

Wippel, John F. Article on Aquinas. In *Cambridge Dictionary of Philosophy,* edited by Robert Audi. (Cambridge: Cambridge UP, 1995).

The Role of Time in *Macbeth*

Macbeth may be described as a man advancing erratically toward power and then to destruction, blundering between indecision and impetuosity. His personal motivations appear to be his ambitions, his fears, and his submission to his wife's stronger character. However, Macbeth also contends with two abstract, intertwined forces: time and religion.

Regarding time, Shakespeare uses that word and its derivatives far more frequently in *Macbeth* than in any other play.[1] Time is indeed important in *Macbeth*, for example, Macbeth's letter to his wife reporting the witches' prediction that he would be King with «the coming on of time» (I.v.9-10), followed by her brutal response to his hesitance to act: «Nor time nor place,/Did then adhere, and yet you would make them both:/They have made themselves, and that their fitness now/Does unmake you» (I.vii.51-4). How does this differ from any other play with a well constructed plot? Does one event not set another in motion just as much in *Hamlet* or *Othello* as in *Macbeth*? Answering these questions— unfolding the role of time in *Macbeth*—is the purpose of this essay.

Regarding religion, Macbeth responds to the discovery of the truth of the witches' initial prediction of his advancement by asking Banquo (emphases are mine): «Do you not <u>hope</u> your children shall be kings,/ When those that gave the Thane of Cawdor to me/<u>Promis'd</u> no less to them?» (I.iii.118-20)[2] The words «hope» and «promise» come from St. Paul, most notably in the Acts of the Apostles, where Paul tells King Agrippa of the resurrection of the dead: «And now I stand and am accused for the <u>hope</u> of the <u>promes</u> made of God vnto our fathers» (26:6).[3] These two words appear also in Ephesians 2:12 and Titus 1:2, in affirmation of God's promise to Christians. Banquo unites the two words in his soliloquy at the start of Act III: «Thou hast it now: King, Cawdor, Glamis, all,/As the weïrd women <u>promis'd</u> ... Why .../May they not be my oracles as well,/And set me up in <u>hope</u>?» (III.i.1-10) Finally recognizing the full deception of the prophecies, Macbeth denounces the «juggling fiends …/That keep the word of <u>promise</u> to our ear,/And break it to our <u>hope</u>» (V.viii.19-22). In other words, Macbeth applies the concepts of his original Christianity to his newfound trust—for he has no allegiance—while Banquo struggles to resist the same temptation. As will be shown, Macbeth's interweaving and replacement of doctrines and ideas applies not only to religion and time, but also to religion, superstition and philosophy.

Regarding the combination of religion and time, Macbeth provides an excellent example at the start of Act I, scene vii, in his soliloquy on whether or not to murder Duncan. Macbeth opens with the consideration that if he could get away with the assassination, «here, upon this bank and shoal of time» (I.vii.6), he would risk the life to come. He continues by remarking that he would still have judgment here on earth, presumably referring to Genesis 9:6, «Whoso shedeth mans blood, by man shal his blood be shed,» reinforced by the fact that Duncan's saintliness will draw heavenly hosts to denounce to all humanity so damnable a deed. Macbeth concludes that the risks are too great, but promptly tells his wife that he must not forfeit the popularity bought by his recent victories.

The soliloquy's opening is a web of evasion and ambiguity, requiring clarification from later lines and scenes, in which it typifies the play's protagonist. To begin with, Macbeth could mean either that in return for success he would willingly risk the life to come, or that the life to come is a risk still to be counted, as indicated by his reference thirteen lines later to «the deep damnation» that would fall on the murderer. Moreover, Macbeth ought to be in no doubt that such a heinous crime would amount to be forfeiting, not risking, the life to come, though his subsequent reference to damnation implies recognition of reality on this point. Then there is Macbeth's chosen pronoun in «We'ld jump [i.e., risk or hazard] the life to come.» Is Macbeth prematurely assuming the royal plural, is he referring to both himself and Lady Macbeth, or is he simply unwilling to say «I»? In any event, he seems prepared to write off one of two divine punishments, as if time ended with his own death—a matter to which he returns later in the play.

The Concepts of Time and Eternity

The concept of time as understood by educated people in Shakespeare's day came from classical philosophy. As no attempt will be made here to show that Shakespeare had personally studied the works in question,[4] a synopsis relevant to the literature of his age will be offered instead. Aristotle taught that time measures motion or change, and would not exist without them; that sleep is outside of time, for no change of consciousness occurs; that certain things are eternal, meaning outside of time, such as mathematical truths; and, paradoxically, that the past and future do not exist, although they did and will, while the present is not part of time as it has no duration, therefore—apparently—time does not exist. Plotinus, expanding on Plato, defined eternity as a state outside of time, in which past and future unite with the present, or, in eternity all three tenses are simultaneous; otherwise, time is the life of the soul as it moves from one act or event to another.

Responding to Aristotle's paradox, Augustine asserts that there is «a present time of past things; a present time of present things; and a present time of future things ... The present time of past things is our memory; the present time of present things is our sight [*contuitus*, «perception»]; the present time of future things our expectation.»[5] Note the similarity of Augustine's explanation of the existence of time to Plotinus's definition of eternity, in that both unite past, present, and future. Finally, Boethius's *Consolation of Philosophy* became the principal means of transmission of this knowledge through the Dark and Middle Ages: translated into English by Chaucer and then others, it was available in print in several sixteenth century editions.[6]

Tudor and Stuart writers counted on their readers' knowledge of the classical heritage on time and eternity. Perhaps the best known example on time and motion is Ralegh's: «tell time it metes but motion»[7]; on eternity, perhaps Milton's: «Him God beholding from his prospect high,/Wherein past, present, future he beholds.»[8]

Shakespeare's views on these essentials feature most prominently in the conversation between Rosalind and Orlando in the Forest of Arden.

When the latter asks, «Who stays it [Time] still withal?», Rosalind's answer covers both the link of time to motion and the extra-chronological status of sleep: «With lawyers in the vacation; for they sleep between term and term, and then they perceive not how Time moves.»[9] The special status of sleep also occurs implicitly in *Winter's Tale*: «I turn my glass, and give my scene such growing/As you had slept between» (IV.i.16-17). Shakespeare's most intriguing passage on eternity comes in *Merry Wives of Windsor*, when Mistress Ford, outraged by Falstaff's presumptuous love letter, remarks that: «If I would but go to hell for an eternal moment or so, I could be knighted» (II.i.49-50). At first glance, her expression, «an eternal moment,» seems a silly contradiction, though quite apt to the humor of the scene. However, on reflection, an eternal moment makes sense. Mrs. Ford's eyes could go blank for a moment or two from the point of view of an observer while she visited eternity—infernal or otherwise—where time does not exist, and where a moment and a century are indistinguishable.

Time in Acts I-III of *Macbeth*

The first three acts of *Macbeth* invoke Time in various ways, often returning to them later in the play, but each act also includes one or more critical decisions or events that foreshadow or shape the plot. Otherwise, Time seems a presence in the play—albeit offstage—that pulls or pushes the characters this way and that, or, to put it another way, Shakespeare seems to be exercising his audiences on the subject of time. Act I serves a threshold, as it were, Act II as the doorknob, and Act III as the hinges. Then, in Acts IV and V, Macbeth challenges Time: Act IV is the door itself, while Act V leads to what lies beyond.

Time's first critical event in Act I is the witches' prediction that Macbeth shall be Thane of Cawdor and then King; the latter motivates the plot, while the former provides a preliminary verification of the witches' reliability. Satan presumably stands behind the witches' words, but the prediction and its resultant temptation operate in Time's framework. Time's second critical intervention is Duncan's decision to spend a night at Macbeth's castle. The choice may be Duncan's, or it could be ascribed to fate, fortune, or chance, but it creates a situation—an opportunity for regicide and usurpation—controlled by the passage of Time.

Otherwise, Macbeth first responds to the witches by allowing his present to be overwhelmed by the future: «Present fears/Are less than horrible imaginings:/My thought, whose murther yet is but fantastical,/ Shakes so my single state of man that function/Is smother'd in surmise, and nothing is/But what is not» (I.iii.137-42). Then, quite sensibly, he returns to honesty or, to put things less favorably, lapses into passivity: «If chance will have me king, why, chance may crown me/Without my stir» (I.iii.143-4); «Come what come may,/Time and the hour runs through the roughest day» (I.iii.146-7); and, writing to his wife, that he shall be King, with «the coming on of time» (I.v.9). Lady Macbeth's first response, like her husband's, is to grasp for the future: «Thy letters have transported me beyond/This ignorant present, and I feel now/The future in the instant» (I.v.56-8). When he loses his nerve after the «bank and shoal of time» soliloquy, she reacts in terms of time: «From this time/ Such I account thy love» (I.vii.38-9). Then she quashes his protests by reminding him that he initiated the matter: «Nor time, nor place,/Did then adhere, and yet you would make them both:/They have made themselves, and that their fitness now/Does unmake you» (I.vii.51-4).[10]

In Act II, some unknown force responds to Duncan's murder by denying future sleep, humanity's refuge from Time, to Macbeth.

Methought I heard a voice cry, «Sleep no more!/Macbeth does murder sleep» ... Still it cried, «Sleep no more!» to all the house;/Glamis hath murther'd sleep, and therefore Cawdor/Shall sleep no more— Macbeth shall sleep no more.» (II.i.30-40).

The voice could arise from Macbeth's own conscience or from various external powers—we do not know which—but this immediate response to murder comes within the domain of Time. Two other time-related items in this Act deserve mention. First, when Macduff asks Macbeth why he slaughtered Duncan's sleeping grooms, Macbeth deftly answers: «Who can be wise, amaz'd, temp'rate, and furious/Loyal, and neutral, in a moment?» (II.iii.108-09) This speech, which asks rhetori-cally, «Who can simultaneously be opposites?», parallels Plotinus's definition of eternity and Augustine's affirmation of the actuality of Time, both of which require the simultaneity of different tenses. Finally, Malcolm's question to his brother, «What should be spoken here, where our fate,/Hid in an auger-hole, may rush and seize us?» (II.iii.121-2), is reminiscent of one of Augustine's puzzles about the past and future: «have they a being also; but such as proceeds out of some unknown secret, when out of the future, the present is made; and returns it into some secret again, when the past is made out of the present?»[11]

In Act III, at least five significant events happen with regard to time, each extending backward in the play as well as forward. Hence, as characterized above, Act III resembles a hinge, or, more precisely, a two-way hinge allowing motion in either direction. The following brief descriptions of the five discuss only the backward movement, with the forward reserved for now.

After his meeting with Banquo, Macbeth launches a soliloquy on the threat posed by his former comrade, including: «For Banquo's issue have I filed my mind,/For them the gracious Duncan have I murther'd, .../Only for them; and mine eternal jewel/Given to the common enemy of man,/To make them kings—the seeds of Banquo kings!/Rather than so, come fate into the list,/And champion me to th' utterance!» (III.i.64-71). The reference to giving his soul to Satan harks back to the «bank and shoal of time» soliloquy, which left in doubt the question of whether Macbeth accepted that his crimes implied damnation. It appears here that he does accept that he is damned, but simply regards it as a cost of getting his way here on earth.

Then, in conversation with his wife, we learn that the prophetic voice that assailed Macbeth after Duncan's murder has come true: «But let the frame of things disjoint, both the worlds suffer,/Ere we will eat our meal in fear, and sleep/In the affliction of these terrible dreams/That shake us nightly. Better be with the dead,/Whom we, to gain our peace, have sent to peace,/Than on the torture of the mind to lie/In restless ecstasy.»

(III.ii.16-22). More on this topic, sleep and its relationship to time, lies ahead.

As a result of becoming unnerved by the appearance of Banquo's Ghost at the feast, Macbeth exclaims that: «Blood hath been shed ere now, i' th'olden time,/Ere humane statute purg'd the gentle weal;/Ay, and since too, murthers have been perform'd/... the time has been,/That, when the brains were out, the man would die,/And there an end» (III.iv.74-9). These words obviously look back to some distant past—the olden time—but they also foreshadow, or alert the audience to, the new belief that Macbeth partially adopts in Act IV: Epicureanism.

Then, after babbling about secret murderers being revealed by stones, trees, and birds, Macbeth suddenly rallies by asking, «What is the night?» (III.iv.125). Very much in command of himself, Macbeth discourses on Macduff's absence from the feast, what his army of spies will tell him on that subject, and then: «I will to-morrow/(And betimes I will) to the weïrd sisters./More shall they speak; ... I am in blood/Stepp'd in so far that, should I wade no more,/Returning were as tedious as go o'er./Strange things I have in head, that will to hand;/Which must be acted ere they may be scann'd.» (III.iv.131-9). The image of stepping through blood[12] recalls the «bank and shoal of time» soliloquy in the sense of picturing time or life as flowing water, as well as in the ambiguities of both passages. Does Macbeth really believe that «returning» through his bloodshed would merely be tedious? What would it mean to return: surely, as Claudius understood, repentance, confession, yielding the fruits of crime, and accepting both human and divine consequences? Macbeth's last two lines reverse his view from returning in time to upcoming events which must be acted ere they be scanned, which anticipates his planned visit to the witches.

Finally, Macbeth's response to his wife's call to sleep has implications that stretch in two directions: «Come, we'll to sleep. My strange and self-abuse/Is the initiate fear that wants hard use:/We are yet but young in deed.» (III.iv.140-3). Somehow, perhaps again anticipating the power of the witches, Macbeth no longer worries about his sleep being destroyed by terrible dreams. Less obviously, Macbeth's reference to self-abuse, like his earlier remark on the olden time, points to the Epicureanism that lies ahead.

In sum, the multiple tentacles of Time extending across, before, and beyond Act III merit the classical term *epitasis*, «that part of a play when the plot thickens,» or, as Ben Jonson put it, «the business of the play.»[13] The references or topics that Time points forward to include: damnation; the security of sleep; the olden times; pausing in a stream of blood; acting deeds before they may be scanned; and self-abuse.

Time in Acts IV-V of *Macbeth*

In Act IV, Macbeth settles upon two courses of action regarding the problem of Time. First, he reveals himself to be a follower of some of the doctrines of the Greek philosopher Epicurus. These include disbelief in any afterlife; hence Macbeth's death will bring an end to Time. Next, he decides that he must keep up with, or travel as fast as Time, lest it leave him behind. These decisions carry over into Act V, along with an unintended consequence: Lady Macbeth falls out of Time and into Eternity. The dramatic effectiveness of these three events depends not only on how the playwright stages them, but also on the audience's awareness of his intent.

Regarding Epicureanism, Shakespeare, as shown in some of his other plays, could rely on the audience's general knowledge, as well as on a scripted sermon that each individual among them should have heard annually. Regarding the other two items, and assuming the audience's general knowledge of Time and Eternity, Shakespeare chose the difficult course of staging a truism and a paradox. On the one hand, Time moves at the same rate for all: sixty seconds per minute, sixty minutes per hour, for both the sluggard and the dynamo. How then does an actor run as fast as Time? On the other hand, how can one actress show past, present, and future all at once?

Epicureanism

Although strongly present earlier in the play, Epicureanism receives its formal introduction in Act V, as Macbeth contemplates English invaders supported by rebellious Scottish nobles:

> Bring me no more reports, let them fly all.
> Till Birnam wood remove to Dunsinane
> I cannot taint with fear. What's the boy Malcolm?
> Was he not born of woman? The spirits that know
> All mortal consequences have pronounc'd me thus:
> «Fear not, Macbeth, no man that's born of woman
> Shall e'er have power upon thee.» Then fly, false thanes,
> And mingle with the English epicures! (V.iii.1-8)

Macbeth's sneer at the English epicures has two meanings, which arise from both the philosophical and vulgar understandings of «epicure.» First, while he openly proclaims himself to be protected by prophecies, the Epicureans scoffed at any sort of soothsaying or omens,[14] and the willingness of the English to attack shows disbelief in Macbeth's prophecies—hence the English are epicures. Macbeth's second meaning results from his military experience, his plan for the coming campaign, and a national stereotype from Shakespeare's day.

In those times, it was held that, although the English were the most valiant of all nations on the battlefield, the English soldier needed plenty of beef and a warm, dry place to sleep, without which he would go home. Consequently, the way to defeat the English was not to confront them face-to-face, but to drag out the campaign into winter, while forcing them to conduct sieges. Contemporary examples of the stereotype are readily found.

In 1519 the Venetian ambassador observed that English soldiers, «insist on being paid monthly, nor do they choose to suffer any hardship; but when they have their comforts [*commodita*], they will then do battle daily, with a courage, vigour, and valour, that defy exaggeration.»[15] Elis

Gruffydd, a Welsh soldier in the Duke of Suffolk's expedition of 1523, recorded that the King of France «did not make much haste to turn back to drive the English from his kingdom since he was sufficiently familiar with them to know that ... as soon as winter came it was sure that they would keep to their custom as they were used to do» and go home, which they did. In 1543, Gruffydd served at the siege of Montreuil, where the French commander responded to the Duke of Norfolk's demand for surrender by telling him to: «take his pleasure in hunting with hawks and hounds about the country while the weather is fine and mild and by winter according to the old English custom you will go home to your kinsmen,» as they did.[16] A specific link of the vice to the nation comes in a 1614 item: «Poysoning to Italie, drunkennesses to Germanie, Epicureanism to England.»[17] English awareness of the stereotype also appears in *1 Henry VI*, where the Duke of Alencon remarks of the English besiegers of Orleans that:

> They want their porridge and their fat bull-beeves:
> Either they must be dieted like mules
> And have their provender tied to their mouths,
> Or piteous they will look, like drowned mice. (I.ii.9-12)

Likewise, on the eve of Agincourt in *Henry V*, when Orleans remarks that the English are out of beef, the Constable replies, «Then we shall find tomorrow they have only stomachs to eat and none to fight» (III.vii.152-4).[18]

As an able general, Macbeth takes his enemy's weakness into account as he waits for them in his fortress on Dunsinane Hill:

> Our castle's strength
> Will laugh a siege to scorn; here let them lie
> Till famine and the ague eat them up.
> Were they not forc'd with those that should be ours,
> We might have met them dareful, beard to beard,
> And beat them backward home. (V.v.2-7)

The last three lines clearly show that Macbeth foresees the English, not the Scots rebels, as the victims of hunger and disease.

Analysis of Macbeth's slap at the English epicures presents two common views of Epicureanism in Shakespeare's age. On the one hand, an epicure was one who followed the teachings of the ancient philosopher Epicurus, which included the non-interest and non-interference of the gods in human affairs by either prophecy or direct intervention; the non-existence of any afterlife, hence the simultaneous death of body and soul; avoidance of public affairs; and asceticism in one's personal life. Given his trust in prophecies, as well as his royal ambitions, Macbeth obviously does not qualify as a full-fledged Epicurean. On the other hand, rival classical schools of philosophy, subsequently joined by Christianity, slandered Epicures as nothing more than hedonists or voluptuaries—atheists who loved luxury. Again, Macbeth does not fit the mold. However, the theology of the Anglican Church offered a simpler picture of Epicures.

Unless a church possessed a minister licensed to preach his own sermon once a month, the ministers of the Church of England read their congregations the prescribed sermon from the *Book of Homilies* every Sunday and holy day, beginning anew each year, thus guaranteeing a high degree of common public knowledge, if not necessarily agreement. The homily for Rogation Week, «That all good things commeth from God,» contains three parts, each read on a different day. The second part concerns those who looked elsewhere for help:

> Epicures they bee that imagine that he [God] walketh about the coastes of the heauens, & hath no respect of these inferiour things, but that all these things should proceede either by chance or at aduenture, or else by disposition of fortune, and GOD to haue no stroke in them. What other thing is this to say, then as the foole supposeth in his heart, there is no GOD?

The fools in question had, however, a supernatural alternative:

I would to GOD (my friendes) that in our wants and necessities, we would goe to GOD ... If wee did, wee should not seeke our want and necessitie of the deuill and his ministers so oft as wee doe, as dayly experience declareth it. For if wee stand in necessitie of corporall health, whither goe the common people, but to charmes, witchcraftes and other delusions of the Deuill? ... If the Merchaunt ... knew that GOD is the giuer of riches, hee woulde content himselfe with so much as by iust meanes approued of GOD, ... hee would neuer procure his gaine and aske his goods at the Deuils hand. GOD forbid ye will say, that any man should take his riches of the Deuill ... And all they that giue themselues to such meanes, and have renounced the true meanes that GOD hath appoynted, haue forsaken him, and are become worshippers of the Deuill ... They be such as kneele downe to the deuill at his bidding, and worship him: For he promiseth them for so doing, that he will giue them the world, and the goods therein. They canno otherwise better serue the deuill, then to doe his pleasure and commandement:[19]

The fundamental Epicurean doctrine of God's indifference or impotence thus leads fools to forsake the divine for the infernal, a reasonable description of Macbeth's philosophy.

Otherwise, Epicureanism is specifically denounced in Acts of the Apostles 17:18, besides being attacked in marginal notes to I Corinthians 15:32 and II Peter 3:5 of the 1560 Geneva Bible,[20] as well as in notes to Luke 6:20, Acts 2:23, and II Peter 3:3 of the 1576 Tomson-Geneva New Testament.[21] The burden of these notes is that Epicureanism is anti-Christian and atheistic, while, as a consequence of denying the afterlife, it promotes hedonism here on earth. Aside from *Macbeth*, Shakespeare stressed the sensualist side of Epicureansim in *Merry Wives* (II.ii.287), *King Lear* (I.iv.244), and *Antony and Cleopatra* (II.i.24), while referring to two of its philosophical aspects in *Julius Caesar* (V.i.76) and *Antony and Cleopatra* (II.vii.52).

As discussed above, Macbeth makes a single remark on Epicureanism with a double meaning in Act V, scene iii, but he clearly adopts part of the doctrines of Epicurus in Act IV, scene i, having already mulled over the topic in Act III, scene iv. After Banquo's Ghost disrupts the feast, Macbeth makes two comments agreeable to Epicureanism, although both may be commonplaces, along with one that is decidedly Epicurean. Marveling at the Ghost's appearance, Macbeth exclaims that if graves reject our corpses, «our monuments/Shall be the maws of kites» (III.iv.71-2), in agreement with a similar remark in one of the most important statements of Epicurean doctrine, *De Rerum Natura*; however, as the Loeb editor notes, the concept was common to many classical and Renaissance authors.[22] At the end of the scene, Macbeth dismisses the reality of the Ghost as a result of «self-abuse,» meaning self-deception, which Shakespeare could easily have picked up as an Epicurean belief from Plutarch's «Life of Marcus Brutus,» the primary source for *Julius Caesar*;[23] however, again, the belief cannot be confined to Epicurus and his followers. On the other hand, right after his complaint about the maws of kites, Macbeth observes that murders occurred «i' th' olden time,/Ere humane statute purg'd the gentle weal» (III.iv.74-5), a puzzling bit of information for which *Macbeth's* editors offer no source.[24] Macbeth's historical knowledge does not come from the Bible, where divine statute, the Sixth Commandment, prohibits murder, nor does it arise from the classical progression of gold, silver, bronze, and iron ages, followed by the flood, as in the opening of Ovid's *Metamorphoses*. Macbeth's belief, however, coincides with human history as narrated in Books V and VI of *De Rerum Natura*, wherein savage primitive humanity first created civilization and then purged it by establishing statutes against homicide.[25]

Macbeth's announcement of his own partial adoption of the teachings of Epicurus comes in his second meeting with the witches, after the two prophecies assure him that he cannot be killed by man nor be vanquished. He then exults that: «Our high-plac'd Macbeth/Shall live the lease of nature, pay his breath/To time and mortal custom» (IV.i.98-100). This statement of satisfaction that he will live out old age and die a natural death is thoroughly Epicurean, and yet such sentiments can hardly be called exclusively Epicurean. For now, however, Macbeth's relief at his prophesied invincibility serves two further purposes. First, in keeping with Epicurus's doctrine, time ends with his own death. Second, Macbeth need no longer be concerned about damnation, as he was in his «bank and shoal of time» and «mine eternal jewel» soliloquies, because he has ceased to believe in the afterlife.

Yet right after being informed that his wife is dead, Macbeth finally rejects the Epicurean view of time.

> She should have died hereafter;
> There would have been a time for such a word.
> Tomorrow and tomorrow and tomorrow
> Creeps in this petty pace from day to day
> To the last syllable of recorded time,
> And all our yesterdays have lighted fools
> The way to dusty death. Out, out brief candle!
> Life's but a walking shadow, a poor player
> That struts and frets his hour upon the stage
> And then is heard no more. It is a tale
> Told by an idiot, full of sound and fury,
> Signifying nothing.
>
> (V.v.17-28)

As Fast as Time

Immediately after meeting with the witches and learning the future, Macbeth discovers that Macduff, whom he intends to kill, has fled to England. He responds:

> Time, thou anticipat'st my dread exploits:
> The flighty purpose never is o'ertook
> Unless the deed go with it. From this moment
> The very firstlings of my heart shall be
> The firstlings of my hand. And even now,
> To crown my thoughts with acts, be it thought and done:
> The castle of Macduff I will surprise,
> Seize upon Fife; give to th' edge o' th' sword
> His wife, his babes, and all unfortunate souls

> That trace him in his line. No boasting like a fool;
> This deed I'll do before this purpose cool. (IV.i.144-54)

On the one hand, Macbeth may be said to recognize his own indecisiveness, and to adopt the motto: he who hesitates is lost. On the other hand, Macbeth directly challenges Time, which he now regards as an adversary.

Lady Macbeth and Eternity

At the start of Act I, scene v, Lady Macbeth reads in her husband's letter that the witches hailed him as Thane of Cawdor and future king, and how he promptly learned that Duncan had granted him the former title. She then reflects on her husband's lack of ruthlessness, which must be made good by her own resolution. Next she learns that Duncan comes to stay for the night and that Macbeth's arrival is imminent, whereupon she appeals to diabolical spirits to fill her with total cruelty. Macbeth enters, Lady Macbeth greets him with his new title, then alludes to greater things to come, concluding, *as noted above* that she has been transported beyond the present into the future. Her assertion of feeling—not of anticipating or expecting, as Augustine puts it—the future in the present amounts to an implication of eternity, a collapsing of the future onto the present. Furthermore, Lady Macbeth's words do not exist in isolation, instead they anticipate her final appearance on stage.

By the time of her sleepwalking scene, Lady Macbeth lives in semi-darkness, as she requires light beside her night and day. Her waiting-gentlewoman and a doctor observe her walking with her candle, repeating or varying speeches uttered at the killings of Duncan, Banquo, and Lady Macduff, but jumbled together, out of their chronological order.

Lady Macbeth has manifestly lost the present tense, especially since she is asleep, in agreement with Aristotle, but she possesses the past—actually the past possesses her—and likewise with the future in hell, to which she refers. In other words, Lady Macbeth has slipped into that timeless eternity so jokingly alluded to by Mistress Ford.

That Lady Macbeth's sleepwalking lies outside of time may be verified by contrasting it to Augustine's definition of the present. He begins by noting that the past and future do not exist, but continues by arguing that «a present time of past things; a present time of present things; and a present time of future things» exist in our souls and nowhere else. Specifically (as noted above): «The present time of past things is our memory; the present time of present things is our sight; the present time of future things our expectation.» Lady Macbeth cannot see or experience the present:

> *Doct.* You see her eyes are open.
> *Gent.* Ay, but their sense are shut. (V.i.24-5)

Lady Macbeth can, on the other hand, both see, smell, and imagine the past: the spot of blood that will not be wiped away. She does not simply remember the past in her speeches and acts, instead she re-lives it. And her words, «Hell is murky,» (V.i.36) [26] remind of the conclusion of her imprecation to diabolical spirits to fill her with cruelty:

> Come, thick night,
> And pall thee in the dunnest smoke of hell,
> That my keen knife see not the wound it makes,
> Nor heaven peep through the blanket of the dark (I.v.50-3)

However, Lady Macbeth saw quite clearly on the night of Duncan's murder, well enough to recognize the sleeping King's resemblance to her own father (II.ii.12-13). Thus, her «Hell is murky» in Act V is not simply a recollection of her words in Act I, but is a response to her current condition. In her sleep, Lady Macbeth does not expect to go to murky hell; as indicated by her use of the present tense, she is already there.

Endnotes

1   On this topic, see Frank Kermode, *Shakespeare's Language* (New York, 2000), 201-16, to whom I am indebted. The relative frequency of «time,» «times,» etc. in *Macbeth* is 0.291, next comes *As You Like It* at 0.219, while the average for all of Shakespeare's plays is 0.15, though for the Sonnets the count is 0.44; Marvin Spevack, *A Complete and Systematic Concordance to the Works of Shakespeare* (Hildesheim, 1968). See also A. C. Bradley, *Shakespearean Tragedy* (London, 1991), note EE, 459-60; and A. R. Braunmuller, ed., *Macbeth* (Cambridge, 1997), 15-24.

2   Unless otherwise noted, all Shakespeare quotations are from *The Riverside Shakespeare, Second Edition*, eds. G. Blakemore Evans and J. J. M. Tobin (Boston, 1997).

3   Unless otherwise noted, all biblical quotations are from *The Geneva Bible, A facsimile of the 1560 edition*, ed. Lloyd E. Berry (Madison, Wisconsin, 1969).

4   Most notably: Plato, *Timaeus*; Aristotle, *Physics*; Plotinus, *Enneads*, 3.7.3,11.

5   *St. Augustine's Confessions*, tr. William Watts (London, 1631) and W. H. D. Rouse (Loeb edition 1912), XI.xx. Other items: I, «Your Father knoweth what you have need of, before you ask» (Matt. 6:8); VI, counting time by syllables, also in XXII, XXVI, and XXVIII; XI, definitions of time and eternity; XIV, defines eternity; XVII, the present comes out of a secret place, then returns; XX, defines the three presents; XXVIII, the three tenses are in the mind. See also *The Teacher* on sleep, madness, the reliability of the senses, and the fact that mathematical truth remains even if the human race sleeps.

6   Boethius, *Consolation of Philosophy*, 1525 (Walton trans.) 1532 (Chaucer). Defines both Time and Eternity.

7   *The Poems of Sir Walter Ralegh*, ed. Agnes C. Latham, «The Lie». For other examples, see *The Poems of George Chapman*, ed. Phyllis Brooks Bartlett, «Hero and Leander,» p. 138, lines 187-8, «Now (as swift as Time/Doth follow Motion)»; and *The Poems of Sir John Davies*, ed. Robert Krueger, «Orchestra»: p. 97, st. 23, «Time the measure of all moving things is»; pp. 123-4, st. 126

8   Milton on eternity *Paradise Lost*, 3.77-8. For other examples, see *Selected Poems of Fulke Greville*, ed. Thom Gunn, «Caelica,» 86, lines 22-4, p. 119, «To see itself in that eternal glass,/Where time doth end, and thoughts accuse the dead,/Where all to come, is one with all that was»; and Sir Thomas Browne, *Pseudodoxia Epidemica* (1645), «For unto God a thousand years are no more than one moment ... for all parts of time are alike unto him, unto whom none are referrible; and all things present, unto whom nothing is past or to come.» (Bk. 7, Ch. 3, p. 493).

9   *As You Like It*, III.ii.330-3; see lines 299-33 for the whole dialogue on time.

10 Cf. *Measure for Measure*: «Had time coher'd with place, or place with wishing» (II.i.11).

11 Augustine, *Confessions* (Loeb), XI.xvii, vol. 2, p. 247.

12 Cf. *Richard III*, IV.ii.63-4: «But I am in/So far in blood that sin will pluck on sin.»

13 J. A. Cuddon, *The Penguin Dictionary of Literary terms and Literary Theory*, Third Edition (London, 1991); Ben Jonson, Argument to *The New Inn of the Light Heart*, *The Complete Plays of Ben Jonson Plays*, intro. Felix E. Schelling (London, 1910).

14 As Cassius says to Messala at Philippi: «You know that I held Epicurus strong,/And his opinion; now I change my mind,/And partly credit things that do presage,» going on to explain the omen of the appearance above their army of birds of carrion, in place of two eagles that had accompanied them on the march (*Julius Caesar*, V.i.76-88).

15 Sebastian Giustinian, *Four Years at the Court of Henry VIII*, tr. Rawdon Brown (London, 1854), 316.

16 M. B. Davies, «Suffolk's Expedition to Mondidier,» *Fouad I University, Bulletin of the Faculty of Arts*, VII (July 1944), 38. Davies, «The ‹Enterprises› of Paris and Boulogne,» *Fouad I*, IX.I (May 1949), 55.

17 *OED*, Epicurism, 2.b.

18 In his footnote to this passage in the Second Arden *Henry V* (London, 1954), J. H. Walter offers several more examples of the stereotype.

19 *Certaine Sermons or Homilies, Appointed to be Read in Churches In the Time of Queen Elizabeth I (1547-1571)*, A facsimile reproduction of the edition of 1623, eds. Mary Ellen Rickey and Thomas B. Stroup (Gainesville, Florida, 1968), The Second Tome, 223, 225. See also Naseeb Shaheen, *Biblical References in Shakespeare's Plays* (Newark, Delaware, 1999), 51, 53, 55-8 on the Homilies, and Appendix C on Shakespeare's dramatic use of them.

20 *The Geneva Bible, A facsimile of the 1560 edition*, ed. Lloyd E. Berry (Madison, Wisconsin, 1969).

21 *The Geneva Bible, The Annotated New Testament, 1602 Edition*, ed. Gerald T. Sheppard (Cleveland, Ohio, 1989).

22 Lucretius, *De Rerum Natura*, eds. W. H. D. Rouse and Martin Ferguson Smith (Cambridge, Massachusetts, 1992), V.993-4, pp. 454-5.

23 *Julius Caesar*, ed. David Daniell (Walton-on-Thames, Surrey, 1998), Appendix, p. 351.

24 Editors on the «olden time»: Wilson (1947) defines «purge,» «humane,» «gentle»; Muir (1951) same as Wilson; Hunter (1967) general explanation, no

source; Foakes (1968) same as Wilson; Brooke (1990) similar to Wilson, cites Empson; Braunmuller (1997) same as Wilson; Miola (2004) defines «weal.»

25 Lucretius, *De Rerum*, V.1136-50.

26 Braunmuller, 1997: «she repeats words that the audience supposes Macbeth said.» Hunter, 1967: quotes Wilson's «abyss at her feet» remark. Muir, 1951/72: Cites Bradley, and «In I.vii Macbeth never appeals to moral principles, and he would jump the life to come.» Wilson, 1950/60: «A sudden glimpse into the abyss at her feet.» Notes the candle and I.v.49. Miola, 2004/xiii, cites Judi Dench's Macbeth apparently returns to Christianity in V.ix, but sticks to «as fast as time.»

Shakespeare's Iago and Santiago Matamoros

Shakespeare's source for *Othello* is a story from Giraldi Cinthio's *Hecatommithi*, in which the villain is simply designated by his military rank, *Alfiero*, meaning ensign or ancient. But Shakespeare chose to name him Iago, Spanish for Jacob or James. As has been noted by various scholars, this name is appropriate for several reasons.[1] In Hebrew it means the one who supplants or undermines,[2] apt for the role of Iago. Further, Saint James or Santiago is the patron saint of Spain, and his name was the national war cry heard by the English from 1585 to 1604, giving it a hostile sound to English ears.

The name of this saint had been invoked as an anti-Protestant battle cry on the English stage a decade before *Othello*. Christopher Marlowe made Saint James the chosen patron of two assassins in *The Massacre at Paris*. During the St Bartholomew's Day Massacre at the start of the play, the murderer Mountsorrell says to a Protestant victim: «*Sanctus Jacobus*, he's my saint; pray to him.»[3] At the end of the play, an unnamed friar stabs Henry III with the cry: «*Sancte Jacobe*, now have mercy on me!»[4] The friar who actually killed Henry III was in fact named Jacques and was a member of the Jacobin order.

But there is further appropriateness that seems to have gone unnoticed in tracing Shakespeare's Iago to Santiago of Spain, which lies in the latter's surname, Matamoros. Santiago's particular role in Spanish history is as the spiritual leader of the Reconquest, and he is said to have appeared over thirty times on the battlefield, mounted and armed, to lead the soldiers of Spain against the Moors.[5] After 1492 Santiago continued to be seen leading Spanish and Portuguese soldiers to victory over the infidels in Africa, Asia, and the Americas. *Matamoros* means the killer of Moors, and the iconography of Santiago often shows his horse trampling on a decapitated Moor. As the symbol of unrelenting enmity towards the Moors, Iago is an excellent name for the nemesis of Othello, the Moor of Venice.

Endnotes

1   The symbolism of the name Iago is discussed in G. W. Knight, *The Sovereign Flower* (1958), 179, and in M. J. Levith, *What's in Shakespeare's Names* (Hamden, Connecticut, 1978), 54.

2   Genesis, 25:26, 27:36.

3   *Christopher Marlowe, The Complete Plays,* ed. J. B. Steane (1969), I.vi.23.

4   Ibid., V.v.34.

5   On Santiago, see T. D. Kendrick, *St James in Spain* (1960), I, particularly p. 24.

A Biblical Echo in *Romeo and Juliet*

When Capulet berates his daughter for refusing to wed Paris, the Nurse protests his harshness, drawing the response: «And why, my Lady Wisdom? Hold your tongue,/Good Prudence! Smatter with your gossips, go» (III.v.170-1).[1] This note identifies Capulet's words as echoing the Book of Proverbs, while providing a context for understanding his reference to «Lady Wisdom.»

Wisdom is personified as a woman in Proverbs, as well as in the apocryphal Wisdom of Solomon and Ecclesiasticus.[2] She is the «eternal worde of God»; «the scholemastres of the knowledge of God»; who understands astronomy, meteorology, and biology; and who comprehends both tables of the Ten Commandments.[3] The unity of the personification across the three books may be seen in their full titles in the Geneva Bible: The Proverbes of Salomon, The Wisdome of Salomon, and The Wisdome of Iesus the sonne of Sirach, called Ecclesiasticus.[4]

Shakespeare knew these three biblical books well, using them in over thirty of his plays.[5] He also cites personified Wisdom in *1 Henry IV*, where Prince Hal paraphrases Proverbs: «wisdom cries out in the streets and no man regards it» (I.ii.87-8).[6]

Capulet's sarcasm to the Nurse echoes the Geneva Bible's translation of Proverbs 8:12, «I wisdome dwell with [d]prudence and I finde forthe knowledge *and* counsels.» The marginal note on prudence adds: «d That is, except a man haue wisdome, w[c] is y[e] true knowledge of God, he can nether be prudent nor good counseller.» Compare Capulet's sequence, «Wisdom ... Prudence ... Smatter with your gossips,» to Proverbs' «wisdome ... prudence ... counsels,» reinforced by the marginal note's «wisdome ... prudent ... counseller.» Note also the contemptuous parallel of «smatter with your gossips» to «finde forthe knowledge *and* counsels.»

Among her counsels, Wisdom provides guidance on raising children. Proverbs advises on bringing up boys, typically: «He y[t] spareth his rod, hateth his sonne» (13:24).[7] Ecclesiasticus adds different rules for girls, essentially: «If thy daughter be not shamefast, holde her straitly, lest she abuse her self thorowe ouer muche liberitie» (26:10).[8] In other words, Capulet implies that the Nurse has failed in her duty as a duenna. Finally, Capulet puts the Nurse in her place socially by demoting her from Lady Wisdom to Good Prudence. The honorific Good or Goody or Goodwife ranked well below Lady, while Prudence was regarded as a lower-class name.[9]

Alternatives to the Geneva text are offered by the Great Bible of 1539 and the Bishops' Bible of 1568. The former reads: «I wysdome haue my dwellyng with knowledge, and prudent cou[n]cell is myne awne.»[10] This translation includes the three key words in the right sequence, «wysdome ... prudent cou[n]cell,» but where the Geneva specifies «prudence» as the companion of Wisdom, the Great Bible offers «knowledge» as the housemate. The Bishops' Bible reads: «I wisedome dwell with counsell, and finde out knowledge and vnderstanding,»[11] which, incidentally, changes the Geneva's «finde for the» to the modern usage, «find out.»[12] This version, however, omits any form of the word «prudence.» The Geneva Bible is significantly closer to Capulet's words than either of the other two possibilities, entitling this passage to join the thirty or so other instances where Shakespeare clearly relied on the Geneva Bible.[13]

Endnotes

1   Shakespeare quotes are from *The Arden Shakespeare Complete Works*, ed. Richard Proudfoot *et al.* (London, 1998).

2   On the female personification, see Proverbs 1-4 and 7-9; all of Wisdom; and Ecclesiasticus 1, 4, 6, 14, 15, 18, 24, 25, and 51.

3   Proverbs 1:20, note «q»; Wisdom 8:4; Ecclesiasticus 43 and Wisdom 7:17-20; and Proverbs 3:3, note «b,» as well as all three books on human conduct generally.

4   *The Geneva Bible, A Facsimile of the 1560 Edition*, intro. Lloyd E. Berry (Madison, Wisconsin, 1969).

5   Richmond Noble, *Shakespeare's Biblical Knowledge* (London, 1935), 287-8,

291-2. Naseeb Shaheen, *Biblical References in Shakespeare's Plays* (Newark, Delaware, 1999), 789-91, 798-800.

6 Proverbs 1:20, 24; Shaheen, 409-10.

7 See also Proverbs 19:18, 22:6, 15; 23:13-14; and 29:15, 17.

8 See also Ecclesiasticus 7:24-5; 36:21; and 42:9-11.

9 On the name Prudence, see Anne Barton, *Ben Jonson, Dramatist* (Cambridge, 1984), 276, and Ben Jonson, *The New Inn,* ed. Michael Hattaway (Manchester, 1984), 59 n. 37.

10 *The Great Bible: A Facsimile of the 1539 Edition,* ed. Yoshio Terasawa (Tokyo, 1991).

11 Bishops' Bible, *The Holy Bible: conteyning the Olde Testament and the Newe* (London, 1595).

12 *OED* «forth,» A. adv., 8. … the adv. was formerly used in many idiomatic combinations with verbs, where for the most part *out* is now substituted. *Obs.*

13 Shaheen, *Biblical References*, 39-40.

Kill, Kill, Kill

Shakespeare repeats the word «kill» at three places in his works. *Venus and Adonis* has «And in a peaceful hour doth cry, ‹Kill, kill!›» (652) *Coriolanus* features «Kill, kill, kill, kill kill him.» (V.vi.130) Finally, *King Lear* provides:

> And when I have stolen upon these son-in-laws,
> Then kill, kill, kill, kill, kill, kill!
> (IV.v. 79 or IV.vi.188, depending on the edition)

It may be added that the French equivalent, *tue, tue, tue,* is found twice in Marlowe's *The Massacre at Paris*, in scenes vii and xii. Edmond Malone asserted that «[t]his was formerly the word given in the English army, when an onset was made on the enemy,» and he offered an example from the 1610 edition of *The Mirrour for Magistrates*:

> For while the Frenchmen fresk assaulted still,
>   Our Englishmen came boldly forth at night,
> Crying St. George, Salisbury, *kill, kill,*
>   And offered freshly with their foes to fight.[1]

Other literary examples of «kill, kill» as an English war cry have been noted in the works of John Cotgrave and Michael Drayton, and in Sir Thomas North's *Plutarch*.[2] The purpose of this article is to show with examples taken from the battlefield, rather than from writers who may never have seen combat, that English and French soldiers of that period actually did use that expression.

The first instances come from a fascinating but little studied work, the memoirs of Elis Gruffydd, a Welsh soldier of long service under Henry VIII and Edward VI.[3] In October 1544, the Dauphin of France (the future Henry II) launched a famous night attack to retake English-held Boulogne. The French overran the lower part of the town, Basse Boulogne, but the English sortied from the houses and then from the citadel above:

Then the Englishmen smote their enemies valiantly and killed them in the cruellest way, at which time the gate of Upper Boulogne was opened and a large number of soldiers dribbled out shouting loudly their warcry «Kill, kill.» These words the Dauphin heard and they abashed the pride of his heart which had been lifted up with the greatest joy while he heard the voice of the French shouting Tuwe tuwe tuwe.[4]

In 1545, the French were holding the fortress of Ardres on the edge of the English Pale, where much of the local population had been French subjects of the King of England for two centuries. They attempted to starve Ardres into submission.

A company of French happened to come with food. The people of Guisnes [an English possession near Calais] got wind of this and went into ambush in the forest between Ardres and Licques. There the French fell into the lap of the men of Guisnes who struck at them crying their cry in English Kil kil kil. This made the French turn and flee back to Licques.[5]

The English cry was recorded in the *Commentaires* of Blaise de Monluc, a Marshal of France. In 1544 de Monluc, then a captain, and a few companions encountered a large troop of Englishmen, who challenged:

Who goeth there? c'est-a-dire: Qui va la? Je leur respondis en anglais: *A friend! a friend!* qui veut dire: amy! amy!... Comme ces Anglois eurent faict d'aultres demandes, et que je feuz au bout de mon latin, ilz poursuyvirent en criant: *quil! quil! quil!* c'est-a-dire: tue! tue! tue![6]

A final French example is found in Motley's *Dutch Republic* concerning the 1583 assault on Antwerp, launched by the Duke of Anjou, longtime suitor to Queen Elizabeth.

Along these great thoroughfares [leading to the center of the city] the French soldiers advanced at a rapid pace, the cavalry clattering furiously in the van, shouting: «Ville gaignee, ville gaignee! vive la messe, vive la messe! tue, tue, tue!»[7]

In short, Malone was substantially correct about Shakespeare's «kill, kill,» though a better definition might be «a war cry used by both French and English.»

Endnotes

1 E. Malone, *The Plays and Poems of William Shakespeare*, (1821), x, 233-4, and 315.

2 P. Brockbank, *The Arden Shakespeare, Coriolanus* (1976), 309-10 and F. T. Prince, *The Arden Shakespeare, The Poems* (1960), 37.

3 M. B. Davies, *Bulletin of the Faculty of Arts, Fouad University* (Cairo), «Suffolk's Expedition to Montdidier» (July 1944), vii, 33-43; «The ‹Enterprises› of Paris and Boulogne» (May 1949), xi, i, 37-95; and «Boulogne and Calais from 1545 to 1550» (May 1950), xii, i, 1-90.

4 Davies, «The ‹Enterprises› of Paris and Boulogne,» 90.

5 Davies, «Boulogne and Calais from 1545 to 1550,» 2.

6 Blaise de Monluc, *Commentaires et Lettres* (Paris, 1864), i, ii, 299. [Who goeth there? that is to say: *Qui va la!* I answered them in English: A friend! that says: *ami! ami!* ... As these English made other questions, and as I was at the end of my Latin (i.e., at my wit's end), they pursued shouting: kill! kill! kill! that is to say: *tue! tue! tue!*]

7 J.L. Motley, *The Complete Works* (1863), v, 301. [The city is won! Long live the mass! Kill, kill, kill!]

Part Two:
An Oxfordian Foundation

The Abysm of Time:
The Chronology of Shakespeare's Plays

The ... use of transcribing these things, is to shew what absurdities
men for ever run into, when they lay down an hypothesis, and
afterward seek for arguments in the support of it.
> Richard Farmer, *An Essay on the Learning of Shakespeare*
> (London, 1767, 1821), 30.

In 1930 Sir Edmund Chambers published the third and final version of
his dating scheme for Shakespeare's plays in Volume I of his *William
Shakespeare: A Study of Facts and Problems*, his two earlier versions being
found in his article on Shakespeare in the 1911 edition of *The Encyclopaedia Britannica* and in Volume III of his 1923 *The Elizabethan Stage*. In
1980 Ernest Honigmann, in *Shakespeare's Impact on His Contemporaries*,
examined Chambers' chronology, noted that nobody had attempted to
replicate the process, pointed out several flaws in it, and said that
Chambers' start date was too late, that the plays really began earlier.

Honigmann's views on Chambers' lateness are supported by many
other scholars; in fact, virtually every post-1930 student of the dating
issue agrees that Chambers' dates are too late. These dissenters include
Peter Alexander,[1] Andrew Cairncross,[2] F. P. Wilson,[3] John Crow, T. W.
Baldwin,[4] William Matchett,[5] Oscar James Campbell and Edward
Quinn,[6] and Russell Fraser[7] —a list that could be expanded considerably.
In fact, it is now completely orthodox to say that Chambers' chronology
is too late, and to grant that his scholarship is a bit dated.

In this article, I will support Honigmann and the others, and it may be
asked what I have to offer, given that I seem to be singing in a chorus of
near unanimity. To begin with, I will add some new points to Honigmann's, both about the chronology as a whole and about some individual plays. Otherwise, I wish to examine an astonishing fact—nearly
every authority who discusses the subject agrees that Chambers' dates
are too late, and yet those dates still stand.

Chambers spreads Shakespeare's plays fairly evenly across the period 1590 to 1613. John Crow revised Chambers' Shakespeare article in the *Britannica* around 1960, noting that recent «scholarship has found a tendency to push back the dates of the earlier plays [from the dates given by Chambers] ... As, however, Chambers' [*William Shakespeare*] remains the standard scholarly life of Shakespeare, it is convenient to retain his order and chronology.»[8] In the 1974 *Riverside Shakespeare*, G. Blakemore Evans moves *1 Henry VI* back to 1589-90 and *Merry Wives* back three years to 1597, but his dates for the other plays stay within one year of Chambers'. The *Britannica's* Shakespeare article was completely rewritten in the early 1980s by John Russell Brown and T. J. B. Spencer, who move the start of the *Henry VI* trilogy back one year to 1589, shift *Twelfth Night* forward one year, and otherwise leave Chambers' scheme intact. The 1986 Oxford *William Shakespeare, The Complete Works*, edited by Stanley Wells and Gary Taylor, does not provide the usual chronological table of the plays, but estimates that Shakespeare's works begin in the late 1580s or early 1590s. However, the prefaces to the individual plays simply rearrange Chambers' sequence slightly, moving *Titus Andronicus*, *Taming of the Shrew*, and *Merry Wives* around a bit; otherwise, Wells and Taylor stick with Chambers.

Moreover, as Honigmann notes (55), no one has attempted to reconstruct the entire dating scheme as Chambers did. Anyone today who wants to see the dating evidence for one of Shakespeare's plays looks in an up-to-date work, such as a recent edition of the play in question, rather than at Chambers. Yet anyone who wants to see the standard dating scheme built up from scratch must still consult Chambers. This point is critically important because so many plays are dated with respect to one another. For example, most editors say that the date of *Hamlet* can be established partly by the fact that it is later than *Julius Caesar*. But when was *Julius Caesar* written? Attempts to date individual plays inevitably rest on assumptions about the solidity of the dating scheme for all of the plays, which carries us right back to Chambers.

In short, Chambers dead is stronger than his successors alive. And now we will look at Chambers' methods and at the flaws in those methods.

We will then consider whether Shakespeare's plays may have begun in the 1580s and whether they continue until 1613. Finally, we will examine the dating evidence for a number of specific plays.

Chambers' «Given»

Chambers explains in his Britannica article that his chronology:

> is certainly not a demonstration, but in the logical sense an hypothesis which serves to colligate the facts and is consistent with itself and with the known events of Shakespeare's external life.

In *Elizabethan Stage*, Chambers offers the «conjecture» that:

> Shakespeare's first dramatic job, which earned him the ill will of [Robert] Greene [in the 1592 *Greene's Groatsworth*], was the writing or re-writing of *1 Henry VI*... in the early spring of 1592. (III.130)

In *William Shakespeare*, Chambers again affirms his belief that Shakespeare's dramatic debut was recorded in *Greene's Groatsworth* (I.58-9), but research performed in the 1920s by Peter Alexander on *2 & 3 Henry VI* forced Chambers to move back his start date. That Chambers was willing to change his widely publicized opinion is to his credit as a scholar,[9] but he changed his start date as little as the new evidences allowed. He first moved the start to 1591, «the earliest year to which there is ground for ascribing any dramatic work by Shakespeare that we know of» (I.59). Yet then, in his table of dates, he puts the two Henry VI plays at 1590-1[10] in the same work. Chambers spoke of:

> fitting this order [of the plays] into the time allowed by the span of Shakespeare's dramatic career (I.253).

He also writes of fitting pieces of evidence:

> into the facts of Shakespeare's dramatic career as given in chapter iii. There is much of conjecture, even as regards the order [of the plays],

and still more as regards the ascriptions to particular years. These are partly arranged to provide a fairly even flow of production (I.269).

In short, the bedrock of Chambers' chronology, the «given» to which all that follows must conform—as in a proof in geometry—is that the sequence of Shakespeare's plays must be spread across the years 1590 to 1613.[11] The unhappy result is the method of Procrustes, described by Ben Jonson to William Drummond as, «that tyrant's bed, where some who were too short were racked, others too long cut short». This is what Chambers' dating scheme amounts to: an attempt to force the plays, in their proper sequence[12]—early, middle, late—into the span of 1590-1613.

I will argue that Chambers' dates for Shakespeare's plays are several years too late from start to finish. In other words, the plays started well back in the 1580s, and, as far as the evidence shows, ended well before 1613. Moreover, I will argue that only one play can be dated with reasonable firmness to a period as narrow as eighteen months, namely *Comedy of Errors* to mid-1587 to December 1588. Any table of dates that assigns each play to a particular year, no matter how environed with cautions and qualifications about the uncertainty of it all, is mere wishful thinking.

Chambers' Errors

Chambers committed four general errors in his construction of Shake-speare's chronology, all of which are neatly summarized by Honigmann (70-8). What is most notable about these four errors is that Chambers knew that he was in the wrong on three of them. Here are the four items: relying on Francis Meres' 1598 list; interpreting Philip Henslowe's «ne» as «new»; treating flimsy earliest possible dates as firm evidence; and assuming that Shakespeare improved other men's plays.

Francis Meres lists six comedies and six tragedies of Shakespeare's in his 1598 *Palladis Tamia,* and Chambers follows Edmond Malone in supposing that 1598 is the earliest possible date for plays not named by

Meres. Consequently Chambers writes «No mention by Meres» against eight plays in his table of boundary dates (I.246-50), despite the fact that he knew or believed that the three parts of *Henry VI* and *Taming of the Shrew*, both omitted by Meres, were earlier than 1598. Moreover, as Chambers could hardly help but know, the symmetrically minded Meres devised his lengthy list of comparisons by balancing exactly so many works of one sort against exactly so many of another, e.g., six comedies against six tragedies. Meres maintains the balance of his entry on Shakespeare by combining the two parts of *Henry IV* together as one tragedy, and so he could easily have listed *Henry VI* as another tragedy and *Shrew* as another comedy—unless he was unaware of these (and other) plays, or unless he was not pretending to be exhaustive.

Philip Henslowe, businessman and theater owner, kept a sort of account book from 1592 to 1603 in which are found hundreds of entries relating to the stage. Several score plays listed by Henslowe have beside them the word «ne», including *1 Henry VI* for 3 March 1592 and *Titus Andronicus* for 24 January 1594. Chambers and his contemporaries took Henslowe's «ne» to mean «new» in some sense or other, even though they were aware that the mysterious term sometimes appears next to plays that were not new, though they might conceivably have been newly revised. As a result, Chambers gained questionable earliest possible dates for two more of Shakespeare's plays, as well as for the non-Shakespearean plays so marked, thereby locking dozens of dramas into the period after 1591.

However, a more complete edition of Henslowe's account book than the version relied upon by Chambers was published in 1961, edited by R. A. Foakes and R. T. Rickert, which includes lengthy extracts from Henslowe's pawnbroking business. Henslowe frequently describes the condition of the pledges left with him by borrowers, often describing clothes and suchlike as «new» or «newe», but never as «ne». Thus, the plausible, if questionable, old assumption that «ne» meant «new» shifts into the category of implausible, particularly given that «ne» was still a current word in English, meaning approximately what it does in French, «not» or «nor». Henslowe's «ne» may mean no more than that something, probably connected with money, did not occur at the performances in question. More to the point, the enigmatic «ne» can no longer be considered to indicate an earliest possible date, and so dozens of plays, including two of Shakespeare's, lose their moorings and are free to drift backward.

It is often observed that the evidence available to scholars for dating plays from Shakespeare's period is of uneven quality. In particular, latest possible dates tend to be hard evidence, such as a record of performance, entry in the Stationers' Register, or a play's actual appearance in print with the year on the title page. Earliest possible dates, on the other hand, tend to be weak in foundation, such as absence from Francis Meres' list, the presence of Philip Henslowe's «ne», dubious topical allusions (on which more later), possible echoes of one writer's words by another author when it is not at all clear who wrote first, and the like. Honigmann (78) tactfully states that Chambers «failed to recognise» this very obvious fact, but Chambers did indeed know it:

> As a rule the initial dates are much less certain than the terminal ones. (I.245)

Chambers goes on to provide examples of what he means, but he gives earliest possible dates to nineteen plays in his table of boundary dates. Ten are from Meres and Henslowe, and most of the others are no better. The exceptions to this rule are *Henry V* (on which see below), *Henry VIII*, and *Two Noble Kinsmen*. The last two plays are generally agreed to have been started by Shakespeare but finished by John Fletcher, and Chambers' earliest possible dates for the two refer to their completion by Fletcher. Unfortunately, we have no evidence that the two men collaborated side by side, so that knowing when Fletcher worked on these plays is of no help in deciding when Shakespeare wrote his parts.

Scholars assumed from the late eighteenth century to the early twentieth that Shakespeare routinely rewrote plays by other authors, that is, that he was something of a plagiarist during the first half of his career. In particular, *2 & 3 Henry VI*, as we find them in the *First Folio* of 1623, were believed to be Shakespeare's upgrades of *The First part of the Contention*, published in 1594, and *The true Tragedie of Richard Duke of Yorke*, published in 1595; that Shakespeare's *Hamlet*, published in 1604, was a revision of what came to be called the *Ur-Hamlet*, a play written no later than 1589 and published in 1603; that Shakespeare's *King John* was based on *The Troublesome Raigne of John, King of England*, published in 1591; and that Shakespeare's *Taming of the Shrew* was a new version of *Taming of A Shrew*, published in 1594. In these matters, Chambers was a man of his era, but scholarship moves on. *The First part of the Contention* and *The true Tragedie* were shown to be inferior versions of *2 & 3 Henry VI*; the 1603 edition of *Hamlet* was proven to be a piracy of Shakespeare's play, not of the mythical *Ur-Hamlet* (see below); Shakespeare's *Shrew* is overwhelmingly viewed by modern scholars as the source for the other *Shrew*; and though the debate still rages on the two plays of *King John*, the balance of opinion is swinging in favor of Shakespeare's play as the original (see below). In short, Shakespeare is now seen as the victim of imitators, and hence another support for Chambers' late dates crumbles.

We have been looking at the earliest possible dates that Chambers used to backstop his late dates, and we have seen that his props collapse one after another. We gain further insight into his chronology by looking at the generally solid latest possible dates for thirty-three of Shakespeare's dramas (I.246-50).[13] In order to cram Shakespeare's plays into the chosen bracket of 1590-1613, Chambers uses his flimsy earliest possible dates to force the great majority of the plays to within one or two years of their respective latest possible dates. More specifically, he assigns the composition of twenty-seven of those thirty-three plays to within two years of their latest possible dates. As the fragile props shatter, common sense tells us that most of those plays must have been written earlier than the dates given by Chambers.

Did Shakespeare's Plays Begin in the 1580s?

We will now turn to the 1580s. Chambers would not place any of Shakespeare's plays earlier than 1590, and the boldest post-Chambers scholars generally do no more than place «?1589» next to one or two of

Shakespeare's earliest plays. Indeed, Chambers might argue that no evidence exists of any Shakespearean activity from the earlier decade. We shall see that this is not entirely true, but first we need to establish the historical context. How much do we know about theatrical activities in the 1580s? If Shakespeare was active in that decade, what traces should we expect to find?

Edmund Chambers provides this description of our knowledge of the history of the English stage before 1592 (that is, Before Henslowe).

> The fragmentary nature of the evidence makes a dramatic history of the period extremely difficult. The work of even the best-known writers is uncertain in extent and chronology, and much of it has come down in mutilated form. Marlowe's authorship of *Tamburlaine* is a matter of inference; it is only by an accident that we know the *Spanish Tragedy* to be Kyd's. (I.55)

F. P. Wilson offered this opinion in 1951.

> Admittedly, few of the plays acted in the fifteen-eighties have survived. So serious are the losses that the historian of the Elizabethan drama—especially of this period, before the practice of printing plays to be read became popular—often feels himself to be in the position of a man fitting together a jigsaw, most of the pieces of which are missing.[14]

Twenty years later G. E. Bentley discussed why he began his examination of playwrights in Shakespeare's era in the year 1590.

> Perhaps I ought to explain the chronological limits which I have set [i.e., 1590-1642]. ... Before 1590 ...records are so scanty, and such a large proportion apply to amateur or semiprofessional theatrical activities, that conclusions about working conditions must be very shaky. One cannot even be sure that a profession of play-writing had yet developed.[15]

Thus, our difficulty in finding evidence of Shakespeare's activities before 1590 is easily explained by the fact that, in terms of theatrical history, the 1580s are the Dark Ages. Yet we have real evidence that Shakespeare was writing in that decade, evidence that was known to Chambers, but which he ignored or distorted because it did not fit his preconceptions.

We may begin with the poem Ben Jonson wrote in praise of Shakespeare for the 1623 First Folio:

> For, if I thought my judgement were of yeeres,
>   I should commit thee surely with thy peeres,
> And tell, how farre thou didst our Lily out-shine,
>   Or sporting Kid, or Marlowes mighty line.

Jonson is saying that in the matter of years, or time, Shakespeare is a peer of Lyly, Kyd, and Marlowe; in other words, they were all contemporary. Most of Lyly's plays are from the 1580s, and though he lived until 1606, his involvement in the theater ended in 1590. Marlowe started as a writer in the 1580s and was killed in 1593. Kyd's plays began in the 1580s, and he died in 1594. Jonson had a strong sense of theatrical development, as indicated by his complaint in the Induction to *Bartholomew Fair* that *Titus Andronicus* and *The Spanish Tragedy* were out of date. In his «Ode to Himself» of around 1629 he made a similar sneer at *Pericles*. Lyly, Kyd, and Marlowe were men whose literary careers ended before Jonson's began, all were writers of the eighties, and these are the men Jonson chose to call Shakespeare's contemporaries.

Titus Andronicus is dated 1593-4 by Chambers, who calls it Shakespeare's sixth play, in which the 1985 *Encylopaedia Britannica* concurs. The Induction to Ben Jonson's *Bartholomew Fair*, written for a performance before King James on «the one and thirtieth day of October, 1614», criticizes, «He that will swear, *Jeronimo* [*The Spanish Tragedy*] or [*Titus*] *Andronicus*, are the best plays yet, shall pass unexcepted at here, as a man whose judgment shews it is constant, and hath stood still these five and twenty or thirty years.» In other words, Jonson is proclaiming that those two plays were written between 1584 and 1589.[16] Moreover,

Jonson's sequence of titles and dates is *Spanish Tragedy*/twenty-five and *Titus Andronicus*/thirty, implying that the former was written around 1589 and the latter around 1584.

Chambers cannot accept Jonson's clear statement, so he dismisses it as «rather vague» (I.319). He and his followers rely on Henslowe's «ne» next to a record of performance of *Titus* in January 1594, but he acknowledges several problems. The title page of the first Quarto of *Titus* states that it was acted by Pembroke's Men, which collapsed in August 1593, being forced to sell their costumes and scripts. Further, *A Knack to Know a Knave*, known to have been performed in June 1592, has a clear reference to *Titus*.[17] The lack of value of this particular example of Henslowe's «ne» is indicated by these items, known to Chambers, as well as by the fact that Henslowe put «ne» next to a performance of *Jeronimo/Spanish Tragedy* of January 1597.

Let us return to the alleged vagueness of Ben Jonson, a writer known as a stickler in matters of detail. We know the date of the royal performance of *Bartholomew Fair* because Jonson put it in the Induction. We have little trouble dating Jonson's early plays because he put the year of first performance for each play in his *Works* of 1616. The Induction to Jonson's *Cynthia's Revels* of late 1600 implies that *The Spanish Tragedy* was then twelve years old, dating it back to 1588. This date is quite consistent with his 1614 statement that *The Spanish Tragedy* was then about 25 years old, and the best estimate of modern scholars is that it was written around 1588 or 1589. The Induction to *Cynthia's Revels* also says that it has been twenty years since «Monsieur» (the brother of the King of France) came to England. Monsieur made two trips to England in pursuit of the elusive hand of Queen Elizabeth, one in 1579, the other in 1581, and so, taking the average, Jonson is right on target. When Jonson died in 1637 he left an unfinished play, *The Sad Shepherd*, and his friend Lord Falkland confirmed that Jonson was working on it just before he died.[18] Its Prologue opens with the announcement that the author has been writing public entertainments for 40 years, and from other sources we know that Jonson's first full play appeared around 1597. Jonson's dates are accurate, even from his deathbed.

In sum, objective scholarship would place *Titus Andronicus* no later than 1589.

I noted earlier that Honigmann refers to most of the earliest possible dates given by Chambers as «soft,» while Chambers himself rates them as «much less certain» than his latest possible dates. Yet it is instinctive to examine a number of solid earliest possible dates that Chambers excluded from consideration, as these reveal most clearly how he operated. I begin with a trivial example to provide contrast to the non-trivial examples that follow.

Romeo and Juliet is based on a poem that was published in 1562, but Chambers omits that datum from his table of earliest possible dates because neither he nor anyone else thinks that *Romeo and Juliet* could have been written anywhere near so early. This particular omission is reasonable, but the spirit behind it calls for ignoring evidence that does not fit one's preconceptions.

Most of Shakespeare's English history plays are based on Holinshed's Chronicles of 1587, which ought therefore to be the earliest possible date for *1, 2, & 3 Henry VI, Richard III, Richard II,* and *1 & 2 Henry IV.* Chambers, however, was unwilling to contemplate the possibility of Shakespeare writing in the 1580s, and so he left all but two of these plays without any earliest possible date. In other words, the earliest possible date is before 1590, therefore, Chambers ignores it. Chambers does give an earliest possible date of March 1592 for *1 Henry VI,* but that date is based on Henslowe's uninterpretable «ne.» Otherwise, Chambers offers 1595 as the earliest possible date for *Richard II* based on a weak theory that Samuel Daniel saw a performance that year. Unfortunately, nothing whatsoever indicates that the performance Daniel may or may not have seen was of a new play or of one written some years earlier.

King John is likewise based on the 1587 edition of Holinshed, but Chambers believed that Shakespeare's play also used *The Troublesome Reign of King John,* published in 1591, as a source. We will return to the relationship between the two King John plays, but, given his assumptions, Chambers should have listed 1591 as the earliest possible date for *King John*. However, Chambers believed that Shakespeare had written twelve plays before *King John*, so he could not contemplate an earliest possible date of 1591, and thus *King John* has no earliest possible date in Chambers' table.

Then there is the interesting case of *Pericles*, published in 1609, which shares two jests virtually word for word with John Day's *Law Tricks*, published in 1608. Chambers' own formidable scholarship proved that *Law Tricks* was written in 1604,[19] and so the earlier assumption that the extremely imitative Day borrowed the two jests from Shakespeare was summarily reversed—Chambers' dating imperatives demanded that Shakespeare be the borrower. That unsupported assumption should at least have provided Chambers with a good earliest possible date for *Pericles*, namely 1604 (see below for further discussion). Yet Chambers' view of the Bard's career required him to date *Pericles* as closely as possible to its publication date, so he put it at 1608-9, and omitted any earliest possible date from his table.

This seems like a good place to summarize what we have seen so far. Chambers' 1930 chronology still stands, despite general agreement that it is too late, because no one has undertaken to redo his work. Moreover, Chambers' dates for individual plays, save for minor adjustments, are still found in the reference books. Chambers insists that Shakespeare's career began in 1590 or '91, despite the fact that he and subsequent scholars regard the 1580s as an unrecorded era in which major playwrights left few traces of their work. Nevertheless, Ben Jonson, a man who was extremely precise about the chronology of the English stage, gives us two very strong pieces of evidence that Shakespeare was writing in the 1580s. He classes Shakespeare with three dramatists whose careers ended between 1590 and 1594, and he testifies that *Titus Andronicus* was written between 1584 and 1589. The full implications of Chambers' *a priori* belief that Shakespeare's plays must be spread evenly across the period 1590 to 1613 become apparent as we examine his table of earliest and latest possible dates for Shakespeare's plays. Chambers buttresses his late dates with the useless evidence of Meres and Hens-lowe, and with the subsequently discredited belief that Shakespeare rewrote the plays of other dramatists, and hence necessarily came after them. Chambers dismisses the earliest possible date of 1587 for most of Shakespeare's English history plays because that date violates his pre-conceptions. Likewise, and even more tellingly, he ignores 1591 as the earliest possible date for *King John* and 1604 as the earliest date for *Pericles*. We already noted Chambers' dismissal of Ben Jonson's com-ment on the date of *Titus Andronicus* on specious grounds of vagueness. We now understand exactly how Chambers' dating methods work. He begins his examination of the evidence with his conclusion already determined, namely that the plays were written from 1590 to 1613, and he discards any evidence disagreeable to this outcome. One last point— virtually everyone says that Chambers' chronology is too late, *but no one has ever said that Chambers' dates are too early.*

I observed that nearly every subsequent commentator agrees that Chambers' dates are too late, and so I should recognize the exceptions. In his 1991 edition of *Shakespeare's Lives*, Samuel Schoenbaum repeats a statement from the original edition of 1970. Noting that some of Cham-bers' scholarship is obsolete, Schoenbaum remarks:

> His chronology has fared better.... His findings with respect to the chronology have worn so well that J. G. McManaway, in «Recent Studies in Shakespeare's Chronology,» *Shakespeare Survey 3* (1950), could offer only a few modifications.[20]

That is to say, in 1991 Samuel Schoenbaum, dean of American Shake-speare scholars, hailed Chambers' 1930 chronology as being pretty much intact as of 1950! I will rephrase that remark—Schoenbaum said in 1991 that Chambers' sixty-one year old chronology was in fairly good shape forty-one years ago! Schoenbaum's sentence on McManaway's article is impossible by its nature to falsify, but it blatantly ducks the problem, which has loomed ever larger since 1950. Yet Schoenbaum's first sentence on how well Chambers' chronology has fared is, in a sense, entirely correct. As I also observed earlier, Chambers' dates for Shakespeare's plays still stand.

Do Shakespeare's Plays Continue to 1613?

What are the implications for Shakespeare's chronology if his *King John* preceded *The Troublesome Reign of King John* that was printed in 1591, and if other arguments in favor of an early start for Shakespeare are accepted? Honigmann acknowledges that Shakespeare's earliest plays cannot be simply moved back a few years while «the rest of the chronology survives intact»:

> But it is not quite so simple: if the first plays are moved back into the 1580s, those of the middle period are also affected, and about half the canon must be re-dated. (54)

Honigmann never suggests that the latter half of the chronology would be unsettled by his strictures on Chambers' methods, but Andrew Cairncross took a more radical approach. Cairncross concludes *The Problem of Hamlet* by proposing a tentative chronology (182-3) that begins before 1589 and closes by placing *Tempest* after 1603. In this section we shall see that Cairncross' boldness in attacking Chambers' end date of 1613 is in full accord with the evidence that Chambers presents, and also with G. Blakemore Evans' 1974 review of that evidence.

Chambers follows his table of boundary dates with a discussion from which I have already extracted several quotes (I.250-69) on the difficulties of fixing Shakespeare's dramatic chronology. He starts by naming the four plays omitted from his table (see note 12), continuing with the remark that:

> for many others, especially in the Jacobean period, a considerable range of dating remains open.

Yet earlier Chambers gives his opinion on the evidence available for dating the plays that follow *Timon of Athens*, which he places in theatrical year 1607-08:

> The chronology of the plays becomes difficult at this point (I.86)

In other words, Chambers tells us that dating evidence begins to thin out after James I came to the throne in the spring of 1603, and it virtually dries up after 1607.

Perhaps subsequent scholarship has firmed things up, and so we turn to Evans' essay on «Chronology and Sources» in *The Riverside Shakespeare*. Evans (47) cites Chambers as providing the authoritative summation of all earlier scholars of the chronology; he also cites J. G. McManaway's 1950 review of Chambers' endeavors, while his table of dating evidence (48-56) includes the fruits of more recent scholarship. In addition, Evans tells us that, «it will be noticed that the dating set forth below [in the table] becomes somewhat firmer beginning with *Richard II* (1595)» (47). As we glance over Evans' dating table after *Richard II*, he seems to be right. Leaving aside the quality of the evidence, we do find more, and seemingly more precise, material for dating *Romeo and Juliet*, *Midsummer Night's Dream*, *Merchant of Venice*, and so on—until we come to *All's Well*, which Evans places at 1602-03, followed by *Measure for Measure* in 1604, and so on to the end, whereupon we realize that Chambers was absolutely correct. For *All's Well* Evans merely records publication in 1623; *Measure for Measure* performed 1604, published 1623; *Othello* performed in 1604, published 1622; *Macbeth* published 1623; *Antony and Cleopatra* registered in 1608, published 1623; *Coriolanus*, *Timon*, and *Tempest* were published in 1623.

One way or another Chambers, Cairncross, and Evans support the fading away of Shakespeare after about 1603 (not that the dynastic change seems to have had anything to do with it), and their testimony is reinforced by Kenneth Muir's *The Sources of Shakespeare's Plays* (1978).

Muir lists about 110 works as certain or probable sources for Shakespeare, of which slightly less than forty had appeared by 1575.[21] Then come almost seventy works that were published or performed during the period 1576-1604. The most notable concentration within the latter group consists of twelve works published in 1586-90, twenty-one works published in 1591-95, and eleven works published in 1596-1600. Then we find four works from 1601-03, followed by six titles from 1604-11.

I will now offer a general observation before going on to the post-1603 items. Shakespeare's reading shows a clear plateau for works published in the period 1586-1600. Even if we fully accept Muir's judgment, Shakespeare's reading or playgoing declined markedly after 1600. Other recent authorities on Shakespeare's sources, most notably Geoffrey Bullough, will be found to agree closely, if not perfectly, with Muir.

Now let us look at the six titles that appeared in 1604-11.[22] Only John Day's *Law Tricks* (performed 1604, published 1608) is called a certain source, namely for two items in *Pericles*. Otherwise we find William Camden's *Remains* (completed by June 1603; published 1605), Samuel Daniel's *Arcadia* (written and performed 1605; published 1606), and three Bermuda shipwreck pamphlets written in 1610 and said to be sources for *The Tempest*. Camden's and Daniel's works are thought to be the sources for two small items in, respectively, *Coriolanus* and *Macbeth*. These five works are said to be probable sources for Shakespeare; none is called a certain source. We can now sharpen the general observation made in the previous paragraph. Muir's scholarship and judgment unite to portray an author who read avidly during the last two decades of the sixteenth century—but who then lost interest in new books and plays.

Muir and various other scholars argue that Shakespeare consulted Camden's *Remains* for one small aspect of the fable of the belly speaking to the other members of the body in the opening scene of *Coriolanus* (I.i.95-139). Shakespeare's version of the fable is believed by Muir and others to represent a fusion of various versions of this tale, which was so well known that Sir Philip Sidney abbreviated it in his *Defense of Poesy* on the assumption that his readers would be familiar with it: «In the end, to be short (for the tale is notorious, and as notorious that it was a tale) ...».[23] Be that as it may, Camden's work was completed by June 1603 (the date on its dedicatory epistle), and so, as noted in the Arden edition of *Coriolanus* (24), Shakespeare could have read Camden's manuscript. Further, Camden's source was *Policraticus*, written by the twelfth century bishop and philosopher John of Salisbury, printed in 1476 and later. So Shakespeare may have known it directly or indirectly from John without the aid of Camden. Given that scholars credit Shakespeare with such extensive reading concerning this fable alone—the Arden edition names three other versions known to Shakespeare (29) — there is nothing improbable about such a contention.

Muir himself noticed a similarity between six lines in Daniel's *Arcadia* and six lines in *Macbeth*. But there are two problems with Muir's claim that Shakespeare «was apparently» echoing Daniel. First, the similarity is not so great as to compel any assumption that the two speeches are connected.[24] Second, as is so often the case in these matters, Muir says absolutely nothing to justify his assertion that Shakespeare echoes Daniel, rather than Daniel echoing Shakespeare.

Muir's contention that Shakespeare relied on the 1610 Bermuda and Virginia reports for various incidents in *The Tempest* can only be sustained by ignoring all the other nautical literature available to Shakespeare. In the discussion below, I show that more parallels to *The Tempest* can be found in two chapters in the Book of Acts of the Apostles (concerning St. Paul's shipwreck) than are claimed for the most important of the Bermuda pamphlets. The same could easily be done with Richard Hakluyt's famous work on voyaging, which, like St. Paul, but unlike the Bermuda pamphlet, did not have to be read in manuscript.

A Statement of the Dating Problem

Everyone agrees that the sequence of composition of Shakespeare's plays—early, middle, late—can be determined with reasonable certainty by considering the evolution of the author's style. A fairly firm chronology could be established if that sequence could be anchored to the calendar at a few widely spaced points—say, one early play, one middle play, one late play—and this is what Chambers tries unsuccessfully to do. When Chambers' chronology is exposed to the full weight of evidence, his seemingly strongest anchors drag easily, and the flow of the current is always backward.

The evidence available for establishing the date of composition of even one of Shakespeare's plays tends to be maddeningly scrappy and unsatisfactory. Some pieces of evidence are strong but vague, for example, the year the play was first put in print, establishing a firm latest possible date, but where everyone is quite sure that the play in question was written years earlier. Other evidence is precise but weak, most notoriously, suggested allusions to the sort of topical events that repeat themselves—riots, storms, political happenings, and the like. As Chambers explains: «both equivocation and coronations were common phenomena, to which any dramatist might refer at any date. So, too, were the plague and tempests and even eclipses» (I.246). Where several items might suggest the earliest possible date for a play, all should be listed; Chambers only took the ones he wanted.

A rule should be laid down that topical allusions should not be taken seriously as dating evidence unless the rarity or particular appropriateness of the suggested allusion is examined. Failure to observe this rule has resulted in a proliferation of absurdly weak topicalities being identified in Shakespeare's plays, for example, *Coriolanus* glancing at a 1609 waterworks project (III.i.95-6). A survey of such trifles leads to the conclusion that Chambers' chronology could be shifted twenty years in either direction—to 1570-1593 or to 1610-1633—and a bit of probing in the archives would produce an equally impressive (or unimpressive) list of topical correspondences to the plays, which is the whole point of Chambers' remark about common phenomena.

Another problem with topical references is that they were frequently added to revived plays, as will be discussed below under *Henry V*. In this case, their dating implications can reverse themselves, with an earliest possible date becoming a latest possible date.

In the same vein, suggestions that Shakespeare borrowed from this or that contemporary English author deserve to be ignored unless the suggester squares up to the possibility that the borrowing went the other way. We have already seen two examples of failure to heed this rule, namely, Chambers' unsupported opinion that *Pericles* borrows from Day's *Law Tricks*, and Muir's equally unsupported finding that *Macbeth* borrows from Daniel's *Arcadia*, and I will offer yet another.

Both *Troilus and Cressida* and Ben Jonson's 1601 *Poetaster* feature armed Prologues, and so, without a hint of argument as to why Jonson may not have borrowed from Shakespeare, scholars assert that Shakespeare was the borrower, and therefore *Troilus* is later than *Poetaster*. Kenneth Palmer in the 1982 Arden *Troilus* candidly explains that the latter's Prologue «is usually taken to be a reference to the Prologue of Jonson's *Poetaster*» (19), while Kenneth Muir in the 1984 Oxford *Troilus* remarks that, «There can be little doubt that the ‹Prologue arm'd› (I.23) is an allsion to the prologue in Jonson's *Poetaster*» (5). That the junior writer might perhaps be expected to borrow from the senior, and that the armed Prologue of *Troilus* is natured in a play about real warfare, as opposed to a play about a squabble between writers, have no force against the inertia of Chambers' dating imperatives.

We have already looked at the evidence for putting a date on *Titus Andronicus*, finding that, at a minimum, it should be dated not later than 1589, but more likely several years before that. We will now consider ten more plays and will see that their conventional dates do not stand up under scrutiny. As for the remaining twenty-seven plays—no precise dating is possible.

Comedy of Errors: France at War with her Heir

Comedy of Errors is dated 1592-3 by Chambers who calls it Shakespeare's fifth play. The 1985 *Encyclopaedia Britannica* dates and sequences it identically. Act III, scene ii includes this exchange: «Where France?», «In her forehead, armed and reverted, making war against her heir.»[25] These words make sense for only one period of French history, spring 1587 to December 1588, or, at latest, to August 1589, and they constitute the strongest internal evidence for the date of any of Shakespeare's plays.

In 1584, King Henry III of France lost his brother and heir, whereupon his brother-in-law and cousin, Henry de Bourbon, King of Navarre, became heir to the throne. Navarre was the leader of the Protestants in France's intermittent religious civil wars, but in 1584 he was residing in his mountain kingdom, at peace with the Catholics. Peace continued through December 1586, when Navarre rejected the King's demand that he change religions. The following spring Catholic armies massed against Navarre in what is known as the War of the Three Henries (the third Henry being the Catholic Duke de Guise), which culminated in Navarre's smashing victory at the Battle of Coutras in October. However, the Catholics rallied and the war continued through 1588. In December of that year Henry III, seeking to escape domination by Guise and desiring peace, had Guise assassinated, whereupon the Catholic forces turned on the King. Catholic France was still at war with the heir, Henry of Navarre, but also with its king, Henry III. This situation continued until Henry III was murdered in August 1589, whereupon Henry of Navarre became Henry IV of France with the dying blessings of Henry III. The war actually continued until Henry IV became a Catholic in 1593, but from the Protestant, English, and moderate French Catholic point of view, France was at war with the King, not the heir. From the ultra-Catholic point of view, Henry IV was neither king nor heir; they selected his elderly uncle as king, with the brother of the murdered Guise as heir.

Shakespeare's words precisely fit the situation between mid-1587 and August 1589, though they would be far less appropriate after December 1588, when «making war against her king» would seem more natural.

In fact, we find confirmatory evidence for this dating a few lines later: «Where America, the Indies?», «all o'er embellished with rubies, carbuncles, sapphires, declining their rich aspect to the hot breath of Spain, who sent whole armadoes of carracks.» Some scholars see here a reference to the Spanish Armada of 1588, which seems very unlikely. Shakespeare is not associating Spanish carracks with war, with danger to England, or with defeat—surely the associations caused in England by the defeat of the Armada—and the word «armada[o]» was in common use in England before 1588. Shakespeare associates carracks with treasure, which would be particularly appropriate after June 1587, when Sir Francis Drake captured the San Felipe, an immensely rich carrack returning from the Indies loaded with jewels, gold, silver, spices, and silks. The San Felipe was carrying a double load of treasure because her sister ship developed a leak and trans-shipped her load to the San Felipe. It took the English over a year to sell all the loot and fully realize the profit. The San Felipe was actually Portuguese, but Portugal was then ruled by the King of Spain, the carrack belonged to him, and her name is Spanish, not Portuguese.

I do not regard the capture of the San Felipe as clinching the case for 1587 as the year of composition of *Comedy of Errors*. Yet it perfectly meets Chambers' view that few topical references «are so definite as to be primary evidence; others at the most come in as confirmatory, after a provisional date has been arrived at on safer grounds» (I.245). As for the San Felipe, the association of Spanish or Portuguese treasure carracks with jewels and with the Indies could be made at any time, while the English captured other treasure ships, but still, there it is in mid-1587, right as the forces of Catholic France were moving against the heir to the throne.

The trouble with Chambers' seemingly cautious position on topical references is that it encourages less meticulous scholars to ignore the background against which the validity of suggested topical allusions must be judged. For example, if we provisionally date *King Lear* at 1605-06, and we note Gloucester's remark about the «late eclipses in the sun and moon» (I.ii.l07), and we further note that such eclipses were visible in Croatia in September and October 1605, being reported in England in February 1606, then we are apt to forget that eclipses occur in literally every year, that eclipses of both the sun and moon took place in 1601, and that astrology was a recurrent topic of discussion and concern in Shakespeare's age, in Shakespeare's plays, and in *King Lear*. Chambers' argument on topical references as confirmatory evidence implies that the topical evidence is strengthened by the fact that it agrees with some other piece of dating evidence, that is, the scholar of chronology need not closely examine the independent strength of the suggested topicality. I hold this implication to be false; each piece of dating evidence must stand on its own merits.

Chambers and later scholars almost unanimously affirm that Shakespeare's words about France refer to the Catholic war against Henry IV between 1589 and 1593, a theory that can be dismissed out of hand. Shakespeare says «heir,» not «king,» and if Chambers was serious, he would have produced examples of the English describing Henry IV as the «heir» after August 1589—that's what scholarship is all about. If he could have, he would have, but he couldn't.

R. A. Foakes in the 1962 Arden *Comedy of Errors* (xix, note 1) gives it a try. Foakes counters Peter Alexander and H. B. Charlton, who state that Henry of Navarre was the heir between 1584 and 1589, by pointing to: «the tracts of the period [1584-9], which refer to Henry always as King of Navarre, not heir to the French throne.» The obvious response to this statement is to note that Foakes conspicuously ignores the real point at issue, that is, the rank that English tracts bestowed on Henry after August 1589—King of France, not heir to the throne. An example is found in a pamphlet to which we will return, Gabriel Harvey's 1592 *Foure Letters and certaine Sonnets*: «That most valorous, and braue king [Henry]... Thrise happy Fraunce; though how vnhappy Fraunce, that hath such a Soueraine Head» (25-6). Otherwise, we see exactly what Richard Farmer meant about the absurdity of putting hypotheses ahead of facts. English tracts during 1584-9 quite properly refer to Henry as King of Navarre because that was his highest title; «heir to the French throne» is not a title at all, it is a condition or status. Even if Henry had (improperly) been made Dauphin, he would still have been called King of Navarre, as the title of King outranks the title of Dauphin. Meanwhile, if we ask why Shakespeare refers to Henry as heir and not King of Navarre, we must trudge through matters that were perfectly well known to Foakes. To say that France is at war with her heir is to call attention to an anomaly, which would not be the case in saying that France is at war with Navarre. Moreover, Shakespeare was obviously punning on heir/hair, for which see any annotated edition of *Comedy of Errors*.

Royal France, like England, had the doctrine that the king never dies, for as soon as one king breathes his last, his heir becomes king. Proclamations and coronations are mere formalities, however symbolically important they may seem. King Henry IV was immediately recognized by

England, and in September 1589 Queen Elizabeth loaned him 20,000 pounds and agreed to send 4,000 troops to his assistance. Objective scholars would date *The Comedy of Errors* during 1587-8.

Romeo and Juliet: The Earthquake

Romeo and Juliet is dated 1594-5 by Chambers and the *Britannica*, and they make it Shakespeare's tenth play. Early in the play the Nurse announces that, «Tis since the earthquake now eleven years» (I.iii.24) and «And since that time it is eleven years» (I.Ui.36). Late eighteenth and nineteenth century scholars noted that there was only one real quake in England in that period, in 1580, and so they dated *Romeo and Juliet* at 1591. Chambers acknowledges his predecessors' views, but cannot accept them, remarking that, «This is pressing the Nurse's interest in chronology—and Shakespeare's—rather hard.» (I.345) Yet Chambers will not deign to give evidence, beyond that odd statement. I call it odd because it amounts to saying that a character—and a play-wright—who take the trouble to give a precise date—twice—can't really be interested in precise dates.

However, Chambers' followers have done some scholarly homework, and are able to produce evidence of other seismic events in England. Unfortunately, the said evidence only highlights the impact of the 1580 earthquake—the other scholars would have done better to have left well enough alone. The 1984 Cambridge *Romeo and Juliet*, edited by G. Blakemore Evans, tells us that there were landslips at Blackmore, Dorset in 1583 and at Mottingham, Kent in 1585, while a line in a book published in 1595 «seems definitely to imply» that an earthquake shook England in 1585, apparently meaning that we can be quite certain that an earthquake either did or did not occur in England in 1585. An earthquake so feeble that its questionable effect on England is possibly implied in one line in one book is hardly the sort of cataclysm that one dates things by eleven years later (actually the 1585 quake was in Geneva). As for the two landslips, we may note that tremors so puny that their effects can be localized to single villages would also not have been exactly memorable to Shakespeare's London audiences.

Now let us turn our attention to the quake of 1580. The event, the damage, and the terror it caused among a populace unused to violent tremors are minutely described in the chronicles of Holinshed and Stow. A volume of letters between Edmund Spenser and Gabriel Harvey was published entitled «Three proper and wittie familiar Letters: lately passed betwene two Universitie men: touching the earthquake in Aprill last, and our English refourmed versifying.» At least four ballads were written on the subject; one begins «Quake, quake, 'tis tyme to quake. When towers and townes and all doo shake.» Another noted, as did Holinshed, that many people were in the theater that Sunday, instead of in church: «Come from the playe, come from the playe, The house will fall so people say.» Arthur Golding, a noted translator, was so shocked that he composed a «Discourse upon the Earthquake that hapned throughe this realme of England and other places of Christendom, the first of April 1580 ...», warning that the quake was God's punishment of wickedness.

Evans and other modern editors argue that, at any rate, *Romeo and Juliet* cannot be earlier than 1593 because Shakespeare's language was influenced by a 1592 work by John Eliot and a 1593 poem by Samuel Daniel. The similarity is slight, and, as usual, Evans and the others say absolutely nothing to justify the theory that Shakespeare was borrowing from Eliot and Daniel, rather than the more sensible idea that they were borrowing from him. One of the implications of defending Chambers' late dates is that everybody else influenced Shakespeare, while he influenced nobody.

I do not believe that the earthquake reference proves that *Romeo and Juliet* was written in 1591; as Chambers would say, it was a phenomenon to which a dramatist might refer at any date. That date, on the other hand, would be taken as rock solid if it suited Chambers' needs.

King John: A Question of Priority

The Troublesome Reign of King John (*TR*) was first published anonymously in 1591, reprinted as by «W. Sh.» in 1611, and reprinted as by «W.

Shakespeare» in 1622. Shakespeare's *King John* was mentioned by Francis Meres in 1598 and was first published in the *First Folio* of 1623. The two plays are so close in plot and characters that one must have borrowed from the other (unless we suppose a common lost source). Back in the days when everyone felt that Shakespeare regularly improved the plays of other men, it was natural to assume that Shakespeare was the borrower, which had the further advantage of agreeing with Chambers' dating scheme.

The first half of the twentieth century saw that judgment reversed, with Shakespeare seen as the victim of pirates. Peter Alexander and Andrew Caimcross both argued in books published in 1936 that *King John* came first and *TR* was the borrower, and, therefore. *King John* was written not later than 1591. In 1954 the second Arden *King John* appeared, edited by Ernest Honigmann, who proved that Shakespeare did extensive research for this play in the chronicles, and who went on to make a full blown case for the priority of *King John*. In 1963, William Matchett's Signet edition supported Honigmann with additional arguments on why Shakespeare's play came first. In *The Sources of Shakespeare's Plays* and elsewhere, Kenneth Muir has strongly supported the traditional view that *TR* came first. In 1974, R. L. Smallwood's New Penguin edition supported Muir against Honigmann and Matchett. In 1982 Honigmann published *Shakespeare's Impact on His Contemporaries*, which includes further arguments for the priority of Shakespeare's play over *TR*. Honigmann also states in his Preface (x-xi) the interesting fact that he abandoned the whole controversy for twenty-five years because (though this is not how he put it) he was warned by higher powers in academia to stop causing trouble. A. R. Braunmuller's 1989 Oxford edition sides with the traditional priority of *TR* over Shakespeare's play. L. A. Beaurline's 1990 New Cambridge edition supports Honigmann's view that Shakespeare's play came first. The most recent contribution to the debate that I have noticed is «*King John and The Troublesome Raigne*: Sources, Structure, Sequence» by Brian Boyd, *Philological Quarterly* (Winter 1995), which argues that Shakespeare's play came first. The battle is fairly joined.

King John is usually listed as Shakespeare's thirteenth play, based on stylistic considerations. If it must be moved back from Chambers' date of 1596-7 to 1591 or earlier, then about twelve other plays must be moved back earlier still, and Shakespeare must start his career around 1585 (which, in my opinion, is about right). Now we have a gap in the standard dating scheme between 1591 or earlier and 1596-7, and so, as Honigmann notes, later plays must be moved back to cover the gap.

I do not pretend that it is proven that Shakespeare's *King John* preceded *The Troublesome Reign*. The jury remains out, and the traditionalists make some valid points, but victory for the progressives on this play alone would finish whatever is still left of Chambers' chronology.

1 Henry IV: Gabriel Harvey's Pamphlet

1 & 2 Henry IV are put at 1597-8 by Chambers and the *Britannica*, and are said to be the Bard's fifteenth and sixteenth plays. Yet Gabriel Harvey in his *Foure Letters and certaine Sonnets* of 1592 uses the epithet «hotspur» three times and also writes that, «some old Lads of the Castell, haue sported themselues with their rappinge bable»,[26] which indicates that *1 Henry IV* may have been in existence in 1592. We will compare these two terms and a couple of others, all taken from Harvey's third and fourth letters, to some expressions from the first two acts of *1 Henry IV*.

The fat knight's original name was Oldcastle, but was changed to Falstaff out of deference to the descendants of the real Oldcastle, a proto-Protestant martyr. In *1 Henry IV* Hal refers to Falstaff as «my old Lad of the Castle» (I.ii.41), meaning a roisterer. Several editors note that John Stow's 1598 *Survey of London* mentions a brothel called the Castle in Southwark, and therefore think that Hal is jesting about Falstaff visiting prostitutes. Yet Stow writes that the twelve brothels of Southwark, including the Castle, were shut down by Henry VIII in 1546. Moreover, Stow refers to these brothels in the past tense, writing he has heard of the prostitutes from «ancient men», so the jest would not have meant much in the 1590s.

Harvey's three uses of «hotspur» in his diatribe against Tom Nashe are all derogatory references to railers: «hypocritical hoat spurres,» «I ... who have made Comedies of such Tragedies; and with pleasure given such hoatspurres leave, to run themselves out of breath,» «wrangling, & quarreling hoatspurres.» Hotspur was the nickname of the historical character portrayed in *1 Henry IV*; the name is used thrice in the first two acts of the play,[27] and, according to the *OED*, the term was restricted to the real character until about 1590, when it became a general term for a hothead or rash person.

The use of one of the two terms, «hotspur» or «old lad of the castle,» in Harvey's pamphlet might not mean much, but both together seem significant, and they are joined by two other expressions that recall Hal and Falstaff. Harvey's first mention of hotspurs is in a series of insults which includes «buckram Giants» (54), meaning false or pretended giants, and that term recurs on the following page (55), while four pages later we find «heir apparent» (59). Shakespeare uses «buckram» once, in *2 Henry VI*, but otherwise has that word only in the first two acts of *1 Henry IV*, where it appears seven times, all concerning the disguises worn by Hal and Poins when they ambush Falstaff and the other three robbers. Falstaff, of course, justifies his cowardice by turning his two buckram clad attackers into four, then seven, then nine, then eleven, and the repetition of the word—used six times in twenty-six lines—certainly imprints it in the auditor's memory.

Save for one place in *2 Henry VI*,[28] Shakespeare only uses «heir apparent» in *1 Henry IV* where it crops up four times in the first two acts, always in the mouth of Falstaff.[29] As with «buckram,» the repetition sticks in one's mind. Harvey's use of «heir apparant» (59) is in no sense idiosyncratic, and would hardly be worth mentioning, except that it comes between his first two mentions of «hotspur.»

These few paragraphs on Harvey's *Foure Letters* and Shakespeare's *1 Henry IV* merely skim a topic that could be developed at greater length. Dr. Gabriel Harvey was a man of whom some good words could be said, but he was also a humorless Puritan bigot and a sycophant toward those in authority. At a guess, I imagine that he stormed out of a performance of 1 *Henry IV* at the end of the second act, enraged both at the slander of a man he regarded as a martyr, and at the portrayal of England's hero king as a youthful rakehell—but that the Bard's words remained in his memory. I do not pretend that this evidence of Harvey borrowing from Shakespeare is conclusive—far from it! Yet it is better than the evidence frequently offered by Chambers and others to support their dates for Shakespeare's plays.

Henry V: Essex in Ireland

The Chorus to Act V of *Henry V* contains six lines to «the general our gracious empress» who is engaged in suppressing rebellion in Ireland (29-34). I share the overwhelming opinion that the general almost certainly must be the Earl of Essex and that those lines were written in 1599, but is this argument strong enough to date the play to that year? May this passage have been a revision? That the Essex passage is an addition to a play written earlier is indicated by the following. The six appearances of the Chorus in *Henry V* are not found in the edition of 1600 and its reprints in 1602 and 1619, but only in the First Folio of 1623. Some lines in the choruses were manifestly revised or added after the play was first written. The Chorus to Act V is corrupt in the lines immediately following the mention of Essex. Furthermore topical revisions were regularly added to revived plays in that age, with prologues and epilogues being the favorite location for such topicalities, while *Henry V* is a patriotic play that is regularly revived in years of national crisis—years like 1599.

The most obvious indication that the choruses of *Henry V* were revisions is found in the last line of the Chorus to Act V: «Unto Southampton do we shift our scene»; these words immediately precede a scene set in London. Much scholarship has been focused on this and other inconsistencies in the choruses, for which the simplest explanation is that Shakespeare wrote or rewrote the choruses after he had forgotten the details of his plot. Moreover lines 34-41 of the Chorus to Act V, which immediately follow the mention of «the general of our gracious empress» are almost universally agreed to contain textual corruption, which could simply indicate incompetent copying of Shakespeare's manuscript, but could also result from an imperfect revision being made at that particular point. In short, the choruses themselves, and the lines concerning Essex in particular, point to very probable revision.

Moreover, as fairly recent scholarship has shown, topical revisions were quite common in Shakespeare's day, and the easiest way to transform an old play into a «new and improved product» was to insert the additional material where it was least likely to foul up the plot and dialogue, namely, in prologues, epilogues, and choruses. G. E. Bentley observes that: «New prologues and epilogues for revived plays and for court performances were already commonplace in [the 1590s]». On the frequency of revision of revived plays, Bentley states that: «As a rough rule of thumb one might say that almost any play first printed more than ten years after composition and known to have been kept in active repertory by the company which owned it is most likely to contain revisions by the author or, in many cases, by another playwright».[30]

So far, I have argued that Shakespeare's reference to Essex in Ireland in 1599 bears the marks of revision of an earlier text, but I have offered no positive evidence for an earlier date for the play. Yet one more item argues that the *Henry V* of 1599 was a revival. The stage history of the eighteenth, nineteenth, and twentieth centuries shows that *Henry V* becomes popular when England is threatened or at war, most famously in Laurence Olivier's 1944 movie, made at the request of Winston Churchill and dedicated to Britain's airborne forces. It so happened that England faced an extraordinary triple threat in the year 1599. England had been at war with Spain since 1585, but in May 1598 her ally France made a separate peace, leaving England and the Netherlands to fight on alone. At the same time, Tyrone's simmering rebellion in northern Ireland threatened to engulf the entire island after the destruction of an English army in August 1598. Essex's departure for Ireland with a new army in 1599 must be seen against the backdrop of the twin disasters of 1598. But then, with most of England's military power deployed to Ireland and the Netherlands in the summer of 1599, a fourth Spanish

Armada assembled and the likelihood of invasion loomed. This last Armada's purpose was actually defensive, but England was seized with a sense of crisis that summer.[31] In addition, as Gary Taylor explains: «Revivals [of *Henry V*] have almost always coincided with wars, rumours of wars, and attendant military enthusiasms;... But *Henry V* has not only been consistently revived in times of national crisis; it has also been, at such times, consistently rewritten.»[32] In short, the theory that the reference to the Earl of Essex was an addition to a play revived during the crisis of 1599 exactly fits the future pattern of *Henry V*.

As You Like It: The Death of Marlowe

Chambers dates this play at 1599-1600, but it contains two references to the death in 1593 of Christopher Marlowe: «Dead shepherd, now I find thy saw of might,/Who ever lov'd that lov'd not at first sight?», and «it strikes a man more dead than a great reckoning in a little room».[33] Shakespeare's ascertainable references to contemporaries are so rare, the Earl of Essex being the only other non-royal Englishman to merit a clear notice, that they deserve close examination. The obvious point about Shakespeare's tribute to the dead shepherd is this: we exclaim upon a man's death when it happens; six or seven years later we simply refer to him in the past tense.

Hamlet: The Question of the Earlier Version

Hamlet is put at 1600-1 by Chambers and the 1985 *Britannica*, both naming it Shakespeare's twenty-second play. A tragic work called *Hamlet* is alluded to in 1589, a performance of a play of *Hamlet* is recorded in 1594, and a play of *Hamlet* is mentioned in 1596. Nineteenth century scholars supposed that all of these references are to a lost play dubbed the *Ur-Hamlet*, written by some other dramatist, possibly Thomas Kyd, which Shakespeare adapted into the *Hamlet* we know. Moreover, the hodgepodge first edition of *Hamlet* of 1603 was regarded as a descendant of the *Ur-Hamlet*. This hypothesis made perfectly good sense up to the 1920s, as Shakespeare was believed to have been a regular reviser of other men's plays. That belief has been reversed for other plays of which Shakespeare was formerly believed to have been an imitator. Furthermore, during the 1920s and 30s, the work of several scholars showed that the inferior 1603 edition of *Hamlet* was not descended from the *Ur-Hamlet* at all, but was a corrupt version of Shakespeare's *Hamlet*. However, Shakespeare's *Hamlet* (II.ii.336-42) mentions controversy caused by child actors, and we know that the War of the Poets—Ben Jonson versus John Marston and Thomas Dekker around 1601—involved the Children of the Chapel. May we not be reasonably confident in the approximate correctness of the conventional date for *Hamlet*? The trouble with this theory is that the Children of Paul's caused such controversy in 1588-9 that they were suppressed in 1590.[34] Thus the props upholding the existence of the *Ur-Hamlet* fall away, one after another; only the necessity of keeping a mature play by Shakespeare near the middle of Chambers' bracket of 1590-1613 remains to date *Hamlet* at 1600-1, when it might better be placed at 1596 or 1594 or 1589.[35]

Macbeth: Equivocation and Gunpowder

Chambers dates *Macbeth* at 1605-06, associating it, as do most scholars, with the Gunpowder Plot of 1605 and the resultant trial of the Jesuit Father Henry Garnet in 1606. Yet Chambers regards that date as probable, rather than certain, in which he is joined by Kenneth Muir in the 1951/84 Arden *Macbeth* and by Nicholas Brooke in the 1990 Oxford *Macbeth*. I will not argue here that an earlier date is indicated for this play (Muir, xvii-xix, summarizes views on this question), but that the alleged connection between *Macbeth* and Gunpowder is fragile.

The best known allusions to Gunpowder in *Macbeth* lie in the word «equivocation,» especially in the Porter's scene, II.iii, an apparent reference to the Jesuit doctrine brought up at Garnet's trial. The weakness of this dating argument was fully recognized by Chambers, who notes that: «the Jesuit doctrine of equivocation had been familiar, at least since the trial of Robert Southwell in 1595» (I.474). Pre-1606 dramatic references to equivocation can be found in Thomas Dekker's *Satiro-mastix*, where the word is not used, but the doctrine is unmistakably enunciated: «there's no faith to be helde with Hereticks and Infidels, and therefore thou swear'st anie thing» (IV.ii.90-1), and also in *Hamlet*: «We must speak by the card or equivocation will undo us» (V.i.133-4). A footnote to the latter passage in the Arden *Hamlet* gives a non-dramatic example from 1584.

On the other hand, it is often maintained that the entire play of *Macbeth* contains matters concerning James I, most especially that its plot about the murder of a Scottish king repeatedly echoes themes from the Gunpowder Plot to murder a King of Scotland who had become King of England. However, Arthur M. Clark offers a strong case in *Murder under Trust* (1982) that *Macbeth* was written in 1601 in response to the 1600 Gowrie conspiracy against James' life. The detailed points presented by Clark are far too lengthy to be considered here, but their strength is attested to by Muir: «If Clark had read H. N. Paul's *The Royal Play of ‹Macbeth›* he could hardly have thought that the Gunpowder Plot was less relevant to the play than the Gowrie conspiracy» (xviii). In other words, Muir's judgment is that Clark's arguments for Gowrie are about equal to Paul's arguments for Gunpowder.

In sum, the firm belief that *Macbeth* glances extensively at the Gunpowder plot withers away when its details are placed in the context of the age.

Pericles: John Day's *Law Tricks*

Pericles was published in 1609 and is dated during 1608-9 by Chambers and the *Britannica*, who call it Shakespeare's thirty-third play.

Pericles contains this passage in II.i, which, unlike the other scenes in Act II, is credited to Shakespeare rather than to a collaborator.

> 3rd Fisherman. ... Master, I marvel how the fishes live in the sea.
> 1st Fisherman. Why, as men do a-land: the great ones eat up the
>   little ones.... Such whales have I heard on a'th'land, who never
>   leave gaping till they swallow'd the whole parish, church,

> steeple, bells, and all.
> 3rd Fish. But, master, if I had been the sexton, I would have been
> that day in the belfry.
> 2nd Fish. Why, man?
> 3rd Fish. Because he should have swallow'd me too; and when I had
> been in his belly, I would have kept such a jangling of the bells,
> that he should never have left till he cast bells, steeple, church,
> and parish up again.

Law Tricks has these passages in two different scenes, I.ii and II.i:

> Joculo. ... But, Madam, do you remember what a multitude of fishes
> we saw at sea? And I do wonder how they can all live by one
> another.
> Emilia. Why, fool, as men do on the land; the great ones eat up the
> little ones...

> Adam. I knew one of that faculty [lawyers] in one term eat up a
> whole town, church, steeple, and all.
> Julio. I wonder the bells rung not all in his belly.

These items were noticed by Day's 1881 editor, A. H. Bullen, who knew that *Law Tricks* was published one year before *Pericles*, and who also noted that Day borrowed heavily from Shakespeare, «Day had evidently made a close study of Shakespeare's early comedies, and studied them with profit»,[36] as well as from Sidney, Spenser, and Lyly. So Bullen concluded that Day had seen the manuscript of *Pericles* or remembered that passage from a performance.

Chambers subsequently proved that *Law Tricks* was written in 1604, which he felt to be impossibly early for *Pericles*, and so he reversed the borrowing. No later editor of *Pericles* has added any justification as to why Bullen was wrong, other than that 1604 is too early.

Let us return to the imitative habits of John Day. In his conversations with William Drummond, right after opining, «That Shakespeare wanted art,» Ben Jonson charged, «That Sharpham, Day, Dekker, were all rogues and that Minshew was one.» What Ben meant by «rogue» becomes evident with a little study. Edward Sharpham was an imitator of John Marston. John Minshew's Spanish dictionary and grammar were based on the earlier work of Richard Percival, which Minshew took over and called his own. Jonson wrote a whole play, *The Poetaster*, against Thomas Dekker and Marston, accusing them of plagiarizing his work. In other words, Jonson was classifying Day as an imitator or plagiarist, and with good reason. *Law Tricks* borrows on a large scale from Jonson's *The Case is Altered*, and borrows from or echoes *Faerie Queene, Venus and Adonis, 2 Henry IV, Julius Caesar, Much Ado, Hamlet,* and *Measure for Measure*. Most of these borrowing are small scraps, but when you see several from the same play, you are justified in claiming borrowing.

Law Tricks is a lively play of some merit, but it is also a motley of shreds and patches filched from better writers. How likely is it that Shakespeare would sit through a performance and decide to imitate the imitator? The presumption must be that Day borrowed the items about the great fish eating the little ones from Shakespeare, in which case 1604 becomes the latest possible date for *Pericles*.

Tempest: Is Bermuda Necessary?

Chambers places *The Tempest* at 1611-12, making it Shakespeare's thirty-sixth play, followed only by *Henry VIII* and *Kinsmen*, and he and others list two or three accounts of a 1609 shipwreck in Bermuda as important sources, especially a long letter by William Strachey and a shorter one by Sylvester Jourdan. *The Tempest* is by far the most important anchor for the latter end of Chambers' chronology, and yet he is cautious when discussing Jourdan's letter in his *Britannica* article: «this *or some other* contemporary narrative of Virginia colonization *probably* furnished *the hint* of the plot» (my emphases). Meanwhile, Muir lists the three Bermuda pamphlets as probable sources for *Tempest*, but warns: «The extent of the verbal echoes of these three pamphlets has, I think, been exaggerated. There is hardly a shipwreck in history or in fiction which does not mention splitting, in which the ship is not tightened of its cargo, in which the passengers do not give themselves up for lost, in which north winds are not sharp, and in which no one gets to shore by clinging to wreckage».[37]

Nevertheless Chambers, Muir, and virtually every other scholar who discuss *The Tempest* believe that Shakespeare was influenced by the pamphlets on the Bermuda wreck of 1609, especially Strachey's. In particular, a detailed case for Shakespeare's use of the latter source is offered in Louis Wright's reprint of Strachey's and Jourdan's letters.[38] Did Shakespeare have any need of these sources? Bermuda's evil name was well established in the sixteenth century; St. Paul's shipwreck at Malta makes a better source for *The Tempest* than any or all of the Bermuda pamphlets, and Richard Hakluyt's popular work on voyaging must be taken into account.

Bermuda's reputation for storms, wrecks, and demons was common knowledge long before *The Tempest* was written. Bermuda is cited as a place of many shipwrecks in Walter Ralegh's 1591 pamphlet about the last voyage of the «Revenge.» Donne's 1597 poem, «The Storme» includes this couplet: «Compar'd to these stormes, death is but a qualme,/ Hell somewhat lightsome, and the Bermuda calme.» Fulke Greville's Sonnet 59, probably written in the early 1580s, makes a similar comment on Bermuda.

Muir notes that «Strachey's account of the shipwreck is blended with memories of St. Paul's—in which too not a hair perished»,[39] so we may ask how much Acts of the Apostles 27-8 shares with *The Tempest*. Without any trouble at all, we find about thirteen items. First, a voyage within the Mediterranean with Italy as the destination. Second, discord and mutiny among the voyagers; the sailors against the passengers. Third, the ship driven by a tempest, that is, forced to abandon course. Fourth, utter loss of hope. Fifth, a supernatural being—an angel in St. Paul, Ariel in *Tempest*—visits the ship. Sixth, desperate maneuvers to avoid the lee shore of an unknown island. Seventh, the ship grounds and splits. Eighth, detailed descriptions of some techniques of seamanship. Ninth, St. Paul gathers wood, like Caliban and Ferdinand. Tenth, a plot against St. Paul's life. Eleventh, the island has barbarous inhabitants, like Caliban. Twelfth, supernatural oversight of the whole episode. Thirteenth, a stay on the island, seeming miracles (St. Paul immune to snakebite), followed by a safe trip to Italy.

So any argument that Shakespeare relied on Strachey for items in his plot can be topped by St. Paul. Furthermore, Strachey's account is quite lengthy, 99 pages in Wright's reprint, while the average Bible covers St. Paul's shipwreck in less than two pages. Thus St. Paul gives a very compressed set of events, making him superior as a potential source; Shakespeare would not have had to wade through 99 pages extracting a detail here, a detail there. Finally, we don't have to speculate about how Shakespeare may have had the opportunity to read his source in manuscript, as with Strachey; we know Shakespeare read his Bible.

However, Wright claims that Shakespeare followed Strachey so closely in certain items that we can virtually see the Bard in the act of borrowing: «When William Shakespeare sat down to write *The Tempest* he had fresh in his memory a vivid description of a hurricane and shipwreck.... The author was William Strachey.»[40] Wright's footnotes to Strachey's text allege about six details borrowed by Shakespeare. For the sake of brevity we will examine only the best known example. Here are the descriptions of St. Elmo's fire from *The Tempest* and Strachey, followed by two descriptions from Volume III of Hakluyt's *Navigations, Voyages, Traffiques & Discoveries*, published in 1600 (numbers indicate parallels in terminology among these publications):

> Now on the beak,/Now in the waist, the deck, in every cabin,/I flamed amazement. Sometimes I'ld divide/And burn in many places; on the topmast,/The yards, and boresprit would I flame distinctly,/ Then meet and join. (*Tempest*, I.ii.196-201)

An apparition of a <u>little</u>[1], round <u>light</u>[2], like a faint star, trembling and streaming along with a sparkling blaze, half the height <u>upon</u>[3] the <u>main mast</u>[4] and shooting sometimes from <u>shroud to shroud</u>[5], tempting to settle, <u>as it were</u>[6], <u>upon</u>[3] any of the four <u>shrouds</u>[5]. And for <u>three or four hours</u>[7] together, or rather more, half the night, it kept with us, running sometimes along the <u>main yard</u>[8] to the very end and then returning... (Strachey)

In the night there came <u>upon</u>[3] the top of our <u>mainyard</u>[8] and <u>main mast</u>[4], a certain <u>little</u>[1] <u>light</u>[2], much like unto the <u>light</u>[2] of a little candle,... This <u>light</u>[2] continued aboard our ship <u>about three hours</u>[7], flying from mast to mast, & from top to top: and sometime it would be in two or three places at once. (From Robert Tomson's account in Hakluyt)

We saw <u>upon</u>[3] the <u>shrouds</u>[5] of the Trinity <u>as it were</u>[6] a candle, which of it self shined, and gave a <u>light</u>[2] .... it was the light of Saint Elmo which appeared on the <u>shrouds</u>[5] ... (From Francisco de Ulloa's account in Hakluyt)

As the underlined, numbered words show, Strachey resembles Hakluyt far more than Shakespeare resembles any of the other three descriptions. Yet the similarity of Strachey to Hakluyt goes further, in that the fire is confined to the upper part of the ship: the masts, yards, and rigging. Only in Shakespeare does the fire travel through the hull: beak, waist, deck, and cabins. Technically speaking, Shakespeare could be charged with error, as St. Elmo's fire visits only the higher parts of a ship. But then, Shakespeare is describing Ariel's supernatural activities rather than the science of atmospherics. Moreover, Muir (280) argues that Strachey's words on St. Elmo's fire are probably based on a passage in Erasmus' colloquy.

In conclusion, St. Paul's shipwreck works better than Strachey as an overall source for *The Tempest*. Further, any argument that Shakespeare borrowed St. Elmo's fire from Strachey is, a fortiori, an argument that Strachey borrowed from Hakluyt.[41] That being the case, and given the much greater availability of Hakluyt's best-selling work than Strachey's unpublished letter, it should be presumed that Hakluyt rather than Strachey was Shakespeare's source—if, indeed, Shakespeare needed a source.

Conclusions

Sir Edmund Chambers' *William Shakespeare: A Study of Facts and Problems* was a truly revolutionary book in its effect on Shakespeare's biography. It demolished the mythology and wishful thinking of many earlier scholars, who produced fantasies based on liberal use of the word «doubtless,» and it forced a return to the primary evidence, no matter how scanty. Chambers' chronology is also of real value, as it represents the strongest case that can be made for the hypothesis that Shakespeare's plays were written between 1590 and 1613. Chambers begins by using biographical considerations to establish his boundary dates, and he then uses the chronological evidence on the plays to spread them between those boundaries. In this regard, Chambers follows the methods of Edmond Malone (see note 11), and both of these scholars explicitly state the assumptions behind their methods.

That said, Chambers' chronology falls apart under inspection.

Chambers' errors, as given by Honigmann, are these. Supposing that Francis Meres' 1598 list of Shakespeare's plays is complete, even though Chambers knew that it was not complete. Assuming that Philip Henslowe's «ne» means «new,» even though Chambers was aware that Henslowe wrote that word against plays that were not new. Treating weak earliest possible dates as strong evidence, even though Chambers discusses that very problem. Believing, in agreement with most scholars of his day, that Shakespeare routinely rewrote other men's plays, a verdict reversed by more recent scholarship.

Yet Chambers' mistakes do not stop there. He treats Shakespeare's absence from the theatrical archives of the 1580s as evidence that the Bard had not yet begun to write, despite his knowledge of the emptiness of those same archives. He ignores or casually dismisses the disagreeable evidence of the punctilious Ben Jonson that Shakespeare was active in the 1580s, specifically, Ben's naming Shakespeare as a contemporary of Lyly, Kyd, and Marlowe, as well as Ben's very precise statement about the date of *Titus Andronicus*. He disregards inconvenient earliest possible dates such as Holinshed's 1587 *Chronicles*. More strikingly, Chambers ignores earliest possible dates dictated by his own logic: 1591 for *King John* and 1604 for *Pericles*. Chambers also fails to consider the implications of his own words to the effect that, in terms of useful dating evidence, Shakespeare starts fading away around 1603, and is virtually gone by 1607-08.

But Chambers' chronological arguments still rule, despite the opinion of so many leading scholars that his dates are too late. On this matter we have the authority of James McManaway in 1950, G. Blakemore Evans in 1974, most especially Ernest Honigmann in 1980, and Samuel Schoenbaum in both 1970 and 1991. This point need not rest on voices of authority, for examination of chronologies of Shakespeare's plays published in the last several decades shows only trivial alterations to Chambers' chronologies of 1911 and 1930.

Despite all this, the errors continue. The last fifty years have yielded impressive comprehensive works on Shakespeare's sources, but these works are invariably organized play by play, as with Kenneth Muir and Geoffrey Bullough, or, for that matter, in the sections on sources in the Arden, Oxford, and Cambridge editions of Shakespeare's plays. Virtually nothing has been done to arrange Shakespeare's certain and highly probable sources in the order in which they appeared, and then to examine that list closely for chronological significance. As for supposed topical references, all the caution of scholars like Chambers and Muir seems to have been wasted, as everyday events in Shakespeare's plays are linked to everyday events in the archives of the age. As Fluellen might have put it: «There is a treason in *Macbeth*, and there is also moreover a treason in 1605-06, and there is equivocatings in both.» Moreover, the implications of Bentley's notice of the frequency of topical allusions being added to revisions seem not to have sunk in. Finally, whenever Shakespeare writes something similar to something by another author, it always seems that the Bard was the borrower, as with armed Prologues in *Troilus* and *Poetaster*, or the jests in *Pericles* and *Law Tricks*.

Where do we stand? The implications of the evidence presented in this essay are: *Titus Andronicus*, circa 1585; *Comedy of Errors*, 1587-8; *King John* circa 1590; *Romeo and Juliet*, 1591; *1 Henry VI*, by 1592; *Henry V*, 1592-9; *As You Like It*, 1593-4; *Hamlet*, ?1594; *Macbeth*, perhaps 1600-01, *Pericles*, by 1604. Yet, though some of the pieces of evidence underpinning this list are strong, others are weak. We have two different ways to propose dates for Shakespeare's plays. We can present evidence of earliest and latest possible (or probable) dates for each play, carefully analyzing every item, or we can exhibit a table assigning each play to a particular year (with, of course, some prefatory caveats on our lack of complete certainty). The latter method soothes our vanity by allowing us to avoid confessing ignorance. The reality of the evidence now available favors the former method, and, as someone said, awareness of ignorance is the first step on the road to knowledge. Any attempt to present a list of Shakespeare's plays, assigning a year of composition to each, no matter how qualified, is pretending to know more than we do.

Endnotes

1   Peter Alexander, *Shakespeare* (London, 1964), 97, and *Shakespeare's Life and Art* (1939, rev. ed. 1964), 57-69 ff.

2   Caincross, *The Problem of Hamlet* (London, 1936,1970), 179-85.

3   F.P. Wilson, *Marlowe and the Early Shakespeare* (Oxford, 1953), 113.

4   T.W. Baldwin, *Shakespeare's Five-Act Structure* (Urbana, Illinois, 1947), 776-84.

5   William Matchett, ed.. *King John*. Signet Classic edition combined with *Henry VIII* (New York, 1986), «Textual Note,» 148.

6   Oscar James Campbell and Edward Quinn, *The Reader's Encyclopedia of Shakespeare* (New York, 1966), article on «chronology,» 113.

7   Russell Fraser, *Young Shakespeare* (New York, 1988), 145-8.

8   John Crow's astonishingly candid statement deserves careful consideration. He is saying, in effect, «I and most scholars think these dates are too late, but they have become the conventional wisdom, the dramatic history of the age has been adjusted to them, and therefore we will keep them,» which, of course, is the whole problem.

9   Indeed, as I hope the quotations in this section show. Chambers also fully meets the scholarly requirement of clearly stating his *a priori* assumptions,

and the same is true of Edmond Malone (see note 11).

10 Edmund Chambers, *William Shakespeare: A Study of Facts and Problems* (Oxford, 1930), Vol. I,270. Further quotations from this work will simply be followed by the volume and page number, thus (I, 270). Chambers dates Shakespeare's plays to theatrical years, so 1590-1 means fall 1590 to summer 1591, not January 1590 to December 1591.

11 In this matter. Chambers is in full accord with Edmond Malone's 1778 essay, «An Attempt to ascertain the Order in which the Plays of Shakespeare were written.» Malone conjectures, to use his own word, that Shakespeare began writing plays in 1591, based on the apparent lack of notice of those works prior to Greene's *Groatsworth*. Moreover, Malone asserts that:

> The plays which Shakespeare produced before the year 1600, are known, and are seventeen or eighteen in number. The rest of his dramas, we may conclude, were composed between that year and the time of his retiring to the country [which Malone put at 1611]. Malone's *Shakespeare*, Third Variorum Edition (1821; AMS reprint. New York, 1966), II.291-302.

12 I agree with Chambers and every other authority that the approximate sequence or order of composition of the plays can be determined on stylistic grounds with reasonable certainty. I further agree with Chambers that attempts to determine an exact sequence by the use of quantitative methods are probably hopeless (I.253). Such methods assume, for example, that Shakespeare's stylistic development was monotonic, to use a mathematical term, that it always proceeded in the same direction, as from more rigid versification to freer versification.

13 Chambers, I.246-50. Chambers' table of boundary dates omits *Shrew, All's Well, Coriolanus*, and *Timon*, and gives no latest possible date for *Two Noble Kinsmen*.

14 Wilson, The Clark Lectures, Trinity College Cambridge, 1951, published as *Marlowe and the Early Shakespeare* (Oxford, 1953), 106. See also Wilson, «Shakespeare's Reading,» *Shakespeare Survey* 3 (Cambridge, 1950), 14-21, esp. 16.

15 Gerald Eades Bentley, *The Profession of Dramatist in Shakespeare's Time 1590-1642* (Princeton, 1971), viii. Bentley later notes (14-5) that Philip Henslowe's business diary, listing hundreds of performances between 1592 and 1602, names about 280 plays, of which about 40 survive today, while «at least 170 would now be totally unknown—even by title—had Henslowe's accounts been destroyed.» Our knowledge of the Elizabethan stage is so dependent on Henslowe's 1592-1602 diary that Schoenbaum calls it «the most valuable single document relative to the early stage» (1991 ed., 127) and «that most

precious of Elizabethan playhouse documents» (1991 ed., 256). As far as the Elizabethan stage is concerned, pre-Henslowe is virtually prehistoric.

16 This argument on *Titus Andronicus* originates with Honigmann, *Shakespeare's Impact*, 67.

17 On the reference to *Titus* in *Knack to Know a Knave*, as well as other indications that *Titus* was written before 1593, see the 1953 Arden, the 1984 Oxford, or the 1994 Cambridge edition.

18 C H . Herford, Percy and Evelyn Simpson, eds., *Ben Jonson* (Oxford, 1925-52), II.213-7 and XI.436.

19 Edmund Chambers, *The Elizabethan Stage* (Oxford, 1923), III.285-6. See also *The Works of John Day*, «Reprinted from the collected Edition of A.H. Bullen (1881) with an Introduction by Robin Jeffs» (London, 1963), xiv-xv.

20 Samuel Schoenbaum, *Shakespeare's Lives* (Oxford), p. 517 of 1991 ed., p. 713 of 1970 ed. Incidentally, Schoenbaum modified the paragraph in which this passage occurs, and he made a minor stylistic change to the passage itself. Therefore, the passage as quoted reflects his considered opinion in 1991, rather than simple failure to review what he wrote in 1970.

21 It is impossible to give a precise count of the titles named by Muir without making arbitrary decisions about how to count an original work and a translation of the same work, or how to count different editions of the same work, or works by one author that are conventionally lumped together as one work. My own count is 113; anyone else's ought to be quite close to that number. I should also note that Muir was not concerned with chronology in this book, while his dating assumptions are pretty much in line with Chambers'. Consequently, when Muir considered a work by another English author that was written slightly before he believed the Shakespearean play in question was written, he naturally assumed that any borrowing was by Shakespeare, when, in fact, the influence could have gone the other way.

22 I omit Samuel Rowley's *When You See Me, You Know Me* (performed 1604, published 1605), a probable source for the subtitle and Prologue of *Henry VIII*, and also John Speed's *History of Great Britaine* (1611), a probable source for items in the latter part of *Henry VIII*, III.ii. These portions of *Henry VIII* are usually attributed to John Fletcher rather than to Shakespeare.

23 Sir Philip Sidney, *Selected Prose and Poetry*, ed. Robert Kimbrough (San Francisco, 1969), 126. *The Defense of Poesy* was first published in 1595, and its version of the fable begins: «There was a time when all the parts of the body made a mutinous conspiracy against the belly.» Shakespeare's equivalent words are: «There was a time, when all the body's members Rebell'd against

the belly,» which gives some idea of the difficulty of sorting out influences in any author's version of this well known parable.

24 Muir's theory about Daniel's *Arcadia* is ignored by Nicholas Brooke in The Oxford Shakespeare *Macbeth* (1990) in his sections Dates and Sources, as well as in the footnotes to the lines in question.

25 III.ii.120-2; this and all subsequent citations from Shakespeare's plays are from the second Arden edition.

26 Gabriel Harvey, *Four Letters and Certeine Sonnets* (New York and London, The Bodley Head Quartos, 1923), «hotspur» is on 54, 63, and 81; «old Lads of the Castell» is on 74.

27 I.i.52, 70; II.iv.l00.

28 I.i.151; the term is also found in the Chorus to Act III of *Pericles*, but those lines are generally not attributed to Shakespeare. *2 Henry VI* uses «buckram» at IV.vii.23.

29 I.ii.56; II.ii.42; II.iv.265, 362.

30 G.E. Bentley, *The Profession of Dramatist and Player in Shakespeare's Time*, 1590-1642 (Princeton, 1971, 1984), 136 and 263. More generally, see 135-6 and 259-63.

31 A synopsis of reports of the invasion scare and the forces raised to meet it in August 1599 can be found in G.B. Harrison, *The Elizabethan Journals* (Ann Arbor, 1955), «A Last Elizabethan Journal,» 13-38.

32 Gary Taylor, ed.. The Oxford Shakespeare *Henry V* (Oxford and New York, 1984), 11. See also Andrew Gurr, ed.. The New Cambridge Shakespeare *Henry V* (Cambridge, 1992), 39 and Oscar James Campbell and Edward G. Quinn, *The Reader's Encyclopedia of Shakespeare* (New York, 1966), article on *Henry V*, Stage History.

33 III.v.81-2 paraphrases a couplet from Marlowe's *Hero and Leander* (I.175-6): «Where both deliberate the love is slight;/Who ever lov'd that lov'd not at first sight?» III.iii.11-12 echoes a passage from *The Jew of Malta* (I.i.36-7): «inclose/Infinite riches in a little room»; Marlowe was killed in a tavern room during a quarrel over the reckoning.

34 Caincross, 105-6.

35 I should note that a date of 1589 or earlier for Shakespeare's *Hamlet* as we know it is not in line with my own views of the evidence on chronology, but I don't believe that awkward facts can be swept away by the mere existence of a plausible alternative explanation. On the other hand, a date of, say, 1594 is perfectly reasonable for Shakespeare's *Hamlet*, and the mention from 1589 could be to an earlier version of Shakespeare's play. My main point is that Chambers' modern followers have no right to treat the hypothesis of a

non-Shakespearean *Ur-Hamlet* as an established fact. That hypothesis is still tenable, but twentieth century scholarship has rendered it far less powerful than it was in the last century, a fact that twentieth century scholars have yet to face.

36 From Bullen's article on Day in the *Dictionary of National Biography*.

37 Muir, Sources, 280. That the stereotyped behavior of passengers in a storm was a byword in those times is seen in an item in Harvey's useful *Foure Letters*, where he compares Fabius Maximus to: «an experte Pilot, that in a hideous tempest regardeth not the foolishe shrickinges, or vaine outcries of disorderly passengers, but bestirreth himselfe, and directeth his mariners, according to the wise rules of orderly Nauigation» (74-5).

38 Louis B. Wright, ed. *A Voyage to Virginia in 1609* (Charlottesville, 1964).

39 Muir, op cit.

40 Wright, op cit, ix.

41 Here are the other items that Wright says Shakespeare borrowed from Strachey (with Wright's page numbers in parentheses)—followed by my responses. Mutinies at Bermuda (xiv) suggested mutinous sailors in *Tempest*—Hakluyt reports several English mutinies, a common accurrence in that turbulent age. Cries of terrified passengers in Strachey (6) suggested the same in *Tempest*, I.i.35-7—a commonplace in nautical literature; see note 37 Strachey speaks of «the glut of water» (7), while *Tempest*, I.i.58, has «to glut him,» Shakespeare's only use of g-l-u-t—Strachey uses glut as a noun, Shakespeare as a verb, as he does with glutted in *1 Henry IV*, and as he does with engluts in *Othello* and englutted in *Henry V* and *Timon*. Strachey discusses a drink made from cedar berries at Bermuda (24), while Caliban speaks of «water with berries in it,» I.ii.336—Strachey lists over forty items of food found at Bermuda, Shakespeare mentions about a dozen wild foods in *Tempest*, and berries are the only common item. Strachey speaks of taking birds at night by «lowbelling» (31), while Sebastian mentions «batfowling,» II.i.180, which Wright says «was another name for ‹lowbelling›»—see the *OED* on the difference between batfowling, scaring birds with light, then clubbing them; and lowbelling, scaring birds with noise, then netting them.

Ben Jonson's «On Poet-Ape»

In 1616 Ben Jonson published the first edition of his works, which included a collection of poems called «Epigrams.» The fifty-sixth of this series is called «on Poet-Ape»:

> Poor Poet-Ape, that would be thought our chief,
> Whose works are e'en the frippery of wit,
> From brokage is become so bold a thief,
> As we, the robb'd, leave rage, and pity it,
> At first he made low shifts, would pick and glean,
> Buy the reversion of old plays; now grown,
> To a little wealth, and credit in the scene,
> He takes up all, makes each man's wit his own:
> And, told of this, he slights it. Tut, such crimes
> The sluggish gaping auditor devours;
> He marks not whose 'twas first: and after-times
> May judge it to be his, as well as ours.
> Fool! as if half eyes will not know a fleece
> From locks of wool, or shreds from the whole piece?

This poem has occasioned a certain amount of comment, but none of Jonson's modern editors are willing to suggest the identity or the subject.[1] There is a tradition that Poet-Ape was Shakespeare, presumably owing to Ben's well known habit of taking potshots at the Bard. However, Jonson's criticism of Shakespeare is pretty well summed up in his comment to William Drummond «that Shakespeare wanted art,» which is to say that Shakespeare didn't follow the rules and regulations of drama as they were conceived by Jonson. But none of Ben's complaints against Shakespeare bear any similarity to the sins that he charges against Poet-Ape.

A much more likely suspect is Thomas Dekker who, along with John Marston, engaged Ben in the 1600-01 Poetomachia or War of the Poets. All three playwrights were establishing their careers around the turn of the century, often working in collaboration with each other or with other writers, when Jonson (for reasons now unknown) decided that Marston and Dekker were mocking him. Jonson apparently aimed some shafts at the other two in *Cynthia's Revels* of 1600, and then heard that they were planning retaliation. So Jonson rushed out *The Poetaster* of 1601, a savage and explicit attack on Marston and especially Dekker. The latter had apparently been working on a tragicomedy set in the reign of William II, to which he added (perhaps with help from Marston) a major subplot in which Jonson is effectively and amusingly satirized. Dekker's and Marston's revenge was performed by the Lord Chamberlain's Men in 1601 and was published under Dekker's name as *Satiro-mastix or The Untrussing of the Humorous Poet* in 1602. Moreover, aside from a much later statement by Jonson that on some unspecified date «he beat Marston, and took his pistol from him,» those are the basic facts of Poetomachia.

In *The Poetaster,* Jonson is represented by Horace (Ben's favorite classical poet), while Marston and Dekker are respectively caricatured in the roles of Crispinus and Demetrius Fannius. Dekker used the same names in *Satiro-mastix*, with Crispinus and Fannius undoing the would-be Horace.

The prologue to *The Poetaster* uses the phrases «no poet apes,/That come with basilisk's eyes» and «illiterate apes» when discussing Jonson's foes. Dekker's play gives Horace (Jonson) the following passage (II.ii.38-43): «as for Crispinus (Marston) that Crispino-asse and Fannius (Dekker) his Play-dresser ... as for these Twynnes, these Poet-apes.» Also in *Satiro-mastix* (V.ii.339), Crispinus (Marston) says sarcastically to Horace (Jonson): «All Poets shall be Poet-Apes but you.» *The Poetaster* puns on Dekker's name, i.e., «decker» equals «dresser» several times (III.i and V.i). Dekker puts the same epithet in Horace's (Jonson's) mouth in *Satiro-mastix* (II.ii.39) and also has Horace refer to him as an «arrogating puffe» (I.ii.155); «to arrogate» means, of course, to take what you are not entitled to. Jonson calls Dekker and Marston «plagiary» several times in *The Poetaster* (IV.i, and V.i). After *Satiro-mastix* came out, Jonson added an «Apologetical Dialogue» to the end of *The Poetaster* in which, speaking as himself rather than as Horace, he attacked Marston and Dekker for «thefts, notable/As ocean-piracies or highway-stands.» Now back to «On Poet-Ape.»

The datable events that scholars have found in Jonson's «Epigrams» are from 1595 to 1609, while *Satiro-mastix* repeatedly depicts Jonson as a maker of nasty epigrams, so dating considerations are consistent with seeing «On Poet -Ape» as a slap at Dekker.

Poet-Ape is denounced with the words «frippery» (i.e., rags or cast-off clothing), «shifts» (i.e., women's slips), «shreds,» and «the whole piece (of cloth),» which words are in accord with Ben's characterization of Dekker as a dresser of plays. Also, the *Dictionary of National Biography* states that a contemporary wrote the words «marchan-tailor» next to Dekker's name in a copy of one of his works, though Dekker has no other known connection with the Merchant Tailors' Company.

The foregoing identification of Dekker as Poet-Ape cannot be called airtight, but I feel that it is a *prima facie* case, unless some flaw can be found in it, or unless a better candidate is put forward.

Endnote

1   I consulted five annotated editions of Jonson's poetry, viz., Herford and Simpson, Newdgate, Johnston, Parfit and Hunter.

A Theory on *The Two Noble Kinsmen*

The Two Noble Kinsmen was first published in 1634 as by John Fletcher and William Shakespeare, and is believed to have been first performed in 1613. Modern scholarship has confirmed the identification of the two authors, but gives no convincing date for the Shakespearean portion of that play, nor any explanation of its motivation—why Shakespeare began it, and why he failed to finish it. I would like to offer such a theory.

By February 1603, Queen Elizabeth was weak, ill, and clearly declining. On March 9, three newsletters (published in the Calendar of State Papers, Domestic) were sent from London to Venice by one Anthony Rivers, who wrote that some of the Court feared that the Queen would soon die, some felt that she would not last past May, while all agreed «that she cannot overpass another winter.» Rivers added that «she cannot abide discourses of government and state, but delighteth to hear old Canterbury tales, to which she is very attentive.» *The Two Noble Kinsmen* is a revision of «The Knight's Tale» from Chaucer's *Canterbury Tales*, and so let us hypothesize that Shakespeare began this play to please the ailing Elizabeth. What other evidence can we find to support this theory?

The Queen died in her sleep on March 24, 1603, and Shakespeare is believed by most scholars to refer to this event in Sonnet 107. He wrote that «The mortal moon hath her eclipse endur'd» (i.e., Elizabeth has died), that «peace proclaims olives of endless age» (i.e., the peace loving King James has peacefully ascended the throne), and that the Fair Youth to whom most of the Sonnets were addressed had been «suppos'd as forfeit to a confin'd doom» (i.e., the Earl of Southampton, almost certainly the Fair Youth, had been imprisoned in the Tower of London since his participation in the Essex uprising of 1601; the new King promptly freed him). If we respect the order in which the *Sonnets* were published in 1609, then we may suppose that Sonnet 106 was written just prior to the Queen's death, and it begins as follows:

When in the chronicle of wasted time
I see descriptions of the fairest wights.
And beauty making beautiful old rime.
In praise of ladies dead and lovely knights

I am hardy the first to suggest that these lines indicate that Shakespeare had recently been reading Chaucer, and the latter's story of Palamon and Arcite (the two noble kinsmen who were sentenced to perpetual imprisonment in a tower) should have reminded Shakespeare of the fate of Southampton. Thus, *The Two Noble Kinsmen* may have been intended as an appeal to Elizabeth on behalf of Southampton.

Another reason for dating *The Two Noble Kinsmen* to early 1603, and, incidentally, for believing that the Earl of Oxford was Shakespeare, is found in *Englandes Mourning Garment*, a pamphlet by a meddling and shady character named Henry Chettle. His pamphlet was published just after Elizabeth's funeral, and it includes a poem calling on specific poets to commemorate the passing of their late, great Queen. The poets are not named, but are clearly identified by references to their works and by being given appropriate classical names. For example, one is described thus:

Neither doth Coryn, full of worth and wit,
That finisht dead Musaeus gracious song . .

The classical Musaeus wrote a poem on Hero and Leander that was an inspiration to Christopher Marlowe, whose own «Hero and Leander» was cut short by his death in a brawl in 1593. It was later finished by George Chapman, who, by 1603, was also famous for his translation of Homer, whose supposed source for the *Iliad* was a poem by the legendary Corinnus. Thus we see that Chettle's «Coryn» is Chapman, and that Chettle's references and allusions identify, rather than conceal, those he calls upon.

According to all authorities, Shakespeare is addressed in the following verse.

Nor doth the silver tonged Melicert,
Drop from his honied muse one sable teare
To mourn her death that graced his desert,
And to his laies opend her Royall eare.
Shepheard remember our Elizabeth,
And sing her Rape done by that Tarquin, Death.

The mention of Tarquin reminds us of Shakespeare's popular epic poem «The Rape of Lucrece» (Tarquin was the rapist), and the references to Melicert's silver tongue and honeyed muse are similar to other tributes to Shakespeare's verse. Orthodox scholars, however, are at a loss in explaining why Shakespeare is named for Melicert, though one suggested that Chettle may have been hard pressed to think of a rhyme for «desert.» As we briefly look at the story of Merlicert, we will see that his name applies very well to Edward de Vere, 17th the Earl of Oxford.

Melicert was the son of Ino, who angered Juno, who drove Ino mad. So Ino threw herself and her child into the sea and both drowned. The gods then took pity on Melicert, and he was made into a god, called Palaemon by the Greeks and Portunus by the Romans. His Roman temple stands in the Forum Boarium. It is hard to see how Chettle could be more helpful.

First, we see that Melicert was also known as Palaemon, which is the name of one of *The Two Noble Kinsmen,* and thus we gain a bit of evidence that Shakespeare was working on that play when Elizabeth died. Next, we see that Melicert was a being with a dual identity, which makes his name apt for Oxford/Shakespeare. Also, we note that if the suffix is dropped from the location of Melicert's temple, then we are left with the English word «Boar»: Oxford's heraldric symbol and the name of the tavern (the Boar's Head) where his acting troupe regularly performed. Lastly, we should consider the full name, Forum Boarium. The latter word, also spelled *bovarium,* means «of the cattle» or «of the oxen,» and the Forum Boarium was Rome's cattle market; thus, we get another symbol for the Earl of Oxenford.

What else in *The Two Noble Kinsmen* supports our theory? The play opens with a song praising the flowers of spring, which seems like appropriate encouragement for a sick person in late winter. Lines 7 and 10 of this song are as follows:

> Primrose, first born child of *of Ver* (Latin for spring, pronounced «vere»).

> Oxlips, in their cradles growing, (emphasis added)

The underlined words may be the concealed signatures of deVere of Oxford. It may also be noted that the Shakespearean portions of *The Two Noble Kinsmen* are unlively and more grand in words than in actions, which makes them well suited for recitation, as opposed to performance by a troupe of actors.

Lastly, we should look at the prologue to this play, which prologue may be by Fletcher, but is certainly not by Shakespeare. Three sentences of the prologue read as follows (Signet Classic edition of *The Two Noble Kinsmen*):

> We pray our play may be so, for I am sure
> It had a noble breeder, and a pure,
> A learned, and a poet never went
> More famous yet 'twixt Po and silver Trent.
> Chaucer, of all admired, the story gives:
> There constant to eternity it lives.
> If we let fall the nobleness of this,
> And the first sound this child hear be a hiss,
> How will it shake the bones of that good man,
> And make him cry from under ground, «O fan
> From me the witless chaff of such a writer
> That blast my bays, and my famed works make lighter
> Than Robin Hood!» . . .

It is usually assumed that the «noble breeder» of the first sentence and «that good man» of the third sentence refer to Chaucer, but his name is set off by itself. Also, if «that good man» is supposed to be Chaucer, then the word «writer» in the third from last line should be plural, that is, Chaucer's ghost should object to the two writers, Fletcher and Shakespeare, who have not done justice to his noble tale. It is just as logical to suppose that the «noble breeder» and «that good man» are references to Oxford/Shakespeare, who might protest Fletcher's chaff.

The theory therefore is that Oxford wrote *The Two Noble Kinsmen* to encourage the ailing Elizabeth and to plead for Southampton's freedom. When the Queen died and Southampton was freed, these motivations collapsed; besides, as Oxford began this play for Elizabeth, he may not have had the heart to finish it for others. When Oxford died in June 1604, the unfinished manuscripts of *The Two Noble Kinsmen* and the likewise incomplete *Henry VIII* should have come under the control of his widow. She died January 1613, and I suspect that it was then that the two manuscripts were discovered by Oxford's theatrically minded sons-in-law and given to Fletcher to complete.

Shake-hyphen-speare

An interesting argument was offered during GTE's televised debate on the Shakespeare authorship question on September 17, 1992, moderated by William F. Buckley, Jr. Professor Gary Taylor, citing the work of Randall McLeod, stated that the Bard's name was hyphenated as «Shake-speare» for typographical reasons. Taylor said that the forward tail of a swash *k* would curl down under the *e* and shove against or crowd out the rearward tail of a swash *s*. The result would be loose type falling out of its frame during the printing process, unless a hyphen was inserted to add more space. Consequently, Taylor maintained, there is nothing suspicious in the spelling of «Shake-speare.»

Let us respond. To begin with, common sense tells us that typecasting technology 130 years after Gutenberg must have been remarkably poor if a simple letter combination like *kes* had to be hyphenated, but let us examine some evidence.

I looked for «Shake-speare» in all of the facsimiles of early Shakespeare works that were readily available: *Shakespeare's Plays in Quarto, A Facsimile Edition of Copies Primarily from the Henry E. Huntington Library*; the original 1609 edition of the *Sonnets*; the title page facsimiles and other illustrations in *The Reader's Encyclopedia of Shakespeare*, edited by O. J. Campbell and Edward G. Quinn; and the *First Folio*.

The first three of these sources give the following hyphenated examples of the author's name: the title pages of the 1603 quarto of *Hamlet* and both quartos of *King Lear*, the cast list for *Sejanus* from the 1616 edition of Ben Jonson's complete works, the title page of the 1640 John Benson edition of Shakespeare's poems, and the 1609 *Sonnets*, where the name is hyphenated on the title page and in the running title printed throughout the book. In all of these examples, the name is printed in normal roman type. Neither the *k* nor the *s* has a tail descending below the line, and it is impossible for the two letters to collide. Professor Taylor's theory does not explain these examples—the name was hyphenated intentionally and not as a typographic accident.

The prefatory pages to the *First Folio* print the author's name 19 times. Five of these are hyphenated, all five being on the page with the commendatory poems by L. Digges and I. M. On all other pages where the name appears, it is not hyphenated. On the Diggs/I. M. page, the name appears six times: first, unhyphenated in the title of Digges' poem; next, hyphenated three times in the body of Digges' poem; next, hyphenated in the title of I. M.'s poem; and last, hyphenated in the body of I. M.'s poem. In four of the five hyphenated cases, the name is in normal roman type, and there is no typographic need for hyphenation. In the title of I. M.'s poem, the name is in swash italic type, and the *k* and *s* have descending tails.

We seem to have found what we were looking for. I measured the width of the hyphen and the horizontal distance between the tails of the *k* and *s* as carefully as possible with dividers. It appears that if the hyphen were deleted, the tails would probably collide. So the Taylor/McLeod theory seems to check out in this example.

But is there an alternative explanation? The oversized italic type used in the title of I. M.'s poem is from the same font as the type used to print the dedication on pages A2r and A2v, the heading «To the great Variety of Readers» at the top of page A3r, and the names of the «Principall Actors in all these Playes» on the last prefatory page. The name «William Shakespeare» heads the list of actors and is not hyphenated, the typesetter having chosen a *k* with a short tail. Further, none of the other material printed with this font contains words with unnecessary hyphens. These facts, coupled with the fact that the italic «Shake-speare» is found on the one page where the name is regularly hyphenated, make it extremely improbable that the italic example of hyphenation resulted from the typesetter being too lazy to place the long-tailed *k* back in its case and replace it with a short-tailed *k*.

Still, let us give this hyphen hypothesis every opportunity to succeed. Suppose the Digges/I. M. page was set up last, and the long-tailed *k* was the only *k* left in the case. Was the typesetter compelled to hyphenate the name? No, he had another option that would detract far less from the appearance of the word.

There was a simple way to gain the minute amount of spacing needed to prevent clashing tails. A font of type includes not only pieces that print letters, numbers, and punctuation marks, but also pieces that produce blank spaces. These «spaces,» as they are called, are mostly of a standard size, about equal to the width of an average letter, and provide the separations between words. There are also longer spaces used to fill out lines that don't reach to the right margin—for example, the last line of a paragraph or a line of verse. Finally, there are shorter spaces, some hair-thin, used to adjust the spaces between words so that the entire line of type fits tightly between the left and right margins. Therefore, the typesetter who prepared the Digges/I. M. page could easily have used a hair-space instead of a hyphen if the tails of the two letters collided. He spelled the name «Shake-speare» because he wanted it that way. In other words, even in the one example that seems to meet Professor Taylor's requirement of colliding tails, there is still no need for a hyphen.

The evidence presented here is only a sample of all the early hyphenations of the author's name. But I feel that it justifies rejecting Professor Taylor's explanation of «Shake-speare» as a typographic accident. The hyphenation was intentional.

The Demolition of Shakspere's Signatures

The 1985 *Shakespeare in the Public Records*, published by the British Public Records Office, includes a chapter on «Shakespeare's Will and Signatures» by Jane Cox (24-34). Ms. Cox reproduces and examines five of the six supposedly authentic signatures of Will of Stratford (she omits the first signature on the will as being too faded to be usable.) She concludes:

> It is obvious at a glance that these signatures, with the exception of the last two [on the Will], are not the signatures of the same man. Almost every letter is formed in a different way in each. Literate men in the sixteenth and seventeenth centuries developed personalized signatures much as people do today and it is unthinkable that Shakespeare did not. Which of the signatures reproduced here is the genuine article is anybody's guess.

We may add that it is anybody's guess whether any of the signatures is genuine. The only orthodox scholar who I know to have responded to Ms. Cox's bombshell is, to his credit, Samuel Schoenbaum,[1] who is cautious about accepting Ms. Cox's verdict, but he does not disagree. In the two works cited and in his *Shakespeare: His Life, His Language, His Theater*,[2] Schoenbaum moves toward what he hopes to establish as the new orthodoxy—that the three will signatures are authentic. However, Professor Schoenbaum has no credentials at all in this field, and is on record as sneering at amateur paleographers.[3] Not to mention the fact that Ms. Cox thinks that three of the witnesses' «signatures» on the will are all by the same hand. Finally, as one remembers, the will was originally drafted to be sealed, not signed. As Ms. Cox says: «But if one must select one of the four signed documents as being the sole example of our greatest playwright's hand, the will has no better claim than the Requests deposition, the mortgage deed or the Guildhall conveyance. As we have seen, the legal sanctity of the signature was not firmly established.»

We no longer have any certain samples of Will signing his name, though we may have one of three. Therefore, the presumption of literacy provided by the signatures vanishes. The man may not have been able to write.

Yet the supposedly authentic handwriting of the Bard was a key part of the evidence used to make the case for him as the author of one scene in the manuscript play of *Sir Thomas More*. Thus, an item drops out of the Shakspere canon. Schoenbaum is not about to proclaim such a loss, but he silently acknowledges it in the 1991 edition of *Shakespeare's Lives*. Page 341 of the 1970 edition includes this sentence, concerning the nineteenth century Shakespeare Society: «Among its notable achievements was the first publication, in Dyce's edition, of *Sir Thomas More* [which in our own century has come to earn a place in the Shakespeare canon by virtue of a single scene].» This sentence appears on page 251 of the 1991 edition, but the bracketed passage has been deleted. Page 696 of the 1970 edition states that several scholars «pooled their expertise and critical powers to make a [persuasive] case for *Shakespeare's Hand in the Play of Sir Thomas More*.» This sentence is on pages 503-4 of the 1991 edition but the bracketed word, «persuasive,» has been downgraded to «impressive.» In short, according to Professor Schoenbaum, the scene in *Sir Thomas More* is no longer part of the Shakespeare canon.

The eighteenth and nineteenth centuries thought they had a real flesh-and-blood Shakespeare. The stories about poaching, horse holding, wit combats at the Mermaid, and the merry meeting with Jonson and Drayton humanized the dry records of the Stratfordian grain hoarder, investor, tax dodger, and bringer of lawsuits. However, these beliefs eroded under scholarly examination and were finally toppled by Sir Edmund Chambers' *William Shakespeare*,[4] which left only a bare-bones Bard or minimalist Shakespeare. Yet now we lose the signatures, the presumption of literacy, and a scene from *Sir Thomas More*—Will continues to play the Cheshire Cat. The Stratfordian professors must be held to have suffered a loss of face for their incompetent handling of the supposed signatures and *Sir Thomas More*.

Endnotes

1   Samuel Schoenbaum, *William Shakespeare: A Compact Documentary Life*, Rev. Ed. (Oxford: Oxford UP, 1987), 326-7. Also, *Shakespeare's Lives* (Oxford: Oxford UP, 1991), 566.

2   Samuel Schoenbaum, *Shakespeare: His Life, His Language, His Theater* (NY: Signet, 1990), 213.

3   Samuel Schoenbaum, *Shakespeare's Lives* (Oxford: Oxford UP, 1970), 616.

4   Sir E. K. Chambers, *William Shakespeare: A Study of Facts and Problems* (Oxford, 1930), 2 volumes.

Experts Prove
Shakespeare Had a University Education

Before 1623 Shakespeare was routinely compared to famous classical writers; after 1623 he was regularly described as unlearned. A serious debate over his education began in the eighteenth century, usually between those who wanted Shakespeare to know virtually everything and those who felt he knew next to nothing. Unlike Ben Jonson, Shakespeare does not indulge classically minded readers with long translations from Latin and Greek, which was the primary way of demonstrating scholarship at the time. Yet, clearly, he had some classical education.

The minimum extent of his learning was charted in the 1940s by Professor T. W. Baldwin of the University of Illinois in his 1,500 page, *William Shakspere's Small Latine and Lesse Greeke*,[1] and by Sister Miriam Joseph, a professor at the University of Notre Dame, in her 400 page, *Shakespeare's Use of the Arts of Language*.[2]

The standard education received by a small percentage of the boys in Elizabethan England was in a grammar school; the wealthy received the same curriculum from tutors. A grammar school began the old medieval trivium of Latin grammar, rhetoric, and logic; the boys were expected to learn to read and write English in a petty school. The grammar school curriculum prepared boys for England's two universities, though most did not pursue higher education. The schoolmasters were university graduates, and the normal course was about seven years. Stratford-on-Avon had a grammar school.

T. W. Baldwin's purpose was to examine in great detail what may be inferred about the grammar school curriculum, particularly the Latin authors studied by the boys, and to demonstrate that Shakespeare's works display familiarity with that curriculum. Baldwin determines to his satisfaction that the Bard's works show certain or probable knowledge of the following Latin authors: William Lily, Ovid, Erasmus,

Quintilian, Cicero, Virgil, Juvenal, Tully, Susenbrotus, Plautus, Horace, Camerarius, Terence, Aphthonius, Livy, Palingenius, Culmannus, Mantuaunus, and maybe Persius, Lucan, Senaca, Pliny, and Cato. This is not to say that Shakespeare read all the works of any of these, save perhaps Ovid, nor even that he read one complete work by each. Many of them were quoted in anthologies and textbooks, and schoolboys were often taught famous sayings rather than whole books. Still, it is an impressive list. Baldwin argues that, regardless of whether Shakespeare ever went to school, he had the equivalent of a complete grammar school education. As Baldwin believed that Shakspere was Shakespeare, he naturally concludes that he took the full course at the Stratford grammar school (II, 378).

As for the upper two thirds of the trivium, Baldwin states that Shakespeare had mastered rhetoric (II, 237-8, 378, 668) and knew some logic, but that a full examination of these matters was beyond the scope of his book. Sister Miriam Joseph undertook that task. Rhetoric and logic had theories behind them, but as Miriam Joseph explains, these two disciplines can be simply defined as mastery of about one hundred and eighty to two hundred figures of speech. Modern Americans know several figures of speech: simile, metaphor, parallel, analogy, hyperbole, pun, and a few more. Classically educated Elizabethans knew prosthesis (the addition of a syllable at the beginning of a word), epenthesis (an extra syllable in the middle), proparalepsis, aphaeresis, syncope, synaloepha, apocope, metathesis, antisthecon, tasis, anastrophe, tmesis, hysteron proteron, hypallage, hyperbaton, epergesis, zeugma, syllepsis, hypozeuxis, and over one hundred and fifty more. Miriam Joseph shows that «with two or three negligible exceptions» the entire theories of rhetoric and logic can be illustrated with examples from Shakespeare's works,» (4) and that «he utilized every resource of thought and language known to his time.» (4)

We now have a clear lower limit to Shakespeare's classical education; he knew the main Latin works taught through the upper levels of a grammar school, and he had fully mastered not only grammar, but also rhetoric and logic. The question asks itself: where did he learn rhetoric and logic? May he not have gone to a university, or mastered part of its curriculum by self study? Sister Miriam Joseph handles these questions by deferring to Baldwin (11), as the greater expert on Elizabethan education. Regrettably, Baldwin handles the matter with falsehood. He wishes to convince readers that a grammar school graduate had a complete knowledge of grammar, rhetoric, and logic, and that the universities were soulless vocational schools.

Baldwin asserts that «[u]niversity training was professional, with literary training only incidental and subsidiary» (II, 662); by «professional» he means Roman law, medicine and divinity. He then meanders through half a page of selected quotations designed to support his view, which actually undercuts it. He then repeats his mantra, «[t]he universities were professional schools» (II, 663), and again twelve pages later, «[u]niversity training was professional training, and only incidentally continued liberal or literary training» (II, 674).

The curriculum of the Stratford grammar school must be inferred, but that of Oxford and Cambridge is well documented, as is the makeup of their student bodies. Most of the students at the universities were in the arts curriculum, enrolled for the B.A., then the M.A. Actually, many of these were uninterested in a degree, and there was no stigma on being what is now called a «drop-out.» Among those who left Oxford or Cambridge universities without a degree were Lord Burghley and Sir Robert Cecil, Sir Philip Sidney and his poet friend Sir Fulke Greville, Anthony and Francis Bacon, and the playwright partners, John Fletcher and Francis Beaumont. Cambridge University had 1,630 members in 1569, rising to 1,950 undergraduates and 657 graduate students in 1597. It awarded 60 B.A.s in 1560, 114 in 1570, and 277 in 1583; thereafter the number declined. Oxford University was somewhat smaller and had similar ratios.

What about the professional disciplines of law, medicine, and divinity? The Roman or civil law taught at the universities had little practical use, as the dominant legal system, the common law, was taught at the Inns of Court in London. Only nine law degrees were awarded by Cambridge between 1544 and 1551. Medical training on the Continent was superior to Oxford and Cambridge, and so prospective English physicians usually studied abroad. Shakspere's son-in-law, John Hall, took his B.A. and M.A. at Cambridge, then went to France for medical training. Cambridge awarded thirty-two medical degrees between 1570 and 1590. Divinity was the most popular academic field after the arts, but it took seven years at Cambridge (five at Oxford) after earning the M.A. to become a Bachelor of Divinity; the Doctorate of Divinity required five more years (four at Oxford). As with divinity, the other professional fields usually required a B.A. and sometimes,

«The Elizabethan Arts course was based firmly on the old medieval *trivium* and *quadrivium*. In his first two years an undergraduate studied mostly rhetoric and Aristotelian logic.» (9)

«Every boy who completed grammar school had worked at Latin (grammar) for seven years and for three or more had studied rhetoric.» (7)

«Some history and geography found their way into the B.A. course, but the main fare in the sixteenth and seventeenth centuries continued to be grammar and rhetoric, logic and philosophy.» (10)

It should not even have been necessary to have written these last few paragraphs, because their contents would have been no surprise to T. W. Baldwin. Nevertheless, his undoubted scholarship led him into a familiar predicament for scholars of the orthodox persuasion. The legend of Stratford clashes with the truth, and so the truth must give way. Baldwin had to misrepresent the truth about the universities—he really had no choice.

The first two years of study at Oxford and Cambridge were in rhetoric and logic; the grammar schools concentrated on grammar (hence the name), and only started their scholars on rhetoric. T. W. Baldwin and Sister Miriam Joseph show that «Shakespeare» mastered Latin rhetoric and logic so fully that he could unobtrusively weave it throughout his

English plays and poems. More to the point, he did this with such art that it went unnoticed for over three centuries. In other words, Shakespeare assimilated the educational equivalent of two years of university study, however and wherever he received it. Moreover, all of us start forgetting the day we leave school—which of us could pass today the final exams of our last year in college? Excellent though his memory may have been, I cannot see Shakespeare's brain as a trap from which nothing ever escaped. If his works display full mastery of the first two years of the university curriculum, then he probably had more than two years of university study.

To reiterate, T.W. Baldwin and Sister Miriam Joseph demonstrated that Shakespeare was completely familiar with grammar, rhetoric, and logic. The study of rhetoric in Elizabethan England began at grammar school but was completed in the first two years at the universities; during the same period the students also learned logic. We now have a university educated Shakespeare on the expert advice of Stratfordian authorities.

Endnotes

1   T.W. Baldwin, *William Shakespere's Small Latine and Lesse Greeke* (Urbana: Univ. of IL Press, 1944), 2 volumes.
2   Sister Miriam Joseph, *Shakespeare's Use of the Arts of Language* (NY: Columbia UP, 1947).

Groatsworth and Shake-scene

Yes trust them not: for there is an Upstart Crow, beautified with our feathers, that with his *Tygers hart wrapt in a Players hyde,* supposes he is as well able to bombast out a blanke verse as the best of you: and beeing an absolute *Johannes fac totum,* is in his owne conceit the onely Shake-scene in a countrey.

Greene's Groatsworth of Wit

On 20 September 1592, a pamphlet called *Greene's Groatsworth of Wit* was registered with the unusual caveat «upon the peril of Henry Chettle,» and was published soon after as the deathbed repentance of Robert Greene. *Groatsworth* contains a letter to three unnamed playwrights, warning them against an actor who is referred to as «Shake-scene» and as «an upstart Crow,» and who is attacked with a paraphrased line from *3 Henry VI.* It was rumored that the true author of *Groatsworth* was Henry Chettle or Thomas Nashe, both of whom publicly denied the accusation, while Chettle also apologized to someone for his role in the publication of *Groatsworth.*

Orthodox Shakespeare scholars insist with near unanimity that we know the following: that Greene wrote *Groatsworth,* that Chettle apologized to Shake-scene, and that Shake-scene was Shakespeare, the actor-turned-playwright from Stratford. But anyone who studies the material without preconceptions will conclude that Chettle must be presumed to be the author of *Groatsworth,* that Chettle apologized to one of the three playwrights, and that even under Stratfordian authorship assumptions, the hit at Shake-scene may very plausibly be explained as an attack on a different actor.

The case for Chettle's authorship of *Groatsworth* can be summarized as follows. Greene died on 3 September, the circumstances of his death became notorious, and his name sold pamphlets,[1] which provided a motive for bogus authorship and prevented Greene from denouncing the same. Chettle admitted that the manuscript of *Groatsworth* was in his hand, but claimed that he had had to copy over Greene's manuscript because the handwriting was bad. Chettle admittted that he had previously published something he had written over the initials of a better known writer, Tom Nashe, but claimed the typesetter was guilty.

Nashe vehemently denied having anything to do with *Groatsworth*, which he dubbed «a scald trivial lying pamphlet,» but he also defended Greene's memory, while distancing himself from Greene. Nashe's words imply that he did not believe Greene to be the author of *Groatsworth*.

Simultaneous with *Groatsworth*, another publisher put out *The Repentance of Robert Greene*, on the same subject. Are we to believe that Greene wrote two deathbed repentance pamphlets with parallel formats? Contemporaries did not question the authenticity of *The Repentance*, but did question *Groatsworth*. Chettle was one of two known suspects, and he did apologize for his involvement.

Greene married some years before 1592 but abandoned his wife around 1586. *The Repentance* says he had a child by her, but otherwise ignores his offspring, which implies that the child died. In London, Greene's mistress bore him a son, Fortunatus, and she was with Greene when he died. Whoever wrote the letter to Greene's wife that was printed at the end of *Groatsworth* was inaccurate about Greene's children. The letter says that Greene sends to his wife their son, which indicates that the author thought that Fortunatus Greene was the child of Greene's wife, unless we are to suppose that Greene carried his legitimate infant son to London while his deserted and virtuous wife went off to Lincolnshire, that he ignored his heir in *The Repentance*, and that the detailed account of his death in Gabriel Harvey's *Four Letters* also missed this child of Robert Greene, by then at least six years old.

In 1969, Professor Warren Austin completed a lengthy statistical comparison of *Groatsworth* to known works of Greene and Chettle, and concluded overwhelmingly that Chettle was the author. Austin's methodology was challenged in a review by R.L. Widmann.[2] This article is too brief to consider Austin's study in detail, but Widmann's review speaks strongly for Austin's hypothesis. Widmann keeps asserting that Austin's methodology is bad without explaining why. She condemns Austin for using photocopies of the original editions of Greene's work without showing that any misreadings resulted. Widmann uses phrases like «such a procedure is not advisable... Austin assumes, probably falsely ... there is no reason to suppose,» and «Austin relies too heavily on,» without providing the slightest justification. She proclaims Austin's data base «inadequate» without telling us how big it should have been, as if the requisite size were a matter of literary judgment rather than mathematics. To anyone with a statistical background, it is clear that Widmann is making superficial arguments, and that she cannot refute Austin.

In short, Greene was dead; a clear motive for fakery existed; the manuscript was in Chettle's handwriting; a previous work of Chettle's had been printed as by a better known writer, contemporaries did not believe Greene wrote *Groatsworth* and Chettle was suspect, while Nashe, another suspect, implied that Greene did not write *Groatsworth*; another deathbed repentance pamphlet appeared and no one questioned its authenticity, the letter to Greene's wife in *Groatsworth* contains a mistake that Greene could not have made; and the modern Shakespeare establishment was unable to undermine Austin's statistical evidence for Chettle as the author. To insist that Greene wrote *Groatsworth* is to defy all notions of scholarship and common sense.

Groatsworth includes a letter to three nameless playwrights, but provided enough intentionally identifying details to show that the first two were almost certainly Marlowe and Nashe. However, the third playwright was clearly given cover; all that can be inferred is that perhaps his first name was George. Chettle said that two of the playwrights were offended; about one he cared nothing, but he extended a handsome apology to the other. Chettle added that the two playwrights regarded him as the author of *Groatsworth* (another point to add to the previous paragraph). Somehow, the Stradfordian establishment transforms this apology to Marlowe, Nashe, or «perhaps George» into an apology to Shake-scene.

One of the few scholars who even attempts to justify the misreading of Chettle's unambiguous words is Sir E. K. Chambers, who argues that of the three playwrights only the first, Marlowe (who is called an atheist), had any cause to take offense. The only other principal who had grounds for being offended was Shake-scene, says Chambers, and therefore the apology must be to him. But even Homer nods occasionally, and so does Sir Edmund Chambers. He gives no explanation of why the apology may not be to Marlowe, who had powerful friends and patrons. He says that Nashe had no reason to be offended because nothing directly defaming him is found in *Groatsworth*. But Nashe's words in *Pierce Penniless* show clearly his anger at being connected to *Groatsworth*, and he also had powerful patrons. The third playwright, «perhaps George,» seems to have had the least ostensible reason for taking offense, but Nashe's anger, the Stationers' Register entry «upon the peril of Henry Chettle,» the latter's forced apology, and the careful concealment of the third playwright's identity all argue that there was genuine scandal somewhere in *Groatsworth*. Merely being alluded to in that pamphlet may have angered the third playwright. The newcomer to Shakespeare studies who takes the trouble to read the pamplets in question can only conclude in bewilderment that Shakespeare experts lose all sense of scholarship when they encounter Elizabethan playwrights with concealed identities. There are no scholarly grounds for doubting that Chettle apologized to one of the three playwrights, except by noting that, given the circumstances, nothing that Chettle says can be taken at face value.

If we assume that Shakespeare's works were written by William Shakspere of Stratford, then taking Shake-scene as Shakespeare makes sense, but there is another equally plausible explanation. Shake-scene is attacked with a line from *3 Henry VI*, and that play and *2 Henry VI* were published in pirated form in 1594 and 1595. The piracy was committed by several of Pembroke's Men, supposedly when that company broke up around September 1593. But there is no reason why the theft of another company's plays by former members could not have occurred in 1592, as Pembroke's was then in existence. The primary suspects were the actors who played Warwick and the doubled role of Suffolk and

Clifford, but the actor who played the Duke of York is also a suspect, and it is his line that is parodied in *Groatsworth*. For all these reasons, I propose that *Groatsworth* attacked one of Pembroke's Men (York?) for pirating two of Shakespeare's plays. This theory is fully consistent with what is known of that piracy and that troupe, with the epithet «Shake-scene,» with the letter and spirit of the full Shake-scene passage, and with the belief of so many scholars over the last two centuries that Shake-scene was charged with theft of some sort.

Endnotes

1   Warren Austin, «A Supposed Contemporary Allusion to Shakespeare as a Plagiarist,» *Shakespeare Quarterly*, 6:4 (1955), 373-80.
2   R. L. Widmann, *Shakespeare Quarterly*, 23 (1972), 214-15.

Masked Adonis and Stained Purple Robes

On October 22, 1593 an obscure poet named Thomas Edwards, apparently a minor courtier, registered a book of four poems which was published in 1595. Edwards' work consists of two major poems, «Cephalus and Procris» and «Narcissus,» each followed by an *envoi*. The work was republished with lengthy commentary by the Reverend W.E. Buckley in 1882, and was extensively discussed by Charlotte C. Stopes, to both of whom I am indebted.[1]

The *envoi* to «Narcissus» consists mostly of praise for six or seven contemporary poets, who are named with the titles or subjects of some of their poems; thus Spenser is called Collyn, Daniel is Rosamond, Watson is Amintas, and Marlowe is Leander. Then follow these three stanzas:

Adon deafly masking thro,	1
Stately troupes rich conceited,	
Shew'd he well deserved to	
Loves delight on him to gaze	
And had not love her selfe intreated,	5
Other nymphs had sent him baies.	
Eke in purple roabes distaind,	
Amid'st the Center of this clime.	
I have heard saie doth remaine,	
One whose power floweth far.	10
That should have bene of our rime	
The onely object and the star.	
Well could his bewitching pen,	
Done the Muses objects to us	
Although he differs much from men	15
Tilting under Frieries,	
Yet his golden art might woo us	
To have honored him with baies.	

Before analyzing these mysterious lines, a few minor points need to be touched on. The word «deafly» (line 1) presumably means «deftly»; of the first six examples of «deftly» in the *OED* (dating from 1480 to 1710), four spell the word without the «t.» The word «baies» (line 6) is middle English for «bays» (laurels). «(T)roupes» (line 2) probably means «tropes,» that is, figures of speech. «Eke» (line 7) is middle English for «also.» The phrase «Tilting under Frieries» (line 16) has elicited no good explanation, and I have none to offer (Edwards is sometimes murky). Edwards was fond of the language of arms, heraldry, and tournaments, and he used the word «tilting» to mean «striving,» particularly with regard to poetic endeavor. «Frieries» could refer to the Blackfriars Theater, but as Mrs. Stopes remarked, the old Blackfriars Theater closed some years earlier (the Earl of Oxford's company being among its last tenants), while the new Blackfriars had yet to open.

«Adon» (line 1) is unquestionably a reference to Shakespeare, whose immensely popular «Venus and Adonis» appeared in early 1593, with an author's dedication signed «William Shakespeare.» Yet Edwards says that Shakespeare was «masking thro» (line 1). There are several sub-definitions of the verb «to mask» in the *OED* (to wear a mask literally or figuratively, to be disguised or concealed, to participate in a masque), but all involve disguise. Stratfordians are cordially invited to explain why Edwards said that the author who published «Venus and Adonis» under the name William Shakespeare was «masking thro.» To Oxfordians the answer is obvious.

Let us peruse the next two stanzas regarding a great poet «in purple roabes distaind» (line 7). Much conjecture was made in the late nineteenth and early twentieth centuries on the identity of this «center poet,» as F.J. Furnivall dubbed him, and I will try to summarize briefly and clearly. First, though this has not been suggested before, the second and third stanzas can be read as a continuation of the first, that is, the «center poet» could be Adonis or Shakespeare. Next, «purple roabes» neatly limits the candidates to two categories, peers and certain high legal officials, including judges. None of the proposed candidates falls into the latter group (Francis Bacon was suggested, but he earned his purple robes some years later), so we are left with four peers who were put forward by orthodox scholars: Lord Buckhurst, the Earl of Oxford, the Earl of Essex (all discussed by the Rev. Buckley), and the 5th Earl of Derby (Mrs. Stopes' candidate).

One small item of evidence, not previously noticed, provides a bit of support for two of these candidates: Edwards' use of the word «star» (line 12). The only charge on Oxford's shield was a star, while the crest of Buckhurst's coat of arms was likewise a star. There was no star on the arms of either Essex or Derby.

All four noblemen were poets, though Oxford and Buckhurst easily overshadow Essex and Derby, both in contemporary reputation and in modern criticism.[2] Oxford, Derby, and Essex were also munificent patrons at the time of Edwards' poem, while Buckhurst's literary involvement had ceased two decades earlier.

Mrs. Stopes' case for Derby rests on her assertion that «(t)here is something against each of» the others, though she does not say what is against them (I will return to this point), and to several particular arguments in favor of Derby. First, Derbyshire is close to the geographical «center» (line 8) of England, though the Earl never lived there and his estates were mostly in Lancashire. Next, Derby's «power flow[ed] far» (line 10) in that the Earls of Derby were also a potential heir to Queen Elizabeth. Finally, Mrs Stopes feels that Derby had a particularly high standing in the eyes of English poets, because Thomas Nashe praised him effusively in 1592 and criticized Edmund Spenser for omitting Derby from the courtiers praised in the dedicatory sonnets in *The Faerie Queene* of 1590. Out of respect for Mrs. Stopes' fairness and industry, I will offer another argument for her candidate. The 5th Earl of Derby was known for most of his life as Lord Strange (he inherited the earldom in September 1593 and died the following April), and perhaps Edwards was referring to this title when he wrote, «Although he *differs* much from men» (line 15). (My emphasis.)

Several weaknesses of Mrs. Stopes' arguments have already been indicated parenthetically, but more counter arguments may be added if I thought that Edwards was talking about geography when he wrote «the center of this Clime.» In response, I would argue that, with a bit of poetic license, Oxfordshire is not far from the center of England. However, it seems to me that Edwards was speaking figuratively, meaning that his poetical peer was the center of England in almost every respect, particularly the cultural, rather than the geographic.

As for his «power floweth far,» Buckhurst and Essex were politically more powerful than Derby, while Oxford was still one of the Queen's favorites. From the point of view of the relatively humble Edwards, all of these men were powerful. Again I think that Edwards was speaking figuratively; earlier in his poem he referred to Spenser's «power,» and I doubt that he meant his political clout. In the world of poesy, Oxford, Derby, and Essex were all powers, while Buckhurst had been one.

As for Nashe's comment, he was presumably bidding for Derby's patronage, and extravagant praise is what most patrons expect. Moreover, not only did Spenser (whom Edwards worshiped above all others) omit Derby from those he lauded in *The Faerie Queen,* he specifically included Oxford, Essex, and Buckhurst. Essex's sonnet comes before the other two, though he is not praised for any connection to literature. Oxford's comes next, and he is proclaimed to be «most deare» to the Muses. After eight more sonnets comes Buckhurst's, who is lauded for his «learned Muse.»

It was presumably the foregoing arguments that Mrs. Stopes had in mind when she wrote that «(t)here is something against» Oxford, Essex, and Buckhurst, but, as has been shown, a close analysis indicates that Derby emerges with no advantage whatsoever. As for my argument about the title Lord Strange, it may be rebutted by noting that the center poet «differs much from men» specifically in that he is engaged in «Tilting under Frieries.» I fear that that phrase is so clipped and cryptic as to deny any confident explanation, though I encourage others to think of one. Also, if Edwards' line 15 favors Derby, the reference to a «star» in line 12 favors Oxford and Buckhurst. So far, all four lords are still viable candidates, with Oxford slightly ahead on points, but there are several more items to consider.

First, Rev. Buckley and Mrs. Stopes note that, for some reason, the «center poet» is not identified by a poetical nickname as are the others that Edwards acclaims. As has been stated, this could be because the two stanzas praising the «center poet» continue the praise for «Masked Adonis»/Shakespeare. Yet there is one word that Rev. Buckley and Mrs. Stopes ignore: «distaind» (line 7). The *OED* gives three sub-definitions for «distain» (which Shakespeare used as a synonym for «rape» in *Richard III*: to discolor, to defile or dishonor, and to deprive of color or brightness). Clearly our «center poet» or poetical peer has suffered some eclipse or loss of honor; there is a stain on his purple robes. As of 1593-95, Essex was the Queen's prime favorite, loaded with glory, honors, and offices. Derby was never touched by scandal (he rejected the one approach made to him by expatriate Catholic conspirators) and held high offices in the north of England. Buckhurst was always the soul of respectability, favored as the Queen's second cousin, was a Privy Councillor, and, following a spell of disfavor in 1587 for political opposition to the Earl of Leicester, recouped by being made a Knight of the Garter in 1589, as well as an ambassador in 1589 and 1591. As regards Edwards' «center poet,» Essex, Derby, and Buckhurst have just been eliminated. It is a different story with Oxford.

Oxford was a prankster and a truant in his youth, repudiated his wife, the daughter of Lord Burghley, in 1576, was at the center of two major scandals in 1580 and 1581, and was expelled from Court for two years, during which time he and his henchmen defended themselves in a murderous feud with the kinsmen of a Maid of Honor that he had made pregnant (though her subsequent career suggests that Oxford may not exactly have been a vile seducer). He re-united with his wife in 1581, though his all-powerful father-in-law continued to complain of him, and was socially rehabilitated in 1583. He served against the Armada and was offered military commands in 1585 and 1588, but neither worked out. From 1589 on, his life seems free of scandal, but the records of his activities are reduced to a suspicious trickle. Dr. A.P. Grosart, a leading nineteenth century Elizabethan scholar, wrote that «an unlifted shadow lies across his memory» while his twentieth century biographer, B. M. Ward, entitled his section on the years 1589 to 1601, «The Recluse.» Oxfordians and Stratfordians alike agree that there was something of a cloud over Oxford.

Mrs. Stopes feels that Edwards' statement «*I have heard* say doth remaine» (line 9) means that the author of «Narcissus» did not personally know the «center poet,» «and was fearful of offending him by giving him a name.» Her first point is plausible but not conclusive, while her second point is less plausible. Edwards' assertion that he is operating on hearsay is more likely an escape hatch in case he had given offense to the authorities, a familiar device in that era (for a contemporary example, see «Hadrian Dorrell's» Introduction to *Willobie his Avisa*). The social customs and taboos of Elizabethan England were complicated, but simply naming Lord So-and-so as a great poet was common enough, e.g., Spenser's dedicatory sonnets to *The Faerie Queene*, and there were several recognized ways of identifying people without naming them, such as references to coats of arms or to a poet's works. In fine, Mrs. Stopes doesn't push her logic far enough. The word «distaind,» Edwards' reference to hearsay, and his failure to identify clearly the «center poet» add up to a strong indication that Edwards was treading on thin ice, which makes no sense for Derby, but does make sense if he was speaking of Oxford.

I do not claim to have proven that the «center poet» in his stained purple robes was Oxford, as I have not considered every other member of the House of Lords, but that he is the only one of the four peers suggested by orthodox scholars who fits the bill. Let us say that Oxford was probably the «center poet,» and let us keep in mind that his praise immediately follows a reference to Shakespeare wearing a mask.

Edwards' mention of a poetical peer with a stain on his robes was presumably written in 1593, and it needs to be considered in the context of that year, during which Nashe and also Thomas Kyd wrote of noble patrons without giving names. Similarly, Edwards' description of «masked Adonis» should be added to the category of Odd Things Said About Shakespeare e.g., Davies of Hereford's mention of the stage staining his pure gentle blood.

Addendum

The Rev. Buckley's discussion of the Earl of Oxford includes an unelaborated statement that Coxeter said that Oxford made a translation of Ovid. Thomas Coxeter (1689-1747) and his works are briefly described in the *Dictionary of National Biography*. The *DNB* gives Coxeter rather low marks for reliability, but presumably his statement about Oxford was based on something tangible. However, I have not been able to locate Coxeter's remark; I suggest that someone with better reference sources follow up on the matter, which tallies nicely with J. Thomas Looney's conjecture that Oxford had a hand in Golding's translation of *Ovid's Metamorphoses*. Coxeter's evidence might amount to nothing, but it could lead us to material of real value; at any rate, it seems that he knew something that we do not.

Endnotes

1   Charlotte Stopes, «Thomas Edwards, Author of ‹Cephalus and Procris, Narcissus,›» *Modern Language Review,* 16, Nos. 3-4 (Jul-Oct 1921). Also, W.E. Buckley (Ed); *Cephalus and Procris; Narcissus.* (Roxburghe Club, 1882.)

2   My argument for Oxford's modern reputation rests on Sir E.K. Chambers' opinion, as given in *The Oxford Book of Sixteenth Century Verse* (Oxford, 1932).

Neglected Praise of the 17th Earl of Oxford

Edward de Vere earned considerable praise, as well as some criticism, during his lifetime, but the several tributes to him after his death are in some ways more interesting, as his power and patronage were no longer in operation.

George Chapman, who is not known as one of Oxford's protégés and who never dedicated anything to him, nevertheless highly commended Oxford in his play *The Revenge of Bussy d'Ambois* (published in 1613). Chapman, however, had more to say about Oxford. In 1609 appeared Chapman's *Twelve Books of the Iliads*, which included dedicatory sonnets to sixteen lords, ladies, and knights. Among these was Oxford's then twenty-two year old daughter Susan, Countess of Montgomery, whose sonnet is followed by this postscript:

> By the long-since admirer of your matchless Father's virtues; and now of your excellent Ladyship's, Geo. Chapman.[1]

None of the other sonnets, with their various prescripts and postscripts, makes any mention of the parents of the subject. Even the sonnet to the Earl of Salisbury neglects his illustrious father. Chapman's 1941 editor, Phyllis B. Bartlett, says in a footnote that Chapman's praise of Oxford «appeared as an afterthought on an extra leaf,» which should be re-phrased as «Chapman felt it important to add an extra page to his book.»

Dr. Bartlett also slips when she confesses her inability to determine the «friend» that Chapman says has also praised the Countess of Montgomery; the obvious answer is Ben Jonson in his Epigram CIV. However, Dr. Bartlett compensates by pointing out an anomaly in Chapman's poem «Pro Vere,» which begins:

> All my yeeres comforts, fall in Showres of Teares,
> That this full Spring of Man, this VERE of VERES
> ... ...

> Famine should barre my Fruites, whose Bountie breedes them,
> The faithlesse World love to devoure who feedes them.

This poem was written in 1622 to celebrate General Sir Horatio Vere, Oxford's first cousin, and, as Dr. Bartlett points out, one or more couplets have clearly been omitted after line 2. The gap may be accidental, but when the only discontinuity in the poems that Chapman published comes after praise of the Veres and is followed by a comment on the world's ingratitude, one suspects censorship. Our British colleagues might find it worthwhile to see if the manuscript of «Pro Vere» can be found.

The unreliable, late seventeenth century gossip monger John Aubrey is best known for a minor piece of smut that he related about Oxford returning from his travels to the English Court, where he publicly suffered a case of flatulence in the Queen's presence. However, one paragraph later, we find Aubrey referring to Edward de Vere as «the great Earle of Oxford.» So Aubrey joins King James and Francis Osborne (both contemporaries at Oxford) in describing the late 17th Earl with the epithet «great.»

Yet Aubrey has more to say. His life of Sir Charles Danvers says that the latter's «familiar acquaintance(s) were the Earl of Oxon; Sir Francis and Sir Horatio Vere; Sir Walter Ralegh, etc. — the Heroes of those times.» Aubrey's life of Ralegh states that, «He was a second to the Earle of Oxford in a Duell. Was acquainted and accepted with all the Hero's of our Nation in his time.»

Aubrey's last item requires a slight digression. An article in *Notes and Queries* contains information of interest.[2] It seems that Ralegh was a member of the Catholic courtier circle to which Oxford belonged at the time of his famous quarrel with Philip Sidney. When Oxford broke with that group in late 1580, there occurred a notorious exchange of charges between him and his former friends, one of whom, Charles Arundell, said that he and Ralegh were employed by Oxford to carry his challenge to Sidney. There are two other accounts of the proposed duel: one says that Oxford challenged Sidney, while the other has it that Sidney challenged Oxford. It seems likely enough that each issued a challenge more or less simultaneously. At any rate, for once there is corroboration for one of Aubrey's anecdotes.

A further digression is needed to consider what Ralegh was doing in Catholic circles. Ralegh's parents were staunch Protestants who suffered for their faith, he fought for the Huguenots in the 1570s, and he left the Court in 1580 to fight Catholicism in Ireland. Peck plausibly suggests that Ralegh may have been motivated by opportunism, but another historian speculates that Ralegh was a spy employed by Burghley or Walsingham. Both motives may, of course, have been in operation.

To conclude, John Aubrey's charge of flatulence is so near to the hearts of many Stratfordians that I am inclined to say, let them have it; but then they must also grant that Aubrey called Oxford «great» and a «Hero.»

Endnotes

1   *The Works of George Chapman, Poems and Minor Translations* (London: Chatto and Windus, 1904) 201.
2   D.C. Peck, «Raleigh, Sidney, Oxford, and the Catholics, 1579,» *Notes and Queries*, October 1978.

The Lame Storyteller, Poor and Despised

This article discusses several items discovered by Professor Alan H. Nelson of the University of California, Berkeley in his examination and transcription of all documents written by or directly about Edward de Vere, the 17th Earl of Oxford. I gratefully acknowledge Professor Nelson's permission to use this material.*

The article starts by demonstrating that a description of Oxford made in 1581 precisely matches Ben Jonson's well-known description of Shakespeare's runaway wit. It will then be shown that Oxford was lame during the latter part of his life, matching Shakespeare's lameness as mentioned in Sonnets 37 and 89. We will see that orthodox scholars reject a literal meaning of «lame» for a very valid reason, namely, that Shakespeare calls himself «poor, lame, and despised,» attributes which do not fit what we know about William Shakspere of Stratford. All three qualities, however, fit Oxford.

Runaway Wit

The first item of interest is an extract from a libel made against Oxford by Charles Arundel in late January 1581 or soon after, which begins: «A trew declaracion of the Earell of oxfordes detestabl[e] vicees, and vnpure life.» Arundel, who went on to become the principal author of the most notorious libel of the Elizabethan Age, *Leicester's Commonwealth*, had been placed under arrest for treasonable activities in December 1580 and was trying to destroy the credibility of his accuser, Oxford. His «Declaration» accuses Oxford of five categories of evil: «impudent, and sencelesse lies,» of being «a most notorious drunkerd,» «a bowgerer of a boye that is his coke,» «detestable practices of hireid murthers,» and

> ffiftlie to shewe, that the worell [i.e., world] never browght forthe suche a villonous Monster, and for a partinge blow to geve him his

---

* See Alan H. Nelson, *Monstrous Adversary: The Life of Edward de Vere, 17th Earl of Oxford* (Liverpool, England: Liverpool Univ. Press, 2003) — Editor

full payment, I will prove against him, his most horrible and detestable blasphemy in deniall of the devinitie of Christ... (all quotations from Charles Arundel provided by Professor Nelson, who cites
Public Record Office, SP12/151[45] ff.100-2)

As Arundel tells it, Oxford's impudent and senseless lies were tall tales
concerning his travels in Flanders, France and Italy. Arundel's previous
libel cited such untruths as that Oxford maintained that St. Mark's
Cathedral at Venice was paved with diamonds and rubies, while the
cobblers' wives at Milan were more richly dressed every working day
than was Queen Elizabeth at Christmas. But in the libel under consideration, Arundel limits himself to Oxford's Münchausen-like war stories,
«as heretofore they have made much sporte to the hereers.»

Arundel claimed that Oxford said that he so impressed the famous
Duke of Alva in Flanders that Alva (who had departed the year before
Oxford's visit) placed him in command of all the King of Spain's forces
in the Low Countries, where he accomplished such mighty feats that his
fame spread to Italy. So, when Oxford traveled to Italy, the Pope gave
him an army of 30,000 men to intervene in a civil war in Genoa. Having
related these matters, Arundel seems, unconsciously, to drop his guard
in wonder, continuing [my emphasis]:

> this lie is verye rife w[i]t[h] him and in it he glories greatie, diverslie
> hathe he told it, <u>and when he enters into it, he can hardlie owte</u>.
> Which hathe made suche sporte as often have I bin driven to rise
> from his table laugheinge so hath my L[ord] Charles howard [of
> Effingham], and the rest, whome I namid before and for the profe of
> this I take them all as wittnises [the witnesses included Lords Wind-
> sor, Compton, Henry Howard, and Thomas Howard, as well as
> Walter Ralegh.]

Arundel is telling us that Oxford was a marvelously imaginative storyteller, who could tell the same tale over and over to the same audience,
convulsing them with laughter every time. Yet in that passage, «and
when he enters into it, he can hardly out,» Arundel describes a personal

characteristic emphasized by Ben Jonson in his description of Shakespeare. Having remarked that the actors praised Shakespeare as having never blotted a line, Jonson said that Shakespeare should have blotted out a thousand, meaning that he let himself get carried away with his wit, not knowing when to stop. Jonson elaborated:

> Hee was (indeed) honest, and of an open, and free nature: had an excellent *Phantasie*: brave notions, and gentle expressions; wherein hee flow'd with that facility, that sometime it was necessary he should be stop'd: *Sufflaminandus erat*; [i.e., he needed a brake] as *Augustus* said of *Haterius*. His wit was in his owne power; would the rule of it had beene so too. Many times hee fell into those things, could not escape laughter: (Herford & Simpson, 8, 583-4)

So Jonson describes a characteristic of Shakespeare that is identical to what Arundel said of Oxford—that once he turned his wit on, he was unable to turn it off. We should also note the emphatic nature of Arundel's and Jonson's comments, as indicating that the personal quality in question was a most salient feature of the man being described. Arundel is putting forth a carefully organized blast of slander, driven by a desire for revenge, as well as to discredit Oxford's accusations against him. But then, weakening the force of his own slander, he depicts Oxford's storytelling ability as if he is simply unable to get over that aspect of Oxford. Jonson, ironically, commits the same fault he criticizes in Shakespeare, being unable to let go of his idea until he has said it four different ways: «wherein he flowed... Sufflaminandus erat... His wit was in his owne power... Many times hee fell...»

Lame

In turning to Professor Nelson's transcriptions of Oxford's letters from 1590 to 1603, we find that Oxford states that he is unable to travel for reasons of bad health or infirmity, in his letters of September 1590 (Fowler, 378), March 1595 (Salisbury, 5, 158), August 1595 (Fowler, 496), September 1597 (Fowler, 524), October 1601 (Fowler, 593), and April 1603 (Fowler, 739). He does not specify the nature of his ailment(s), yet in a letter to his father-in-law, Lord Burghley, dated 25 March 1595, Oxford writes: «I will attend yowre Lordship as well as a lame man may at yowre house» (extract in Salisbury, 5, 154; this quote from Professor Nelson). On 27 November 1601, Oxford wrote to his brother-in-law, Sir Robert Cecil, closing with, «thus desyring yow to beare w[i]th the weaknes of my lame hand, I take my leaue» (Fowler, 607; this quote from Professor Nelson). In January 1602, he wrote again to Cecil, noting, «thus wythe a lame hand, to wright I take my leue» (Fowler, 653).

Shakespeare's Sonnet 37 contains these lines:

> So I, made lame by Fortune's dearest spite, (3)
> ....
> So then I am not poor, lame, nor despised, (9)

Sonnet 89 returns to this theme: «Speak of my lameness, and I straight will halt» (3).

Recent editors of the *Sonnets* insist that the obvious conclusion that the poet might literally have been lame cannot possibly be true, but they cannot be bothered to give the modern reader good arguments to support their ideology. W.G. Ingram and Theodore Redpath's 1964 edition begins its notes on Sonnet 37 by sneering at the idea that the lame poet is someone other than the actor from Stratford, and then goes on to explain that the word «lame» can be taken metaphorically. Ingram and Redpath imply that the existence of a figurative meaning excludes the possibility of a literal reading. John Kerrigan's 1986 edition makes the same argument.

Stephen Booth's 1978 edition of the *Sonnets* is notable for exceeding all others in finding an absurdly large number of multiple meanings in Shakespeare's words. As Kerrigan puts it, Booth works on the «principle that any extractable meaning is significant» (65). Yet when he comes to Sonnets 37 and 89, Booth will allow «lame» to have only one meaning—the poet is apologizing for his poor meter. Booth offers five examples of poets using «lame,» «limping,» or «halting» to indicate bad

meter, examples which utterly disprove Booth's interpretation of Shakespeare's words. To add a sixth example, John Donne begins the poem
«To Mr. T. W.:» «Haste thee harsh verse as fast as thy lame measure/Will
give thee leave.» As with Donne, all five of Booth's examples apply the
modifier «lame/limping/halting» to the poet's verse, not to the poet
himself. In no case does a poet write, «I am lame,» expecting readers to
understand the words as an apology for bad meter.

Now, it is true that words can have both literal and figurative meanings
as well as special meanings within the conventions of poetry. However,
Ingram and Redpath, Booth and Kerrigan all fail to give us a valid
reason for not taking Shakespeare's words literally.

Older editors of the *Sonnets* showed more respect for their readers'
intelligence. Hyder Rollins' 1944 New Variorum edition offers in its
notes to Sonnet 37 this quotation from Edmond Malone's edition of 1790
(my emphasis):

> If the words are to be understood literally, we must then suppose
> that... [Shakespeare] was also <u>poor</u> and <u>despised</u>, for neither of
> which suppositions there is the smallest ground.

Rollins also makes this argument concerning line 9 of Sonnet 37 (my
emphasis):

> Literalists might note that, even if he was lame, Sh. could not have
> been <u>poore</u>, for he had jewels which ([Sonnet] 48.1-5), during his
> absences from London, he put in a sort of safe-deposit vault.

Now here is good sense. Malone and Rollins are telling us that the
author of Sonnets 37 and 89 does not match what we know of William
Shakspere of Stratford, who became quite well-to-do from a modest
beginning, and who could hardly be said to be poor if he owned jewels
of value, as indicated in Sonnet 48. On the other hand, the author of
these Sonnets certainly matches what is known of the Earl of Oxford,
who was never in real poverty, but who was disgracefully poor for an
earl.

Poor and Despised

Owing to extravagant habits and unlucky financial speculation, Oxford was forced to sell most of his inherited lands by 1585 (Ward, 353). In 1586, the Queen granted him an annual pension of 1,000 pounds, to continue «until such time as he shall be by Us otherwise provided for to be in some manner relieved» (Ward, 257). After Oxford's death in 1604, his widow and son received a much smaller pension from King James. She petitioned that the annuity be raised to 500 pounds a year, noting:

> The pension of 1,000 pounds was not given by the late Queen to my Lord for his life and then to determine [i.e., cease], but to continue until the Queen might raise his decay by some better provision. (Salisbury, 16, 258)

Elsewhere in the letter, she referred to her «ruined estate... desolate estate... greate distresse... miserable estate» (copy of original letter from Matus, 261).

About the same time, James was having to fend off a debt-ridden baron who felt that a grant of 1,000 pounds a year was too small. The King commented, «Great Oxford when his [e]state was whole ruined got no more of the late Queen» (Salisbury, 16, 397). Some time after Oxford's death, Sir George Buck, Master of the Revels, made a note on Oxford's magnificence, learning and religion, adding that in the promise of his youth, Oxford seemed «much more like to raise... a new earldom, than to decay... waste & lose an old earldom» (Miller, 394).

So, we know that Oxford was poor as well as lame, and we also know that he was despised accordingly. When Queen Elizabeth was dying, the Earl of Lincoln tried to enlist Oxford in some scheme of opposition to King James. Sir John Peyton, Lieutenant of the Tower of London, found out about Lincoln's activities, but failed to report them. Peyton excused himself for this dereliction by saying that he took the matter seriously until he found out that Lincoln's alleged accomplice was Oxford, on whom Peyton passed this verdict (my emphasis):

> I knewe him to be <u>so weake in boddy, in friends, in habylytie,</u> and all other means to rayse any combustyon in the state, as I never feered any danger to proseyd from so feeble a fowndation. (O'Conor, 107)

Peyton's words merit a close inspection. He calls Oxford weak in body, a reference to that infirmity cited in Oxford's letters that led him to describe himself as «lame.» Peyton next notes that Oxford lacked friends, which is a way of saying that he was despised or looked down on (*OED*). Peyton then says that Oxford lacked «ability... to raise... combustion in the state,» which in the context of potential for raising insurrection, means (*OED* definition 4 of «ability»): «Pecuniary power; wealth, estate, means.» Or, in other words, Peyton is saying that Oxford was poor.

Shakespeare also frequently laments that he is old in the *Sonnets*, which would be appropriate coming from Oxford. Shakespeare says that his career has brought him shame and disgrace by virtue of his association with the public stage in Sonnets 110 and 111, and by his literary career in Sonnet 72. Such matters would hardly have brought disgrace to Shakspere of Stratford. Shakespeare alludes to life at Court in several sonnets, especially 125. He repeatedly castigates the highborn friend to whom the first 126 sonnets are addressed, something not done by poets of humble origins to their patrons back then. Moreover, when the *Sonnets* appeared in print in 1609, the publisher's dedication referred to the author as «OVR.EVER.LIVING.POET»—unambiguously meaning that he was dead (see endnote). Oxford died in 1604; Shakspere in 1616.

In conclusion, when we match Ben Jonson's description of Shakespeare's runaway wit to what we know of the phantom of Stratford-on-Avon, we find nothing to work with. When we match that description to what Charles Arundel said about the Earl of Oxford, we get a perfect fit. When we match Shakespeare's words in Sonnets 37 and 89 to what we know of the affluent burgher of Stratford, we find such a mismatch that orthodox scholars must take one of two courses: either they twist Shakespeare's meaning into something no sensible reader can accept, or else, as with Malone and Rollins, they tell us that Shakespeare's autobiographical words cannot apply to Shakspere of Stratford. This latter explanation we can very well accept, especially when we discover that the Earl of Oxford was «poor, lame, and despised.» Moreover, the author of the *Sonnets* indicates that he is old, shamed by his literary and theatrical career, and a courtier of high enough station to sharply criticize his aristocratic friend, while his publisher said that he was dead by 1609.

Both Oxford and the author Shakespeare were superb tellers of imaginative stories, possessed of an extraordinary wit, and they were poor, lame and despised. Further, Oxford matches the author of Shakespeare's *Sonnets* on a number of other points where the Stratford man does not fit. The odds against such similarity resulting from sheer coincidence are formidably long.

Endnote

In 1926, Colonel B .R Ward published a list of 23 examples of use of the term «ever-living,» compiled from concordances and major dictionaries (Miller, 211-14). All the examples refer to deities, abstractions and dead people. I would like to take this opportunity to provide an update on Colonel Ward's work.

No scholar of the Stratfordian persuasion has found a single example of «ever-living» being applied to a living person, though at least one tried. Professor Donald Foster writes: «In a fairly extensive search, I have not found any instance of ever-living used in a Renaissance text to describe a living mortal, including, even, panegyrics on Queen Elizabeth, where one should most expect to find it—though it does appear sometimes in eulogies for the dead.» («Master W.H., R.I.P.,» *PMLA* [Jan. 1987] 102, 1:46)

Miller's version of Ward's list contains an error. The example printed as: «In that he is man, he received life from the Father as the foundation of that <u>everliving</u> Deity. (Hooker, 1593)» Should read: «In that he is man, he received life from the Father as from the fountain of that <u>ever living</u> Deity, which is the Person of the Word.» (Hooker's *Of the Laws of Ecclesiastical Polity*, V, lvi, 4, 1593)

In the meantime, I have encountered a few more examples. Henry Brinklow's 1542 *Complaynt of Roderyck Mors* and *The Lamentacyon of a Christen agaynst the Cytye of London* (Early English Text Society, Extra Series, 1874, no. 22) use the term «everlyving God» six times (53, 56, 76, 93, 94, 98). The statute 1 Mary I, St. 2, c. 1 has the phrase, «wee beseeche Thalmightye and ever lyving God» (*The Statutes of the Realm*, IV, 200). The anonymous 1591 *Troublesome Raigne of King John* includes:

> Thus hath K Richards Sonne performde his vowes.
> And offered Austrias bloud for sacrifice
> Unto his fathers everliving soule. (VI, 1044-46)

Gabriel Harvey's 1592 Sonnet XIII in *Foure Letters and Certeine Sonnets* provides a variant usage of particular interest as showing clearly that «live ever» meant «dead» if applied to a human being. The sonnet appeals to Fame on behalf of ten recently deceased knights (the Bacon in question being Sir Nicholas), beginning:

> Live ever valorous renowned Knightes;
> Live ever Smith, and Bacon, Peerles men:
> Live ever Walsingham, and Hatton wise:
> Live ever Mildmayes honorable name.
> Ah, that Sir Humphry Gilbert should be dead:
> Ah, that Sir Philip Sidney should be dead:

Works Cited

William Plumer Fowler, *Shakespeare Revealed in Oxford's Letters* (Portsmouth, NH: Peter Randall, 1986).

C.H. Herford, Percy Simpson, & Evelyn Simpson, *Ben Jonson* (1947), «Timber: or, Discoveries.»

Irvin Leigh Matus, *Shakespeare, In Fact* (NY: Continuum, 1994).

Ruth Loyd Miller, Volume II to J. T. Looney's «*Shakespeare*» *Identified*. 3rd ed. (Jennings, LA: Minos Press, 1975)

Norreys Jephson O'Conor, *Godes Peace and the Queenes* (London: Oxford UP, 1934).

Manuscripts of the Marquess of Salisbury; H.M.C. Series.

B. M. Ward, *The Seventeenth Earl of Oxford* (London: John Murray, 1928).

Shakespeare's Astronomy

Despite a few references to astrology, Shakespeare seems to have had little interest in physics or mathematics (in contrast, for instance, to John Donne). However, he did write one well known passage on astronomy, spoken by Ulysses in *Troilus and Cressida* (I.iii.85-91):

> The heavens themselves, the planets, and this center   85
> Observe degree, priority, and place,
> Insisture, course, proportion, season, form,
> Office, and custom, in all line of order:
> And therefore is the glorious planet Sol
> In noble eminence enthron'd and spher'd   90
> Amidst the other; ...

Most annotated editions of *Troilus and Cressida* assert that this passage shows that Shakespeare believed in the ancient Ptolemaic theory of the heavens, in which the stationary Earth is orbitted by the sun and the planets. The basis for this assertion is the final phrase of line 85 («this center»), which places the Earth amid the other celestial bodies. But a few observers, including Charlton Ogburn, argue that lines 89-91 support the Copernican theory (announced in 1543) that the immobile sun is circled by the Earth and the other planets.

In fact, Ulysses' statement cannot be reconciled with either theory; lines 89-91 are at variance with Ptolemy, while line 85 contradicts Copernicus. Also, the sun («Sol») is called a planet, literally meaning «wanderer,» which further disagrees with Copernicus. Actually, wise Ulysses is describing the compromise between Ptolemy and Copernicus that was devised by the Danish astonomer Tycho Brahe in the 1580s. In Tycho's system, the Earth is the fixed center (consistent with line 85), about which the sun orbits (consistent with the word «planet» in line 89), while the remaining planets circle round the sun (consistent with lines 89-91).

It may seem a pity to deny the possibility that Shakespeare was advanced enough to support Copernicus, but it must be remembered that there were several very real objections to the Copernican theory that were not solved until Kepler and Galileo modified that theory in the early 17th Century.

When and how Shakespeare came to know Tycho's planetary system is hard to say. The theory originated in 1583 and was published in 1588 in a limited edition that Tycho sent to friends and correspondents. The work in question, *The Second Volume About Recent Appearances in the Celestial World*, was finally offered to the public in 1603. However, in 1588, another astronomer, Reymers Baer, published a similar theory, and Tycho, always a wrangler, charged Baer with theft. In addition, in 1598 Tycho published a short work describing his famous instruments and his leading discoveries. Actually, it was unnecessary for Shakespeare to have read any of these books, as Tycho was the most famous astronomer of his day (King James of Scotland visited him in 1590), and he had correspondents in England and other countries, so Shakespeare could have learned of Tycho's system any time after 1583. It is interesting to note that the 17th Earl of Oxford may have met Tycho Brahe in Italy, as both were in Venice in mid to-late 1575.

Suffolk's Head and Royal Behavior

In Act IV, Scene i of 2 *Henry VI*, William de la Pole, Duke of Suffolk and lover of Queen Margaret, is beheaded. In Scene iv Margaret brings his head to a conference at the palace, where she weeps over and embraces it. Margaret's behavior is denounced as unqueenly by Louis Auchincloss, who adduces her misconduct as evidence that Shakespeare was ignorant on the subject of royal deportment.[1] The unhistorical incident of Suffolk's head probably derives from an event during Shakespeare's lifetime.

In 1574, the French Court was convulsed by a treason plot that involved two Princes of the Blood, but only two lesser figures, Joseph de La Mole and Hannibal de Cocconas, were punished. They were tortured, tried, and beheaded. These men were, respectively, the lovers of Margaret of Valois, Queen of Navarre and of the Duchess of Nevers. A few hours after the executions the two heads disappeared, and it was said that Margaret's chamberlain brought them to the two ladies who «wept over them that night and then had them enbalmed and placed in jeweled caskets».[2] Whether this story is true is not at issue; the point is that it was told, and its similarity to 2 *Henry VI* is striking.

In both cases there is a queen named Margaret who is French and who receives the head of her decapitated lover in order to weep over it. There is also the resemblance between the names de la Pole and de La Mole. The likelihood that Shakespeare had the executions of 1574 in his mind when he wrote 2 *Henry VI* is strengthened by the fact that he knew a good deal about Margaret of Valois and her husband Henry of Navarre (later King Henry IV of France); *Love's Labour's Lost* is based on an episode in their lives. Also, the fate of de La Mole was of interest to the English Court as he had charmed Queen Elizabeth on an embassy in 1572. She unsuccessfully interceded on his behalf through her ambassador to France, and also expressed her regrets after the execution.

The 17th Earl of Oxford was at Elizabeth's Court at the times of de La Mole's embassy and execution, and he visited the French Court in early 1575, thus being well placed to hear the story of Queen Margaret and de La Mole's head.

Endnotes

1   Louis Auchincloss, *Motiveless Malignity* (Boston: Houghton Mifflin, 1969) 107. See also Charlton Ogburn Jr. *The Mysterious William Shakespeare* (New York: Dodd, Mead, 1984), 256.

2   E.R. Chamberlin, *Marguerite of Valois* (New York: Dial Press, 1974) 129. See also Charlotte Haldane, *Queen of Hearts*, (London: Constable, 1968) 68-74; and the Calendar of State Papers.

The Fable of the World, Twice Told

Author's Note: The McKeldin Library at the University of Maryland holds nearly one hundred volumes of the Historical Manuscript Commission (HMC) Reports. These books consist mostly of transcripts and abstracts of letters of leading British families. The set at McKeldin is incomplete, but it does include nineteen of the twenty volumes of the Salisbury Manuscripts, the papers of the Cecil family. The entire HMC collection has a three-volume general index, which I realized was incomplete. Consequently, I went through the indexes of the nineteen volumes of the Salisbury Manuscripts, and then through the indexes of the other eighty or so volumes. In the former, I found a great deal on the Earl of Oxford, mostly routine matters, and in the latter a few odds and ends. In the quotations that follow, additions made by the HMC compilers are shown (thus) in single parentheses, while my own additions are ((thus)) in double parentheses.

On 3 July 1575, Sir Walter Mildmay congratulated Lord Burghley on the happy delivery of Lady Oxford.[1] In 1594 Burghley drew up a historical chronology of his family, which states that his granddaughter Elizabeth Vere was baptized at Theobalds on 10 July 1575.[2] The date of the former item and the location of the latter (Theobalds was close to London) virtually rule out the possibility that Lady Oxford delivered in September (which would have implied illegitimacy), which Lord Oxford should have been able to confirm easily. The ruin of his marriage had a different cause.

Burghley had Oxford spied upon while in Italy, with one spy's report being written on 23 September 1575.[3] B.M. Ward publishes the report on page 106 of his biography of Oxford, though he does not identify it as such.

On 25 April 1576, Burghley penned a memorial on Oxford's separation from his wife,[4] most of which is reported by Conyers Read and Charlton Ogburn Jr.[5] On 27 April, Oxford wrote his harsh letter to Burghley, insisting on the separation of himself from his wife, making a pointed reference to Lady Burghley, and regretting that Burghley's indiscretion has made this scandal into «the fable of the world.»[6]

On 29 April, Burghley wrote a memo, summarized in HMC Salisbury, which I quote in its entirety:

> «The communication I had with my Lord of Oxford.» Contains various complaints made by the Earl, such as «His money not made over to him according to his directions,» «his followers not favoured by me,» «his letter showed to the Queen of set purpose to bring him into her Majesty's indignation» etc. With respect to Oxford's wife, Burghley's daughter, «taken away from him at Wivenhoe and carried to London, he means not to discover anything of the cause of his misliking, but he will not come to her until he understands further of it; also that «my wife hath ever drawn his wife's love from him, and that she hath wished him dead»; and that «at Wivenhoe she caused a division in his house, and a slander to be raised of him for intention of killing of his men.»[7]
>
> In Burghley's hand. 1 page.

Before discussing this extraordinary item, I will summarize a few more. At an unknown date in 1576, Burghley drew up a list of six complaints made by Oxford against him; Burghley denied or justified all of them.[8]

> «1. That Clopton and Faunt ((Oxford's men)) were ... maintained ((by Burghley)). 2. That Denny, the French boy, and others that lay in wait to kill Clopton, were punished by the Lord Treasurer ((Burghley)). 3. That he ((Oxford)) had not his money made over sea so speedily as he desired. 4. That his wife was most directed by her father and mother. 5. That Hubbard would not deliver to the Earl his writings ((concerning his debts)), wherein he was maintained by the Lord Treasurer. 6. That his book of entail was not enrolled whereby the estates were void.»

These two-and-a-half pages in Burghley's hand close as follows: «1576. His own good nature. Pleasing of Almighty God wherein is contained *omnes charitates*» etc, etc, «The greatest possession that any man can have is honor, good name, good will of many and of the best sort.»

There is also a summary of a statement in Burghley's handwriting refuting «certain slanderous reports as to his conduct towards the Earl of Oxford,» namely items 3 and 6 above.[9] The HMC dates this at 10 July 1570, but it refers to Oxford's trip to Italy of 1575-76. Lastly is a one page document of uncertain date (the HMC guesses 1577) which is summarized as: «Memoranda by Lord Burghley of the good offices rendered by him from time to time to the Earl of Oxford and of the latter's subsequent ingratitude.»[10]

The items above relating to Clopton, Faunt, and Denny presumably refer to the Gad's Hill episode of 1573.[11] Ward speaks of Wotton rather than Clopton, but my guess is that these are the same men, and either Ward or the HMC compiler misread the name. In other words, the Gad's Hill attack was intended to kill or terrorize two spies that Burghley placed in Oxford's household. Burghley's spying tendencies are well established. He spied on his son Thomas during his travels in 1561-3, as he spied on Oxford; he apparently placed John Florio as a spy in Lord Southampton's household in the early 1590s; and Robert Lacey's 1974 biography of Sir Walter Ralegh argues for several reasons that the Protestant Ralegh was acting as a government spy when he joined the Catholic courtier circle to which Oxford belonged in 1579. The six-page article on Burghley in the *Dictionary of National Biography* (*DNB*) sadly acknowledges that Burghley's domestic spying was dishonorable. Conyers Read's sycophantic two-volume biography ignores this distressing matter.

As for the five-year break in Oxford's first marriage, it appears that Lord and Lady Burghley's domineering habits were the cause. One may imagine the scene at Wivenhoe for oneself. Oxford's initial suspicions of infidelity could have been satisfied, but he must have been enraged by the spying, by Lady Burghley trying to raise a mutiny among his servants, and by the carrying away of his wife. Another cause of resentment indicated by these old documents is that it took Oxford

years to pry his full estate out of the hands of Burghley, his former
guardian. So the clumsiness of the Burghleys wrecked the marriage that
they wished to save. It may be added that Lady Burghley showed
hostility toward Oxford as early as 1572.[12] The only known quarrel
during the final seven-year phase of the marriage, during 1581-8, occurred in 1587 as a result of Lady Oxford siding with her father against her
husband.[13]

I interpret the remainder of the 29 April memo as follows. The letter
shown to the Queen to excite her indignation is likely to be Oxford's
letter of 27 April, which was written at Greenwich. Lady Burghley's
slander aimed at upsetting Oxford's servants has a double ring of *déjà vu*
about it—something like this happened twenty-three years earlier, and
then again twenty-one years later. Servants in those times were not mere
employees; they were part of the household and were supposed to be
utterly loyal to their master. In fact, their loyalty included the duty of
keeping their master from committing crime or folly. Upon the death of
Edward VI in 1553, the 16th Earl of Oxford declared his support for
Lady Jane Grey as Queen, whereupon his servants mutinied in favor of
Princess Mary Tudor, whereupon the Earl wisely changed his mind. It
was difficult for a master to oppose the unified will of his household.

The sense of the item on Lady Burghley's slander must be something to
the effect that Oxford, knowing or suspecting more Burghley spies in
his household, threatened them to Lady Burghley's face, and that she
then rushed to tell the servants that Oxford planned to kill them in order
to unite them against him.

We will now move on, passing over Oxford's travel intentions in 1577,
various aspects of his marital situation, his attempts to regain Havering
House and Waltham Forest, a touching reference «to the sweet little
Countess of Oxford,» a tournament, real estate deals, a dedication of
«Caesar and Pompeius» to the Countess by a prisoner, the total disap-
pearance of Oxford from the Cecil Papers between 2 June 1590 and 9
March 1595, and his tin mine letters, until we reach the marriage of his
daughter Elizabeth to William Stanley, Earl of Derby in January 1596.

There exist a number of letters from 1595 and 1596 in which Oxford shows normal fatherly affection for his daughter Elizabeth, two of which have not, I believe, been noticed before. The first is from 24 April 1595 to Sir Robert Cecil[14] and contains little of note save that the new Countess of Derby had somehow offended her great-aunt Elizabeth, Lady Russell. The latter was sister to the by now deceased Lady Burghley, and she was very easy to offend. The papers of that age are full of Lady Russell dashing about, starting trouble, and picking fights in all directions. A third sister was the widowed Lady Ann Bacon, who preferred to stay at her home at Gorhambury, nagging her middle-aged sons Anthony and Francis by mail. The second letter is from 17 September 1596,[15] also to Sir Robert Cecil from Oxford, who describes himself as «far off as I cannot be at Hand.» The letter contains the following warning of trouble brewing:

> «You know her youth and the place wherein she lives ((at Court attending the Queen)), and how much to both our houses it imports that she carry herself according to her honour. Enemies are apt to make the worst of everything, flatterers will do evil offices, and true and faithful advice will seem harsh to tender ears,» but as Oxford is far away «I commit unto you the authority of a parent in mine absence.»

Now the plot thickens. In July 1597, the Earl and Countess of Derby went from London to the Earl's home in Lancashire. In their train was Sir Edward Fitton (father of Mary), a fiftyish knight from Cheshire, whose wife was from Lancashire. In these counties and beyond, the Stanleys had been the paramount noble family for centuries. In 1485, they brought over 6,000 men to Bosworth Field and threw their support to Henry Tudor, which gave him victory over Richard III. For this critical aid, Henry raised the head of the family, Lord Stanley (Henry's stepfather), to the dignity of Earl of Derby. Queen Elizabeth called the Stanleys the richest subjects in her kingdom, and Oxford's son-in-law, the 6th Earl, had inherited royal blood and a claim to the throne from his mother. As of 1597, the 6th Earl was a mature, well-traveled man of thirty-five years. During the Civil War of the 1640s, his son the 7th Earl was said to have raised 60,000 men in Lancashire and Cheshire for King Charles. I dwell on the wealth and power of the Stanleys to highlight the significance of what is about to happen.

Sir Edward Fitton's family allegiance was to the Stanleys, but in 1578[16] and again in 1588 (*DNB*), he sought financial relief from Lord Burghley, to whom he was therefore beholden. After the Earl and Countess reached the Stanley mansion of Knowsley, Lancashire, Fitton sent a report to Sir Robert Cecil, by now thirty-four years old and his father's full partner in running the Queen's government.[17] Fitton mentioned Cecil's «honorable and virtuous niece» and her husband being met as they entered Cheshire by Fitton's cousin, who was sheriff of the county, various other Fitton kith and kin, and 500 horsemen. The party then crossed into Lancashire where they were greeted by 700 horsemen, who banqueted them and escorted them to Knowsley. Fitton then discussed some unsettled financial aspects of the marriage, and suggested that Cecil get his father involved. So far everything seems routine, but then comes, «I beseech you, keep this to yourself until I see you. It is better for me to speak all I know than write. I have appointed all the names of the gentlemen that met my Lord ((Derby)) to be set down for you.»

On 9 August Edward Mylar (Miller), another of Cecil's agents in Derby's household, reported to Cecil in a letter from which I must quote at length.[18] I know little about Miller but that he was a gentleman follower of the Earl of Derby who rode with him from London, his home was in Derby's area, and he was under obligation to Burghley:

> The Countess of Derby hath by courtesy and virtue got the love of all here ((Knowsley)).

> This journey hath also disseevered ((i.e., severed or ended)) my lord's humour of frenzy, for when her ladyship lived at Court in the eye of the world, then you know, and with grief I witnessed his ((Derby's)) violent course. But now here yesterday, upon letters from my lord Cobham, the Countess of (Warwick?) and my Lady Raleigh, he is in such a jealous frame as we have had such a storm as is wonderful. But such it appeareth, though (her ladyship) lived in a cell unseen,

all is one ((meaning that it would not matter if the Countess was isolated in a cell, she would still be slandered)). Mr. Ireland the lawyer did in wisdom, upon conference with me, prevail so much with all my lordship's officers seeing my lord's madness and my ladyship's patience, whose only defense was patience with tears, as they all went to my lord when he was looked to go to the Court and leave my lady here to shift for herself, and told him that as they had served him and his father and been the same by them, if he held this jealousy in that force as he did, themselves, seeing my lady's carriage of herself and managing my lord's estate with that honourable care of his house and himself that never any the like, if he would hate her and (not) desist from this jealousy and bitterness to her ladyship, and not dishonour himself, or else they would hate him: and bring her to my lord ((Burghley)) and you ((Cecil)), if all ((Mr.)) Ireland had would do it. If my lord ((Derby)) had come ((to London)) I think scarce one many had come with him to attend him. You, Sir, in my simple opinion, you may do well (to incite) my lord Treasurer ((Burghley)) to write to my lord ((Derby)) without knowing of this: assure yourself my lady wanteth not friends, friends firm to our purposes, wise, and experienced in this humorous house.

Thus having nakedly delivered the truth, for the honour I bear to your old father, who I love about any subject, keep this from him till I see you, for now all is well: but write to my lady to comfort her, and direct your letters to me; you may always send them to the manor for Chester who will convey them safe to me. I have not seen my own house yet, but should have been gone yesterday, it this had not been. — Knowsley, this 9th of August.

One reads this with awe, particularly in light of the debacle at Wivenhoe in 1576. Sir Robert Cecil was obviously better at managing this sort of thing than his parents, or perhaps the Cecil family knew how to learn from its mistakes. Besides, by 1597, Cecil dominance was taken for granted, and their domestic espionage network was better established. The Stanleys were bound to be spied upon as they combined great wealth, Catholic leanings, and a claim to the English throne.

With a storm developing around his niece, little hunchbacked Sir Robert, generally referred to as Master Secretary, hustles her and her husband back to their country estate, with his agents in Derby's household carefully reporting back to him. When the storm breaks upon the arrival of slanderous letters, the Earl goes into a jealous frenzy and prepares to abandon his wife and return to Court. Whereupon the officers of the Derby household (attorney, chamberlain, steward, etc.) band together behind their recently acquired mistress in defiance of their hereditary master. Thus, the Earl of Derby, the richest lord in England, of royal descent, whose family could summon armored horsemen in the thousands to follow their standard, submits within one day to the man that Queen Elizabeth called her «elf» or «pygmy» and that King James later addressed as «my little beagle.» In addition, all of these things are kept from old Lord Burghley.

I will briefly finish discussion of events in Lancashire before returning to London. On 11 August, Miller wrote to Cecil that all continued well, and that Derby's uncle the Earl of Cumberland had arrived to support the Countess. Cumberland was not so rich as Derby, but he was a powerful sea warrior who led or sent a fleet of private warships against Spain every year. As regards financial arrangements that were being made, the Countess would do as Burghley and Cecil directed.[19]

On 22 August, the Earl and Countess of Derby wrote to Cecil to say how well they were getting along, signed «Your loving niece and nephew.»[20] On 14 October, Fitton let Cecil know how much the Countess appreciated Cecil's kind letters and deeds.[21] On 24 July 1598, Fitton reported to Cecil on Derby's financial arrangements for the Countess.[22] On 30 July 1598, Derby's attorney Thomas Ireland informed Cecil that relations between the Earl and Countess were still a bit shaky.[23] In January 1599, Derby wrote Cecil on behalf of his wife, requesting that a «poor young man» who stole a small silver handbell from her chamber be spared hanging.

We will now turn to the cause of Lord Derby's jealousy. On 1 December 1596, Lady Ann Bacon, a woman of very strict morals, wrote a letter to her son Anthony, the Earl of Essex's spymaster, to be delivered to Essex. The letter accused Essex of the sin of fornication involving the «infaming of a nobleman's wife,» who «is utterly condemned as bad, unchaste, and impudent,» and who should be «delivered to her husband, and the Court cleansed by sending away such an unchaste gaze and common by-word.» In short, Essex was commanded to reform his ways.

The Earl responded graciously that he took «it as an argument of God's favour in sending so good an angel to admonish me.» However, Essex protested that he had abstained from such sin since his departure for Cadiz on 1 June. He also firmly denied having an affair «with the lady you mean»; he could hardly admit such a thing in writing to someone like Lady Bacon. He added that «I live in a place where I am hourly conspired against and practised upon,» and he ended with, «Burn, I pray you.»[24] This seems like what we are looking for, particularly given that Lady Ralegh and Lord Cobham were bitter enemies of Essex. Yet Essex was a man of many loves and there were other noblemen's wives. Both Essex and Lady Bacon avoided naming the noblewoman, nor did Lady Bacon give any indication that it was her own great-niece that she was condemning.

That we are on the right track is proven by a newsletter written by Thomas Audeley in London to Edward Smythe in Paris.[25] The letter is dated 20 September 1597, but was clearly written that December. It contains the following passage:

«My lord of Essex is in no great grace, neither with Queen or Commons: with the Queen for that he lay with my Lady of Derby before he went ((to the Azores from August to October)), as his enemies witness.»

So Thomas Audeley dared to put in writing what everyone in the know only spoke of, but still failed to make it publicly known, for his letter ended up in the Cecil papers along with so many other letters not addressed to the Cecils. It was presumably intercepted and Volume VII of the Salisbury Manuscripts places it immediately after twelve undated drafts of political intelligence reports in the hand of Archibald Douglas, the Scottish Ambassador to England (presumably Cecil had a spy in the embassy). One sees why Lady Bacon and Essex refrained from naming the noblewoman and why Essex asked for his letter to be burned.

We can conclude that the infidelity of the Countess of Derby is not fully proven, and note that, as her mother's example shows, accusations can be false. What matters is that the slanders against her were widespread and serious. We see one of the reasons for the enmity that was building between Cecil and Essex. The Cadiz voyage of 1596 was Essex's greatest triumph and represented a political victory over the Cecils. Burghley acknowledged as much by currying favor with Essex, and Anthony Bacon crowed that Essex «hath made the old Fox to crouch and whine.»[26]

Sir Robert Cecil did not for, in September 1596, Essex wrote to Anthony that he «was more braved by your little cousin ((Cecil)) than ever I was by anyone in my life.»[27] «To brave» means to defy or challenge, as in *King John*, «Out, dunghill! Darest thou brave a nobleman?» We also see Cecil's friends and allies, Cobham and the Raleghs, striking at Cecil's niece as a means of striking at Essex. After assisting Essex in his course of self-destruction, Cecil secretly dug Ralegh's grave. When Cobham and Ralegh fell together, Cecil offered aid to neither. Cobham's deceased sister had been Cecil's beloved wife, and after her death their son was raised by Sir Walter and Lady Ralegh. I have never seen a good explanation of why Cecil stabbed Ralegh in the back, though we may have the beginning of an explanation in the defamation of Cecil's niece; Cobham, like Essex, destroyed himself.

With regard to the Earl of Oxford, we now know a bit more about his life; as for the authorship controversy, we gain several points. Orthodoxy maintains that Oxfordians have a paranoid obsession with conspiracies and cover-ups, to which our reply should be that the Elizabethan Era was an age of plots and secrecy. The master plotter was master Secretary Robert Cecil; the word secretary is rooted in the Latin *secretus*, a secretary being one who keeps secrets. We have seen Cecil subdue the richest lord in England with a wave of his hand, as he covers up what was an open secret, trying to prevent even his father from knowing what was gossiped about at Court.

With regard to my theories on the *Sonnets,* I had assumed that Oxford must have resented Essex for displacing him as commander of the English cavalry in 1585, which post started Essex on the road to glory, but that was years earlier. Oxford had fresher reasons for resentment. On 20 October 1595, Oxford wrote to Cecil about his suit to recover Waltham Forest and Havering House.[28] He said that Lord Burghley had advised him to ask Essex to drop his efforts to get possession of this Vere property, but this Oxford «cannot do in honour, having already received divers injuries and wrongs from him.» Moreover, Oxford must have been infuriated by slander about Essex's seduction of his daughter.

In an earlier article, I dated Sonnets 78 to 100 as between late 1597 and early 1599 by tying them to events in the lives of Southampton and Essex, with little reference to Oxford. Let us now look back to Sonnets 66 to 70, a cluster of woe, bearing in mind that the Countess of Derby's troubles apparently began in the fall of 1596, coming to a head in August 1597.

Sonnet 66 is a lament without any particular addressed, which complains of «gilded honour shamefully misplaced, And maiden virtue rudely strumpeted.» Sonnets 67 and 68 are both about a man in that masculine pronouns are used. Sonnet 67 begins «Ah, wherefore with infection should he live,» and goes on to associate Shakespeare's friend with «impiety,» «sin,» and the «false painting» of cosmetics. I take these as references to Southampton's friend Essex. Sonnet 67 closes, «In days long since, before these last so bad.»

Sonnets 69 and 70 are addressed to «thee,» who is said to be the victim of slander, who, however, is partly at fault. Now things get a bit complicated. Shakespeare always addresses the Dark Lady as «thee,» but Sonnets 1 to 126 are sometimes to «you» and sometimes to «thee.» No one has ever given a good explanation for these pronoun shifts, but some of them could result from a change in the person being addressed. I have always believed that the first 126 Sonnets were to or about the same person, the Earl of Southampton, but Sonnets 69 and 70 can be plausibly explained as to Elizabeth, Countess of Derby.

In February 1597, there was a quarrel between the Earls of Northumberland and Southampton, of which the only record is a letter by Northumberland to Anthony Bacon.[29] Northumberland wrote that Southampton slandered him behind his back, that Northumberland then gave him the lie, whereupon Southampton sent a gentleman bearing his rapier to Northumberland, who embraced him and asked if he bore a challenge. The gentleman did not, he only brought the rapier to measure its length against Northumberland's, so the latter sent him away. The gentleman returned within thirty minutes with a challenge but with what Northumberland felt were «strange conditions,» one of which was that they fight with single rapier rather than with rapier and dagger, because Southampton had hurt his left arm in a ball game. Northumberland replied disdainfully that he knew Southampton did not play with his left hand, but that he would wait until Southampton recovered. The Queen promptly summoned them before the Privy Council, where they made up and parted friends. It seems that Northumberland was the one who was slandered (one regrets not having both sides of the story), but then he called Southampton a liar and implied he was a coward. Thus, Sonnets 69 and 70 could well refer to what Northumberland said of Southampton, bearing in mind that Southampton brought this upon himself. Sonnet 70 mentions that «slander's mark was ever yet the fair,» which refers to some other slander of a fair person. This could be a generalization, but it could also look at the recent slander of Oxford's daughter.

Sonnets 71 and 72 are both to «you,» 73 and 74 are both to «thee,» and all four anticipate the poet's death. Sonnet 72 closes «for I am shamed by that which I bring forth, And so should you to love things nothing worth.» I had before and still do see these lines as referring to Shakespeare's plays and poems, but we now have a plausible double meaning: Oxford's shame at his daughter's misconduct.

At any rate, the infection, bad days, shame, and slander of Sonnets 67 to 72 are doubly appropriate for Oxford from late 1596 to fall 1597. I have said that I take «infection» as a reference to Essex, who interestingly ended up of the same opinion. When Essex repented and confessed his crimes after his trial, he said that he «was like a leprosy that had infected far and near,» and on the scaffold he asked «God to forgive him his great, his bloody, his crying, and his infectious sin.»[30]

There is still much to be uncovered. I have not seen the originals of the documents that I discuss but, at best, transcriptions, more often abstracts and summaries. In Volume II of the Salisbury Manuscripts (58) is a summary of a four-and-a-half page document: «1573, Sept. 2. — Concerning the affairs of the Earl of Oxford: enclosing articles relating to the same, with the Earl's answers thereto.» I have not been able to confirm the handwriting and date on Sir Walter Mildmay's letter to Burghley. The document describing the Wivenhoe fiasco is a combination of abstract and summary. Thus, whoever is able to visit Hatfield House and view the originals of the documents mentioned in this article is bound to find more information about Oxford.

I have not seen Vol. XI of the Salisbury Manuscripts, nor a complete set of the HMC Reports, nor the Lansdowne Manuscripts, the Stanley Papers, nor the papers of people such as Anthony Bacon and Lord Henry Howard. It is absurdly unlikely that everything of significance is in the volumes I was able to inspect. Oxford's tin mining letters of March and April 1595 do not say that he has been to Devon and Cornwall, but presumably he had. Oxford's tin letter of 20 March 1595 says that he has been looking into the tin business for «This last year past.» Earlier in that letter, speaking of his «unfortunate estate,» he said that he has «consumed four or five years in a flattering hope of idle words,» which period exactly coincides with his disappearance from the papers of the Cecils. Oxford's letter of 17 September 1596 says «but sith my fortune hath set me so far off as I cannot be at hand in this her ((his daughter's)) troublesome occasions.»

I may be reading too much into these words, but they seem to speak of some purposeful mission rather than a casual visit to a country house. Evidence of travel in this period jibes well with references to travel and separation in Sonnets 27 to 51, though not much can be made of so weak a point. A letter of military advice from Sir Francis Vere to Essex on 7 March 1596 recommends as a fortifications engineer one «Edward Hamnum... sometimes belonging to my lord of Oxford, who ((Hamnum)) is not ignorant of architecture.» So Oxford must have done some building, someplace, sometime. We need to try to clarify these matters and fill in the gaps.

Endnotes

1 HMC Salisbury 9/2, 101.
2 HMC Salisbury 9/5, 70.
3 HMC Sals. 9/2, 114.
4 HMC Sals. 9/2, 131-2.
5 See Conyers Read, *Lord Burghley and Queen Elizabeth* (NY: 1960), 134-5 and Charlton Ogburn Jr., *The Mysterious William Shakespeare* (NY: Dodd, Mead, 1984), 556.
6 HMC Sals. 9/2, 132-3; see also Bernard Ward, *The Seventeenth Earl of Oxford* (London: John Murray, 1928), 121-2 or Ogburn, 559.
7 HMC Salisbury 9/13, 128.
8 HMC Sals. 9/2, 145-6.
9 HMC Sals. 9/1, 474.
10 HMS Sals. 9/2, 171.
11 See Ward, 90-2 or Ogburn, 528-9.
12 See Ward, 78 or Ogburn, 510-1.
13 See Ward, 285 or Ogburn, 701.
14 HMC Sals. 9/5, 181.
15 HMC Sals. 9/6, 389.
16 HMC Sals. 9/2, 183.
17 HMC Sals. 9/7, 327.
18 HMC Sals. 9/7, 339.
19 HMC Sals. 9/7, 344.
20 HMC Sals. 9/7, 363.
21 HMC Sals. 9/7, 430.
22 HMC Sals. 9/8, 275.

23 HMC Sals. 9/8, 281.
24 Quotations in the prior and current paragraphs are from Daphne du Maurier, *Golden Lads* (London: Gollancz , 1975), 151-2.
25 HMC Sals. 9/7, 391-2.
26 Dictionary of National Biography article on Robert Devereaux, Earl of Essex.
27 Read, 523.
28 HMC Sals. 9/5, 426-7.
29 Thomas Birch, *Memoirs of the Reign of Queen Elizabeth*, Vol. II (NY: AMS Press, 1970), 274.
30 Francis Bacon, «A Declaration of the Practices and Treasons of the Late Earl of Essex, etc.» *The Works of Francis Bacon*, Ed. James Spedding, Vol. IX (London: Routledge, 1996), 285.

The Earl of Oxford and the Order of the Garter

In August 1995 Professor Alan H. Nelson, acting at my suggestion, microfilmed the records of the elections to the Order of the Garter for the years 1569 to 1604 from the register in the British Library, where it is identified as Additional Manuscript 36,768. The purpose of this article is to examine the tale that these elections tell about the standing of Edward de Vere, 17th Earl of Oxford during his adult years.

I have never seen the Garter elections cited in history books as evidence of the standing of English courtiers, though they say a great deal about who a courtier's friends were, about the formation of factions and alliances, not to mention who had the monarch's favor. For example, the nineteenth century myth that the poet Earl of Surrey detested Sir Thomas Seymour collapses in the face of Surrey's votes for Seymour in 1543 and 1544.[1] Other old stories from the history books can receive support or refutation from the evidence of the Garter elections, but new evidence often does much more than simply providing approval or disapproval on the received wisdom. We often find entirely new motives, twists, and dimensions in old tales of who, what, when, where, how, and why. The Garter elections could add a great deal, for example, to our understanding of court factions in the reign of Henry VIII.

The information about the Earl of Oxford's life that is currently in print (1996) is highly incomplete given the available records, and new material is becoming available.[2] Moreover, as with Surrey, myths have proliferated, such as that Oxford cruelly rejected his wife in 1576. Both B.M. Ward and Conyers Read, biographers respectively of Oxford and Lord Burghley, concealed their knowledge of a memorandum in Burghley's hand showing that Lady Burghley carried off her daughter after she reunited with her husband upon his return from Italy.[3] We must expect more surprises.

We will begin by considering what the Order of the Garter is and how members were selected. We will then take a look at some other nominees besides Oxford; the Garter elections are of particular interest at the end of a reign when a transfer of power is imminent, and Elizabeth's reign is no exception. Finally, we will examine the record on Oxford. The purpose of considering other nominees before taking up Oxford is twofold. First, we cannot make much sense out of the Garter elections or, for that matter, anything else that happened four centuries ago, without establishing the historical context. Second, we shall discover interesting things about people who are part of the story of Oxford's life.

The Order of the Garter was founded by Edward III in the 1340s and consists of the sovereign and 25 Knights of the Garter (KGs). Membership in the Order remains the highest honor bestowed by the British monarch. The great prestige of the Order is due in large measure to its exclusiveness; no one may be elected KG unless the death or degradation of an incumbent creates a vacancy. During the period 1569-1604 there were about sixty peers, so the Order of the Garter was far more exclusive than the peerage. In contrast, the French Order of St. Michael was debased in the mid-sixteenth century by being awarded to all and sundry, and so in 1578 Henry III created the Order of the Holy Spirit, limited to one hundred knights. Given the much larger population of France in those days, the Holy Spirit was about as exclusive as the Garter. Relevant to this discussion is that the ninth, eleventh, thirteenth, fifteenth, and twentieth de Vere Earls of Oxford were Knights of the Garter.

Selection of KGs were initiated whenever a vacancy existed, and an election would then be held to select a new member, normally at the annual meeting or chapter on St. George's Day, 23 April, at St. George's Chapel, Windsor Castle. Each KG present voted for nine men, three in each of the following categories: princes, barons, and knights. «Princes» means earls, marquesses, dukes, and royalty (or, earls and above), while «barons» and «knights» are self explanatory. A viscount, who ranks between an earl and a baron, could be nominated under either category, «prince» or «baron.» In Queen Elizabeth I's reign, the heir to an earl or above could be nominated under his courtesy title, while a duke's younger son could be nominated as a «baron.» If ten Knights of the Garter were present at a given election, with each KG listing nine nominees, then as many as ninety names could be listed, though the more likely result would be about twenty. Then the votes were tallied and presented to the Queen, who picked whomever she pleased or no one at all.

As an example, we may consider the election of 1572. Nine members were present, and they voted for seventeen names. The top finishers were the French Duke of Montmorency, the newly created Lord Burghley, and the Queen's first cousin, Sir Francis Knollys, each of whom received nine votes; Sir James Croft received eight; the Earl of Oxford and Lord Grey of Wilton each obtained seven; four other men gained either six or five votes; and Walter Devereux, Viscount Hereford received four. Three places were vacant, so the Queen selected Burghley, Grey, and Hereford as the new KGs; later that year Burghley became Lord Treasurer and Hereford was created Earl of Essex. Hereford's wife was the Queen's first cousin once removed (the daughter of Francis Knollys), and Hereford had shown great energy opposing the Northern rebellion of 1569-70, hence the Queen's favor.

Who received votes and how did the Queen make her choices? The category of «princes» included about twenty Englishmen, though a significant number of them were already KGs, but also included favored foreign royalty and near-royalty, as well as Irish earls. Twelve KGs voted in the election of 1590, and Henry IV of France and James VI of Scotland were up for the first time, and so all twelve KGs made Henry their first pick and James their second; four English earls split the remaining twelve votes. The category of «barons» included about fifty men, less those who were already KGs, but they didn't have to compete with foreigners. There were three or four hundred knights in England at this time, but the nominations for the category «knights» were confined to a very tight circle of high Court officials, military commanders, and the Queen's viceroys for Ireland, Wales, and the North. In the elections of 1578 and '79, all voters listed Sir Francis Knollys, Sir James Croft, and Sir Christopher Hatton, in that order. It is easy to see which knights received votes, namely the Queen's closest servants, and the number of votes received is a good index of a knight's standing.

Why noblemen received those votes is not so easy to say. Mere rank was not enough. In 1576 William Paulet succeeded his father as third Marquess of Winchester, and Paulet lived until 1598. During that time England had no dukes and no other marquesses, so Winchester stood alone above the earls, yet he received only twelve votes for the Garter during the entire period. His record is particularly sad compared to that of his cousin Sir Hugh Paulet, Governor of Jersey, Vice-President of Wales, and second-in-command at the defense of Le Havre, who received twenty-eight votes in the last five years of his life, 1569-73. Sir Hugh's son, Sir Amias Paulet was Governor of Jersey, ambassador to France, and jailer to Mary of Scotland; he received twenty-three votes in the period 1580-85. The Marquess of Winchester's problem was that he was a stay-at-home, whose best Garter year, four votes in 1580, coincided with his only significant office, Lord Lieutenant of Dorset.

Family connections helped. The second Earl of Essex received his first Garter vote in 1587 from his stepfather, the Earl of Leicester. In 1603 Lord Howard de Walden was able to cast all three of his «baron» votes for fellow Howards. The only votes ever received by the dissident Catholic second Earl of Southampton were cast by his father-in-law and coreligionist, Viscount Montague, in the elections of 1574-78. Montague was not present to vote in 1579. Southampton rejected his wife in early 1580, and so he failed to get Montague's vote in that year and the next, whereupon he died.

The Queen's choices seem to have been influenced by three factors besides personal favor: rank, service, and good behavior (from her point of view). As Sir Robert Naunton remarked, Queen Elizabeth was partial to the nobility (including noblemen by courtesy), and it shows in her Garter selections. In the first three decades of her reign, only one «knight» received the Garter, Sir Henry Sidney in 1564. But in her later years the Queen grew more democratic: Hatton finally got it in 1588, Knollys in 1593, and Sir Henry Lee in 1597. Barons were more than twice as numerous as earls, but Elizabeth selected slightly more earls for the Garter, showing again her preference for rank. Separating service to the Queen from her personal favor is difficult for she combined the two. Her leading favorites over the course of her reign were the Earls of Leicester and Essex, Sir Christopher Hatton, and Sir Walter Ralegh. All received offices of great responsibility, and the first three were also Privy Councillors and KGs (Sir Walter just missed on both counts).

Among the men whose standing can be judged by the Garter elections are Thomas and Robert Cecil, Henry Howard, Walter Ralegh, and the third Earl of Southampton.

The *Dictionary of National Biography* (*DNB*) is quite scornful of Thomas Cecil, Lord Burghley's older son, though it allows that he eventually received the Garter in 1601 for helping to suppress the Earl of Essex's rebellion, which the *DNB* calls a «foolish riot.» However, Thomas Cecil regularly received votes from 1590 on, with the numbers steadily increasing; in 1601 he was picked by eleven out of thirteen members. Robert Cecil never received a vote until 1604, when he obtained fourteen votes out of sixteen, being finally elected in 1606. What is truly remarkable is that Robert, by then Lord Cecil, didn't get a single vote in the election of June 1603, with King James on the throne and Lord Cecil clearly confirmed as the new King's right hand man. Presumably, the Knights of the Garter respected the frequently displayed military skills of Thomas, while the Queen valued his abilities enough to make him President of the North in 1599. Meanwhile, the KGs probably resented Robert's status as his father's understudy, and the Queen failed to put in a word to help him garner some votes.

Lord Henry Howard, Oxford's enemy in 1580 and 1581, held the rank of younger son of a duke, but never received a vote during Elizabeth's reign, though he picked up five out of six as James' favorite in June 1603, and was elected unanimously in 1604. (Incidentally, one must be careful with names and titles when examining the Garter register, especially when the prolific Howard clan is involved. The «Lord Howard» who received numerous votes in 1599 and 1600 is the same «Lord de Effingham» who received votes in 1601 and 1603, that is William, Lord Howard of Effingham, heir to the Earl of Nottingham. Lord Henry Howard was son of the Earl of Surrey, who was heir to the third Duke of Norfolk. Lord Henry's brother became the fourth Duke of Norfolk, and Henry was treated as a duke's son.)

Sir Walter Ralegh's rising political power at the end of Elizabeth's reign and his sudden collapse may be seen in the Garter elections. He received single votes in 1590, '92, '96, and '97, then four out of nine in 1599, eight out of thirteen in 1600, and nine out of twelve in 1601. Reeling under the new King's disfavor, Ralegh received a sole vote from his friend the Earl of Northumberland in June 1603, shortly before being arrested for treason (Lord Henry Howard had been poisoning James' mind against Ralegh for several years). As a Virginian, I rather like seeing Ralegh's prosperity, but the Earl of Oxford felt otherwise. It will be recalled that he said of Ralegh's rise, apparently at the time of Essex's execution, «When jacks start up, heads go down.» Ralegh's rise in Garter votes exactly coincides with Essex's fall, 1599-1601.

Biographers have remarked on the popularity of the third Earl of Southampton, which is borne out in the Garter elections. He received four out of twelve votes in 1595 at age twenty-one and ten votes out of twelve in 1596. In 1597 all ten voters picked the Duke of Württemberg, thereby reducing the votes available for English earls, but Southampton managed to secure two, including Lord Burghley's vote for the first time. On the other hand, Southampton did not get the Earl of Essex's vote in 1597 (though he did in '95 and '96); the attachment of Southampton to Essex begins with the Azores voyage later that year. The theory of an Essex-Southampton social circle going back to the early 1590s is a myth originating in a misdated letter. G. P. V. Akrigg's *Shakespeare and the Earl of Southampton* provided the evidence to puncture the myth, but Akrigg failed to realize its significance; the Garter election of 1597 provides more evidence. In 1599, newly arrived in Ireland, Southampton was decidedly in the Queen's disfavor owing to his begetting a child by one of her maids of honor, whom he secretly married, but he still received four out of nine votes. In 1600, presumably even more deeply in disfavor with the Queen as a result of the Irish campaign, Southampton yet polled six votes out of thirteen. In 1603, only six KGs voted, all selecting James' Scottish favorites, the Duke of Lenox and the Earl of Marr, as two of their three «princes.» Of the six remaining ballots in the «prince» category, Southampton and the Earl of Pembroke each got three, and James selected both English earls as KGs.

We now turn to the Earl of Oxford. With regard to the Garter elections, Oxford's life can be divided into four phases: 1569-80, 1581-4, 1585-8, and 1590-1604.

Oxford received numerous votes from 1569 to 1580 and probably would have received the honor, except that the Queen preferred someone else. In 1569 and '70 the underaged Oxford received the vote of William, Lord Howard of Effingham. In 1571, Oxford was chosen by all ten voters.

In the eight elections from 1572 to 1580, Oxford averaged close to eight votes annually and never less than four. Oxford's supporters included not only the Earl of Sussex, as one would expect, but also the Puritan leader, the Earl of Leicester. The various misdeeds and alleged misdeeds of Oxford's youth—such as trying to rescue the Duke of Norfolk in 1571, or running away to the Low Countries in 1573—seem to have had no effect on his standing with the KGs, though they may have prevented the Queen from selecting him. Lord Burghley always voted for Oxford as his first choice among English «princes» (foreigners were always listed first), even during his separation from his wife from April 1576 to 1582. Burghley's forbearance stands in marked contrast to Viscount Montague's reaction to the rejection of his daughter by the second Earl of Southampton. Burghley's various writings on the breakup of the marriage invariably take a hurt or defensive tone, rather than expressing outrage, presumably reflecting the primary role of Lady Burghley in the separation. Incidentally, Lady Burghley's invasion of Oxford's house at Wivenhoe, trying to raise his servants against him and carrying off his wife, occurred in April 1576 while Oxford and Lord Burghley were at Windsor Castle for the chapter of the Garter.

Oxford was forbidden from Court until June 1583 as a result of having a son by Anne Vavasour in March 1581. Moreover, during 1582 and 1583, Oxford and his followers had to defend themselves against attacks by Vavasour's kinsmen and their men. Moreover, Oxford was involved in a scandal of charges and countercharges with Lord Henry Howard and Charles Arundel starting in December 1580, though we have little evidence how seriously the charges against Oxford were taken. Oxford received no votes in the four Garter elections during 1581-4. The Queen's anger explains the results for 1581-3, but Oxford's failure to receive any votes in 1584 (an election that Burghley missed) indicates that he was still not fully rehabilitated. His disfavor in these years may be contrasted to the third Earl of Southampton's situation in 1599-1600, when he continued to receive votes despite his sexual misconduct. Clearly Oxford's standing with his fellows was seriously damaged.

Oxford was allowed to return to Court in June 1583, but the Queen was not fully mollified. In May 1583, she was still concerned about the charges made by Howard and Arundel, and she permitted Oxford's return to Court only after «some bitter words and speeches.» Oxford's standing presumably improved further after Charles Arundel fled to France in the wake of the discovery of the Throckmorton plot in November 1583, which resulted in the reincarceration of Lord Henry Howard. Arundel was further discredited in September 1584 by being named as one of the co-authors of the libelous book, *Leicester's Commonwealth*. That Oxford was fully restored to the proper status of his rank in the period 1585-8 is shown by the Garter elections and proffers of two military commands.

In April 1585, Oxford received five votes out of thirteen for the Garter, while that summer he was offered command of the cavalry contingent of the English expeditionary force to the Netherlands. In 1587, Oxford earned four votes out of eight, and he received three out of seven in 1588. In the summer of 1588, Oxford was offered command of the key port of Harwich during the fight against the Spanish Armada, and he was prominent in the victory celebrations in November. Lord Burghley voted for Oxford in all three elections, always naming him first among the «princes.» Two recently made KGs who voted for Oxford were the seventh Lord Cobham and the third Earl of Rutland. Oxford's other supporters had all voted for him before 1581, namely Henry Stanley, fourth Earl of Derby, Henry Herbert, second Earl of Pembroke, and Charles, second Lord Howard of Effingham and Lord Admiral (the future Earl of Nottingham).

It is worth noting that Oxford's daughter Elizabeth married Derby's son William in 1595, Oxford's daughter Bridget almost married Pembroke's older son William in 1597, and Oxford's daughter Susan married Pembroke's second son Philip in 1605. These marriages seem to have been arranged by the Cecils, and the fathers were dead in several cases, but the Garter votes support a connection between Oxford and the other two earls. Charles Arundel had accused Oxford of plotting to murder Lord Howard of Effingham, who was the first cousin of Lord Henry Howard's father, the poet Surrey. Yet Effingham's three subsequent votes for Oxford seem to indicate that he didn't take the charges seriously. Derby, Pembroke, and Howard of Effingham had one obvious thing in common — they were all patrons of major acting companies (see the *DNB* or *The Reader's Encyclopedia of Shakespeare* for dates and other details of their troupes).

The Garter election of 1589 produced two new KGs, Lord Buckhurst and the fifth Earl of Sussex, but the votes were not recorded. Buckhurst was the Queen's cousin, a Privy Councillor, and several times an ambassador, and presumably benefitted from the death of his enemy Leicester in 1588. Sussex was the military commander of Portsmouth, and he emptied his magazines to replenish the English fleet with powder and shot during the Armada fight the previous year. Lord Admiral Howard of Effingham and Lord Hunsdon had previously been Sussex's leading supporters for the Garter, the Admiral being Sussex's first cousin, Hunsdon his first cousin once removed, both were present for the 1589 election, and so Sussex was selected.

Oxford received one vote throughout the period 1590 to 1604, that of his brother-in-law, Thomas Cecil, second Lord Burghley, in 1604. Oxford's loss of his father-in-law's vote is easily explained by Anne Cecil's death in 1588, but his failure to get anyone else's vote seems to indicate that he was living under something of a cloud in this period. The least dramatic explanation of Oxford's disrepute would be his financial collapse around 1590, accompanied by the loss of his daughters to Burghley, their guardian after 1588 (and Robert Cecil became their guardian when Burghley died in 1598).

Nevertheless, Lord Sussex was even more broke than Oxford. Between his election as KG and his installation, Sussex wrote a letter to the Queen explaining that his inherited estate yielded but 450 pounds per year, while he owed her a debt of 500 pounds per year. Sussex begged that his annual payment be reduced to 200 or 250 pounds. Oxford had his 1,000 pound pension from the Queen, he also had lands worth at least several hundred per year, though we do not know the size of his debts. On the other hand, his second wife was a woman of some wealth.

To judge Oxford's lack of votes during 1590-1603, we must compare him to his peers. Twenty-five other Englishmen held the rank of marquess or earl in that period, and fifteen of them were KGs by 1603. One of the remaining ten, the fifth Earl of Derby, died a few months after inheriting his title, and there was no election during his short period as an earl. Thus, we are left with nine earls and marquesses besides Oxford who never became KGs. Yet several of them, such as the Earls of Kent and Hertford, regularly received a respectable number of votes, as Oxford did during 1585-8. Those who did worst were the third Earl of Bedford and the second Earl of Lincoln, who received three votes each from 1590 to 1603 and one vote each in 1604, followed by the fourth Marquess of Winchester, who received two votes under his courtesy title in 1590 and '91, and no votes after that, even after becoming a marquess in 1598. Last we find the third Earl of Bath, who received zero votes in the entire period 1590 to 1604. So Oxford comes in behind Bedford, Lincoln, and Winchester, and barely beats Bath.

Lords Winchester, Bath, Bedford, and Lincoln were all nonentities. None of them rates an entry in the *DNB*, nor even the kind of sub-entry given to the sixth Earl of Derby at the beginning of the entry on his son, the seventh Earl. Examination of GEC's *The Complete Peerage* confirms the *DNB*'s verdict on these four lives of non-achievement, especially that of Lord Bath, whose invisibility must set the record for Tudor earls. Oxford, however, was anything but a nonentity, and he didn't go into rural hibernation after 1588.

B. M. Ward entitles the final section of his biography of Oxford «The Recluse,» stating that «[f]rom 1589 onwards the life of Lord Oxford becomes one of mystery» (299). From 1589 to about 1593 we are indeed in some doubt as to Oxford's activities, but we know where he was after that—at Court and living in or near London. He was still in the Queen's good graces, so it seems, he had a new wife and son, his daughters were getting married, and he was in the picture. Nonetheless, from the point of view of the Knights of the Garter, he seems to have become a pariah. Ward quotes Oxford's first modern editor, Dr. A.B. Grosart: «An unlifted shadow somehow lies across his memory.»[4] As the Garter elections show, Grosart hit the nail squarely on the head.

In the autumn 1995 issue of *The Elizabethan Review*, I discussed the appropriateness of Shakespeare's self-description in Sonnet 37, «lame, poor, [and] despised,» as applied to Oxford. Regarding the word «despised,» I quoted Sir John Peyton's 1603 comment that Oxford lacked friends. The Garter elections powerfully reinforce Peyton's evaluation. The 17th Earl of Oxford had been a man of popularity and prestige, but he fell from favor and honor twice, first in 1581, then again after 1588. Shakespeare's personal sense of disgrace is found throughout his Sonnets: the poet is barred from «public honour and proud titles» (25), he wants his name buried with his body (72), he knows himself to be «vile esteemed» (121). Finally, Shakespeare alludes to the cause of his dishonor several times, most clearly in Sonnet 110: «I ... made myself a motley to the view.»

Endnotes

1   Letters and Papers of Henry VIII, 18.2.517 and 19.1.384.

2   See Alan H. Nelson, *Monstrous Adversary: The Life of Edward de Vere, 17th Earl of Oxford* (Liverpool, England: Liverpool Univ. Press, 2003) — Editor

3   See H.M.C. Salisbury, 13.128; also, B. M. Ward, *The Seventeenth Earl of Oxford* (London: John Murray, 1928), 123; and Conyers Read, *Lord Burghley and Queen Elizabeth* (London: Jonathan Cape,1960), 136.

4   B. M. Ward, *The Seventeenth Earl of Oxford* (London: John Murray, 1928), 389.

Oxford in Venice: New Light on an Old Question

I wish to congratulate Professor Alan Nelson for discovering new material on Edward de Vere, 17th Earl of Oxford, namely the poetry of Nathaniel Baxter. At the same time, I must disagree with his interpretation of the meaning of the second verse of Baxter's acrostic poem to Oxford's daughter, the Countess of Montgomery. Prof. Nelson argues that Oxford caught syphilis in Italy in 1575 or 76, and that Baxter said as much in these lines:

> Never omitting what might pastime bring,
> Italian sports, and Syren's Melodie:
> Hopping Helena with her warbling sting,
> Infested th' Albanian dignitie,
> Like as they poysoned all Italie.

My disagreement has two causes. First, it would have been utterly unthinkable for Baxter to say that Oxford had syphilis in a dedicatory poem to Oxford's daughter, from whom Baxter was hoping for a gratuity. Second, the last three lines of this verse clearly refer to poisoning rather than to venereal disease.

Professor Nelson correctly tells us not to judge Baxter's intentions by «the political correctness which rules in 1995.» What we should rather be interested in are the rules of political correctness of 1606, which, as it happens, are precisely explained with regard to syphilis in John Graunt's 1662 *Natural and Political Observations Upon the Bills of Mortality*.[1] Graunt analyzed the weekly Bills of Mortality published by each parish of London from 1603 to 1624, giving the cause of death for a total of 229,250 people. Graunt was astonished to discover that only 392 of them were reported to have died of the dreaded pox, that is, syphilis. Graunt says that he considered suppressing this information, lest men be led to believe that they could sin without danger, but then he looked into his evidence a bit further:

upon inquiry I found that those who died of it out of [i.e., in] the Hospitals (especially that of *King's-Land*, and the *Lock* in *Southwark*) were returned of *Ulcers*, and *Sores*. And in brief I found, that all mentioned to die of the *French-Pox* were returned by the *Clerks* of Saint *Giles's*, and Saint *Martin's in the Fields* onely; in which place I understood that most of the vilest, and most miserable houses of uncleanness were: from whence I concluded, that only *hated* persons, and such, whose very *Noses* were eaten of[f] were reported by the Searchers to have died of this too frequent *Maladie* ...

In other words, only two poor parishes, out of a total of 114,[2] reported any deaths caused by syphilis, and those were of outcasts, derelicts, and persons so visibly eaten by the disease that the cause of death could hardly be hidden. The remaining 112 parishes and all of the hospitals (Kingsland and the Lock being leper hospitals[3]), disguised the true cause of death. So even the poorest of Londoners, so long as they had any family and place in society, and didn't live in the parishes of St. Gile's and St. Martin's, were officially protected in death from revelations of syphilis.

We now see something about the political correctness of the early seventeenth century (and we also see how well that society could conduct cover-ups). The consequences of indiscretion on this subject could be unpleasant. In 1594 Dr. Roderigo Lopez, physician to the Queen, was convicted of treason and executed, largely at the instigation of the Earl of Essex. However, it was later reported that Lopez had let out professional secrets concerning Essex, «which did disparage to the Earl's honour,» presumably meaning that Essex had a venereal disease.[4]

We may now ask what is implied by the theory that Baxter was publicly proclaiming that Oxford had syphilis, bearing in mind that a husband can pass this disease to his wife, and she to a child in the womb. We would have to suppose that Baxter, his publisher, Edward White, and the printer Edward Allde had literally gone mad. Baxter, trying to curry favor with and patronage from the powerful Herbert family, would be saying, in effect: «Most wonderful and exalted Countess, I was with your wonderful and exalted father in Venice when he contracted syphilis, and soon thereafter he begot your Ladyship (which means that there's a good chance that your Ladyship is also syphilitic, as was your late mother). Would your Ladyship please reward me for my praise of your most noble family?»

It's probably unnecessary to add that under laws passed in the reigns of Edward I and Richard II, not repealed until 1887, slandering the nobility was punishable through an action of *scandalum magnatum*.[5] Even if I had no idea what Baxter's words meant, I would have to reject the syphilis theory.

Yet Prof. Nelson also reports that Charles Arundel testified in December 1580 or January 1581 that Oxford had annual visitations of the «Neapolitan maladye,» which did indeed mean syphilis. A full evaluation of the testimony of Charles Arundel is far beyond the scope of this article, but a few points may be noted. Among the other grotesque charges, Oxford is accused of attempting to murder Rowland York, Lord Howard of Effingham (Oxford's best friend, according to Arundel), the Earl of Worcester and all of his servants, Sir Christopher Hatton, John Cheke (twice), the Earl of Leicester (twice), Sir Henry Knyvet, Philip Sidney, Arthur Gorges, Walter Ralegh (twice), and one Denny. As a result of all these charges, Oxford was not brought to trial, he was not imprisoned (unlike his accusers), he did not even lose the Queen's favor (though he did lose that in late March as a result of his extra-marital liaison with Anne Vavasour). In short, the charges were not taken seriously by the Queen's Government, much to Arundel's chagrin.

Arundel made two later depositions against Oxford, and Arundel's co-slanderer, Lord Henry Howard, made several depositions of similarly lurid crimes against Oxford, but none of these other depositions mentions the Neapolitan malady. Meanwhile, the third accomplice, Francis Southwell, tried to distance himself and Howard from Arundel, and attempted to persuade Howard to abandon his bizarre charges in favor of some others (unspecified) that might have a chance of being believed.

In short, Charles Arundel's slanders against Oxford were not believed in 1581 by those in the best position to know the truth, and I do not see how Arundel's credibility improves with age.

That Oxford was not regarded as diseased, even by his enemies, is clearly implied by the opening clause of Thomas Vavasour's challenge to Oxford of 1585: «If thy body had been as deformed as thy mind is dishonourable ...».[6] The animosity displayed throughout the letter makes its opening a remarkable testimony to Oxford's physical health and excellence.

Incidentally, spreading the word that one's enemy (or the enemy's mistress) had the pox was a commonplace slander for centuries. When Sir Robert Cecil, Earl of Salisbury, died in 1612, his enemies rejoiced and composed a vicious ballad in his dishonor. It ends,

> But now in Hatfield lies the Fox
> Who stank while he lived and died of the Pox.[7]

No historian takes such smears seriously without corroboration.

Even if I could not give any other interpretation to Baxter's odd lines about Hopping Helena and the Albanian dignity, I would have to dismiss the syphilis theory for the reasons already given. Yet the meaning of Baxter's words is not hard to decipher. He is saying that as long as Oxford was in Italy, regarded by Englishmen, especially Puritans, as the Land of Poisoners, his life was in danger, so the Queen ordered him home to save him.

The Italian for Helena is *Elena* (feminine) or *Eleno* (masculine). John Florio's 1611 Italian dictionary defines *Eleno* as:

Dogs-grasse or Deadly-dwale which is used to poison arrowheads.[8]

I do not know how this definition came about, but the Italian for «poison» is *veleno*, defined by Florio as:

any kind of poison, venome, bane, or infection. Used also for witchcraft or sorcery by drinkes.

The *OED* mentions «dog-grass» under «grass» 2.b., without saying anything about it, but «dwale» turns out to be deadly nightshade or belladonna. The *OED*'s first two examples of usage of «belladonna» (from 1597 and 1757) associate the term specifically with Venice. *Florios Second Frutes* of 1591[9] translates *Piu tira un sol pelo d'una bella donna* to «Than doth one haire of Helens tresse,» so John Florio links «belladonna,» which means «fair lady,» to Helen of Troy, the fairest of all ladies. In short, the Italian for Helen means belladonna, a poison used on arrows, and when Florio wanted to translate *bella donna*, meaning «fair lady,» into English he chose the word Helen. So when Baxter uses that name in a Venetian context, we do well to start thinking of poison, and, sure enough, Baxter directly mentions poison in the last line of his verse. Before finishing this line, I will move on to the next one, concerning the Albanian dignity.

Thomas Coryat toured Europe in 1608, describing the sights he had seen in *Coryat's Crudities* of 1611.[10] At Venice, by the Doge's palace and St. Mark's Cathedral, Coryat reports of

> The pourtraitures of foure Noble Gentlemen of Albania that were brothers, which are made in porphyrie stone with their fawchions [falchions] by their sides, and each couple consulting privately together by themselves, of whom this notable history following is reported.

The four brothers sailed to Venice from Albania in a ship full of treasure. Upon arrival two went ashore, while two stayed aboard ship, and each pair conspired to murder the other to enrich themselves. Rejoining for supper, each pair served the other a poisoned dish, and all four died, whereupon Venice seized their riches, «the first treasure that ever Venice possessed, and the first occasion of inriching the estate.» So Baxter gives us another image of poison in Venice.

Note that, as Prof, Nelson points out, «infested» meant «infected,» and Florio associates infection with poison.

Let us now return to the Hopping Helena line. «Warbling» is the song made by a bird, a creature that flies through the air, as does an arrow. The word «sting» had a much more deadly and venomous connotation back then than it does today, because we say a snake «bites,» while Shakespeare and his contemporaries used the word «sting,» for instance, «envenomed and fatal sting» (*2 Henry VI*, III.ii.267) or «lurking serpent's mortal sting» (*3 Henry VI*, II.ii.15).

Before explaining the full meaning of Baxter's verse, one last chore remains, namely a quick look at his punctuation. Baxter reserves the period for the end of each verse. When he completes a sentence within a verse, he places a colon (a modernizing editor would replace his colons with periods). So the last three lines of Baxter's verse do not refer back to the first two. In other words, «pastimes ... Italian sports, and Syrens Melodie» is one sentence, while «Hopping Helena ... th' Albanian dignitie, ... they poysoned all Italie» is another.

We can now explain the verse. While in Venice Oxford took part in Italian sports and was lured by sirens, but he was in danger of poison. Hopping Helena, that is, an arrow poisoned with *eleno* or belladonna, sings as it flies through the air (warbling), bearing its poisoned sting. The four noble Albanian brothers poisoned themselves at Venice, presumably with belladonna, and introduced this evil habit throughout Italy. I agree with Prof. Nelson on the next verse, which says that Oxford was summoned home by the Queen.

In conclusion, the theory that Baxter was trying to gain the patronage of the Countess of Montgomery by announcing to the world that her father had syphilis can be rejected out of hand. More important, a little research makes clear that the Puritan Baxter was playing up the perils caused by Oxford's sojourn in the Nation of Poisoners.

Endnotes

1 See *The World of Mathmatics,* ed. James R. Newman (New York, 1956), III, 1420-35.

2 John Stow, *The Survey of London* (London, 1987), 437.

3 *Ibid.,* 441.

4. *DNB* article on Lopez. The source of this information is Bishop Godfrey Goodman's *Court of James I,* written in the 1650s. Goodman is considered an honest historian, but the item on Essex and Lopez could well be a baseless rumor. The point, however, is that Goodman believed it helped to explain why Essex pursued Lopez with such ferocity; in other words, Goodman thought it plausible in his society that such a canard could cause a murderous vendetta.

5 *The Statutes of the Realm* (1817), 3 Edw. I c. 34, 2 Ric. II c. 5, 12 Ric. II c. 11.

6 B. M. Ward, *The Seventeenth Earl of Oxford* (London: John Murray, 1928), 229.

7 David Cecil, *The Cecils of Hatfield House* (Boston, 1973), 160.

8 *Queen Anna's New World of Words, or Dictionarie of the Italian and English Tongues,* facsimile (Menston, England: Scolar Press Limited, 1968).

9 John Florio, facsimile, *Theatrum Orbis Terrarum* (Amsterdam, Holland: 1969), 183/Aa4r (there are two pages 183, the one in question follows 182, the other comes four pages later, following 178).

10 Reprint, Glasgow University Press (Glasgow, Scotland: 1905), I, 331-2.

Claremont McKenna College's Shakespeare Clinic: Who Really Wrote Shakespeare

In 1990, the Shakespeare Clinic of Claremont McKenna College, headed by Ward Elliott, a professor of political science, released statistical results from its three-year study of the Shakespeare authorship problem. The Clinic used a computer to compare selected linguistic tendencies in Shakespeare's poetry to fifty-eight of his contemporaries, including Edward de Vere, 17th Earl of Oxford. The conclusion is that none of the other poets wrote like Shakespeare, hence it was highly unlikely that any of them was the true author of Shakespeare's works.[1]

The Clinic's tests are of two types, one being nine «conventional» tests, which this article is concerned with.

The nine tests are as follows. «Line Beginnings» tests word choice at the start of sentences and lines of verse. I have not seen an explanation of how it works, but the *Report* says that the Earl of Oxford matches Shakespeare, so I didn't pursue it. «Feminine Endings» counts the percentage of verse lines that end with an unstressed syllable; Oxford received a tentative mismatch on this test. «Open Endings» counts the percentage of verse lines that have no punctuation mark at the end. Oxford reportedly matches Shakespeare on this test. Oxford reportedly mismatched Shakespeare on the remaining six tests. «Hyphenated Compound Words» counts the rate of such words per thousand words in the verse of each author. «Relative Clauses» counts the rate per thousand words of relative pronouns and clauses beginning with such words as «that,» «which,» «who,» and «whom.»

«Percentage Word Length» counts the number of words of each poet that are made up of one letter, two letters, three letters, etc., up to twelve-letter words, expressing each as a percent of the total. As no poet uses many words of thirteen or more letters, the summed percentage of one-to-twelve letter words should amount to almost 100%. «Exclamation Points» counts the rate of occurrence of this punctuation mark for each author. «Reading Ease» and «Fog Index» are unexplained combinations of sentence length and word length. Incidentally, Professor Elliott remarked to me that his group regards hyphenated Compound Words, Relative Clauses, and Exclamation Points as their best tests.

Before looking further into the nine tests, I would like to express several reservations to this procedure. First, William Shakspere of Stratford-on-Avon is not tested, maintaining his status as the Teflon candidate. Second, when scientists or engineers devise a new metric or other measuring device, it is normally validated on known distances before being used to measure a disputed or unknown quantity. The Shakespeare Clinic's nine conventional tests therefore have not been validated. Third, the canon of poems for Oxford is small and uncertain, as he had no known involvement in the publication of fifteen of them.

Fourth, the Shakespeare Clinic's *Report* ignores the factor of time. Shakespeare's poetry was published from 1593 to 1609 and was probably not initiated until the early 1590s. Nine of Oxford's poems had been published by 1576, three more were quoted in a book that appeared in 1582, the next three are of uncertain date, while the last was responded to by Sir Philip Sidney, who died in 1586. There is an interval of about fifteen years between the bulk of the Oxford canon and the start of Shakespeare's non-dramatic verse and three important events occurred during or just before this gap. Oxford traveled extensively in Italy and France in 1576, which should have greatly increased his knowledge of the languages and literature of those nations; on his return he was regarded as an Italianized Englishman. This trip followed the writing of his first nine poems and possibly some of the others. Next, the English language was in a process of transition throughout the period. Not only was its vocabulary increasing exponentially, but it was changing in more fundamental matters, such as pronouns, possessives, punctuation, and verb forms. To quote from A. C. Patridge's valuable *Orthography in Shakespeare and Elizabethan Drama*:

> In vocabulary, accidence, syntax, colloquial usage, spelling, punctuation, and handwriting, the period from Spenser's ‹Sheperd's Calen-

dar› (1579) to the closing of the theatres (1642) was one of great flexibility, fluidity and change. A writer who began his literary career in one writing style might end it in another markedly different in its details.[2]

* * *

Sir Edmund Chambers' preface to *The Oxford Book of Sixteenth Century Verse* describes the poverty of English poets during the middle decades of that century, concluding:

> The most hopeful of them was Edward de Vere, Earl of Oxford, a real courtier, but an ill-conditioned youth, who also became quite mute in later life. The revival begins with Edmund Spenser's ‹Shepherd's Calendar› in 1579. And thereafter, of course, there is God's plenty.[3]

The Clinic feels that one of its best tests is its exclamation mark count; Shakespeare's works show some exclamation marks, and May's edition of Oxford's poems show none. But, again, the Clinic neglected the time factor. According to Partridge, the exclamation mark was not used in England until the 1590s, that is, after Oxford's poetry was written.[4]

Alert readers may have wondered how the Clinic could judge Shakespeare's use of exclamation marks, as there is no presumption that the punctuation in Shakespeare's early texts is his, rather than that of a scribe or publisher. The answer is that the Clinic took its punctuation for Shakespeare straight from the 1974 Riverside edition of Shakespeare's works, edited by Professor G. Blakemore Evans of Harvard University. The clinic did not bother to study Elizabethan punctuation, nor did they notice Professor Evans' careful description[5] of his unusual, intentionally archaic approach to punctuation. Three of the Clinic's nine tests are direct counts of punctuation (Open Endings, Hyphenated Compounds, and Exclamation Marks), while two more are also dependent on punctuation (Reading Ease and Fog Index depend on sentence length, which depends on the placement of periods, question and exclamation marks).

On the matter of hypens we may note another item. Over 99% of the Shakespeare poetry analyzed by the Clinic was originally printed by two publishers, Richard Field printed *Venus and Adonis* and *Lucrece*, while George Eld printed the *Sonnets* and *A Lover's Complaint* (for Thomas Thorpe). The Clinic's *Report* shows some significant differences in hyphenation between these two publishers, with Field using about 70% more hyphens per thousand words. Does this reflect Shakespeare's word use changing over time or genre; does it capture punctuational differences between Field and Eld; does it simply pick up variations in Professor Evans habits; or is it something else? These are the sort of questions the Clinic should have asked before making assertions like «Shakespeare ... loved compound words.» (Prof. Elliott to the Washington Post, April 17, 1990)

I wrote earlier that the Clinic's nine conventional tests had not been validated, to which the Clinic might reply that the high rate of consistency among different blocks of Shakespeare's poetry is validation of sorts. Yet it is not validation of the conventional tests' ability to distinguish different poets, rather than distinguish different editors.

English punctuation in Shakespeare's day was evolving rapidly with printers being far ahead of the educated public (save for Ben Jonson). Most surviving manuscript letters, poems, and plays are very lightly punctuated, and punctuation was then added by scribes, play directors, and printers. Expert conjecture on Shakespeare's punctuation is tentative and conflicting. Commas, semi-colons, colons, periods, and question marks are used today according to a logical grammatical system. But we simply accept the dictionaries' authority on «already,» «all-around,» and «all right,» which, so far as I can see, reflects no particular logic, but rather the usage dictated by a few authoritative books like the King James Bible and standard editions of Shakespeare, and a few authoritative lexicographers like Samuel Johnson and Noah Webster. Any study of Shakespeare that has a punctuational basis must consider these matters in detail. The Clinic failed to do so.

Let us consider the four non-punctuation dependent tests. The Clinic passed Oxford on Line Beginnings and, as we have seen, he also passes on Percentage Word Length once the Clinic's faulty data is corrected, but he allegedly falls on Relative Clauses. This test has two main subtests, Relative Pronouns and Relative Clauses. Oxford is within Shakespeare's range and within two standard deviations of Shakespeare's mean on Relative Pronouns, so he passes that subtest. The Relative Clause subtest is broken into six categories, and Oxford is well within Shakespeare's range on five of them; he is outside Shakespeare's range in having too many relative clauses beginning with the word «that.»

On the total Relative Clause subtest score, Oxford shows 60 relative clauses, but would have passed had he had only 58. In other words, Oxford matches Shakespeare on six of seven subtests, but is given a «mismatch» for two too many «that's.» This outcome could be reversed by a small change in Oxford's canon, but let us accept the methodology and improve the test by considering the time factor.

Casual inspection reveals that the number of «that's» falls off sharply with the later poems. In other words, the youthful Oxford was already moving in Shakespeare's direction, and so when the time factor is taken into account, Oxford passes on Relative Clauses.

We now consider the final test, Feminine Endings. Oxford has virtually no feminine lines, while about 10% of Shakespeare's lines are feminine. Clearly Oxford mismatches Shakespeare, but that is to be expected if the time factor is considered. Poetry in that period first sought to achieve regularity of meter and then moved toward studied irregularity. This trend is found in sixteenth century English poetry in general, in dramatic verse in the second half of the century, and in Shakespeare's works. Feminine lines are a form of irregularity, and so we should not expect to find as many in Oxford's youthful poetry as in Shakespeare's mature poetry.

In conclusion, the *Report* of the Shakespeare Clinic has the following initial faults. Shakspere is not even tested, the methodology has not been validated, Oxford's small and uncertain canon makes a treacherous basis for statistical analysis, and the time factor has been ignored. As we begin to examine the tests in detail, they crumble. Serious bias is seen in setting up the scoring system, as Relative Clauses and Relative Pronouns are lumped together as one test, when they are really two different things, while Reading Ease and Fog Index, which really measure the same thing, are counted as two tests.

I do not think that this bias was intentional; errors in counting up the basic data are found with ease and one of them, Daniel's word count, is egregious. Moreover, Oxford is faulted for lacking exclamation marks though his poems were written before there were any such marks. Further, all of the five punctuation tests simply capture the usual pointing of the Riverside Shakespeare. The Clinic failed to standardize its data, to use the technical term for removing the effects of extraneous variables. The four tests not based on punctuation might hold some interest if the data could be trusted, which is not presently the case. But even if they were redone properly, they would only have the status of evidence, data, or tendencies subject to interpretation rather than decisive tests. At any rate, and for what they're worth, they support the theory that the Earl of Oxford wrote Shakespeare.

Endnotes

1   For the most recent report on the Clinic's project, see Ward Elliott and Robert Valenza, «Oxford by the Numbers: What are the Odds that the Earl of Oxford Could Have Written Shakespeare's Poems and Plays?», *University of Tennessee Law Review*, 72 (1), Fall 2004, 323-453 — Editor

2   A.C. Partridge, *Orthography in Shakespeare and Elizabethan Drama* (Univ. of Nebraska Press, 1964), 106.

3   Sir E.K. Chambers, *The Oxford Book of Sixteenth Century Verse* (Oxford: Clarendon Press, 1932), vii.

4   Partridge, 124-26.

5   *The Riverside Shakespeare*. Ed. G. Blakemore Evans (Boston: Houghton Mifflin, 1974), vi and 39-40.

Demonography 101:
A Review of Alan Nelson's
Monstrous Adversary

Professor Alan H. Nelson of University of California, Berkeley has produced *Monstrous Adversary, The Life of Edward de Vere, 17th Earl of Oxford* [Liverpool, England: Liverpool UP, 2003], which offers a mass of new documentary information on his subject. Nelson deserves thanks and praise for this research, as well as for his openness in sharing his archival discoveries on his website, socrates.berkeley.edu/~ahnelson/authorsh.html.

In six of his chapters (29, 45, 46, and 75-7) Nelson analyzes Oxford's poetry, literary patronage, and sponsorship of acting companies. The contents of these chapters should remind readers that Nelson hails from the English Department of one of America's leading universities. When analyzing metrical conventions, the niceties of dedications, or the history of theatrical troupes, he shows the sure touch of an expert in his field. I do not imply that readers must accede to Nelson's every judgment on these matters, though I find little to disagree with, but readers should recognize an obvious professional. Unfortunately, Nelson cannot do history.

Monstrous Adversary is a documentary biography composed of extensive quotations from contemporary letters, memoranda, legal records, and the like, stitched together with Nelson's comments. Nelson asks in his Introduction that we let «the documentary evidence speak for itself» (5). His request fails for two reasons. First, documentary evidence rarely makes sense without the appropriate context, which includes not only historical background information on the religious, legal, social, or cultural practices of a much earlier era,[1] but also personal information, such as establishing who struck the first blow in a fight, or whether a witness was truthful in other matters.[2] As I will show, Nelson totally botches the context of event after event. Secondly, Nelson, who with some justice refers to Oxford's first biographer, B. M. Ward, as a hagiographer (250), pushes much further in the opposite direction, so much so, that his study of Oxford may well be dubbed demonography.

The 17th Earl of Oxford was anything but a model nobleman of his time. He threw away his family fortune, he failed to develop the career expected of an earl by shouldering his share of local and national responsibilities, and he fathered a child out of wedlock. Quite possibly he also drank too much as a young man. On the other hand, he excelled in his generosity, he earned praise for his writings, and he retained the favor of his famously headstrong and moralistic Queen. These facts have long been known. What does Nelson add to them? Quite a lot of detail and color: Nelson's persistence and skill as a document sleuth flesh out both major and minor events of Oxford's story. Unfortunately, Nelson the analyst relates to Nelson the researcher as Hyde relates to Jekyll—moreover, Nelson's obsessive denigration of Oxford carries him from error into fantasy.

I. A Nelson Sampler

In support of my criticism, I will begin by discussing Nelson's treatment of five episodes of Oxford's life. I will then discuss Oxford's most significant scandal, the accusations between him and his sometime friends, Lord Henry Howard and Charles Arundel, before proceeding to the peculiarities of Nelson's writing style. Finally, I will discuss some of the positive aspects of Oxford's story that can be extracted from Nelson's work.

My first example offers a very simple case of Nelson's historiographic ineptitude. His Chapter 13, «Necromancy,» begins with quotations from Oxford's friends-turned-accusers in 1580-1, Howard and Arundel, to the effect that Oxford copulated with a female spirit, saw the ghosts of his mother and stepfather, and often conjured up Satan for conversations. Nelson then explains in detail where, when, and, above all, how Oxford carried out these ungodly deeds. Unfortunately, Nelson neglects to inform his readers that Howard and Arundel listed these items among the outrageous lies regularly told by Oxford.[3] In other words, although neither Howard nor Arundel expected their contemporaries to believe that Oxford actually committed such acts, they failed to anticipate the stunning gullibility of Nelson.

We can find out why Oxford told these horrendous falsehoods by turning to some of the documentary evidence found on Nelson's website, though omitted from the biography. After relating yet another of Oxford's tall tales—about peacefully ending a civil war in Genoa—Charles Arundel continued: «this lie is very rife with him and in it he glories greatly; diversely hath he told it, and when he enters into it, he can hardly out, which hath made such sport as often have I been driven to rise from his table laughing, so hath my Lord Charles Howard [the admiral who defeated the Spanish Armada] and the rest».[4] Not only does this remarkable testimony reveal a side of Oxford's character that Nelson studiously ignores, it also indicates the unbalanced nature of Oxford's foes, who thought they could damn him as a liar by describing his brilliance as a raconteur.

After concealing the unbalanced nature of Oxford's enemies, Nelson attributes insanity to one of Oxford's friends. Nathaniel Baxter accompanied Oxford on his trip to Italy in 1575-6, which he described in a 1606 poem to Oxford's daughter, the Countess of Montgomery (138-9). Baxter's poem includes this seemingly cryptic stanza: «Never omitting what might pastime bring,/Italian sports, and Syren's Melodie:/Hopping Helena with her warbling sting,/Infested th'Albanian dignitie,/ Like as they poysoned all Italie.» Without the slightest hint that another interpretation might exist, Nelson informs us that «Albania» means England, while «Hopping Helena» indicates a prostitute whose «warbling sting» is venereal disease. Thus, according to Nelson, Baxter publicly «reveals» that the Countess of Montgomery's father caught syphilis in Venice.

Another interpretation emerges by assuming that «Albania» means the nation of that name, and that Baxter's «poysoned» means poisoned. Such an interpretation agrees with Venetian lore on four noble Albanian brothers who poisoned each other in Venice, especially given that John Florio's Italian dictionary defines «eleno,» the Italian masculine form of the name «Helena,» as deadly nightshade or belladonna, while Florio elsewhere translates the Italian «bella donna» as «Helen.» I lack the space to work through two rival interpretations, particularly when a far greater threat hangs over Nelson's reading.[5] Baxter's verse was published in his popular work, *Sir Philip Sidney's ‹Ourania,›* along with commendatory poems to other aristocrats. The next stanza in Baxter's poem informs the Countess that her father promptly hurried home to England in order to beget her upon her «everlasting faire» mother (actually the Countess was conceived ten years later). If we accept Nelson's interpretation, then we must conclude that Baxter and his publisher had literally taken leave of their senses by publicly proclaiming that the recently deceased Earl of Oxford carried a disgraceful and loathsome disease, which he presumably passed on to his first and second wives and their three children: the Countess of Montgomery, the future Lady Norris, and the eighteenth Earl of Oxford. The *Dictionary of National Biography* notes that Baxter's commendatory poems in *Ourania* were «evidently written with a view to some pecuniary reward.» On the contrary, according to Nelson, those poems were evidently written with a view to ostracism—if not specifically intended to provoke savage reprisals.

Oxford's departure from the Netherlands campaign for unknown reasons in October 1585 provides the next example of Nelson's slipshod methods (296-8). English support for the Dutch rebels fighting for independence from Spain became urgent as the Spanish gained ground that summer, and several thousand troops were raised and dispatched pell-mell in August, with the size and organization of the army still undetermined. This advance force was led by Sir John Norris (misidentified by Nelson as his brother Henry Norris), with Oxford apparently commanding the cavalry contingent. Meanwhile, fierce political maneuvering over the top command positions continued at Court, with the Earl of Leicester being selected, unselected, then re-selected as commander-in-chief in September and October. Leicester naturally wanted his own choices, such as his nephew Sir Philip Sidney, for subordinate commands, but he yielded one position to pressure from Oxford's father-in-law, Lord Treasurer Burghley, on behalf of his son,

Sir Thomas Cecil.[6] On October 21, Oxford returned to England. Leicester's commission as commander was signed on October 22, and he arrived in December with his twenty-year-old step-son the Earl of Essex, who received command of the cavalry.

Although no one knows exactly why Oxford returned, we find something of an explanation in a letter printed by Nelson: Oxford had «letters of my Lord Treasurer's to him wherein he wrote of her Majesty's grant of the commanding of horsemen» (298). Nelson mistakenly refers to these letters as Oxford's «commission from Burghley» (299), but the Lord Treasurer had no authority to award military commissions. These were granted by the Queen in letters patent stamped with the privy seal, and no such commission exists for Oxford. Apparently the Queen sent Oxford without a commission, and then he lost out in the jockeying for position at Court. He may have returned because he had been superceded or simply to lobby on his own behalf—no one knows. Nelson, however, pretends otherwise: «As of mid-October, Oxford's loyalties were put to the test. Would he cooperate with Leicester and Sidney to advance the Queen's interests in the Low Countries? He would not.» As far as Nelson is concerned, Oxford simply «quit his post in a fit of pique.» Thus, evidentiary complexity and uncertainty dissolve before Nelson's inability to distinguish between private letters and the Queen's commission.

My fourth example of Nelson's strange ways with evidence deals with the Spanish Armada, which reached England on July 19, 1588, fought its way to Calais only to be expelled by fire-ships in the night of July 28-9, followed by a day of battle, and finally turned north for its homeward voyage on July 30.[7] Oxford played a small part in these great events. He was with the Earl of Leicester's army at Tilbury near the mouth of the Thames, then sailed out to the fleet, returning to Tilbury on July 27. On August 1, Leicester, still expecting to give battle at Tilbury, wrote that Oxford disliked the Queen's proposal that he take command of the north Essex port of Harwich, a potential Spanish landing place, and so he went to Court to protest. According to Leicester, Oxford objected to being ordered away from the anticipated combat. And that is the last we know until Oxford took a conspicuous role, suitable to his rank, alongside the Queen at the November victory celebration. Nelson records these details (316-8), concluding that Oxford should have been severely punished for disobeying Leicester's order. This judgment fails on several grounds. First, Leicester says nothing about giving Oxford an order, rather than informing him of the Queen's intention; Leicester certainly says nothing about Oxford disobeying an order. Next, Nelson has no business assuming that Oxford did not end up at Harwich anyway, as the Queen may have overruled his protest. In the course of his researches in England, which included the Essex Record Office (xvii-xviii), Nelson could easily have tried to discover who did command at Harwich in early August, but he did not bother. Finally, Oxford's place beside the Queen at the victory celebration seems to dispel any imputation of disgrace, particularly given Elizabeth's notoriously strong opinions and sharp tongue.

My fifth example concerns reports that Oxford plotted against the succession of King James while Queen Elizabeth lay dying in March 1603 (409-18). A few days before the Queen's death the Earl of Lincoln informed Sir John Peyton, commander of the Tower of London, that Oxford proposed that they support Lincoln's nephew, Lord Hastings, as heir to the throne rather than James of Scotland; both Lincoln and Peyton subsequently reported this information to the authorities. Nelson supplies the following essential information to help us sort out this issue. Lincoln was an «erratic and violent» man; it was his close kinsman, not Oxford's, who was being pushed for the crown; and Lincoln, not Oxford, had discussed the matter with the French Embassy, which opposed James. Peyton wrote of Lincoln that, «his fashion is to condemn the world if thereby he might excuse himself.» After the proclamation of James as King of England, and the arrival in London of his advance man, Lord Kinloss, Peyton told Lincoln to inform Kinloss. Peyton later explained that he did not tell Kinloss himself, out of fear that Lincoln would deny his conversations with Peyton.

Nelson urges Oxford as the instigator of this sedition, but the foregoing details, as well as others that I have omitted, allow sensible readers to identify Lincoln as the probable culprit. My principal objection to Nelson's treatment of this episode lies in these words: «Lincoln and Peyton agreed on one point: the most active opponent of James among English noblemen at the time of the Queen's death had been Oxford» (411). Peyton agreed to no such thing; he simply reported what Lincoln told him while making clear his mistrust of Lincoln. Readers unfamiliar with this affair have no real way of spotting Nelson's dereliction. Otherwise, I will note three more objections. First, Nelson insinuates, as he says nothing at all about any other nobles opposing James, much less that Oxford—or Lincoln—was «the most active.» Next, Nelson displays hopeless naivety in using denigration of Oxford as his main criterion for source reliability. Finally, Nelson seems incapable of fitting together pieces of historical evidence into a coherent whole, preferring simply to snatch up any item that he can twist against Oxford.

The foregoing examples display Nelson's methods and limitations. The next is similar but on a much larger scale.

II. The Howard-Arundel Affair

We now come to the scandal of Oxford's life, the mutual accusations between him and his former friends, Henry Howard, Charles Arundel, and Francis Southwell. After his return from Italy in 1576, Oxford became a Catholic, until Christmas 1580, when he denounced his three co-religionists for subversion. Howard and Arundel—but not Southwell—replied by accusing Oxford of a non-stop crime spree. Nelson utterly ignores the historical context of this affair, which may be summarized as follows.[8] During the 1560s, Queen Elizabeth temporized with the Papacy and other Catholic powers, while generally turning a blind eye to the practice of Catholicism in England. That policy ended with the 1570 papal decree that Elizabeth had no right to the throne and that her subjects owed her no allegiance, followed by the infiltration into England of hundreds of English priests fresh from continental seminaries. The Queen and her Councilors watched with alarm as Catholicism grew in the later 1570s, and then the dreaded Jesuit order arrived in England in June 1580. The government's ultimate fear, which actually went back to the late 1530s, was invasion by a French, Spanish, or Imperial army, supported by a rebellion of English Catholics. The periodic Catholic-Protestant warfare in Europe and around the world of the early and mid-sixteenth century turned continual in 1567 and stayed that way until 1648.

These facts, of which Nelson seems unaware, would have occupied the mental foreground of the Queen and her ministers as they evaluated Oxford's charges of subversive or treasonous activities against Howard and Arundel, as well as their countercharges of criminal conduct and personal misbehavior against Oxford. The simplest way to evaluate the government's reaction to the various accusations is to note that Howard, Arundel, and Southwell were placed in confinement, while Oxford remained at liberty—until he was locked up from late March through June 1581 for fathering a child by one of the Queen's maids of honor. Subsequently, as discussed above, Oxford was twice chosen for military commands against Spain, while Henry Howard spent most of the remainder of Elizabeth's reign in obscurity.[9] Charles Arundel fled England for France in fall 1583 in the wake of the Throckmorton plot, which sought to combine a French invasion of England with a domestic Catholic rebellion. Once in France, Arundel helped author the book later called *Leicester's Commonwealth,* a massive slander aimed at the Queen's favorite, the Earl of Leicester, which Elizabeth Jenkins summarizes as follows:

> This pungent, racy piece of journalism gives a sensational picture of Leicester as a master criminal, with his tribe of poisoners, bawds and abortionists, his Italian ointments and aphrodisiacs, the bottle at his bed's head worth £10 the pint, «his good fortune in seeing them dead who, for any cause, he would not have to live,» the list of his victims beginning with his wife and ending with the Earl of Sussex.[10]

That one of Oxford's two accusers turned into a professional slanderer does not seem relevant to Nelson, who buries his sole mention of *Leicester's Commonwealth* in a footnote, which gives no explanation of this notorious libel beyond mislabeling it a «satire.»[11]

I turn now to the charges made by Charles Arundel against Oxford, specifically: seven counts of atheism; sixteen counts of lying; thirteen counts of setting one person to kill another or setting two men against each other; approximately eight counts of attempted murder; several counts of sodomy and bestiality; continual drunkenness; six counts of bearing grudges against Arundel, Howard, and Southwell; and sixteen counts of undutifulness to the Queen.[12] Henry Howard's charges bear enough similarity in organization and wording to Arundel's for Nelson to recognize that the two men were obviously collaborating (259). It is hardly possible now to determine whether Oxford actually did say, «that the cobblers' wives of Milan are more richly dressed every working day than the Queen on Christmas Day,» or whether he did «break into my Lord of Worcester's house with an intent to murther him and all his men,» as Arundel affirmed. We may, however, look at how several contemporaries responded.

Francis Southwell's hand appears only once in the numerous documents of accusation, but that one instance is highly significant. Howard smuggled an abbreviated set of his charges against Oxford to Southwell, with these instructions: «Add to this what particulars soever you have declared of him and they shall be justified. Here is nothing in this paper but may be avowed without danger as hath been determined.» Southwell replied with several annotations and an addendum.[13] Howard's document lists four items under the heading «Atheism,» thirteen under «Dangerous practices,» and four under «Buggery.» Southwell writes the Latin word «Audivi,» that is, «I heard [it],» next to two of the blasphemy items, then adds two more remarks by Oxford: that Solomon was blessed with 300 concubines, and that the Bible was written to keep men in obedience. In the dangerous practices category, Southwell ignored five charges of attempted murder, while placing his «Audivi» against three instances of Oxford's railing about the Queen, English Catholics, and the late Duke of Norfolk. Southwell added in the margin that Oxford «promised to sack London, and give me [Alderman] Day['s] house.» Under buggery, Southwell ignored two specific charges, while posting a denial against a third, along with his «Audivi» regarding hearsay of Oxford's tendencies.

Thus far, Southwell indicates that Oxford talked big, but nothing else. Now, however, we come to the addendum, in which Southwell makes clear his enmity toward Oxford. He discusses at some length charges related to prophecies, presumably subversive. Then he takes up dangerous matters:

> I cannot particularly charge my Lord [Oxford] with pedication [pederasty], but with open lewdness of his own speeches, neither with Tom Cooke, nor Powers, nor any else.

> I pray, my good Lord [Howard], in any matter of treason he [Oxford] may justly be charged withal let us have care of misprision [concealment]. By my intelligence I hear the Queen's Majesty hath clearly forgiven him, and therefore let us wisely and safely disable him.

> I hear by you [that] Mr. Charles [Arundel] is my dear friend. In faith, my Lord, it is not best, for if the Earl could get one man to aver anything, we were utterly overthrown.

Thus, in his secret communication with Henry Howard, Southwell specifically states that he cannot accuse Oxford of homosexual acts, but only with having a foul mouth. Further, he warns that he and Howard will be implicated in any accusations of treason they might make against Oxford; I should add that the extent to which Catholic activities in the 1570s might be held treasonous in 1581 would have depended heavily on their context and implications, as well as on the authorities' attitude toward the accused. Finally, Southwell clearly indicates that Arundel faced the greatest danger of prosecution, probably for treason, of any of the four.

However Southwell also says, in the middle quotation above, that he and Howard should «disable» Oxford, for an explanation of which we must turn to the heading of Arundel's principal document of charges against Oxford.

> The strength of this monster's evidence against my Lord Henry [Howard], Mr. Southwell, and myself weakened and taken down by

> the <u>sufficient proof</u> of <u>the man's insufficiency to bear witness</u> against any man of reputation. For these respects [the accusations that follow] no less warranted by laws of honor and of arms than by the civil laws and <u>the laws of our own country</u>. [my emphases]

Although no lawyer, Arundel advances a legal argument based on three current statutes that required two witnesses for proof of treason, with one statute calling specifically for «two lawful and <u>sufficient witnesses</u>.»[14] The first two groups of charges after Arundel's heading are atheism and lying. Thus, rather than defending against Oxford's focused charges of sedition or treason, Arundel countercharges with the aim of preventing Oxford from bearing witness. Arundel's delusion about eliminating Oxford's testimony crops up later in three letters, which contrast his own seven to eight months of confinement to the freedom of Oxford, «a person convicted of great beastliness.»[15] Arundel failed to grasp that Oxford had been convicted of nothing; to put it another way, Arundel, like Nelson, confuses accusation with proof. Meanwhile, Southwell—also aware of the two witness rule—warns Howard that Oxford plus one further witness will destroy them. Southwell apparently uses «disable» in the sense of *OED* definition 2, «to incapacitate legally ... to hinder or restrain (any person...) from performing acts ... which would otherwise be open to them,» such as bearing witness. One wishes for more testimony from Francis Southwell.

One witness remains on the topic of Oxford's alleged homosexuality, Orazio Coquo, a Venetian singing boy who came with him from Italy, remained for eleven months in Oxford's house, and then returned home. Henry Howard wrote that «touching buggery» Coquo «complained how horribly my Lord [Oxford] had abused him,» while Arundel added that Coquo «made it [buggery] the quarrel of his departure» (140-1).[16] Thanks to Nelson's impressive research we are able to read the interview of Coquo by the Venetian Inquisition that followed his extended trip to heretic England (155-7). That Coquo said nothing about homosexuality proves little, as he might have preferred to avoid that topic, while the Inquisition's interest centered on threats to his religion.

Nevertheless, Coquo himself brought up his reason for leaving England, which was that a Milanese merchant in London advised him that his Catholicism would be endangered if he remained longer. Otherwise, Coquo associated freely with other Italian musicians in London, performed before and spoke to the Queen (who tried to convert him), attended mass at the French and Portuguese Embassies, and reported Oxford as offering religious freedom to those in his household. In short, where Howard and Arundel can be checked against Coquo, their testimony turns out to be false.

On the other hand, how did the Queen react to Howard and Arundel's accusations that Oxford tried to murder her favorite, the Earl of Leicester; her Principal Secretary, Sir Francis Walsingham; her Vice Chamberlain and favorite, Sir Christopher Hatton; Lord Worcester and all his household; Lord Windsor and all his household; as well as a string of other prominent courtiers, including Sir Walter Ralegh and Philip Sidney; not to mention the accusations of buggery, atheism, sedition, disrespect to her own person, etc.? Although, as noted above, the Queen swiftly and sharply punished Oxford's fornication with a maid of honor in the spring of 1581, she refused to take action on the basis of Howard and Arundel's charges. Her predecessors and successors were certainly capable of punishing crimes committed by peers against lesser folk. Her father hanged Lord Dacre for felony murder and beheaded Lord Hungerford for sodomy and soothsaying, while her sister hanged Lord Stourton for murder. James I hanged Lord Sanquhar for murder, and allowed his favorites, the Earl and Countess of Somerset, to be convicted of murder by poisoning, although he punished them with lengthy imprisonment rather than death, while Charles I beheaded the Earl of Castlehaven for sodomy.

Elizabeth did not ignore Oxford's misdeeds, although the surviving records fail to clarify the extent to which her disfavor was caused by his dalliance with the maid of honor and his subsequent feud with her kinsmen, or by the accusations of Howard and Arundel. Oxford was forbidden from the Queen's presence from spring 1581 until May 1583, then restored to favor.[17] His rehabilitation was presumably enhanced by

Throckmorton's arrest that October, along with Arundel's flight to France, the expulsion of the Spanish ambassador, and the reincarceration for a year and a half of the ambassador's hired informant, Lord Henry Howard. Oxford's fall and rise may also be seen in his standing with the Knights of the Garter and in his military record. Although Oxford received numerous votes in the annual elections for membership in the Order of the Garter from 1571 to 1580, he secured not a single vote in the elections of 1581-4. Clearly, the combination of the Howard-Arundel affair, the illegitimate child and subsequent feuding, and the Queen's disfavor all caused a heavy drop in his prestige. Yet just as clearly, his respectable showings in the next three elections, 1585, 1587, and 1588, mark his rehabilitation. Apparently the six peers who voted for Oxford in these elections placed little trust in the Howard-Arundel smear.[18] Meanwhile, Oxford received offers of military commands in 1585 and 1588, while Howard's 1587 request to serve against Spain was rejected.[19]

I have tried in the preceding paragraphs to present the principal evidence on the credibility of the accusations against Oxford in 1580-1. To say that Nelson offers nothing equivalent actually understates the case. Nelson obliterates the whole issue of credibility by spreading most of the accusations across his earlier chapters, with titles like «Necromancy,» «Atheist,» «Sodomite,» and «Prophet.»[20] Nelson's Chapter 48, «Tables Turned,» discusses the charges as a whole in barely one page,[21] including: «We have already considered both the form and substance of most of these charges» (259). This statement is perfectly true, as long as we realize that Nelson's «substance» simply means «content.» The question of credibility never arises in Nelson's text. The critical testimony of Francis Southwell does not appear, even in a footnote.[22] The disagreement between Orazio Coquo's statement to the Inquisition and what Howard and Arundel said about him goes unnoticed.[23] Arundel's connection to the Throckmorton plot is ignored, while his later profession as a manufacturer of defamation against Leicester is hidden in an uninformative footnote. Henry Howard's life of machinations, especially his role as a paid agent of Spain in the early 1580s, and as accomplice to his great niece, the murderous Countess of Somerset, go unmentioned. Although Howard died the year before the Countess's sensational trial, the obscenity of his letters, which were read in court, stunned contemporary observers, a point of particular relevance to our evaluation of the obscenities Howard charged against Oxford.[24] Moreover, Queen Elizabeth, in Nelson's telling, comes across as a spineless ninny, quite at variance with the portrait painted by her many biographers.

Nelson maintains his evasiveness in his recitation of the charges made by Oxford and Thomas Norton against Howard and Arundel (254-8),[25] which have nothing to do with bizarre personal behavior, but everything to do with Catholic invasion and rebellion. Nelson's verdict is that Oxford was guilty of betrayal, hypocrisy, petty-mindedness, and a lack of mental control (258). Only readers sensitized to Nelson's ways will notice his failure to say that Oxford's charges were false—and herein lies a mystery. It could be that even Nelson recognizes the fatuity of denying that Henry Howard and Charles Arundel were Catholic conspirators—or it could simply be an oversight? The latter possibility, that is, lack of authorial control, draws support from the final sentence of Chapter 47, which accuses Oxford of «cramming his paper with ... hatred and resentment of the whole Howard clan» (258). Oxford's two page paper makes no mention of the Howard family, but only names Henry Howard, along with one neutral reference to his brother. Despite Nelson's frenzy concerning Oxford's alleged hatred of his Howard cousins (249 and 251), Charles, Lord Admiral Howard of Effingham, voted for Oxford in the Garter elections from 1585 to 1588.

No responsible historian would ignore the political and religious context of Oxford's quarrel with Howard and Arundel. No real historian would fail to compare Howard and Arundel's accusations against Oxford to their subsequent conduct: Howard's record as a paid agent of Spain, and Arundel's pack of lies in *Leicester's Commonwealth*. Finally, no historian would both suppress and misrepresent the critical evidence of Francis Southwell. Nelson falls short on all counts.

III. Nelson's Style

I now turn from specific events to Nelson's style, in particular his penchant for suppression of evidence, insinuation, and «cheap shot.» Before offering examples, I will expand the quotation from his Introduction that I placed at the start of this article: «I beg the open-minded reader to join me in holding the mature Oxford responsible for his own life, letting the documentary evidence speak for itself» (5). As we shall see, Nelson is unwilling to let the evidence speak freely to the reader, presumably because he will not get the outcome he desires. The examples that follow could easily be multiplied tenfold. Incidentally, identifying the quirks of Nelson's style offers a peculiar charm to readers who succeed in overcoming the notion that *Monstrous Adversary* should be regarded as a genuine work of biography or history.

Thomas Fowle, the Cambridge M.A. who had been Oxford's tutor in 1558, was among a group of Puritan clergymen that committed a disorderly protest in Norwich Cathedral in 1570, and Fowle later participated in the lawful suppression of Catholicism and promotion of Puritanism. Nelson informs us that this background «suggests that [Oxford] was tutored during his formative years by a religious fanatic of violent temper» (25). The sight of a professor from Berkeley, of all places, growing hysterical over a protest demonstration is truly amusing. Then, of course, Nelson's target is not Fowle, but Oxford, as Nelson adumbrates his ominous future. I would also like to single out Nelson's weaselly verb, «suggests,» apparently designed to deflect criticism, as in: «I only suggested ...»

In June 1563, Lawrence Nowell wrote that his instruction of Oxford, then age thirteen, «cannot be much longer required.» Nelson comments: «Perhaps Oxford had surpassed Nowell's capacity to instruct him. More likely—since nothing indicates that Oxford was an enthusiastic student, and much indicates that he was not—Nowell found the youth intractable» (39). Here Nelson at least allows for both good and bad possibilities, although he provides no support for the opinion he places inside the hyphens. But later in the book Nelson returns to this episode:

«Lawrence Nowell ... declare[d] the 17th Earl incapable of further instruction» (437). So much for the pretence of objectivity.

Oxford experienced illness for a few months in 1569-70, then headed north to join the Earl of Sussex's punitive raid into Scotland. From Oxford's medical expenses, plus the fact that a few of his later book dedications came from apothecaries, Nelson opines that, «we may infer that Oxford was chronically sickly, hypochondriacal, or both» (51). Once again Nelson qualifies his childish logic with a weaselly verb, «may infer»—after all, he may infer whatever he likes—but the plural subject, «we,» means that Nelson refuses even to accept responsibility for the inference.

The concluding paragraph of Nelson's chapter on Oxford's marriage in December 1571 opens thus: «It is difficult to believe that the happiness of the couple was complete» (77). The supporting evidence is the fact that Oxford's bride was a virgin, along with Nelson's opinion that Oxford was a «buck,» although Nelson offers no evidence that the buck was not also a virgin. Note that Nelson's unmeasurable requirement for happiness is absolute, not merely that happiness might be very great or almost complete. Note also the passive voice, which prevents us from knowing who finds it difficult to believe that this unmeasurable absolute requirement was met. In short, Nelson's verdict is meaningless.

In 1572, Oxford gained possession of his inheritance, drawing Nelson to remark: «On May 30 the license Oxford had anticipated for most of his conscious life was finally issued» (83). No weasel verb here! Nelson forthrightly presents opinion as fact, but, alas, we are not informed whether the alleged fact is based on tangible evidence or on mind reading.

Nelson's Chapter 21 consists of miscellaneous items from January to June 1573. He concludes with the observation that Oxford's wife, age seventeen and a half years, had yet to become pregnant after two and a half years of marriage. Nelson insinuates: «To the extent that Oxford had been sexually active since December 1571, it was evidently with partners other than his young, pretty, and lawful wife» (107). Again the passive voice, along with an insinuation of adultery without a scrap of supporting evidence.

Speaking of the «sodomitical multiple sins ... laid against Oxford,» Nelson avers that we have «active witnesses in the figures of Henry Howard, Charles Arundel, and Francis Southwell (before he got cold feet)» (214). Nelson's words clearly imply that Southwell said something implicating Oxford in sodomy, but then got scared. In fact, Southwell's only comment was, as given in the previous section: «I cannot particularly charge my Lord [Oxford] with pedication,» etc. In this instance, Nelson not only suppresses evidence, he misrepresents the suppressed denial as an affirmation.

Oxford's first wife died of a fever on June 5, 1588 and was buried at Westminster Abbey on June 25. Nelson quotes an account of her funeral which lists two groups of participants in the ritual: mourners and carriers of banners. Nelson then cites the observation of Lord Burghley's biographer, Conyers Read: «It is not recorded that her husband was among those present» (309). Thus Nelson would have us conclude that Oxford deserted his wife in death. The trouble with this conclusion, which probably explains why Nelson hides behind Read's authority, is that neither Lord Burghley nor his two sons are recorded among those present, and so it seems that the Countess of Oxford was also deserted by her father and brothers. Actually, all of them may have been there, but not in the two recorded categories of mourners or banner carriers.[26] Their absence, on the other hand, might be explained by the fact that the Spanish Armada sailed from Lisbon for England in May, although, unknown to the English, it was regrouping in Corunna on the date of the funeral.

In September 1595, Oxford received a letter of thanks from King Henry IV of France for assisting in some unknown business with Queen Elizabeth. Nelson's conclusion on this episode: «Similar letters sent on the same day to Burghley and the Lord Admiral [Howard of Effingham], and an even longer letter to [the Earl of] Essex, suggest that Oxford's letter had no personal significance» (349). A minimally competent historian would have noted that Oxford's association in the eyes of the King of France with the three most powerful and prestigious noblemen in England indicates that Oxford remained a figure of some consequence.

IV. Reading Nelson Against the Grain

Despite Nelson's efforts to portray Oxford's life as a half century of unbroken shame and disgrace, some positive aspects may be gleaned by readers who know where to look—and who possess the requisite background knowledge. To begin with, save for the period 1581-3, Oxford remained in favor with his hard-to-please sovereign Queen Elizabeth until her death. Moreover, her perception of his ability and loyalty caused her to choose him for military commands against Spain in 1585 and 1588.

Nelson meticulously records the fairly impressive vote totals that Oxford received for the prestigious Order of the Garter during 1569-80 and 1585-8.[27] Nelson predictably invents an unpleasant explanation for Oxford's failure to gain any votes thereafter until 1604. Regarding his presumption that Oxford refused the Harwich command in 1588, Nelson imagines that: «the Queen did not forget the truth: while she lived, Oxford never received another vote for the Order of the Garter» (319). Aside from the lack of any evidence supporting this assertion, Nelson supposes Elizabeth as a moral coward who was unable to forbid Oxford from taking a prominent place in her victory celebration, but who chose instead to secretly blackball him with regard to the Knights of the Garter. Rather out of character for Elizabeth Tudor, especially as Nelson knows that she regularly ignored the vote totals and picked whomever she preferred for the Garter, while her deep disfavor for the Earl of Southampton did not prevent him from garnering a goodly number of Garter votes in 1599 and 1600.[28] More can be profitably said on this topic.

Perhaps Oxford did not go to Harwich in 1588. Military history is full of soldiers, including some famous ones like U. S. General George Patton, who used any method to get to the battle zone and avoid the rear echelon. The superiors of such men may well have regarded them as infernal nuisances, but no one calls them shirkers—except Nelson. Yet Nelson's contextual ignorance spills over into areas of his supposed competence. In 1589, the year after Oxford's supposed disgrace, Edmund Spenser wrote dedicatory sonnets to fourteen men, one of whom was Oxford, for the first edition of *Faerie Queene*. Nelson prints the sonnet to Oxford (383) but misses the context. The other thirteen men were Hatton, Burghley, Northumberland, Cumberland, Essex, Ormond, Howard of Effingham, Hunsdon, Grey of Wilton, Buckhurst, Walsingham, Sir John Norris, and Ralegh. Aside from Grey and Norris, to whom Spenser had personal connections, the other eleven were the top movers and shakers at Elizabeth's Court.[29] Like the supposedly deluded Henry IV of France, Spenser somehow managed to insert Oxford into this roll call of the mighty.

Oxford maintained relations, both friendly and unfriendly, with Sir Walter Ralegh over a period of twenty-five years, but Nelson bungles their last known connection. After Essex's rebellion and execution in February 1601, Ralegh rose to the peak of his power and influence with the Queen, thereby eliciting from Oxford a witticism about upstarts, which was recorded by Francis Bacon and Sir Robert Naunton. Nelson reports these facts, but somehow twists them into a tale of Oxford gloating over Ralegh's downfall (397), which actually took place in 1603, and about which Oxford is not known to have expressed any opinion. Ralegh's destruction, incidentally, was engineered by the viperous Lord Henry Howard, who poisoned the mind of King James against Ralegh, naming him, among other things, «the greatest Lucifer that hath lived in our age,» in a series of letters from 1601-03.[30]

I will end this section by mentioning several of Oxford's friends. During his separation from his first wife, 1576-81, Oxford formed a double connection to Catherine Bertie, dowager Duchess of Suffolk, whom Nelson mistakenly calls a Countess (172-3, 176-7). In summer 1577, Oxford's sister and the Duchess's son decided to marry, but Oxford objected to the match, reportedly threatening death to his sister's fiancée, while the Duchess objected to Oxford's religion, unbridled tongue, and general demeanor. Nelson misses the obvious problem, which is that Oxford had become, or was soon to become, a Catholic, while the Duchess was a staunch Puritan who had fled England during Queen Mary's reign. However, by December the Duchess said to Oxford's sister that, «now I wish to your brother as much good as to my own son.» Meanwhile, the Duchess tried to arrange a seemingly accidental meeting between Oxford and his infant daughter as a prelude to repairing his marriage. Otherwise, the wedding of Oxford's sister to the Duchess's son proceeded, and Oxford became the friend of his new brother-in-law.[31]

The poems in Nathaniel Baxter's 1606 *Ourania* include three eulogistic stanzas on Oxford (430-1), which merit examination as an acquaintance's reflection on Oxford's life. Baxter's first stanza essentially hails Oxford's prowess in tournaments which occurred in the 1570s and 80s. The first three lines of the second stanza allow that Oxford wasted his fortune, while lauding him as learned, just, affable, and plain (presumably meaning honest or candid; *OED*, adjective, iv). The next four lines refer to the Howard-Arundel affair, denying that Oxford plotted against the Queen, but only that he put his trust in men who proved unjust. The third stanza returns to Oxford's learning, which displayed his honor as fruits prove the goodness of a tree. Baxter earns credit for his candor and courage, first by admitting that Oxford was a wastrel, secondly by defending Oxford in the Howard-Arundel matter, as Henry Howard had by then become Earl of Northampton, a privy councilor, and a confidant of King James. Otherwise, Baxter gives us four positive adjectives, perhaps appropriate tokens of a life that fell short of its promise.

Nelson spends a considerable number of words trying to portray Oxford as a sex fiend, although, prior to the appearance of Nelson's book, Oxford was known to have strayed only once in his life: his affair with the maid of honor in 1580-1. Nelson manages to double the count: a lighthearted letter from an English knight in Venice in 1587 reveals an old liaison between Oxford and the knight's neighbor, one Virginia

Padoana, whom Nelson identified as a courtesan or high class prostitute (138-9). I also award him credit for printing the courtesan's reaction, as recorded by the knight, to a man she knew eleven years earlier: «Virginia Padoana ... honoreth all our nation for my Lord of Oxford's sake.» Not a bad compliment.

V. Conclusion

There is a maddening disparity between Nelson the diligent research assistant and Nelson the puerile demonizer. An objective scholar could have transformed Nelson's materials on Oxford's turbulent and messy life into an illuminating study of Elizabeth's Court. Instead, readers of *Monstrous Adversary* end up asking who went further off the rails: Oxford or Nelson? Yet Nelson's approach—his belief that historical texts can be made to say whatever he wants them to say—did not arise from a void.

I noted at the start of this essay that Nelson cannot do history, but after all, he is a literature professor, not a historian. Nelson's treatment of historical texts is, in a surreal sense, a product of his academic discipline. Frederick Crews, one of Nelson's colleagues at the Berkeley English Department, lampooned the wackier tendencies in modern literary criticism in his two bestsellers, *The Pooh Perplex* (1963) and *Postmodern Pooh* (2001). Each book describes an imaginary conference where a group of academic critics analyzes the Winnie-the-Pooh stories, with each critic following his or her own specialty: Freudianism, Marxism, new historicism, post-colonialism, and so on. The critics regard Pooh as belonging to them individually, to be supplied with authorial intention, context, and meaning to suit each critic's tastes. In other words, the critic owns the text. One of Crews's characters, a cyberporn expert, justifies his approach to his colleagues: «If you want to make something else out of it, be my guest—just so you don't call your idea the point of the poem. The same rule applies to *Winnie-the-Pooh*, which is so easy to jam your own thoughts into that you can do it on autopilot after a while ... The sky's the limit if you cheat a little by leaving out whatever doesn't fit your theory.»[32]

There, in a nutshell, is *Monstrous Adversary*: the application to historical documents of such fashionable lit-crit inanities as «the author is dead» and «all reading is misreading.» Nelson wrenches his documents from their backgrounds, which he then replaces with his own commentary to support his thesis that Oxford was a monster. Nelson no more acknowledges an obligation to the normal rules of historical scholarship than a deconstructionist recognizes rules of literary scholarship. Just as the post-structuralist believes that texts are infinitely malleable, so Nelson feels entitled to recreate the past to suit his fancies.

Endnotes

1   As a distinguished historian recently explained: «Common sense is prone to assert that ‹the facts speak for themselves›. Historians know that this is just what they don't do. Facts ... have to be scrutinized against a background, a setting, in a context.» Richard Fletcher, *Bloodfeud: Murder and Revenge in Anglo-Saxon England* (Oxford, 2003), 6.

2   Nelson's introductory remark on his documents adds that he, «felt dutybound to point out their significance for an accurate estimation of Oxford's character.» As it turns out, this does not mean establishing the documents' contexts, but only asserting their implications.

3   See documents 3.1[3] and 4.2[2] on Nelson's website socrates.berkeley.edu/~ahnelson/authorsh.html

4   This passage is in Nelson's document 4.3[1.2], which he mentions on p. 206 as «(LIB-1/2).» I have modernized this and subsequent quotations.

5   See my Response to Alan Nelson's «Oxford in Venice: New Light on an Old Question» on page 275-281 of this book.

6   Conyers Read, *Lord Burghley and Queen Elizabeth* (New York, 1960), 322-4. See also Elizabeth Jenkins, *Elizabeth and Leicester* (New York, 1961), 303-6.

7   Nelson and I both give the Old Style (O.S.) dates used in Elizabethan England, while the Spanish and most modern books use the New Style (N.S.) introduced in 1582, which adds ten days, e.g., July 19 O.S. is July 29 N.S.

8   See Anne Somerset, *Elizabeth I* (New York, 1991), 385-94.

9   Howard was readmitted to Elizabeth's presence around 1597; see Linda Levy Peck, *Northampton: Patronage and Policy at the Court of James I* (London, 1982), 15.

10 Elizabeth Jenkins, *Elizabeth the Great* (New York, 1958), 257.

11 Reference to «satire,» p. 275. On p. 472, Chapter 51, note 3, Nelson attempts to overturn the judgment of the modern editor of *Leicester's Commonwealth*, D. C. Peck, on Arundel's authorial involvement, without offering the least justification for his bare opinion.

12 See Nelson's website documents 4.2 by Arundel and 3.1, 3.2, and 3.6 by Howard.

13 Nelson's documents 3.6.1 and 3.6.2.

14 *Statutes of the Realm*, 1 Edward VI, c. 12, §22; 5&6 Edward VI, c. 11, §9; 1&2 Philip & Mary, c. 10, §11, my emphasis. See my «Hamlet and the Two Witness Rule,» on page 33-43 of this book.

15 Nelson's documents 2.3.3, 5.7, and 5.8. On the treason statutes and witnesses, see Sir William Blackstone, *Commentaries on the Laws of England* (Oxford, 1765-9), 3.363-70; 4.350-2.

16 See also Nelson's documents 3.6.1[3] by Howard and 4.2[6.4] by Arundel.

17 Nelson understates the period of Oxford's disfavor by having the Queen award him a tournament prize in November 1581 (177-8); the tournament was actually in 1584. See Roy Strong, *The Cult of Elizabeth* (Berkeley, 1977), 134; and Jenkins, *Elizabeth the Great*, 258.

18 See my article, «The Earl of Oxford and the Order of the Garter,» on page 263-274 of this book.

19 *Dictionary of National Biography*, Howard, Henry, Earl of Northampton.

20 Chaps. 13, 40-2. See also pp. 140-1, 166-7, Chaps. 31, 35, 37-9, and 44.

21 Chap. 48 is slightly over two pages long, but half of it consists of quotations; the half written by Nelson is a little over one page.

22 The suppression of Southwell's evidence is on pp. 204, 214, and 259. Actually Nelson does cite Southwell's refusal to charge Oxford with pederasty, but changes the verb from Southwell's «can not» to «will not» (214).

23 Compare pp. 140-1, 213, and 215 to pp. 155-7.

24 See Peck, *Northampton*, 11 and 220, n. 17, on Howard as a Spanish spy; and 38-40 and 225, nn. 70-2, on his role in the poisoning of Sir Thomas Overbury. I should add that while Howard clearly arranged for the false imprisonment of Overbury, he may not have been involved in the actual murder.

25 See also documents 2.1.1, 2.1.3, 2.1.4, and 2.2.1 on Nelson's website.

26 Sir Philip Sidney's funeral procession is detailed in a book of 32 plates showing 320 men, while indicating an actual total of 484. Seven men, including Sidney's two brothers, are designated as «mourners,» while nine men carry flags. Sidney's widow and sister are omitted, probably because the women waited for the procession at the cathedral. Katherine Duncan-Jones, *Sir Philip Sidney, Courtier Poet* (New Haven, 1991), 308-39.

27 See Nelson's Index under «Garter.»

28 «The Earl of Oxford and the Order of the Garter,» on page 263-274 of this book.

29 *Faerie Queene* was printed in 1590, but was registered for publication in Dec. 1589. Spenser had been Grey's secretary in Ireland, while Norris was governor of Munster, the province where Spenser lived. Of the thirteen men, all were or became Knights of the Garter, save Ralegh, Walsingham, and Norris. Fourteen of England's eighteen earls (as of Dec. 1589; Leicester, incidentally, died in 1588) did not get dedicatory sonnets.

30 Peck, *Northampton*, 19-21.

31 See Nelson's Index entries for Bertie, Peregrine, and Vere, Mary.

32 Frederick Crews, *Postmodern Pooh* (New York, 2001), 137.

The Stella Cover-Up

If «William Shakespeare» was, as many of us believe, the 17th Earl of Oxford, one implication seems inescapable: Oxford's contemporaries — courtiers, writers, and theater people — must have maintained a remarkable conspiracy of silence. We can go further. The silence must have been maintained well into the next generation, long after Oxford was dead.

At first glance, this seems implausible. Moreover, orthodox Stratfordians scoff at the idea of so extensive a cover-up. As one of them put it, the required conspiracy is so large that it is difficult to see who was left to be deceived.

Yet anyone familiar with human history or modern American society knows that some things are not discussed in public, and that open conspiracies of silence are common events. The number of examples — political, military, or social — that could be cited is endless. We might begin with the motto of the New York Times, «All the News That's Fit to Print,» which clearly implies that some news is not fit to print. American journalists have often suppressed what they knew about the sex lives of politicians they reported on — though we may well ask whether this amounts to a «cover-up» or is simply a matter of respecting privacy. When issues of decorum are at stake, it can be misleading to think of suppression purely in terms of sinister «conspiracies.» Thomas Bowdler became infamous for producing a censored edition of Shakespeare in 1807, but it was discovered in 1966 that Bowdler's sister Henrietta was really responsible for ridding the Bard of ribaldry. The motive behind the Bowdler cover-up was a simple matter of sexual modesty. If Henrietta admitted reading and understanding the bawdy parts of Shakespeare that she excised, then she could no longer be a decent woman, and so her physician brother pretended to be the editor.

However, a cover-up far more relevant to the Shakespeare authorship question occurred in Elizabethan England, spread to the English colonies in America, and continued into the twentieth century.

Sir Philip Sidney wrote his sonnet sequence, *Astrophel and Stella*, around 1582 and circulated it in manuscript. It was published in 1591, five years after his death, and became an immediate and much-imitated best seller.

«Stella» was Penelope Devereux, Lady Rich. Various writers covertly but unmistakably alluded to this identity, but nobody directly said so in print until 1691, a full century after the sequence was published. What is interesting for our purpose is that the Stella cover-up (to call it that) involved the same society, the same mores, and even the same literary genres and stratagems as the conspiracy of silence that Oxfordians posit in the case of «William Shakespeare.» It offers a convincing reply to the Stratfordian complaint that such a conspiracy is too far-fetched to be believed.

Most of the literary history in my article comes from Hoyt H. Hudson's essay, «Penelope Devereux as Sidney's Stella,» which I recommend to all readers.[1] I can only give a summary of Hudson's arguments, but will add a few items of which he was unaware.[2]

Even though much of the story he tells may be imaginary, Sidney's sonnets do not describe a disembodied poet in love with an abstract woman. That Sidney is Astrophel is clearly indicated by, among other things, Sonnet 30's reference to his father's rule in Ireland as the Queen's Lord Deputy; by Sonnet 41's description of a 1581 tournament; and by the closing line of Sonnet 65, «Thou bear'st the arrow, I the arrow-head,» an arrowhead being the sole device on the Sidney coat of arms.

Stella's identity is made clear for initiates by Sidney's puns on the word «rich» in Sonnets 24, 35, and 37; by references to her unhappy marriage in several sonnets; by praise of her black eyes and curly golden hair, which were echoed by other poets and which may be seen in her surviving portrait; and by Sonnet 13's mention of her coat of arms as «roses gules ... borne in silver field.» The Devereux shield was white (which heralds call silver), with a horizontal red (gules) stripe across the middle, above which were three red disks in a horizontal line.

In order to assess the implications of the Stella cover-up, we need to examine the principals. Sidney died in 1586, immediately becoming a cult figure of astonishing dimensions: the perfect English, Christian, Renaissance knight, virtually the Protestant Saint George. Sidney's sonnets to Stella are extremely chaste; he woos her, and, taking her by surprise on one occasion, manages to steal a kiss, but she is true to her husband. Sidney's incredible cult lasted through the seventeenth century. It flagged a bit in the eighteenth, but revived mightily in the Victorian age.

Lady Rich's reputation went the other way. Beautiful and highly educated, she was shoved into an arranged marriage with the dull and detestable Lord Rich in 1581 when she was only 18. While bearing her husband five children in nine years, she managed to be active in society and politics, and in time became a patron of poets.

In 1590 she took as her lover the dashing Charles Blount, Lord Mountjoy, by whom she had six more children. Her husband acquiesced in her adultery, being in awe of her brother, the Earl of Essex. After the latter's execution in 1601, Lord Rich cast his wife out. Meanwhile, Mountjoy had replaced Essex as commander in Ireland and was methodically destroying the rebellion that had cost Essex his reputation. When King James came to the throne in 1603, Mountjoy returned from Ireland as a hero, and Lady Rich moved in with him as his wife. Mountjoy and Lady Rich had both supported the cause of James, and he made them favored courtiers, promoting both, and seemingly indifferent to their blatant adultery. Mountjoy became Earl of Devonshire; Lady Rich, daughter of a junior earl and wife of a junior baron, was given precedence of all barons' wives and almost all earls' daughters.

In 1605 Lord Rich sued for divorce, and Lady Rich confessed to committing adultery with a stranger. Lord Rich wanted a new wife, and Lady Rich and Devonshire wanted to marry and legitimize their children. Divorce was granted, but remarriage was forbidden, and legitimizing the children was out of the question. King James was infuriated by the divorce proceedings, banished Lady Rich from his court, and reprimanded Devonshire. The two lovers made an illegal marriage and continued to live as husband and wife until Devonshire died in April 1606. Lady Rich died in July 1607 and was buried in a London church without any marking on her grave. The register simply recorded the burial of «A Lady Devereux.»

James had no objection to adultery among his nobles, but he did expect them to maintain appearances, and was enraged when one of them publicly admitted her offense. After her divorce Lady Rich was regarded as a notorious woman, but that made it all the more important to prevent her name from contaminating the cult of Sir Philip Sidney.

Enough evidence survives to anatomize the cover-up of the 1590s. The three unauthorized editions of *Astrophel and Stella* that came out in 1591 omitted Sonnet 37, the poem that most clearly says that Stella's name is Rich, while a key line in Sonnet 35 was reworded to make the name less apparent.[3] One of these editions included ten songs that are part of the cycle, but cut from one a passage in which Stella confesses her love for Astrophel, and cut from another Astrophel's anticipation of kissing Stella.[4]

This could have been the work of the publishers, but more likely reflected the manuscripts they had obtained. Sonnet 37, the correct text of 35, and the full text of all ten songs were provided in the 1598 folio edition of Sidney's works that was published by his sister, the Countess of Pembroke. In other words, the Countess, who idolized her brother, saw no need to censor his works to hide Stella's identity. No one up to that point had publicly named Stella, and if the Countess assumed that the cover-up would continue—well, continue it did.

In 1595, Edmund Spenser published a batch of poems in praise of Sidney entitled «Astrophel.» Two of the «Astrophel» poems clearly imply that Stella was Sidney's wife, which seems like a deliberate deception. Yet Spenser's poem says that Stella died of grief immediately following Astrophel's death. Sidney's widow, Frances Walsingham, had by then remarried, becoming the Countess of Essex, and Spenser's «Astrophel» is dedicated to her. Spenser was obviously creating a pleasant fiction, and as Hudson points out,[5] no one even pretended to believe that Stella was Sidney's wife until 1655. Further, Spenser's «Astrophel» puns several times on the word «rich» and describes Stella's hair as yellow; Frances Walsingham was a brunette. One of the «Astrophel» poems, by Matthew Roydon, provides the only further comment on the matter, saying to Stella: «Sweet saints! it is no sin nor blame,/To love a man of virtuous name.»

Meanwhile, as Hudson shows, a number of other poets glanced at the relationship, usually in poems or dedications to Lady Rich. For example, Gervase Markham dedicated a work to Lady Rich and her sister in 1597, which concluded that if the two ladies approved his writing, then his pen would be «stellified.»[6] Or, in 1603, Matthew Gwynn wrote a sonnet in her honor saying that «HE» praised Lady Rich, followed by ten compliments lifted verbatim from Sidney's sonnets to Stella. As Ringler notes, five out of seven dedications to Lady Rich written between 1594 and 1606 found a way to hint unmistakably at her being Sidney's Stella, without, of course, deliberately saying so.[7]

One contemporary actually stated what so many knew and hinted at: that Stella was Penelope Devereux Rich, but this item went unnoticed until the twentieth century. Sir John Harrington, godson to Queen Elizabeth, copied Sidney's first sonnet to Stella into a manuscnpt volume, headed with these words: «Sonnettes of Sr Phillip Sydneys <uppon> to ye Lady Ritch.»[8]

The cover-up evolved during the following decades and generations, but the central taboo remained. After Lady Rich's divorce, public compliments virtually ceased and private slurs on her character multiplied, but her rank sheltered her from public attack long after her death. For example, an obscene epitaph penned shortly after she died was published in 1640, but with her name removed. As the generation that knew her in life died off, the attacks subsided, and the fact that she was Stella was gradually forgotten.

It may seem remarkable that her name was protected through the 1640s, a decade of civil war during which pamphleteers of all persuasions freely libelled the characters and families of their enemies. Even here Lady Rich enjoyed posthumous good luck: thanks in part to her adultery, she had, on both sides of the strife, allies with an interest in sparing her reputation.

Lady Rich's oldest legitimate son had become the Earl of Warwick, Lord High Admiral of England and a leading figure among the Parliamentary forces opposing King Charles. Her other legitimate son was the Earl of Holland, a powerful politician who kept changing sides, until Parliament settled things by beheading him in 1649. Lady Rich's oldest illegitimate son was the Earl of Newport, a general fighting for the King.

Other families might also have taken umbrage at full disclosure of the story of *Astrophel and Stella*. Sidney, a moderate Puritan, was a hero to both sides, and his widow's children had a stake in his reputation, if only to deny that he wronged their mother by loving Lady Rich during his marriage negotiations. Frances Walsingham's older son was the Earl of Essex (he was also Lady Rich's nephew), a leading Parliamentary general, while her younger son was the Marquess of Clanricard, one of the King's strongest supporters in Ireland. Frances Walsingham's daughter by her Irish husband was the Marchioness of Winchester, a heroine of the Royalist cause in England. Another man who might have taken offense was the Countess of Pembroke's son, Sidney's nephew and godson, the Earl of Pembroke and Montgomery, a political supporter of the Parliament. Lastly, there was Sidney's brother's son, the Earl of Leicester, the then head of the House of Sidney. He was disaffected from the King but wouldn't oppose him, so he stayed neutral, while his son and heir, Viscount Lisle, was active in support of Parliament.

Hudson's article does not make clear when the first public attack was made on Lady Rich's character. He cites only Clarendon's massive *History of the Rebellion*, written in the 1670s and published thirty years later, which implies she was immoral without actually saying that she committed adultery, a thing she had admitted in open court in 1605.

Other seventeenth century discussions of Lady Rich's offense are instructive. The Jesuit Father John Gerard attempted to convert her during his years in the Catholic underground in England, but was foiled by Devonshire. After his return to the Continent in 1606, Gerard wrote a Latin account of his missionary work, intended for confidential use within the Jesuit order. It was published in 1870. He described his dealings with Lady Rich and the scandal of her affair with Devonshire, but named neither of them. She is called a «sister to the Earl of Essex»; Devonshire is identified as the conqueror of Ireland. Lady Rich and Lord Devonshire were openly named and their scandal was discussed by a contemporary historian, Robert Johnston, but his Latin account was published in the Netherlands in 1655. Archbishop George Abbot wrote a lengthy essay on political and religious affairs in 1627 which was published in 1659. Abbot has a paragraph on the scandal, but calls the participants «the Earl of D» and «the Lady R.» Peter Heylyn published a biography of Archbishop William Laud in 1668; Laud had been Devonshire's chaplain in 1605 and conducted the illegal marriage of the two lovers, Heylyn does name names, but the whole point of his account is that Lady Rich's 1581 marriage was improper, hence she and Devonshire could rightfully wed.

From the time Sidney died through the late seventeenth century, biographical books and articles kept appearing, none of which mentioned Penelope, Lady Rich. These included an inspiring account of Sidney's last days, written by George Gifford, a clergyman who attended at his bedside. Gifford wrote that Sidney was insufficiently sure of salvation, but then God delivered him: «There came to my remembrance a vanity wherein I had taken delight, whereof I had not rid myself. But I rid myself of it, and presently my joy and comfort returned within a few hours.» In 1964, Jean Robertson found a manuscript version of Gifford's memoir, and discovered that between these two sentences was a third which had been deleted from the published versions: «It was my Lady Rich.»

In 1638, Anne Bradstreet of Massachusetts, a distant cousin of Sidney's, wrote a poem in his praise which was published in London in 1650. The poem mentions their kinship, describes Stella and mildly condemns her, but insists that her love for Sidney was not adulterous. Bradstreet died in 1677, and her poems were republished in Boston in 1678; the reference to kinship to Sidney had been removed as had been the attack on Stella. The revised version cites Spenser's claim that Stella was Sidney's wife.

In 1691, Anthony A. Wood published *Athenae Oxoniensis*, which included a simple, unsupported statement that Stella was «the Lady Rich.» This assertion was not treated as a scandalous revelation, it was simply a few words in a large book, and it was ignored. Not until the mid-nineteenth century was the literary and social history of Shakespeare's England sufficiently reconstructed in detail for scholars to begin building the case for Lady Rich as Stella. Then a new obstacle arose to complicate objective scholarship.

The letters of John Chamberlain were published from 1848 to 1861, providing a mine of information on Shakespeare's era. One letter described the death of the Earl of Devonshire, and stated that his will provided for only three of his alleged five surviving children by Lady Rich. The clear implication was that Devonshire was not the father of the other two, which was widely believed in the last century. The matter was not cleared up until Devonshire's will was found. It provided quite generously for all five of his children. Sylvia Freedman also shows that Lady Rich's two sets of children did not overlap, as had previously been believed. She broke off marital relations with Rich before taking up with Blount. The false belief that Lady Rich mingled her husband and lover, and was not even faithful to the latter, caused her to seem more wicked than ever. To many Victorians and some post-Victorians, Lady Rich's scarlet sins absolutely confirmed that the saintly Sidney could have had nothing to do with her.

In 1934, Professor James Purcell published a book purporting to prove that Lady Rich was not Stella. That provoked Hoyt Hudson's forty-page response, which crushed Purcell (who withdrew and revised his book), and has been considered the definitive article on the subject ever since. Subsequent research has strengthened Hudson's arguments.

Yet one more group continued to hold out: overly zealous professors of English literature of the school called the New Criticism (now obsolete), a powerful force in academia in the early and mid-twentieth century. The New Criticism insists that a poem «stands alone» and must be examined without regard to any background—historical, cultural, or linguistic. There is something to be said for this approach, if it is not carried to excess. There is no reason why a Literature professor needs to study the Battle of Balaclava in order to appreciate Tennyson's «The Charge of the Light Brigade,» but we would surely be astonished if the professor heatedly insisted that there had been no such battle.

Some of the New Criticism professors felt that verse was polluted if its background was analyzed, or, for that matter, if it was even admitted to exist. Judging by the quotations from Purcell that are given by Hudson, the former was motivated by New Criticism. My own copy of Sidney is the 1969 *Sir Philip Sidney, Selected Prose and Poetry*, edited by Robert Kimbrough of the University of Wisconsin. Kimbrough's introduction to *Astrophel and Stella* complains that «scholars have fastened on partial and inconclusive evidence to identify Stella as Penelope Devereux Rich,» which Kimbrough dismisses as an «extraliterary controversy» which would prevent us from «open[ing] our ears to ... some of the finest music achieved by English poetry.»

We can now characterize the Stella cover-up. That Lady Rich was Sidney's Stella was known to many people, including courtiers and poets. There appears to have been no active attempt to suppress the truth. Indeed, Spenser's 1595 pretense that Stella was Sidney's widow was intended to be taken as a fiction, while Sidney's sister's 1598 edition of *Astrophel and Stella* strengthened the identification. Meanwhile, from 1591 to 1619, various writers (Hudson cites about fifteen) published works that made the identification in a manner that was covert but perfectly clear to those in the know. These writers meant to compliment Lady Rich for the honor of inspiring Sidney's sonnets, but decorum required that the compliments be veiled. Presumably, the truth was discussed in private. Vested interests in the reputations of Sidney and Lady Rich kept the truth from being uttered openly until exactly a century after Sidney's sonnets were first published. By then, the matter was stale and uninteresting; there was no follow-up. Not until the mid-nineteenth century did scholars begin to assemble the various pieces of evidence, but they still met with decades of opposition from defenders of the cult of Sir Philip Sidney, who were eventually joined by certain English professors of the New Criticism school.

Sexual propriety was the simplest motive behind the Stella cover-up, as, in a different way, it was the motive for the Bowdler cover-up. Sidney's poetical niece, Lady Mary Wroth, had two illegitimate children by her cousin the Earl of Pembroke (Sidney's nephew), a matter that was managed so discreetly that it escaped notice until the twentieth century. Sex probably had something to do with the cover-up of the story behind *Shakespeare's Sonnets*, which make Sidney's seem positively tame. Of course, other factors presumably affected Shakespeare's works, such as the stigma of print, which kept all of Sidney's works in manuscript until after his death.

The Stella cover-up offers remarkable parallels to what we infer concerning the Earl of Oxford and William Shakespeare. It should become the standard response to sneers about conspiracy theories.

Endnotes

1   Hoyt H. Hudson, «Penelope Devereux as Sidney's Stella,» *Huntington Library Bulletin*, No. 7 (April 1935).
2   W. A. Rigler, *Sidney's Poems* (Oxford, 1962), 435-48; Roger Howell, *Sir Philip Sidney: The Sheperd Knight* (London, 1968), 181-82; and Sylvia Freedman, *Poor Penelope, Lady Penelope Rich, An Elizabethan Woman* (London, 1983).
3   See Hudson, 92.
4   See Ringler, 448.
5   See Hudson, 121.
6   See Hudson, 96.
7   See Ringler, 436.
8   Further details are found in Ruth Hughey's *The Arundel Harington Manuscript of Tudor Poetry* (1960), i, 254-55; ii, 352-55.

Developments in the Case
for Oxford as Shakespeare

(Presented at the annual conference of the Shakespeare Oxford Society in October 1996)

> If this book succeeds in its purpose, it will have no future except as an historical curiosity. (91)

> But surely, it will be argued, there must have been persons acquainted with the identity of the man behind the name Shakespeare who risked confiding their knowledge to personal letters or private papers—why then have these not come to light? ... Speaking for myself, I can say only that I hope, not without optimism, that such documents will be turned up among the masses of Elizabethan manuscripts that have been inadequately combed by investigators knowing what to look for, if combed at all. Indeed, my guess is that an enormous opportunity beckons young scholars. (184)
>
> Charlton Ogburn, *The Mysterious William Shakespeare* (1984).

Charlton Ogburn's first statement, given above, has not yet come true. His monumental work is still the foundation for those of us seeking to establish the identity of the author known as William Shakespeare. On the other hand, his second statement has, to some extent, come to pass. We do not yet have the long sought smoking gun, but, in consequence of standing on Ogburn's shoulders, we and he know much more now than he knew in 1984, especially about the life story of the Earl of Oxford. Yet many of our public utterances, written and spoken, seem to show no awareness of the progress that has been made.

Ogburn discusses the problem of presenting the Oxford case in short and long magazine articles and books; there is so much to say, and a few thousand words, or a couple of hundred pages, are not enough. Eventually he decided that a long book was necessary to tell the whole story, even if its bulk deterred some readers. So came about the 900 pages of

The Mysterious William Shakespeare. In those pages, Ogburn gives us just about every argument that's ever been made concerning the authorship controversy, which, as far as I'm concerned, is of inestimable value. But this is not how you argue the case in a limited presentation such as an oral debate. We need to sort out the stronger points from the weaker, and then focus on the former. We must lead from strength, not from weakness. We also need to alter or discard aspects of our arguments that are wrong or simply of no value. The rest of this paper discusses improvements we need to make, the essentials of the case for Oxford as I see them, and recent and not-so-recent developments that have gone unnoticed.

Needed Improvements

1. Abandon the notion that Shakespeare was a universal genius, which is a relic of nineteenth century bardolatry that we inherited from the Baconians. We must define what Shakespeare didn't know, just as well as what he did. Shakespeare clearly had a working knowledge of Latin, French, and Italian, though he preferred English translations to the originals in those languages. Given those tongues, it would be easy enough for him to read Spanish if he had to. Given the education that we know Shakespeare had, he was almost certainly taught the Greek alphabet and the rudiments of Greek, and the Greek alphabet alone is enough to pick out words here and there in a Greek text, as I know from my own experience.

However, if Shakespeare was fluent in Spanish, Greek, or any other tongue, he concealed it quite well. Shakespeare had excellent legal knowledge, a matter to which I will return, but I see no evidence that he possessed advanced knowledge of astronomy or medicine. Playing the Universal Genius gambit as a means of eliminating a man with, at best, a grammar school education is not the same thing as pursuing the truth. Moreover, the Universal Genius is no more a believable human being than the fuzzy Everyman/No-Man from Stratford. Finally, while it is true that Oxford was an above average student who maintained intellectual interests all his life, we would have a tough time trying to prove—with evidence—that he was a universal genius.

2. Clean up and expand Oxford's biography. The Gad's Hill episode of 1573 was no prank; the breakup of his marriage in 1576 was the Puritan Lady Burghley's response to Oxford's conversion to Catholicism; «the Lord Chamberlain with his white staff … the people began to laugh» of 1581 is not about Oxford, who was on the run or in prison concerning Anne Vavasour at that date; the man on the footcloth nag of 1581 was an opponent of the Queen's proposed French marriage, of which Oxford was a leading supporter; the 1,000 pounds per year was not secret service money; Oxford did not oppose the execution of Mary of Scotland; the 1603 letter by Captain Edward Vere to «kinde father» was to Sir William Browne, not to Oxford; etc. Oxford was a significant but minor figure at Elizabeth's court. Arguments about «Poet-Ape» (probably Thomas Dekker) aren't worth making.

On the other hand, arguments about the «Not Without Mustard» section of Jonson's *Every Man Out* are definitely worth making. Incidentally, trying to strengthen your arguments with a lot of adjectives and adverbs is about as effective as trying to strengthen them by raising your voice—it doesn't work in serious debate. For example, a statement like, «It is absolutely and utterly inconceivable that a total tightwad like Elizabeth I would ever give anyone 1,000 pounds per year without expecting something extraordinary in return» is no good. All I need to do in response is to point out her grants to other people, and to note that she gave 200 pounds per year to Lord Henry Howard (a much lower ranking figure than Oxford) in compensation for detaining lands that he should have inherited, which she was also doing to Oxford.

3. Present the cover-up as a tacit conspiracy like the Stella Cover-up, not as The Greatest Secret Ever Kept, that is, a directed cover-up with oaths of secrecy, death threats, etc. Understand that Shakespeare wasn't deified until the eighteenth century; the seventeenth century regarded him as an excellent playwright and the equal of Ben Jonson and Beaumont and Fletcher. Oxford himself was part of the cover-up, and he didn't litter his works with secret signatures. As Joe Sobran puts it, «Oxford didn't write the plays and poems for the sole purpose of proving that he was Shakespeare.»

4. Face reality on the «Prince Tudor» theory, and submit it to proper historical scrutiny. Always try to make the strongest arguments you can against your own theory, or ask your friends to do so (as I was taught to do as a graduate student in economics). It's far more unpleasant to have your enemies shoot holes in you in public, than to have your friends do it in private. If you can't make or listen to the strongest arguments that can be made against your own theories, then you'd better keep them to yourself (this also applies to some Stratfordian professors).

5. Understand that Oxford's autobiography is in the *Sonnets*, not the plays. Autobiographical arguments can be made concerning *Hamlet*, *All's Well*, and the bed trick in *Measure for Measure*, but the Eva Turner Clark approach of seeing Oxford's autobiography all over the plays simply makes it easy for the other side to discredit us.

6. Prioritize the arguments for Oxford as Shakespeare and against the Stratfordian. Emphasize the strong arguments, de-emphasize the weaker ones, and get rid of the arguments of zero value. Using every argument imaginable is a poor tactic, which simply guarantees that the strong arguments will be diluted and lose impact. Furthermore, it allows the Stratfordians to limit their response to refuting the weak arguments, and we should not aid them in their well developed technique of dodging the issue. Irvin Matus' book, *Shakespeare, In Fact*, is a complete exercise in undermining all of our weak arguments and errors, while totally evading all of the strong arguments. I've met Matus a couple of times, and I couldn't even get him to discuss the strong arguments in private. Here are some simple examples of strong, weak, and zero arguments: «EVER-LIVING POET» is a strong argument, «Shake-speare» is a weaker argument, «Shakspere» versus «Shake-speare» is a zero argument, the Droeshout engraving and the Stratford monument are weak arguments at best, while John Benson's question marks offer a very strong argument.

a. We have discovered many examples of usage of the term «ever-living» and none applies to a living person. Moreover, Prof. Donald Foster of Vassar has done us the enormous favor of confirming our findings in «Master W. H., R.I.P.», *PMLA*, vol. 102, no. 1 (January 1987), 46, making it impossible for Stratfordians to sneer at the fruits of amateur research.

b. The Stratfordians have come up with a few examples of ordinary names being hyphenated in that period, which weakens the argument that «Shake-speare» indicates recognition of a pen name. Hyphenation of real names was a rarity, and our argument is not valueless, but the few exceptions require recognition on our part and deprive the argument of much of its power.

c. The spelling of family names was extremely variable in Elizabethan times. Smith, Smyth, and Smythe were all the same name, as were Moore, More, Moor, and Muir. Even if it could be determined beyond doubt that the name in question—Shakspere—was pronounced with a short ‹a› in the first syllable in sixteenth century Warwickshire, the fact remains that it was regarded as a variant of Shakespeare, as indicated by the shield and crest granted to John Shakspere by William Dethicke.

d. Arguing that the Stratford monument and the Droeshout engraving are obvious frauds is also pointless, though contrasting the two different personas, the gentleman and the actor, is of value.

e. The question marks in the frontispiece in John Benson's 1640 edition of Shakespeare's poems make a very strong argument that Benson regarded the First Folio's identification of the author as a fraud. Incidentally, I once read in a Stratfordian source that Benson's question marks mean nothing because question and exclamation marks were used interchangeably in those days. This argument is false. They used the question mark in exactly one place where we would use an exclamation mark, namely a rhetorical statement put as a question. For example, if I say, «I worked hard under the hot sun all day; was I ever tired,» I would close with an exclamation mark because I'm not really asking a question (for another example, see S. Schoenbaum's statement beginning «What would we not give...!», below). However, Shakespeare's contemporaries would probably have used a question mark, because, after all, the statement is put in the grammatical form of a question. John Benson's words are exactly the opposite case. You can verify this old use of question marks in Percy Simpson's *Shakespearian Punctuation* (Oxford, 1911), 85-6, or by simply looking at the question and exclamation marks in the 1609 edition of the *Sonnets*. Or, see Stephen Booth's edition of the *Sonnets*, notes to numbers 95.3, 97.2-4, and 148.1-2.

Essentials

The essentials of the case for Oxford and/or against Shakspere are these six items:

1. The author's background and education as revealed by his works: Shakespeare's works were written by someone with an instinctively aristocratic outlook, who had detailed familiarity with hunting with horses, hawks, and hounds, who had traveled in France and Italy, who possessed considerable legal knowledge, who had completely assimilated the first two years of the university curriculum, and who seems to have had some military and nautical experience. These things are true of the Earl of Oxford. The state of the art Stratfordian response to this unpleasant reality is given in the Shakespeare article by John Russell Brown and T. J. B. Spencer in the current *Encyclopaedia Britannica*:

> In lieu of external evidence, such extrapolations about Shakespeare's life have often been made from the internal «evidence» of his writings. But this method is unsatisfactory: one cannot conclude, for example, from his allusions to the law that Shakespeare was a lawyer; for he was clearly a writer, who without difficulty could get whatever knowledge he needed for the composition of his plays. (15th edition, 1995)

No author who ever lived, especially a man of humble origins and educational attainments 400 years ago, ever got whatever knowledge he needed without difficulty. In other words, Shakespeare was super-human, and the age of miracles was still alive circa A.D. 1600.

2. The obscurity of William Shakspere of Stratford: His early obscurity is understandable, but not after *Venus and Adonis* (1593) and *Lucrece* (1594). Then he becomes one of Lord Chamberlain's Men, later the King's Men, and has, according to the authorities, a stable career of over fifteen years as London's leading playwright. Yet we only know where he lived for a short part of this period because of records of tax evasion and a law suit. Ogburn is quite good on this topic. Edmund Chambers notes that Shakespeare's acting company became more prominent after James came to the throne in 1603, averaging over ten court performances annually, far more than all the other play companies put together (I.77). Chambers also says that putting dates on Shakespeare's plays becomes more difficult after 1603 (I.85-86). Why should this be so? Why should greatly increased popularity for the acting company coincide with increased invisibility for the playwright? No one paid attention to his death; compare to Spenser (1599), Beaumont (1616), Donne (1631), Drayton (1631), Jonson (1637), and Burbage (1619) (see Ogburn 52, 112).

3. The *Sonnets:* Shakespeare's autobiographical *Sonnets* pose such problems for the Stratford theory that since around 1960 the story behind them has been declared off-limits by the orthodox authorities. When the *Sonnets* were published in 1609, the editor's dedication clearly said that the author was dead. Most of the *Sonnets* address a handsome young man, promising him immortality through verse. But the young man is never named, and the *Sonnets* seem to have been suppressed after the first edition—why the mystery? Shakespeare in the *Sonnets* repeatedly refers to himself as old, which fits Oxford (1550-1604), but not Shakspere (1564-1616). Shakespeare says that he is lame in Sonnets 37 and 89—Oxford was lame. Shakespeare repeatedly speaks of being involved in shame and disgrace, which makes sense coming from an aristocrat who violated the rules of his caste, but makes no sense coming from Shakspere. Shakespeare complains of poverty in several sonnets, but speaks of his jewels in 48 and of his rich clothes in 146, which makes sense coming from an earl who was relatively poor, but not from a successful man like Shakspere. The young man addressed by Shakespeare was clearly a man of rank, but is nevertheless castigated by Shakespeare at several places in the *Sonnets.*

An examination of leading editions of the *Sonnets* since 1780 provides an instructive look at the establishment's changing views. W. G. Ingram's and Theodore Redpath's edition of 1964 discusses eleven annotated *Sonnets* from Malone's edition of 1780 to Hyder Rollins' of 1944. All of these editors thought that the story behind the *Sonnets* was important and said so. Then the Penguin edition of 1961, edited by Douglas Bush and Alfred Harbage of Harvard, opined that the wise reader ought to ignore the story altogether, a view endorsed by Ingram and Redpath, both of Cambridge. W. H. Auden in the Introduction to the Signet edition of 1964 denounced anyone interested in the story behind the *Sonnets* as an invader of Shakespeare's privacy. Stephen Booth in the 1977 Yale edition sneered at the very idea that there was a story behind these poems. John Kerrigan of Cambridge in the New Penguin edition of 1986 followed the orthodox line by announcing that the «*Sonnets* are not autobiographical in a psychological mode,» (11) whatever that means. Yet Kerrigan's scholarship got the better of him later in his commentary, in which he cites recent articles strengthening the argument that the 1609 Quarto prints the *Sonnets* in the right order (66, 71, 430). Moreover, Kerrigan's notes to Sonnet 107 provide the best short discussion I've seen on the date of that sonnet, concluding that it was almost certainly written on the death of Queen Elizabeth in 1603. Most recently, in the Cambridge edition of 1996, G. Blakemore Evans of Harvard ignores the scholarship of Kerrigan and others and dismisses the whole story with, «the question of the documentary nature of the *Sonnets* is largely irrelevant.» (28)

We find a combination of the attitudes mentioned in the last two paragraphs in the writings of Samuel Schoenbaum. At the close of his 1970 *Shakespeare's Lives*, Schoenbaum laments:

> Perhaps we should despair of ever bridging the vertiginous expanse between the sublimity of the subject and the mundane inconsequence of the documentary record. What would we not give for a single personal letter, one page of diary! (767)

And then, in some preliminary remarks on the *Sonnets* in his 1977

William Shakespeare: A Compact Documentary Life, Schoenbaum refers to them as:

> sporadic entries, as it were, in a poet's rhyming diary (180).

The *Sonnets* could also be called letters, as most address the recipient, and so at last we seem to find a Stratfordian scholar who wants to know what Shakespeare's autobiographical poems have to say. But then we get to Schoenbaum's main section on the *Sonnets*, only to read:

> All of the riddles of the *Sonnets* — date, dedication, sequence, identity of the dramatis personae — elude solution, while at the same time teasing speculation. *This writer takes satisfaction in having no theories of his own to offer.* (271, my emphasis)

Note the extraordinary implications of that last sentence; Shakespeare's leading biographer was actually proud of his ignorance.

4. The evidence on the dates of the plays: Most reference books say that Shakespeare's plays were written between about 1590 and 1612, and they place perhaps a dozen plays after Oxford's death in 1604. But the orthodox dating scheme is primarily the work of Edmond Malone in the late eighteenth century and Sir Edmund Chambers in the early twentieth century. Both Malone (*Shakespeare's Works*, 1821 ed., I.291) and Chambers (I.253) explicitly state that they based their dating schemes on the assumption that it had to be made to fit into the presumed working career of Shakspere of Stratford. Since Chambers published his final dating scheme in 1930, a large number of eminent Shakespeare scholars have said that Chambers' dates are too late, and that the plays were written earlier. These dissenters include Peter Alexander, Andrew Cairncross, F. P. Wilson, E. A. J. Honigmann, John Crow, William Matchett, John Russell Brown, T. J. B. Spencer, Russell Fraser, and Richard Hosley (the list could be expanded considerably). In fact, it is now completely orthodox to say that Chambers' dates are too late, and I could be criticized for attacking Chambers' obsolete scholarship. The trouble is that the establishment is unable to act on its knowledge,

because to do so would wreck the Stratford theory. No play by Shakespeare can be proven to have been written after Oxford's death in 1604, including *Macbeth* and *The Tempest*, though, on the other hand, we can't prove that the late plays were written earlier than 1604.

Various Stratfordians have charged that we don't offer an alternative dating scheme, to which I will make two responses. First, it is a major scholarly sin to pretend to know more than you do, as is the case with any dating scheme for the plays that assigns each to a particular year. Second, my guess is that the plays as we know them were written in their conventional order from about 1585 to 1604; rather than 1590 to 1613, as Chambers proposed. Another thing that must be understood about the whole dating picture is that the history of the English stage before about 1590 is the Dark Ages, as noted by Chambers, F. P. Wilson, and G. E. Bentley. In other words, our ignorance of the history of the Elizabethan stage before 1590 may explain why Shakespeare and his works weren't noticed until after that date.

Edmund Chambers on the history of the English stage before 1592: «The fragmentary nature of the evidence makes a dramatic history of the period extremely difficult. The work of even the best-known writers is uncertain in extent and chronology, and much of it has come down in mutilated form. Marlowe's authorship of *Tamburlaine* is a matter of inference; it is only by an accident that we know *The Spanish Tragedy* to be Kyd's.» *William Shakespeare: A Study of Facts and Problems* (Oxford 1930), 55.

F. P. Wilson: «Admittedly, few of the plays acted in the fifteen-eighties have survived. So serious are the losses that the historian of the Elizabethan drama—especially of this period, before the practice of printing plays to be read became popular—often feels himself to be in the position of a man fitting together a jigsaw, most of the pieces of which are missing.» The Clark Lectures, Trinity College Cambridge, 1951, published as *Marlowe and the Early Shakespeare* (Oxford, 1953), 106. See also Wilson, «Shakespeare's Reading», *Shakespeare Survey* 3 (Cambridge, 1950), 14-21, esp. 16.

Gerald Eades Bentley: «Perhaps I ought to explain the chronological limits which I have set [i.e., 1590-1642]. … Before 1590, moreover, records are so scanty, and such a large proportion apply to amateur or semiprofessional theatrical activities, that conclusions about working conditions must be very shaky. One cannot even be sure that a profession of play-writing had yet developed.» *The Profession of Dramatist in Shakespeare's Time 1590-1642* (Princeton, 1971), viii.

But the Stratfordian position continues to evolve. They now deny our assertion that the dates of the plays have been made to fit Will's life, but they don't face up to what Malone and Chambers say because we haven't forced them to. Also, some of them—specifically, the ones who use computers—are trying to prove that the Malone-Chambers dates are completely in line with developments of other English playwrights. In other words, no one wrote like Shakespeare in his later plays until after 24 June 1604.

5. The oddity of contemporary comments on Shakespeare: A fair number of contemporary writers commented on Shakespeare, but only one did so in a way that implied that he actually knew the man, that one being Ben Jonson. Others spoke of him respectfully, but often strangely, in a way that would make sense if he were a nobleman who lost caste by association with the public stage. What else are we to make of: «And though the stage doth stain pure gentle blood, yet generous [i.e., aristocratic] ye are in mind and mood»? Edmund Spenser (Pleasant Willy in «Tears of the Muses» and Aetion in «Colin Clout»), Ben Jonson (revision of *Sejanus* and *Epigram 77* «To one that desired me not to name him»), Thomas Edwards (the «center poet» in the prologue to «Cephalus and Procris»), Sir John Davies («Orchestra»), and John Marston (a great writer «whose silent name/one letter bounds» in *Scourge of Villanie*) all mention some important writer who had to be referred to by a pseudonym or who could not be named at all. Meanwhile, Puttenham and others discuss the discretion that surrounded the writings of the aristocracy. Ben Jonson included a well known description of Shakespeare in «Timbers or Discoveries,» in which he said five times that Shakespeare let his wit run away with him—that he couldn't control it. Somebody said exactly the same thing about Oxford in 1581.

6. The discredited academic establishment. Since about 1960, the establishment has declared that looking for Shakespeare's background in his works is not allowed (see item 1, above), and the story behind the *Sonnets* is a taboo (see item 3). The conventional biographies of the Bard that keep appearing, some written by professors, are best classed as fiction (see 2). The establishment clings to a Procrustean dating scheme that everyone knows is false, because they feel they have no choice (see 4). All contemporary references to Shakespeare are twisted and contorted to fit the Stratford theory (see 5), save one, which is so damaging that it is ignored. In 1613 Francis Beaumont wrote a poem to Ben Jonson with a six-and-a-half line evaluation of Shakespeare. Beaumont implied that Shakespeare had considerable scholarship, that is, Latin, but that the ignorant future would proclaim him to be a simple child of nature. Beaumont was, of course, completely right, with the new party line being announced in 1623 by Jonson. The 1966 *Reader's Encyclopedia of Shakespeare* makes no mention of Beaumont's verse, neither does the standard scholarly biography of the Bard, Samuel Schoenbaum's *William Shakespeare: A Documentary Life*. The 1986 Oxford *William Shakespeare: The Complete Works* omits Beaumont's lines from its section of «Commendatory Poems and Prefaces (1599-1640).» Edmund Chambers, in his *William Shakespeare*, remains, to the best of my knowledge, the only Stratfordian authority to print Beaumont's words, which Chambers flagrantly misinterprets in his discussion of them.

But perhaps the most striking example of scholarly dereliction on the part of the establishment concerns *Greene's Groatsworth*. They cannot bring themselves to admit the obvious facts that Henry Chettle must be presumed to be the author; that Chettle's apology was to one of the three playwrights, not to Shake-scene the Upstart Crow; and that, even under Stratfordian authorship assumptions, Shake-scene need not be Will Shakspere (see Ogburn, 56-64, or see my article «Groatsworth and Shake-scene»). They are so vulnerable on the matter of *Groatsworth* that we are obliged to keep on hitting them.

Developments

1. Shakespeare had a University Education

The foundation of formal education in sixteenth century England was the old medieval trivium, consisting of Latin grammar, rhetoric, and logic, which were studied in that order. The standard works on the amount of formal education found in Shakespeare's plays and poems are *William Shakespeare's Small Latine & Lesse Greeke* by Prof. T.W. Baldwin (Univ. of Illinois Press, 1944) and *Shakespeare's Use of the Arts of Language* by Prof. Sister Miriam Joseph (Columbia Univ. Press, 1947). Baldwin shows that Shakespeare had fully mastered grammar, which is to say that he knew most of the grammar school curriculum. But Baldwin did not in any way place a cap on Shakespeare's educational attainments, as by showing that he knew only grammar and not the other two subjects. In fact, he states that he believes that Shakespeare knew some rhetoric and logic, but that investigating those matters was beyond the scope of his book. Sister Miriam Joseph shows that Shakespeare had fully mastered rhetoric and logic. Like Baldwin, she does not cap Shakespeare's education; nothing shows that he went no further.

Baldwin falsely asserted that university education was mostly professional (i.e., civil law, medicine, and theology) (II.662), and that therefore Shakespeare missed little by not going to a university.

Most important of all, if Shakespeare had this grammar school training, he had the only formal literary training provided by society in his day. University training was professional, with literary training only incidental and subsidiary. (Baldwin goes on to give two quotes from Roger Ascham, noting that the universities produced professionals, as if Ascham was saying that they produced nothing but professionals.) The grammar school gave the linguistic basis of grammar, rhetoric, and logic. The university perfected the logic, together with some rhetoric and made the application to the professions of physic, law, and divinity. The universities were professional schools.

Sister Miriam Joseph declined to tackle the question of how far Shakespeare's education went. Baldwin's blatant falsehood has been embraced by orthodox scholars (see, for example, Schoenbaum's *Compact Documentary Life*, 71), but the curricula of Oxford and Cambridge are well known and are easy to look up. The great majority of students at both universities were in the arts curriculum; only a minority were in professional studies (which, in any case, required a B.A. or M.A. first). Prof. Craig Thompson in *Universities in Tudor England* (1959), published for the Folger Shakespeare Library, states (9): «The Elizabethan Arts course was based firmly on the old medieval trivium and quadrivium. In his first two years an undergraduate studied mostly rhetoric and Aristotelian logic and some arithmetic and music.» In other words, rhetoric and logic were only mastered after two years at a university. Thompson also remarks: «Every boy who completed grammar school had worked at Latin [grammar] for seven years and for three or more had studied rhetoric.» (7) Also: «Some history and geography found their way into the B.A. course, but the main fare in the sixteenth and seventeenth centuries continued to be grammar and rhetoric, logic and philosophy.» (10)

Baldwin's *obiter dictum* is a good example of a Stratfordian *modus operandi*. He is the official expert on Shakespeare's education, grammar schools, and university education, so the other scholars can hide behind his falsehoods. The same is true with Shakespeare's legal knowledge. Likewise with statistical knowledge, to include not only the recent Elliott-Valenza foolishness, but also R. L. Widmann's vapid attack on Warren Austin's study of *Groatsworth* (*Shakespeare Quarterly*, xxiii (1972), 214-15. You must always try to get behind these «experts.» In the case of the statistics, I know enough to do it myself. I don't know enough about law, but Arthur Underhill gave the game away (see 3, below). As for Baldwin, it just took a bit of research, because you don't need to be an expert on the Elizabethan grammar school and university curricula.

Sister Miriam Joseph shows that Shakespeare had fully assimilated at least the first two years of the university arts curriculum, however he got it, and she offers no evidence that his education stopped there.

2. Stratford Theory at Stake in Unnoticed Debate Over *King John*

Shakespeare's *King John* was written between 1587 (second edition of *Holinshed's Chronicles*) and 1598 (mentioned by Francis Meres); Chambers dates *King John* at 1596-97. A related play about King John, *The Troublesome Reign*, was published anonymously in 1591. From the eighteenth through the early twentieth century, it was assumed that Shakespeare regularly borrowed and fixed up other men's plays, and so *King John* was taken to be adapted from *Troublesome Reign*. But then in the 1920s, Peter Alexander showed that the bad, early versions of 2 and 3 *Henry VI* were not sources for Shakespeare's plays, but rather were piracies of them; what came to be called «bad quartos.» Subsequent work on other plays reversed the old belief, which went back to Tyrwhitt's discovery of and theory about *Greene's Groatsworth*, and so Shakespeare came to be seen as a victim of pirates, not a pirate himself. Stratfordian views on *Groatsworth* changed without fanfare; Robert Greene was now seen as charging Shakespeare with presuming to compete with his betters, rather than with stealing the plays of others.

In 1954, the Arden series released its *King John*, edited by E. A. J. Honigmann, who showed that Shakespeare had done a great deal of research on that play, research that is not reflected in *Troublesome Reign*. Honigmann went on to argue that Shakespeare's play was the source for the anonymous play, hence Shakespeare's *King John* had to have been written by 1591. The next important *King John* was William Matchett's Signet edition of 1966, which offered further arguments in support of Honigmann's position on the priority of the two plays. Since then, R. L. Smallwood in the New Penguin *King John* of 1974, Kenneth Muir in *The Sources of Shakespeare's Plays* 1978, and A. R. Braunmuller in the Oxford *King John* of 1989 have argued that *Troublesome Reign* came first, while L. A. Beaurline in the Cambridge *King John* of 1990 supports Honigmann and Matchett. The most recent contribution to the debate that I've noticed is «*King John* and *The Troublesome Raigne:* Sources, Structure, Sequence» by Brian Boyd, *Philological Quarterly* (Winter 1995), which argues that Shakespeare's play came first. Boyd, like most of his predecessors, avoids any mention of the dating issue.

In short, for over forty years some quite eminent Stratfordian experts have been debating whether *King John* was written by 1591, with the experts evenly divided. But no one outside the debate seems to have noticed its implications, which are that if *John* must be moved back to 1591 or earlier, then about a dozen other plays must be moved back earlier still, and the Stratford theory goes up in a puff of smoke. We can continue with Honigmann's story.

In 1954, Ernest Honigmann had recently received his doctorate, having done a dissertation criticizing Edmund Chambers' dating scheme for Shakespeare's plays. Honigmann recognized the drastic implications of his research into the sources of *King John*, but he withheld comment.

Honigmann's next significant Shakespeare publication was «The Date of Hamlet,» *Shakespeare Survey* (1956), 24-34, in which he followed the establishment's line, offering up stale arguments to place *Hamlet* at its conventional date of late 1599 to early 1600.

By 1980, Honigmann was a major Shakespeare establishment figure, so he published *Shakespeare's Impact on his Contemporaries*, in which he greatly added to the case against Chambers' dating scheme and also strengthened the case for the priority of Shakespeare's *King John* over the 1591 version. He also offered empty arguments to the effect that we could be pretty sure that Shakespeare's play was written in 1591, with the pirated play being written and published immediately after, and not in 1590, 1589, 1588, or 1587, though any of those years is just as likely as 1591. He argued that the «dozen or more» earlier plays could be crammed into a few years immediately preceding 1591. Plus he recognized the implied void of five years or more in Shakespeare's production of plays, so he proposed that the later plays be «thinned back» from their conventional, Chambers dates to cover the gap.

Honigmann also told, in a very understated manner, what happened in 1954:

> the relationship of the two King John plays, one by Shakespeare and the other anonymous, a tale of a tub that fascinated me from 1948 to

1954, and that I then abandoned (as Swift might have said) to divert the whales. The whales sported happily and spouted mightily, but solved no problems. Returning now to *King John* after a quarter of a century I am particularly conscious of my debt to three brilliant teachers ... I can only hope that, had they lived, they would have given their approval not only to a thesis presented in 1950 but also to its belated afterbirth. (x-xi)

In other words, Honigmann was told by his superiors to stop causing trouble, and the warning was serious enough to drive him away from his stunning academic breakthrough for twenty-five years.

The debate about which King John play came first has not stopped since 1954, and it won't go away. But those involved tiptoe around or ignore altogether the implications with regard to the orthodox dating scheme of Shakespeare's plays. Oxfordians should not be part of this conspiracy of silence. Incidentally, I have the utmost respect for those Stratfordian scholars who have argued for the priority of Shakespeare's *King John*. They are in no position to emphasize what's really at stake, but the same cannot be said of us.

3. Shakespeare and the Law; the Testimony of Arthur Underhill

The first scholar to argue that Shakespeare had a legal background was Edmond Malone, himself a lawyer, who proposed that young Shakespeare might have been a lawyer's clerk. That idea was shot down in 1859 by Lord Chief Justice Campbell in *Shakespeare's Legal Acquirements Considered*, but Campbell maintained that Shakespeare's legal knowledge was flawless. His opinion was fully supported in 1883 by Cushman K. Davis in *The Law in Shakespeare*, which analyzes several hundred legal passages in Shakespeare's works, and includes over 600 legal terms in its index. But other lawyers can be found to argue against Shakespeare's legal knowledge, permitting Stratfordian professors to shrug off the whole matter. Indeed, how can any of us laymen be sure, especially given that lawyers are trained to argue both sides of a case? It is notorious that members of different professions, hobbies, and religions all want to argue that Shakespeare was their fellow, and so perhaps the Stratfordian bias of the lawyers who argue against Shakespeare's legal knowledge is balanced by Malone's, Campbell's, and Davis' desire to claim that «Shakespeare was just like me.»

But one Stratfordian lawyer showed his hand, revealing both his motives and the emptiness of his arguments, namely Arthur Underhill, one of the Conveyancing Counsel to the High Court of Justice and author of the chapter on the law in the 1916 *Shakespeare's England*. This work, now slightly out of date, consists of thirty essays by leading authorities on various aspects of Elizabethan England and how they appear in Shakespeare's works. Underhill, who proudly records his descent from the man who sold New Place to Will Shakspere, opens his chapter:

> Despite Shakespeare's frequent use of legal phrases and allusions his knowledge of law was neither profound nor accurate. (I.381)

Underhill does not try to rebut Shakespeare's legal knowledge with a direct show of counter-evidence, instead, he artfully distributes three-and-a-half objections to Shakespeare's knowledge across his chapter. Underhill's most interesting hit at the Bard's law is the one I referred to as a «half» objection.

King Lear orders law to sit with equity (III.vi.39-41), and Underhill remarks that «[b]ut for [this] passage, Shakespeare gives no hint that he knew of the existence of Courts of Equity as distinguished from Courts of Law» (I.395). We might just as well say that, but for one remark in *1 Henry IV* (I.iii.60-62), we would have no idea that Shakespeare knew that saltpeter is used in making gunpowder. But the remark is there, and so obviously Shakespeare did know that saltpeter is used in gunpowder, just as he knew about the judicial system called equity. So what's Underhill's point? Underhill won't say, but the point is that Francis Bacon was a specialist in equity who ended up achieving his goal of becoming Lord Chancellor, that is, the head of equity. In other words, Underhill is arguing the case against Francis Bacon. The three objections Underhill made to Shakespeare's law are these:

a. *Love's Labour's Lost* (II.i.220-21): Where Maria rejects Boyet's request for a kiss with: «My lips are no common, though several they be.» Underhill natters that Shakespeare did not know the two meanings of the word «several.» Any annotated edition of *Love's Labour's Lost* will explain that Maria is playing on the two meanings. Any Shakespeare concordance, such as Alexander Schmidt's, which was available to Underhill, will show that Shakespeare, like everyone else, knew both meanings of «several.»

b. *Hamlet* (V.i.110-18): Where Hamlet in the graveyard remarks on the technicalities of buying land, including «statutes and recognizances,» Underhill sneers: «What ‹statutes and recognizances› had to do with the buying of land is not evident to a lawyer, and may suggest that Shakespeare's knowledge of the law of property was neither accurate nor extensive.» (I.406) Any annotated, university-level edition of *Hamlet*, such as Arden, Oxford, or Cambridge, will explain exactly what statutes and recognizances had to do with buying land. Notice how Underhill words his statement in a evasive manner, instead of simply saying that statutes and recognizances had nothing to do with real estate.

c. *All's Well* (II.iii.58-59): When the King of France proposes to marry Helena, «a poor physician's daughter,» to his ward, Count Bertram, Underhill complains about the requirement «that the spouse must be of equal rank with the ward, which Shakespeare had ignored.» Underhill is really getting desperate when he brings up this nonsense. One need not even look at the footnotes in the Arden edition. Just read on a few more lines to Bertram's objection to Helena's low rank, and then note the King's answer: «I can build up [her title].» In other words, Shakespeare was perfectly well aware of the requirement.

Incidentally, every one of these four items is clearly explained by Cushman Davis, who, like Lord Campbell, found no faults in Shakespeare's legal knowledge. Underhill, with the advantage of over a century of accumulated research into Shakespeare's law, and with Campbell's and Davis' books in front of him, was unable to point out a single defect in that knowledge.

We must always be aware of the importance of knowing and using our opponent's work: what Malone and Chambers say about dates, Sister Miriam Joseph on Shakespeare's classical education, Prof. Foster on «ever-living,» Honigmann and others on *King John* and other dating issues, Underhill on the law. It is difficult for Stratfordians to dismiss the testimony of experts from their own camp. Also, these and similar sources, each of which must be searched out, can give us accurate evaluations of the extent and accuracy of Shakespeare's knowledge of Latin, the law, etc. Typical Stratfordian sources tend to say that Shakespeare knew all that he needed to know about such subjects, but really didn't know very much, which tells us exactly nothing.

4. The Demolition of Shakspere's Signatures

The 1985 *Shakespeare in the Public Records*, by David Thomas, published by the British Public Records Office, includes a chapter on «Shakespeare's Will and Signatures» by Jane Cox (24-34). Ms. Cox reproduces and examines five of the six supposedly authentic signatures of Will of Stratford (she omits the first signature on the will as unusable). She concludes:

> It is obvious at a glance that these signatures, with the exception of the last two [on the will], are not the signatures of the same man. Almost every letter is formed in a different way in each. Literate men in the sixteenth and seventeenth centuries developed personalized signatures much as people do today and it is unthinkable that Shakespeare did not. Which of the signatures reproduced here is the genuine article is anybody's guess.

We may add that it is anybody's guess whether any of the signatures is genuine. The only orthodox scholar that I know to have responded to Ms. Cox's bombshell is, to his credit, Samuel Schoenbaum in his 1987 *William Shakespeare: A Compact Documentary Life* (326-7) and his 1991 edition of *Shakespeare's Lives* (566). Schoenbaum is cautious about accepting Ms. Cox's verdict, but he does not disagree. In the two works cited and in his 1990 *Shakespeare: His Life, His Language, His Theater* (213),

Schoenbaum moves toward what he hopes to make the new ortho-doxy—that the three signatures on the will are authentic. But Prof. Schoenbaum has no credentials at all in this field, and is on record as sneering at amateur paleographers (*Shakespeare's Lives*, 1970 ed., 616), not to mention the fact that Ms. Cox thinks that three of the witnesses «signatures» on the will are by the same hand. Moreover, the will was originally drafted to be sealed, not signed. As Ms. Cox says:

> But if one must select one of the four signed documents as being the sole example of our greatest playwright's hand, the will has no better claim than the Requests deposition, the mortgage deed or the Guild-hall conveyance. As we have seen, the legal sanctity of the signature was not firmly established.

We no longer have any certain samples of Will signing his name (though we may have one or two). Therefore, the presumption of literacy provided by the signatures vanishes. The man may not have been able to write.

But the supposedly authentic handwriting of the Bard was a key part of the evidence used to make the case for him as the author of one scene in the manuscript play of *Sir Thomas More*. So an item drops out of the Shakespeare canon. Schoenbaum was not about to proclaim such a loss, but he silently acknowledges it in the 1991 edition of *Shakespeare's Lives*. Page 341 of the 1970 edition includes this sentence, concerning the nineteenth century Shakespeare Society: «Among its notable achieve-ments was the first publication, in Dyce's edition, of *Sir Thomas More* [which in our own century has come to earn a place in the Shakespeare canon by virtue of a single scene].» This sentence appears on p. 251 of the 1991 edition, but the bracketed passage has been deleted. Page 696 of the 1970 edition states that several scholars «pooled their expertise and critical powers to make a [persuasive] case for Shakespeare's Hand in the *Play of Sir Thomas More*.» This sentence is on pages 503-4 of the 1991 edition, but the bracketed word, «persuasive,» has been down-graded to «impressive.»

The eighteenth and nineteenth centuries thought they had a real, flesh and blood Shakespeare. The stories about poaching, horse holding, wit combats at the Mermaid, and the merry meeting with Jonson and Drayton humanized the dry records of the Stratfordian grain hoarder, investor, tax dodger, and bringer of lawsuits. These beliefs eroded under scholarship, and were finally toppled by Sir Edmund Chambers' 1930 *William Shakespeare*, which left only a bare-bones Bard or minimalist Shakespeare. But now we lose the signatures, the presumption of literacy, and a scene from *Sir Thomas More*—Will continues to play the Cheshire Cat, and the Stratfordian professors must be held to have suffered a loss of face for their incompetent handling of the supposed signatures.

It is quite understandable that the overwhelming majority of Stratfordian scholars lack the courage to acknowledge the expert testimony of Jane Cox. After all, they wouldn't want the newspapers to notice this horrible embarrassment with its implication of illiteracy. But it is truly astonishing that most Oxfordians also want to look the other way. Too many of us have gotten too comfortable in attacking the six famous signatures, as if literary ability had something to do with good handwriting. Those who feel this way are no different from Stratfordians who can't let go of the late seventeenth and early eighteenth century legends about Gentle Will. We must become accustomed to adjusting our theories to new evidence, not demanding that all new finds be forced to fit old theories.

Bibliography

«The Rival Poet of *Shakespeare's Sonnets*»
  Shakespeare Oxford Society Newsletter, v.25, n. 4 (Fall 1989), 8-11.
«Dating Shakespeare's Sonnets 78 to 100»
  Shakespeare Oxford Society Newsletter, v.26, n.1 (Winter 1990), 11-13.
«Every Word Doth Almost Tell My Name»
  Shakespeare Oxford Society Newsletter, v.26, n.2 (Spring 1990), 12-15.
«The Order of *Shakespeare's Sonnets*»
  Shakespeare Oxford Society Newsletter, v.26, n.4 (Fall 1990), 9-13.
«*Hamlet* and the Two Witness Rule»
  Notes and Queries v.44, n.4 (December 1997), 498-503.
«Ophelia's False Steward»
  Notes and Queries v.41, n.4 (December 1994), 488-489.
«*Hamlet* and Surrey's Psalm 8»
  Neophilologus v.82, n.4, (July 1998), 487-498.
«*Hamlet* and *Piers Plowman*: A Matter of Conscience»
  Cahiers Elisabethains n.65, (Spring 2004), 11-24.
«The Nature of *King Lear*»
  English Studies v.87, n.2 (April 2006), 169-190.
«The Role of Time in *Macbeth*»
  Manuscript.
«Shakespeare's Iago and Santiago Matamoros»
  Notes and Queries v.43, n.2 (June 1996), 162-163.
«A Biblical Echo in *Romeo and Juliet*»
  Notes and Queries v.51, n.3 (September 2004), 278-279.
«Kill, Kill, Kill»
  Elizabethan Review v.2, n.2 (Autumn 1994), 19-22.
«The Abysm of Time: The Chronology of Shakespeare's Plays»
  Elizabethan Review v.5, n.2 (Autumn 1997), 24-60.
«Ben Jonson's ‹On Poet-Ape›»
  Shakespeare Oxford Society Newsletter v.24, n.3 (Summer 1988), 7-9.
«A Theory On *The Two Noble Kinsmen*»
  Shakespeare Oxford Society Newsletter v.24, n.1 (Winter 1988), 9-11.
«Shake-hyphen-speare»
  Elizabethan Review v.1, n.1 (Spring 1993), 57-59.
«The Demolution of Shakespeare's Signatures»
  Shakespeare Oxford Society Newsletter v.30, n.2A, (Spring 1994), 1-2.

«Experts Prove Shakespeare Had a University Education»
«Stratfordians Prove the Bard had a University Education», *Shakespeare Oxford Society Newsletter* v.30, n.4 (Fall 1994), 1-3.

«Groatsworth and Shake-scene»
The Shakspeare Newsletter v.41. n.4 (Winter 1991), 56.

«Masked Adonis and Stained Purple Robes»
Shakespeare Oxford Society Newsletter v.25, n.3, (Summer 1989), 9-12.

«Neglected Praise of the 17th Earl of Oxford»
Shakespeare Oxford Society Newsletter v.24, n.4 (Fall 1988), 7-8.

«The Lame Storyteller, Poor and Despised»
Shakespeare Oxford Society Newsletter v.31, n.3, Summer 1995, 17-22.
revised version in: *Elizabethan Review*, v.3, n.2 (Autumn 1995), 4-10.

«Shakespeare's Astronomy»
Shakespeare Oxford Society Newsletter v.24, n.3 (Summer 1988), 4.

«Suffolk's Head and Royal Behavior»
Shakespeare Oxford Society Newsletter v.25, n.1 (Winter 1989), 4-5.

«The Fable of the World, Twice Told»
Shakespeare Oxford Society Newsletter v.27, n.3 (Summer 1991), 8-10 and n.4 (Fall 1991), 5-9.

«The Earl of Oxford and the Order of the Garter»
«Oxford, the Order of The Garter, and Shame,» *Shakespeare Oxford Society Newsletter* v.32, n.2 (Spring 1996)

«Oxford in Venice: New Light on an Old Question»
Shakespeare Oxford Society Newsletter v.31, n.2B (Spring 1995), 8-11.

«Claremont McKenna College's Shakespeare Clinic: Who Really Wrote Shakespeare?» *Shakespeare Oxford Society Newsletter* v.26, n.3 (Summer 1990), 7-10.

«Demonography 101: Alan Nelon's *Monstrous Adversary*»
Shakespeare Oxford Society Newsletter v.40, n.1 (Winter 2004)

«The Stella Cover-Up»
Shakespeare Oxford Society Newsletter v.29, n.1 (Winter 1993), 12-17.

«Developments in the Case for Oxford as Shakespeare»
«Recent Developments in the case for Oxford as Shakespeare,» *Ever Reader* (online at www.shakespeare-oxford.com) v.4 (October 1996)